Advances in

THE STUDY OF BEHAVIOR

VOLUME 43

Advances in
THE STUDY OF
BEHAVIOR

Edited by

H. JANE BROCKMANN
Department of Biology, University of Florida, Gainesville, Florida

TIMOTHY J. ROPER
*School of Life Sciences, University of Sussex, Falmer, Brighton
Sussex, United Kingdom*

MARC NAGUIB
*Department of Animal Ecology, Netherlands Institute of Ecology (NIOO-KNAW),
Wageningen, The Netherlands*

JOHN C. MITANI
Department of Anthropology, University of Michigan, Ann Arbor, Michigan

LEIGH W. SIMMONS
*Center for Evolutionary Biology, The University of Western Australia,
Crawley, WA, Australia*

————————————*VOLUME 43*————————————

AMSTERDAM • BOSTON • HEIDELBERG • LONDON
NEW YORK • OXFORD • PARIS • SAN DIEGO
SAN FRANCISCO • SINGAPORE • SYDNEY • TOKYO
Academic Press is an imprint of Elsevier

ELSEVIER

QL
750
.A38
V.43

Academic Press is an imprint of Elsevier
32 Jamestown Road, London NW1 7BY, UK
225 Wyman Street, Waltham, MA 02451, USA
525 B Street, Suite 1900, San Diego, CA 92101-4495, USA
Radarweg 29, PO Box 211, 1000 AE Amsterdam, The Netherlands

First edition 2011
Copyright © 2011 Elsevier Inc. All rights reserved

Permissions may be sought directly from Elsevier's Science & Technology Rights Department in Oxford, UK: phone (+44) (0) 1865 843830; fax (+44) (0) 1865 853333; email: permissions@elsevier.com. Alternatively you can submit your request online by visiting the Elsevier web site at http://elsevier.com/locate/permissions, and selecting, *Obtaining permission to use Elsevier material*

Notice
No responsibility is assumed by the publisher for any injury and/or damage to persons or property as a matter of products liability, negligence or otherwise, or from any use or operation of any methods, products, instructions or ideas contained in the material herein. Because of rapid advances in the medical sciences, in particular, independent verification of diagnoses and drug dosages should be made

ISBN: 978-0-12-380896-7
ISSN: 0065-3454

For information on all Academic Press publications
visit our website at www.elsevierdirect.com

Printed and bound in United States of America
11   12   13   14   10   9   8   7   6   5   4   3   2   1

Contents

Polyandry, Sperm Competition, and the Evolution of
Anuran Amphibians

J. DALE ROBERTS AND PHILLIP G. BYRNE

The Role of Coloration in Mate Choice and Sexual
Interactions in Butterflies

DARRELL J. KEMP AND RONALD L. RUTOWSKI

Hormone-Behavior Interrelationships of Birds in Response
to Weather

JOHN C. WINGFIELD AND MARILYN RAMENOFSKY

Conflict, Cooperation, and Cognition in the Common Raven

BERND HEINRICH

Communication Networks and Spatial Ecology in Nightingales

MARC NAGUIB, HANSJOERG P. KUNC, PHILIPP SPRAU,
TOBIAS ROTH, AND VALENTIN AMRHEIN

Direct Benefits and the Evolution of Female Mating Preferences:
Conceptual Problems, Potential Solutions, and a Field Cricket

WILLIAM E. WAGNER

Contributors

Numbers in parentheses indicate the pages on which the authors' contributions begin.

VALENTIN AMRHEIN (239) *Research Station Petite Camargue Alsacienne, Rue de la Pisciculture, Saint-Louis, France, and Zoological Institute, University of Basel, Basel, Switzerland*

PHILLIP G. BYRNE (1) *Institute for Conservation Biology and Management, School of Biological Sciences, University of Wollongong, Wollongong, New South Wales, Australia*

BERND HEINRICH (189) *Department of Biology, University of Vermont, Burlington, Vermont*

DARRELL J. KEMP (55) *Department of Biological Sciences, Macquarie University, Sydney, Australia*

HANSJOERG P. KUNC (239) *School of Biological Sciences, Queen's University Belfast, Belfast, United Kingdom*

MARC NAGUIB (239) *Department of Animal Ecology, Netherlands Institute of Ecology (NIOO-KNAW), Wageningen, The Netherlands*

MARILYN RAMENOFSKY (93) *Department of Neurobiology, Physiology and Behavior, University of California, Davis, California, USA*

J. DALE ROBERTS (1) *Centre for Evolutionary Biology and School of Animal Biology M092, University of Western Australia, Crawley, Western Australia, Australia*

TOBIAS ROTH (239) *Research Station Petite Camargue Alsacienne, Rue de la Pisciculture, Saint-Louis, France, and Zoological Institute, University of Basel, Basel, Switzerland*

RONALD L. RUTOWSKI (55) *School of Life Sciences, Arizona State University, Tempe, Arizona, USA*

PHILIPP SPRAU (239) *Department of Animal Ecology, Netherlands Institute of Ecology (NIOO-KNAW), Wageningen, The Netherlands*

WILLIAM E. WAGNER (273) *School of Biological Sciences, University of Nebraska, Lincoln, Nebraska, USA*

JOHN C. WINGFIELD (93) *Department of Neurobiology, Physiology and Behavior, University of California, Davis, California, USA*

ADVANCES IN THE STUDY OF BEHAVIOR, VOL. 43

Polyandry, Sperm Competition, and the Evolution of Anuran Amphibians

J. Dale Roberts* and Phillip G. Byrne[†]

*Centre for Evolutionary Biology and School of Animal
Biology M092, University of Western Australia,
Crawley, Western Australia, Australia

[†]Institute for Conservation Biology and Management, School of
Biological Sciences, University of Wollongong, Wollongong,
New South Wales, Australia

I. Introduction

A long-held notion of sexual selection theory is that only males enhance their reproductive success by mating with multiple females (Bateman, 1948; Trivers, 1972). However, recent advances in molecular techniques for assigning paternity have revealed that polyandry, in which females mate with more than one male, is widespread among animals (Birkhead, 1995). Copulation is potentially costly to females as a result of time and energy expenses (Sih et al., 1990), exposure to predators (Fairbairn, 1993), increased risk of disease transmission (Thrall et al., 1997), and mechanical damage (Eberhard, 1996). Consequently, understanding why females routinely mate with multiple males is now one of the most compelling questions in evolutionary biology (Andersson and Simmons, 2006; Simmons, 2005).

Polyandry may have evolved in two main contexts. First, it may be a male-driven phenomenon with females mating with multiple males as a consequence of persistent harassment. In these instances, females may be incapable of controlling whether a mating takes place (forced copulation), or they may submit to superfluous matings because this is less costly than attempting to resist them (convenience polyandry) (Rice et al., 2006; Rowe, 1992). Second, females may solicit matings with multiple males because this behavior provides adaptive advantages.

1

0065-3454/11 $35.00
DOI: 10.1016/B978-0-12-380896-7.00001-0

Arguments about the benefits of polyandry to females fall into two categories: direct benefits and indirect "genetic" benefits. Direct benefits arise if females obtain parental care from more than one male (Birkhead, 1995), acquire extra nutrients for progeny (Zeh and Smith, 1985), or reduce the consequences of male infertility or sperm depletion (Byrne and Whiting, 2008; Walker, 1980). Indirect or genetic benefits will arise if polyandrous females experience fitness gains when multiple paternity (i) increases the likelihood that females obtain compatible partners (either at the point of fertilization or developmentally; Zeh, 1997), (ii) supplies "good genes" for their progeny, or (iii) enhances the genetic diversity of their progeny (Yasui, 1998).

Irrespective of the underlying causes, polyandry can have far-reaching evolutionary consequences because it usually results in sperm from multiple males being simultaneously available to fertilize eggs. The outcome, sperm competition (Parker, 1970), can have profound impacts on the reproductive behavior, physiology, and morphology of both sexes (e.g., Simmons, 2001). The primary impact on females is selection for traits that permit discrimination against fertilization by suboptimal sperm: cryptic female choice (Eberhard, 1996). In males, selection should favor traits that enhance the competiveness of their sperm, or traits that inhibit the successes of rival sperm (Simmons, 2005). The drive for males to win fertilizations, and for females to control paternity, can also conflict, resulting in one sex imposing significant costs upon the other (sexual conflict: e.g., Arnqvist and Rowe, 2005). Sexual conflict might be resolved in favor of either males or females; however, the struggle to avoid costs imposed by the opposite sex can often escalate into a coevolutionary arms race where the sexes enter a cycle of adaptation and counter adaptation as they struggle to maximize their reproductive success. This process can lead to very rapid change in mating behaviors and potentially speciation (e.g., Hosken et al., 2009; Martin and Hosken, 2003). Understanding the causes and consequences of polyandry may give us key insights into the evolution of sexual reproduction, and the evolution of reproductive isolation and speciation.

A large amount of empirical work on polyandry has focused on animals with internal fertilization (e.g., Birkhead and Møller, 1992, 1998; Simmons, 2001). Polyandry is common in internal fertilizers because the sperm from multiple males can be stored and/or mixed in the reproductive tract of females, providing extended opportunities for sperm competition and fertilization by multiple males. Polyandrous mating systems are also known in many external fertilizers (e.g., Brockmann et al., 1994; Oliveira et al., 2008; Taborsky, 1998), which have been used in critical analyses of models of the evolution of polyandry (e.g., compatibility, Evans and Marshall, 2005; Marshall and Evans, 2005a,b). External fertilizers present a range of unique characteristics that simplify investigation of the evolutionary causes and consequences of polyandry: (1) there are limited time delays between ejaculation and fertilization; (2) there are no order effects due to male mating sequence; (3) direct access to unfertilized eggs provides the opportunity to experimentally manipulate paternity; (4) lack of nutrient investment by males eliminates the need to control for this confounding variable (though ejaculate components may affect sperm properties, sperm/egg interactions, or competitive fertilization success, cf. Chapman, 2008; Karn et al., 2008); and (5) there is no opportunity for females to select sperm or manipulate ejaculates in the reproductive tract (Byrne and Roberts, 2000). Anuran amphibians, almost universally, have external fertilization (but see Wells, 2007 for some notable exceptions) meaning they also potentially offer many of these advantages in analyzing the evolution of polyandry and build on the already extensive analysis of sexual selection in anurans.

Over the past 30 years, studies on anuran amphibians have generated pivotal data in rekindling and building our current understanding of sexual selection. Wells (1977) summarized an impressive data set on anuran social systems, and that was quickly followed by some key studies on sexual selection within single species (e.g., Howard, 1978a, 1980; Ryan, 1980, 1983). Those studies demonstrated the importance of direct benefits (e.g., resources defended by males as critical to egg development, Howard, 1978b) and documented patterns of mating success in relation to male size, call structure, or mating tactics (reviewed by Gerhardt and Huber, 2002; Halliday and Tejedo, 1995; Sullivan et al., 1995). Work on anuran amphibians also led to some important theoretical contributions, such as sensory exploitation (e.g., Ryan, 1998). These specific studies focused on mate choice, particularly female preference patterns and cues that might allow choice. Intentionally, or by chance, they have chosen study species where polyandry did not occur or, at least, was not detected.

There have been two major reviews on sperm competition in amphibians that have included short discussions on polyandry in anurans: Halliday and Verrell (1988) and Halliday (1998). There are additional relevant comments in reviews of anuran or amphibian mating systems and alternative mating tactics by Halliday and Tejedo (1995), Sullivan et al. (1995), Wells (2007), and Zamudio and Chan (2008), including several examples that involve polyandry. Polyandry was not prominent in these earlier reviews as there were few reports of behaviors consistent with its occurrence, though both Halliday and Verrell (1988) and Halliday (1998) suggested polyandry might be more common in anurans than reported.

For anurans with external fertilization, polyandry can be either simultaneous or sequential. Simultaneous (or synchronous) polyandry was used by Roberts et al. (1999) to define matings where a female mates with multiple males at the same time. However, for external fertilizers such as anurans, males do not necessarily have to be present at a mating because they may gain fertilizations by releasing their sperm into the environment before a female releases her eggs (e.g., Limerick, 1980) or very soon after deposition (cf. Vieties et al., 2004), or sperm may survive for extended periods (Edwards et al., 2004; Sherman et al., 2008a) in and around egg masses despite males attending sequentially. Therefore, for anurans, and external fertilizers in general, we define simultaneous polyandry as any egg deposition event where sperm from two or more males may be in competition to fertilize eggs. Sequential polyandry occurs when a female mates with a series of males over hours, days, weeks, or months where there is no risk of sperm competition, for example, where eggs are deposited at several different locations with different males (Backwell and Passmore, 1990). Both forms of polyandry are known in anurans.

In this chapter, we do not discuss sequential polyandry. The evolution of sequential polyandry may involve many of the genetic issues outlined above (e.g., compatibility, genetic variation, good genes), but it may also have a strong ecological component related to optimizing egg survival. There is a developing literature on sequential polyandry in anurans, but so far this is largely descriptive (e.g., Backwell and Passmore, 1990; Byrne and Keogh, 2009; Pröhl, 2002) and inadequate to make any clear conclusions about why this pattern of breeding might have evolved. Byrne and Keogh (2009) make some strong arguments about the role of unpredictability in egg survival as a generic explanation for the evolution of sequential polyandry, and these and other issues related to sequential polyandry are considered elsewhere (Byrne and Roberts, in review).

Based on direct observation of mating behaviors or genetic data from egg clutches, simultaneous polyandry is known in seven frog families: Bufonidae (1 genus), Hylidae (1 genus), Leptodactylidae (1 genus), Myobatrachidae (1 genus), Leiopelmatidae (1 genus), Rhachophoridae (4 genera), and Ranidae (1 genus; Table I). The systematic spread of examples may indicate

a. very limited, independent evolution of this trait;

b. that polyandry is more widespread but largely unreported—this view is consistent with recent observations reporting polyandry in *Bufo bufo* and *Rana temporaria*, both species that have had previous extensive studies of their mating systems (*B. bufo*, e.g., Davies and Halliday, 1977, 1979; *R. temporaria*, e.g., Elmberg, 1990; Ryser, 1989); or

c. given 4 genera in the family Rhacophoridae contain several polyandrous species, polyandry might be a basal character in some clades.

TABLE I

SUMMARY OF THE OCCURRENCE OF SIMULTANEOUS POLYANDRY IN ANURANS

Species	Distribution	Proportion polyandrous matings	Number of males per mating	Evidence	Mechanism	Reference
Agalychnis callidryas	Southern Mexico to Panama	Unknown	2	Two males amplexed dorsally on top of each other or side by side. DNA fingerprint data from two matings	Simultaneous amplexus. Males fight for cloacal apposition	D'Orgeix and Turner (1995)
Agalychnis saltator	Central America	Unknown	4 attempting amplexus, 2 during egg deposition	Multiple males amplex single female, all dorsally.	Presumed simultaneous sperm release	Roberts (1994)
Ascaphus truei	USA	Unknown	2, a male in dorsal and a second male in ventral amplexus	In laboratory matings, males mated sequentially from similar pairings	Sequential copulexus: sperm are stored internally allowing sperm competition	Stephenson and Verrell (2009)
Bufo americanus	USA	Unknown	2	Small males maintain contact with cloaca of larger males in amplexus, sitting behind but moving with the amplexed pair	Presumably simultaneous sperm release	Kaminsky (1997)
Bufo bufo	Austria, United Kingdom	25–33% in field	1–2	Multiple males amplexing single female, simultaneously. Microsatellite data from individual egg clutches	Presumably simultaneous sperm release	Sztatecsny et al. (2006)

(Continued)

TABLE I (*Continued*)

Species	Distribution	Proportion polyandrous matings	Number of males per mating	Evidence	Mechanism	Reference
Chiromantis dudhwaensis	North India	Unknown	1–6	Multiple males amplexing female dorsally	Presumed simultaneous sperm release into foam egg masses	Biswas (2000)
Chiromantis rufescens	Liberia	Unknown	3	Multiple males amplexing female dorsally	Presumed simultaneous sperm release into foam egg masses	Coe (1967)
Chiromantis xerampelina	Southern Africa	Uncertain	Mean of 5.5 per egg mass	Foam egg masses in trees, multiple males per foam nest from a single female. Female amplexes one male but may switch males between bouts of egg deposition in a single foam nest. Exclusion of amplexed male sperm results in fertilization by peripheral males	Presumed simultaneous sperm release	Jennions et al. (1992) and Jennions and Passmore (1993)

Crinia georgiana	South-western Australia	Varies between populations: 33–73% (6–96 matings per site) Allozymes: 50% Microsatellites: 27–75%	1–8	Observation of matings involving multiple males, dorsal and ventral amplexus plus other peripheral males. Allozyme data: two matings. Two fathers (≈50% each). Microsatellites: 4–13 clutches analyzed per sites, 10 sites	Males simultaneously release sperm	Roberts et al. (1999), Byrne (2002), and Dziminski et al. (2010a)
Kurixalus eiffingeri	Taiwan	60% (5 clutches)	1–2	Peripheral males amplex behind inguinally amplexed male. Genetic analysis of four microsatellite loci	Males presumably simultaneously release sperm	Chen et al. (personal communication, 2009)
Leptodactylus podicipinus	Brazil	Unknown	Up to 8	Focal large male amplexes female, build foam nest, peripheral smaller males presumed to release sperm into foam nest	Presumed males release sperm into foam	Prado and Haddad (2003)

TABLE I (*Continued*)

Species	Distribution	Proportion polyandrous matings	Number of males per mating	Evidence	Suggested Mechanism	Reference
Osteopilus septentrionalis	Introduced populations in Florida, native to Cuba	Unknown	Unknown	Possibility inferred from close proximity of unpaired males to amplexed pairs	Suggested unpaired males might release sperm close to amplexed pairs depositing eggs	Salinas (2006)
Phyllomedusa distincta	Brazil, Atlantic Rainforest	Unknown	1–4	Multiple males join an amplexed pair during egg deposition. Additional males released sperm onto and lateral to amplexed male	Simultaneous amplexus, presumed all males released sperm onto eggs	Prado et al. (2006)
Phyllomedusa rohdei	Brazil, Atlantic Rainforest	≈2%	1–3	Male joined an amplexed pair and stayed amplexed—normally displaced	Simultaneous amplexus during egg deposition	Wogel et al. (2005)
Polypedates leucomystax	SE Asia	Unknown	3	Multiple males amplexing single female dorsally. Cloacae of all three males engulfed in foam forming nest	Presumed all males released sperm into foam	Feng and Narins (1991)
Rhachophorus arboreus	Japan	Unknown	3–4	Multiple males amplexing single female dorsally	Simultaneous sperm release into a foam nest	Kusano et al. (1991)

Species	Location	Multiple paternity	No. of sires	Mating behavior	Fertilization notes	Reference
Rhacophorus megacephalus Note: reported as *Polypedates megacephalus*	Taiwan	31% of 61 matings	2–5	Multiple males amplexing single female dorsally	Simultaneous sperm release into a foam nest: arboreal or on bank above water	Yang (1998) and Zhang (1988)
Rhacophorus moltrechti	Taiwan	One mating	2–4	Multiple males amplexing single female dorsally	Presumed simultaneous sperm release into a foam nest on ground	Wen (2001)
Rhacophorus schlegelii	Japan	44.4%	1–4	Multiple males amplexing single female dorsally	Peripheral males insert cloaca into foam nest made by amplexed pair	Fukuyama (1991)
Rhachophorus taipeianus	Taiwan	10.3% of 87 matings	2–4	Inferred from observations of mating behavior	Presumed simultaneous sperm release into a foam nest on ground	Yang (1987, 1998)
Rhachophorus smaragdinus	Taiwan	12.9% of 70	2–3	Multiple males amplexing single female dorsally	Presumed simultaneous sperm release into a foam nest on ground	Chen (1991)
Rana arvalis	Sweden	14% (Colony1.2) or 29% (Gerud)	1–2	Microsatellite genotypes (9 loci). Paternity assessed using Gerud, or Colony1.2 software. No behavioral observation	Unknown, collected freshly deposited egg masses	Knopp and Merilä (2009)

(Continued)

TABLE I (*Continued*)

Species	Distribution	Proportion polyandrous matings	Number of males per mating	Evidence	Mechanism	Reference
Rana dalmatina	France	Varies between populations, higher if predation on males is lowered experimentally	1–2	Allozyme data: segregation patterns in egg clutches. No behavioral observation	Unknown	Lodé and Lesbarrères (2004) and Lodé et al. (2004)
Rana temporaria	Sweden	48–55%	No observations of matings	Allozyme data: segregation patterns in egg clutches estimating relatedness and minimum number of parents for genotype distributions	No observations: speculated about multiple males releasing sperm or free-swimming sperm in water at communal egg deposition sites	Laurila and Seppä (1998)
Rana temporaria	Spain	84%	1 initially,1 sequentially but sometimes ≥ 2 sequentially	Microsatellite analyses of single clutches	Clutch piracy where males pirate males enter clutch post deposition and improve fertilization success	Vieites et al. (2004)

In some cases, names of species and/or genera have been changed from the original names to conform with usage in Frost et al. (2006) and as updated at "Amphibian Species of the World 5.4, an Online Reference" (http://research.amnh.org/vz/herpetology/amphibia/index.php—last accessed April 13, 2010).

Polyandry may be a strong selective pressure on anuran mating systems with considerable potential to generate the same patterns of postcopulatory sexual selection seen in many other organisms (e.g., Andersson, 1994; Andersson and Simmons, 2006; Simmons, 2001). It is plausible to believe that our knowledge of anuran polyandry is about where knowledge of polyandry in birds was more than 40 years ago, when Lack (1968) claimed that over 90% of birds were monogamous and only a small number of species were polyandrous. Genetic work with birds has now demonstrated polyandry in more than 90% of bird species (Griffith et al., 2002). No current study on sexual selection in birds would ignore the possibility of polyandry. Polyandry now needs to be seriously considered in anurans, and possibly reconsidered, in the context of several classic studies on anuran sexual behavior and sexual selection. As with birds, targeted application of genetic techniques to analyze patterns of parentage will be a critical step in those evaluations.

This chapter covers four major areas: (i) how and when simultaneous polyandry occurs in anurans; (ii) the costs and benefits of polyandry; (iii) the impact of polyandry on sperm and testis evolution; and (iv) the impact of polyandry on the evolution of sperm storage organs and strategic ejaculation, body size, call structure, and anuran diversity. Our review has a strong focus on work on the Australian Myobatrachid frog, *Crinia georgiana*, as the breeding biology of this species, including acoustic behavior, egg physiology, polyandry, systematics, maternal provisioning of eggs, and plasticity of tadpole development, has been reported in 29 publications since 1995 (Ayre et al., 1984 to Dziminski et al., 2010a). Research into the occurrence and the evolution of polyandry in anurans is still in its infancy. Therefore, this chapter necessarily contains a lot of observational data and natural history information which we use to suggest problems and research directions.

II. Simultaneous Polyandry: Mechanisms

In anurans, simultaneous polyandry or behavior that is likely to lead to sperm competition occurs in a large number of species, from seven anuran families (Table I). Across these species, the number of males involved in a mating usually ranges between two and five, but the number of males involved can occasionally be extreme. For example, in the African frog, *Chiromantis xerampelina*, a female may mate with 12 or more males at once (Byrne and Whiting, 2008; Byrne and Whiting, 2011), and in the Australian quacking frog (*C. georgiana*), females may mate with up to eight males at once (Roberts et al., 1999). At least five forms of simultaneous polyandry have been described or speculated about in anurans, and each is discussed below.

A. MULTIPLE-MALE AMPLEXUS

This form of polyandry occurs when a female is amplexed (grasped) by multiple males at the same time. Multiple males attempting to amplex a single female are sometimes referred to as "mating balls" or "group spawnings" (e.g., Byrne and Roberts, 2004; Crump and Townsend, 1990), and this phenomenon is the most common form of simultaneous polyandry in anurans (Table I). Mating balls occur when unpaired males deliberately join an amplexed pair to gain fertilizations (e.g., Sztatecsny et al., 2006; Zamudio and Chan, 2008). However, it is important to recognize that apparent "mating balls" will not always result in polyandry because an amplexed male may successfully repel his competitors and ultimately fertilize an entire clutch (cf. Davis and Roberts, 2005; Zamudio and Chan, 2008). The amplectant positions adopted by secondary males vary considerably between species. In *C. georgiana*, secondary males preferentially clasp females in a ventral position, and additional males then clasp the female dorsolaterally. In matings that involve large numbers of males, secondary males may also clasp a female's head or appendages (Byrne and Roberts, 2004; Roberts et al., 1999). Similar ventral and dorsolateral amplexus by secondary males has been reported in "mating balls" of the common toad *B. bufo* (Sztatecsny et al., 2006). However, in most anurans that display multimale amplexus, secondary males adopt a dorsal position alongside or behind the focal male. This behavior has been reported in several phyllomedusine hylids, leptodactylid frogs, and in several species of foam-nesting rhacophorids (Table I).

B. CLOSE POSITIONING WITHOUT AMPLEXUS

Kaminsky (1997) suggested that in the American toad *Bufo americanus*, satellite males might achieve a paternity share because they sit in close proximity to amplexed pairs, position themselves so that their cloacae appose the cloaca of the amplexed male, and move synchronously with the amplexed pair, maintaining the same relative position of the cloacas of both males. A similar mechanism was suggested in the Cuban treefrog *Osteopilus septentrionalis* where nonamplexed males observed in the water adjacent to spawning pairs might release sperm and achieve paternity (Salinas, 2006). At present, this form of polyandry is only supported by the apparently deliberate behavior of satellite males, but importantly, these observations raise the possibility that polyandry might be achieved by quite subtle means—behaviors that may easily be overlooked.

C. Sperm Leakage

Laurila and Seppä (1998) argued that sperm leakage may occur between adjacent mating pairs in communal breeding assemblages of *R. temporaria* leading to simultaneous polyandry. Similarly, Krupa (1994) suggested that communal egg deposition in *Bufo cognatus* may serve to deliberately promote sperm competition. Simultaneous, communal foam nesting, as seen in *Physalaemus pustulosus*, may also allow sperm mixing especially given that communal nesting seems to be a preferred egg deposition mode in this species (Ryan, 1985, illustrated in Ryan's Fig. 3.14). Sztatecsny et al. (2006) found no evidence of stray sperm fertilizing eggs in *B. bufo*, but given that anuran sperm can retain fertilizing capacity over several hours (Hettyey and Roberts, 2006, 2007), or even days (Edwards et al., 2004; Sherman et al., 2008a), sperm leakage cannot be ruled out as a mechanism when egg masses are deposited close together. Demonstration of sperm leakage requires genetic evidence of polyandry, direct observations of egg deposition and a guarantee that additional males neither deliberately join amplexed pairs nor attend egg masses post-egg deposition. Detection of viable sperm at egg deposition sites would at least allow the possibility of sperm leakage. This problem could also be approached experimentally by placing unfertilized eggs into breeding sites (e.g., for communal breeders), or close to recently deposited egg clutches, and determining fertilization rates in the absence of males, or by detecting multiple paternity in clutches deposited in matings observed to be behaviorally monandrous.

D. Multiple Males in a Foam Nest

Polyandrous matings have been reported in arboreal, terrestrial, and aquatic foam nesters from the families Racophoridae and Leptodactylidae (Table I). In the African treefrog *C. xerampelina*, females are amplexed by a male, ascend into trees, and are joined by multiple males while the amplexed pair forms a foam nest as eggs are deposited (Jennions et al., 1992). Males jostle, though not intensely, to gain cloacal apposition with the female, which presumably improves their chances of fertilizing eggs. Females descend into ponds to rehydrate between bouts of egg deposition and may switch focal males between successive egg deposition bouts (Byrne and Whiting, 2008; Jennions et al., 1992). In *Rhacophorus schlegelii*, amplexed pairs excavate an egg deposition chamber several centimeters underground in moist soil along the shores of ponds or rice fields (Fukuyama, 1991). Other males then join this pair by breaking into the egg deposition chamber from above and inserting their cloaca into the foam nest, or joining in dorsal amplexus and immersing themselves in the foam

(Fukuyama, 1991). In the South American frog *Leptodactylus chaquensis*, an amplexed pair forms in a small water body, and when they begin to deposit eggs in a foam nest, smaller males position themselves around the pair and may shed sperm into the foam without directly contacting the amplexed pair (Prado and Haddad, 2003).

Foam nests offer a very different environment for polyandry as sperm are released directly into the foam which is likely to reduce sperm loss, maximizing the chances of sperm competition occurring.

E. POSTMATING EJACULATION (CLUTCH PIRACY)

This form of simultaneous polyandry occurs after a pair has completed mating and a second male visits an unattended clutch and releases sperm on, or inside, the already deposited egg clutch. Vieites et al. (2004) showed that amplexed pairs of *R. temporaria* rapidly deposited eggs in a single clutch, but then other males either physically entered the centers of the clutch or hung on the outside of a discrete clutch. The second, pirate, male improved fertilization success by approximately 15% if they entered the clutch but had little impact on mean fertilization levels if they remained outside the egg mass. Pirate males entered clutches within 1 s, but up to 2 h post-egg deposition. Seven of 16 pirated clutches had eggs fertilized by the pirate male with successful pirates having an average paternity share of 26% (but up to 100%). This behavior has also been reported in Romanian populations of *R. temporaria* (Demeter and Benko, 2007), indicating it is not a phenomenon unique to the high-altitude populations studied by Vieites et al. (2004). Clutch piracy contains both elements of simultaneous and sequential polyandry. The outcome is multiple paternity, but the uncertain feature is whether sperm from the first male are still present and capable of fertilizing eggs when the second ejaculation occurs. Given sperm of some frogs can survive and maintain fertilization capacity for several hours or days (e.g., Edwards et al., 2004; Sherman et al., 2008a), this seems plausible.

F. REPEATED COPULATION AND INTERNAL FERTILIZATION

In the tailed frog, *Ascaphus truei*, males have an intromittent organ and copulate with females to transfer sperm. Males in "copulexus" (Sever et al., 2001 coined "copulexus" to distinguish amplexus leading to copulation from conventional, anuran amplexus) clasp both dorsally and ventrally, and two males clasping a single female has been seen in the field (Stephenson and Verrell, 2003). In laboratory mating trials, two male copulexus also occurs and the dorsal and the ventral males both copulated, sequentially, leading to internal fertilization, sperm storage (Sever et al., 2001), and the potential for sperm competition. Internal fertilization occurs in other frog groups (e.g., Sever et al., 2001; Wake, 1980), and there is potential for polyandry because in at least one bufonid species (*Nectophrynoides malcolmi*), multiple males have been reported to associate with females in amplexus (Wake, 1980).

III. GENETICS OF PATERNITY

Multiple paternity occurs when the sperm of several different males fertilizes a clutch of eggs produced by one female. Jennions and Passmore (1993) took a rudimentary, but effective, approach to estimating the potential for multiple paternity in *C. xerampelina* by using a plastic bag to exclude the sperm from a focal male and showed that eggs were still fertilized by peripheral males. While such techniques can be used to demonstrate that secondary males have the capacity to fertilize eggs, they cannot be used to accurately establish normal paternity contributions because the absence of sperm from the focal male is unrealistic. In these situations, it could be argued that sperm from the focal male, who is physically positioned in closer proximity to the cloaca of the female, may normally out-compete the sperm of secondary males. Therefore, unequivocal evidence for multiple paternity can only be gained using molecular techniques to assign parentage to offspring.

A. PATTERNS OF PATERNITY

Molecular approaches have taken three basic approaches: (i) assessment of segregation patterns in whole egg clutches collected in the field. Deviations from average patterns of relatedness across multilocus genotypes (expected to be 0.5 for a single father) define the occurrence of polyandry (e.g., Laurila and Seppä, 1998); (ii) direct assessment of paternity based on genotypes of the mother and all possible fathers (e.g., D'Orgeix and Turner, 1995); and (iii) assignment of paternity from field-collected egg masses using multilocus genotypes that define a likely maternal genotype and then evaluate the number of possible fathers (e.g., Dziminski et al., 2010b). Data on paternity patterns are given in Table I, and from these we make three points.

1. Proportion of Polyandrous Egg Masses

The genetic data are limited with only studies on *C. georgiana*, *R. temporaria*, and *Rana dalmatina* having sufficient data to make any general statements. In these three examples, highest proportions of polyandrous clutches vary from < 25% to 84% of egg masses sampled, but in the first two species, values were often > 50%. Importantly, in all three examples, polyandry is a routine occurrence: not a once-off aberration. In *C. georgiana*, genetic data and behavioral observations indicate similar rates of polyandry. Using microsatellite markers, Dziminski et al. (2010b) reported an average of 47% (range: 27–75% across sites) of all clutches sampled were polyandrous—very comparable to rates of polyandry estimated from observations of mating behavior in the field (Roberts et al., 1999, 44%; Byrne, 2002, 50%). In *R. temporaria*, Vieites et al. (2004) analyzed paternity in 16 clutches where pirate males were present but detected polyandry in only seven, emphasizing the importance of genetic analysis of polyandrous outcomes.

2. Fathers per Clutch

The number of fathers per clutch ranged from a minimum of two in several species, to a maximum of four in *C. georgiana* (Dziminski et al., 2010b). For *C. georgiana*, this is well below the maximum number of males attempting simultaneous amplexus (up to 8, Table I). Of critical interest here is what predicts a male's success when in competition: mating position, body size, or time in amplexus? This has not been investigated.

3. Position and Time Effects

The share to known fathers in the normal amplexus position, and ventral or additional dorsal or ventral males, is about equal in *Agalychnis callidryas* and *C. georgiana*, but males amplexed in the normal axillary position may have an advantage in *B. bufo* (Table I). A similar bias to one of two fathers occurred in *R. dalmatina*, but Lodé and Lesbarrères (2004) did not directly observe matings, so position effects are unknown. With clutch piracy, paternity share to pirate males was highest (100% and 95%) when piracy occurred 1 min after egg deposition, or when a pirate carried the clutch away while the parental male was still releasing sperm (Vieites et al., 2004).

B. Prospects for Analysis of Paternity Patterns

Neff and Pitcher (2002), Neff et al. (2002), and Jones (2005) have all outlined analytical techniques to define minimum numbers of fathers of an egg mass or proportions of masses that are polyandrous. These techniques generally assume a single mother, which is a reasonable assumption for many anuran species with discrete egg masses, but the techniques can also be used to analyze data with totally unknown parentage (e.g., Jones, 2005; cf. Dziminski et al., 2010b where several, apparently discrete clutches were excluded due to multiple mothers). The increasing availability of microsatellite markers for anuran species makes broad scale analysis of patterns of paternity feasible. More extensive data sets across more anuran species need to look at one simple question: what are the rates of polyandry measured in discrete egg masses across a systematic sample of frog species across frog families? The absence of data is not evidence for the absence of polyandry. Rhacophorids, where polyandry appears repeatedly in several genera of arboreal and terrestrial foam nesters as well as in species with more conventional egg masses, might be a particularly fruitful group for investigation.

IV. The Evolution of Simultaneous Polyandry in Anurans

The two broad competing explanations for the evolution of polyandry in animals are (i) males force matings and (ii) females' solicit matings to gain benefits (e.g., Simmons, 2005). While the evolution of polyandry has gained considerable research attention in vertebrates, our understanding of why female anurans mate with multiple males has received very little empirical attention. Nevertheless, there is a limited, but growing body of evidence to suggest that simultaneous polyandry in anurans could be an outcome of forced matings in some species, but be an adaptive female strategy in others.

A. Biased Operational Sex Ratios and Forced Mating

For most animals, males invest much less in gamete production and parental care than females and therefore have a much higher potential reproductive rate (Clutton-Brock and Vincent, 1991; Parker and Simmons, 1996). Consequently, males typically compete vigorously for access to mates, while females are discriminating in their choice of mating partners (e.g., Andersson, 1994). One way to predict this sex-related difference in behavior is the operational sex ratio (OSR): the ratio of fertilizable females to males available to mate (Emlen and Oring, 1977). Heavy male bias in the OSR is often linked to intense male–male competition and female selectivity. The opposite pattern, high female bias, will reverse those sex-specific roles (e.g., Andersson, 1994). Where there is heavy male bias in the OSR, subordinate males may force matings, may not mate, may plastically adopt alternative mating tactics, or may evolve fixed alternative mating tactics (e.g., see a recent summary of models in Shuster, 2008). Alternative mating tactics range from female mimicry to males forming coalitions (Oliveira et al., 2008), but if males gain matings against female interests, then matings can be defined as forced (e.g., Andersson, 1994). Among external fertilizers, forced matings by sneak and satellite males are a common model used to explain simultaneous polyandry in several fish (Taborsky, 2008) and to explain group spawning in horseshoe crabs (Brockmann, 1990; Brockmann et al., 1994).

Anurans are well known for forming massive breeding aggregations and having choruses with OSR values that are heavily biased toward males (Wells, 2007). These biases often manifest in intense male–male competition, with males competing acoustically and physically to gain access to oviposition sites and females (Wells, 2007). In many anurans, males will struggle to displace males already in amplexus (e.g., Sullivan et al., 1995). Male bias in the OSR selecting for forced matings and convenience polyandry for females is a likely explanation for simultaneous polyandry in many anurans, but empirical evaluation of this model has been limited to relatively few species. We examine available data below.

B.   BIAS IN THE OPERATIONAL SEX RATIO

For *R. dalmatina*, the OSR is strongly affected by predation pressure because calling males are preferentially eaten by European pole cats, *Mustela putorius* (Lodé et al., 2004, 2005). Normally, the OSR at breeding ponds is male biased. If pole cats can freely enter ponds, the OSR bias is reduced and polyandry is uncommon, but if pole cats are experimentally excluded, the male bias in the OSR is strong, and polyandry is more likely to occur (Lodé et al., 2004). In *B. bufo*, experimental manipulation of the OSR in laboratory settings generated higher rates of multiple paternity when males were more common, and Sztatecsny et al. (2006) suggested that females may passively accept polyandry with small numbers of males to avoid male harassment, but there were no data on the OSR in field situations.

In *R. temporaria*, Vieites et al. (2004) argued that clutch piracy evolved under conditions with a strong OSR bias toward males, because over 3 years, there were consistently more males than females present at breeding sites. They also argued that clutch piracy was probably a consequence of the OSR bias and males adopting alternative mating tactics.

The impact of OSR on mating behavior and polyandry has been intensively studied in *C. georgiana*. Multiple-male amplexus arises from noncalling "sneaks" joining an amplexed pair formed by a female choosing a calling male, or because additional males join pairs that initially form when larger males search the chorus without calling, and forceably clasp females (Byrne and Roberts, 2004). Increasing frequencies of polyandrous mating, and increasing numbers of males per mating, are both positively correlated with a shift in the bias of the OSR toward males (Fig. 1). The cause of variance in the OSR bias in *C. georgiana* is unknown, but there may be multiple contributing factors, related to energetics, adult sex ratios, and chorus attendance. The potential importance of these causes is discussed below.

1.   Energetics

Over a breeding season, males captured in breeding choruses of *C. georgiana* showed little change in mass (mean of 0.41% decline; Smith, 2001), suggesting no major costs of calling, sperm production, or other mating tactics. This

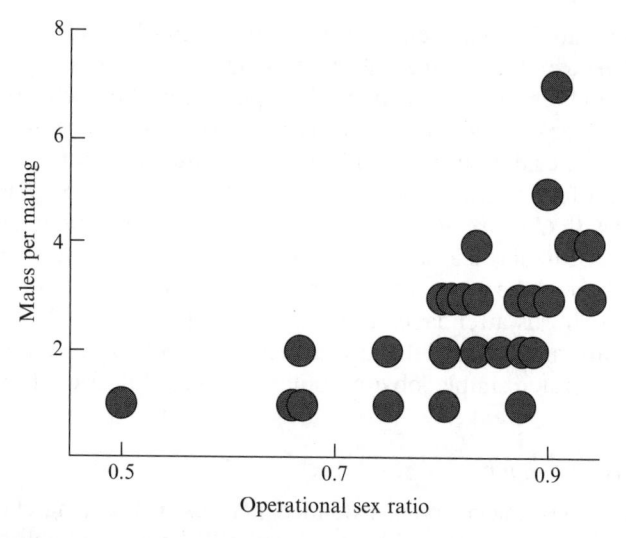

Fɪɢ. 1. Relationship between males per mating and the operational sex ratio (OSR calculated as the number males not physically grasping a female)/[(number gravid females not grasped by a male)/(number of males not grasping a female)] (modified and redrawn from Byrne and Roberts, 2004).

contrasts with average body mass losses of 33% and 36% in males of *Crinia signifera* and *Crinia parinsignifera* over an extended breeding season (Mac Nally, 1981). Male *C. georgiana* do invest in mating tactics not involving calling, for example, searching for and intercepting females (Byrne and Roberts, 2004), and the costs of movement or fighting might be relatively high, or at least not very different from the costs of calling (cf. Table 5.3 in Wells, 2007). Although not losing mass, males are also not growing at their potential because Smith and Roberts (2003a) demonstrated that males can make big gains in weight between breeding seasons: three smaller males grew an average of 12.7 mm, approximately a 50% increase in snout-vent length, in 12 months. There is no evidence of strong energetic constraints on chorus attendance in *C. georgiana*, which should bias the OSR more strongly toward males.

2. Adult Sex Ratios

A bias in the OSR might arise if the adult sex ratio itself is skewed toward one sex. The available data for *C. georgiana* are contradictory. In an intensive mark-recapture study of *C. georgiana* at a long-term study site, the sex ratios of frogs collected across a single breeding season was heavily male biased (5.6:1; Smith and Roberts, 2003a). But, in laboratory rearing studies, 36 females and 26 males survived to sexual maturity from a starting set of 96 eggs (not significantly different from a 1:1 ratio, $\chi^2 = 1.61, p > 0.05$; Smith and Roberts, 2003a). The field data collected by Smith and Roberts (2003a) are likely to be biased toward collection of males, as females appear to enter choruses and breed in a single night. Irrespective of the adult sex ratio, the OSR will still be dependent on patterns of chorus attendance by both sexes. Determining the adult sex ratio and defining the interplay between that ratio and factors affecting chorus attendance to determine the OSR has not been attempted with *C. georgiana* but is a challenging task that might help explain patterns in OSR bias leading to polyandry in this, and other frog species. Rainfall, phase of the moon, and number of females have all been implicated in affecting chorus attendance in *C. georgiana* (Byrne, 2002; Smith et al., 2003), but attempts to model chorus attendance and mating tactics in frogs have not generated simple, obvious outcomes (e.g., Lucas et al., 1996).

3. Chorus Attendance

In many frogs, males spend extended periods in breeding choruses but females only attend once in a season so there will almost inevitably be a strong male bias in the OSR, but this may actually be relieved at high densities when the proportion of females can increase (e.g., Ryan et al., 1981; Tejedo, 1993). In an intensive mark-recapture study of *C. georgiana* over a 3-month study period, Smith et al. (2003) reported a modal stay in the chorus for males of 1 night, a mean of 3.41 nights, and a maximum attendance of 19 nights which could still be enough to bias the OSR if female attendance per night was relatively constant. However, females not only enter choruses in large numbers on a very small number of nights per season but also trickle in over the whole season (Byrne, 2002; Smith et al., 2003). OSR increases with chorus density (Fig. 1), suggesting male persistence in a chorus has little impact on OSR values, and that both sexes may be responding to common environmental cues.

Bias in the OSR in anuran choruses may be an obvious outcome of higher potential reproductive rates in males manifest as higher chorus attendance rates, or generated by explicit causes such as predation on one sex. Irrespective of the cause, bias to males in the OSR is positively associated with increased rates of polyandry in several anuran species.

C. Direct Benefits

Because females may receive direct benefits from males, such as insurance of fertilization, nutrients, or other critical compounds in ejaculates, females may deliberately solicit polyandrous mating if those direct benefits accumulate with more males per mating, or polyandrous matings have site-specific properties that improve egg survival.

1. Switching Partners

If males supply specific benefits to females, such as ejaculate components that enhance egg survival (cf. spermatophylax nutrients in tettigoniid grasshoppers, Gwynne, 1988), females may mate with multiple partners to enhance these paternal impacts. In *C. xeramplina* and *A. callidryas*, females often switch males between bouts of egg deposition: females may actively solicit some degree of sequential polyandry in these species (D'Orgeix and Turner, 1995; Jennions et al., 1992). In *Chiromantis*, and indeed many other species discussed above, females move through or deposit eggs in areas where multiple nonamplexed males are present. This may be a deliberate decision by females to maximize the chance of mate switching or polyandry occurring, but the particular benefits are not obvious in any of these examples.

2. Egg Survival and Physical Attributes of Egg Deposition Sites

Low oxygen tensions generally have detrimental effects on egg development in anurans (Seymour and Bradford, 1995; Wells, 2007). Seymour and Roberts (1995) suggested that site quality, measured by dissolved oxygen levels at egg deposition sites, might affect mate preference in *C. georgiana*, raising the potential for direct benefits arising from improved quality of egg development site (e.g., as occurs in *Rana catesbiana* with reduced predation by leeches or optimal temperatures for development; Howard, 1978a,b). Males may aggregate at high-quality sites for egg deposition, leading to localized increases in the OSR and polyandry. Byrne and Roberts (1999) found no evidence that polyandrous matings were more likely to occur at well-oxygenated sites, or that oxygen tensions had any significant impact on fertilization success. Seymour et al. (2001) showed that *C. georgiana* sometimes deposits eggs at sites where oxygen tension is too low to allow egg survival, suggesting frogs cannot discriminate variation in this variable. There is no evidence of parental care in this species and the reduced, rather than enhanced, fertilization rates in polyandrous matings all argue against any direct, environmental benefits of polyandry (Byrne and Roberts, 1999).

3. Fertilization Success

In the foam-nesting frog *C. xerampelina*, polyandry improved fertilization rates by > 20% between 1 and 12 males (regression line in Fig. 3(a) of Byrne and Whiting, 2008), but the reasons why poor fertilization occurred in monandrous matings was not certain. This pattern is complicated as there was high variance in fertilization success with one or two males, but the mean was higher, and the variance lower, with three or more males. Byrne and Whiting (2008) argued that poor fertilization might be a common property of foam nesters. They argued this might arise from (a) repeated mating by males who were consequently sperm depleted; (b) because the viscous nature of foam inhibited sperm movement; or (c) because males actively allocate sperm in ways that limit their capacity to fertilize a whole clutch. We consider each of these explanations below.

a. **Sperm Depletion**   Sperm depletion is a real possibility because group spawning events in *C. xerampelina* permit males to engage in multiple spawning events within breeding nights. In one instance, an individual male was observed to engage in six separate matings over a period of approximately 7 h (Byrne, personal observation). Sperm depletion has been reported in frogs allowed to mate repeatedly (e.g., *B. bufo*, Hettyey et al., 2009), but those data were not based on sequential, natural matings, and there are no data for any foam-nesting frog species. Sperm depletion has also been considered an explanation for poor fertilization success in frog pairs mismatched by body size, where it is possible that smaller males have too few sperm to fertilize high clutch sizes in larger females (e.g., Bourne, 1993; Robertson, 1990), but there is no evidence of this in any *Chiromantis* species. Foam nesting may favor reduced sperm investment under conditions of monogamy, but foam nesting under conditions of polyandry, and sperm competition, may strongly favor the evolution of increased sperm investment reflected in the relatively large testes found in *C. xerampelina* (Jennions and Passmore, 1993).

b. **Foam and Sperm Movement**   This seems an unlikely explanation as Muto and Kubota (2009) showed rhacophorid sperms were adapted for optimal performance in viscous media comparable to egg foam, and foam nests occur in several rhacophorid clades, so we would expect sperm properties and foam to have coevolved for optimal performance (Grosjean et al., 2008; Li et al., 2009).

c. **Sperm Allocation**   Byrne and Whiting (2008) considered several allocation models. Males may allocate sperm (a) according to the perceived risk or intensity of sperm competition (Ball and Parker, 1996) but may misallocate if some males in an aggregation do not release sperm; (b) to improve sperm economy because males mate repeatedly over a relatively long breeding season risking sperm depletion (Shapiro et al., 1994); or (c) to strategically allocate sperm between matings, as has been shown in coral reef fish (Shapiro et al., 1994). Sperm allocation in anurans has only been investigated in relation to the risk and intensity of sperm competition. In a manipulative, laboratory study using *C. georgiana*, Byrne (2004) found no evidence of selective allocation of sperm, contrary to theoretical predictions (Ball and Parker, 1996).

The prevalence of poor fertilization in foam nesters could be tested with limnodynastid species from Australia, rhacophorid species from Africa and Asia, or foam-nesting leptodactylid species from South America, with known polyandrous species available for comparison in the latter two of those groups (Table I).

D. Indirect Benefits

Indirect benefits of polyandry might arise in two ways. First, males may provide higher-quality genes, or a variety of genes, that directly affect survival (e.g., genes conferring resistance to disease or parasites, or that affect mating success indirectly because male offspring have phenotypes preferred by females, or genes that improve sperm performance when in competitive environments). Neff and Pitcher (2005) termed these collectively additive genetic benefits. Second, there may be compatibility effects where certain combinations of sperm and eggs improve fertilization success, or developmental compatibility improves offspring survival or performance: nonadditive genetic benefits (Neff and Pitcher, 2005). For indirect effects without compatibility, individual males or females should consistently perform better across matings, irrespective of the genotype of a mating partner. When compatibility effects are present, some combinations of females and males will perform well, but the same individuals may perform poorly with alternative mates (Neff and Pitcher, 2005). Neff and Pitcher (2005) and Simmons (2005) discussed several examples of experimental approaches that can be used to detect the presence of compatibility effects. External fertilizers are good candidates for analyzing compatibility effects as they reduce, but do not eliminate, the likelihood that females can exert cryptic female choice. In natural matings, females may still exert preference by selective allocation of eggs to particular males (cf. Reyer et al., 1999) or because eggs, egg jelly, or material released with eggs, selectively affect sperm performance (e.g., Rosengrave et al., 2008; Simmons et al., 2009). We note that both compatibility and additive genetic variance effects may influence the outcomes of particular matings—they are not mutually exclusive.

1. Male-Specific, Indirect Benefits

Generally, data on this problem have been obtained by comparing performance of females mated to one male, ideally mated twice to maintain a constant effect of ejaculate volume or effects of mating, and females mated to two different males (cf. Simmons, 2005). Using exactly that design, Byrne and Roberts (2000) found no evidence of indirect benefits in *C. georgiana* when they analyzed egg survival, and in a separate experiment, tadpole growth and survival from clutches raised when fertilized by one versus two fathers. Eggs were raised in water or on moist substrates, and tadpoles were reared in constant or declining water levels. Egg and tadpole rearing conditions simulated extremes of field conditions where ponds dry out over several days between rain events (Seymour et al., 2001). However, this design cannot logically distinguish male effects from compatibility effects as males were only ever mated to one female (cf. Zeh, 1997; Neff and Pitcher, 2005). This species might be adapted to coping with extreme conditions of water availability as ponds frequently dry over winter (Seymour et al., 2001), but in both cases, simulated drying conditions increased mortality, suggesting offspring were pushed beyond normal limits. The value of genetic variability in offspring may only be truly tested in novel and challenging growing conditions or with novel selection pressures. In a similar data set, Byrne and Whiting (2011) compared the viability of offspring derived from naturally formed monogamous and polyandrous matings in *C. xerampelina* and found that offspring from polyandrous matings had higher mean survival. However, as with other correlational studies designed to investigate the genetic benefits of polyandry, it is possible that the fitness benefit reported may have been linked to maternal effects or material benefits. For example, polyandrous females may have been of higher genetic quality, or eggs in polyandrous matings may have received added nutrients transmitted via the seminal fluid.

2. Compatibility Effects

The demonstration of compatibility effects is best approached by designs that cross a set of males, and a set of females, in all possible pairwise combinations and then measure fertilization success and developmental outcomes (Neff and Pitcher, 2005; Simmons, 2005; Zeh, 1997). There are then two effects that can be analyzed: additive effects due to male or female quality and nonadditive effects representing the interaction between male and female genotypes. These designs incorporate cryptic female choice effects, and if they simulate polyandrous matings with two males per mating, also incorporate sperm competition effects or outcomes. Two data sets for frogs have addressed these problems. In *C. georgiana*, compatibility was studied using North Carolina II breeding designs (cf. Neff and Pitcher, 2005), using four blocks of four females and four males mated in all possible pairwise combinations within a set (Dziminski et al., 2008). These data demonstrated significant effects of yolk volume on fertilization rates (interestingly negative—bigger eggs had lower fertilization success), and on several developmental outcomes, including size and time to metamorphosis, and survival to initial metamorphosis. There was only a single individual effect of females on percentage of tadpoles developing abnormally. There were strong male–female interaction effects consistent with compatibility effects on fertilization rates (38%), percentage hatch (68%), percentage reaching initial metamorphosis (emergence of front legs—59%), percentage initial metamorphs deformed (46%), proportion completing metamorphosis (28%), size at metamorphosis (55%), and time to metamorphosis (67%) (% in brackets represents the proportion of total variation in each variable due to incompatibility effects; Dziminski et al., 2008). Fertilization success and subsequent developmental success were positively correlated (except for time to metamorphosis where the correlation was negative, indicating faster metamorphosis), suggesting improved fitness outcomes from compatible matings. Dziminski et al. (2008) used only single-male crosses and the results might differ if males were involved in sperm competition (cf. Dziminski et al., 2009a). Compatibility gains should be favored even when there are high costs to females, even if the gains are only marginal, but they may still be a relatively small compensation for the average high costs of polyandry in *C. georgiana* (Byrne and Roberts, 1999).

Sherman et al. (2008b) also produced some evidence of compatibility effects in frogs. They crossed females to each of two males: one from their own and one from another, geographically distant population. They found extreme variation in fertilization success with significant male effects on fertilization success but no effect of population. These patterns are consistent with compatibility effects but might also have been caused by sperm concentration differences which were not controlled.

3.   Selective Fertilization—Mechanisms

The mechanism that would allow selective fertilization to exploit the sort of compatibility effects reported by Dziminski et al. (2008) is not known, but there are several options.

a.   Egg Jelly Proteins   Simmons et al. (2009) demonstrated strong individual female effects of extracts of egg jelly on sperm motility. Egg jelly proteins always raised sperm motility, but there were no significant male–female interactions analogous to the compatibility effects noted above (Simmons et al., 2009). Egg jelly effects on sperm motility are well known in fish, and a recent study on chinook salmon demonstrated significant interaction effects, suggesting females or males can selectively influence fertilization outcomes in external fertilizers (Rosengrave et al., 2008).

b.   Genetic Similarity   Sherman et al. (2008c) suggested relatedness might be a mechanism promoting selective fertilization by compatible gametes. In experimental studies of polyandry with the Australian tree frog, *Litoria peronii*, Sherman et al. (2008c) showed that in competitive fertilization trials that mixed sperm from two males, competitive fertilization success was biased toward males that had higher genetic similarity (measured by shared alleles at eight polymorphic microsatellite loci) to the female, although that result was not replicated in an independent data set for the same species reported by Sherman et al. (2009a). In a similar competitive fertilization trial with *C. georgiana*, Dziminski et al. (2009a) found no effect of relatedness (also assessed using multilocus microsatellite genotypes).

To show that genetic similarity and relatedness are important determinants of fitness, individual case studies need to examine the fitness consequences associated with different levels of outbreeding. Only if fitness is affected by genetic similarity and/or relatedness should we expect selection to favor fertilization biases toward, or against, related or similar genotypes. Markers other than neutral microsatellites, such as major histocompatibility complex genotypes (MHC), that have been implicated in selective mate choice in a variety of organisms (e.g., Drury, 2010), might produce very different results, but they also need to be measured in realistic contexts, incorporating the impacts of interactions between males and females before mating, which can modify female preferences (Drury, 2010; Garner et al., 2010).

c. Genetic Compatibility   At a broader level, Sherman et al. (2008b, 2009a, 2010) determined fertilization outcomes using sperm mixtures from males from geographically separate populations of *L. peronii* and sperm from *L. peronii* mixed with sperm from *Litoria tyleri*, a sympatric congener. Sherman et al. (2008a, 2009, 2010) argued that local populations, or different species, would be genetically distinct or developmentally incompatible, favoring local population or conspecific sperm at fertilization. However, own population and even own species sperm did not have a competitive advantage in *L. peronii* contrary to the expectations of genetic similarity and compatibility arguments, and despite strong evidence of postfertilization, developmental incompatibilities (Sherman et al., 2008b, 2010). Contrarily, Reyer et al. (2003) ran competitive fertilization trials with frogs in the *Rana ridibunda, R. lessonae, R. esculenta*, complex, where mixed sperm from the first two species did not differ in their fertilization ability in sperm mixtures with females of either species. Sperm from both *R. ridibunda* and *R. lessonae* outcompeted sperm from *R. esculenta*, and eggs fertilized by *R. esculenta* sperm generate offspring with lower viability. Competitive fertilization can give an advantage to sperm of one or two species in trials mixing sperm from two or three anuran species, indicating that there are mechanisms for species level sperm–egg recognition in some anurans (e.g., Berger and Rybacki, 1992; Reyer et al., 2003).

d. Sperm Size and Motility   Using IVF techniques, Dziminski et al. (2009a) found no evidence that sperm swimming velocity, the proportion of motile spermatozoa, sperm head and tail length, or the proportion of live spermatozoa had any impact on fertilization success in *C. georgiana* when eggs were fertilized by a single male. In competitive fertilization trials reported by Dziminski et al. (2009a), slower swimming speeds and the proportion of motile sperm best predicted competitive fertilization success. Dziminski et al. (2009a) argued that slower swimming sperm and persistence might be critical factors allowing sperm to penetrate the multiple jelly layers around frog eggs. Reyer et al. (2003) found no effect of sperm morphology or swimming speed on fertilization success during competitive fertilization trials in the *R. ridibunda*, *R. lessonae*, *R. esculenta* complex. Their sample sizes for speed were small, and lower speeds were reported in *R. esculenta* (hybrid) males, suggesting a possible mechanism for their poor performance in competitive fertilization trials.

Two studies by Sherman et al. (2008b, 2010) also analyzed outcomes of competitive fertilization trials in *L. peronii*, and relative male performance in competitive trials was consistent across crosses to two different females as well as in mixed and single-male fertilization trials. These results are inconsistent with compatibility effects, but might be anticipated in a species where there has been no selection to improve performance in competitive situations, which may be the case in this species (cf. calculations in Reyer et al., 2003). The breeding system for *L. peronii* is poorly known, with the only clue to the occurrence of polyandry being the observation by Sherman et al. (2008b), that multiple males have been observed trying to amplex females, and that amplexing pairs are often surrounded by satellite males as they move into the water to spawn: neither condition necessarily leads to polyandry (see Section III.A).

External fertilizers, including frogs (e.g., Dziminski et al., 2008; Evans and Marshall, 2005; Marshall and Evans, 2005a,b; Neff and Pitcher, 2005), have produced a strong body of evidence that compatibility effects may be an explanation for the evolution of polyandry and provide tractable models for answering questions about the evolution of polyandry and associated issues such as the heritability of sperm performance (e.g., García-González, 2008). Polyandrous frog species with larger clutch sizes and less variation in yolk volume than *C. georgiana* offer particular advantages, as they could be crossed to more males or use larger sample sizes to assess effects.

E. Costs of Polyandry

Polyandry generates high costs, often for females, in many animal species (e.g., Table 4.1 in Arnqvist and Rowe, 2005). This is also true in the mating system of *C. georgiana* where matings involving two or more males impose very high costs: dramatic reductions in fertilization rates (around 30% for matings with two males and higher for matings with more than two males) (Fig. 2). The cause was not clear, but Byrne and Roberts (1999) suggested that reduced fertilization success was most likely the outcome of intense competition between struggling males interfering with sperm transfer because males physically obstructed sperm from reaching eggs, males prevented other males from adopting optimal fertilization positions, or males were unable to adopt optimal sperm allocation strategies. Importantly, the mismatch in male–female body size ratio leading to a reduction in fertilization success that has been reported in other frogs (e.g., Bourne, 1993; Robertson, 1990) did not occur in *C. georgiana* (Byrne and Roberts, 1999). Byrne and Roberts (1999) also reported a 1 in 50 female death rate due to drowning of females involved in polyandrous matings. Deaths of females by drowning in polyandrous mating attempts also occur in *B. bufo* (Sztatecsny et al., 2006), and Sztatecsny et al. (2006) suggested that *B. bufo* females may accept polyandrous matings by two males out of convenience to avoid risks of drowning imposed by larger aggregations of males. Deaths of females as a result of competition among males scrambling for access to

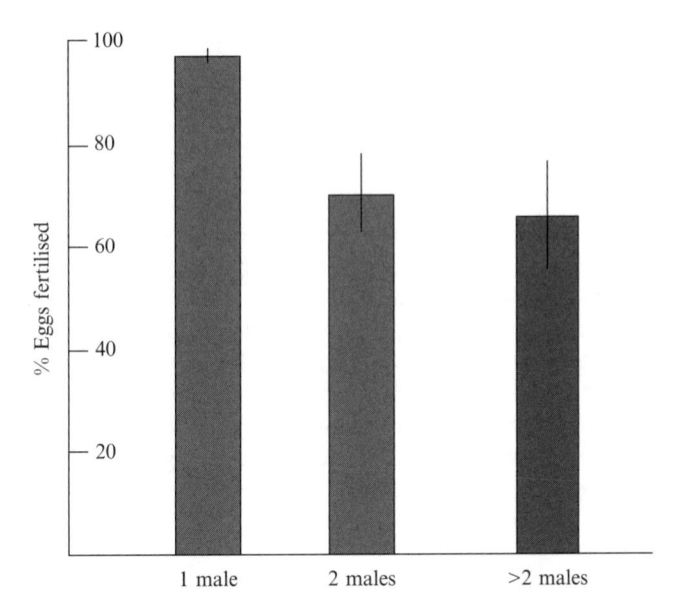

FIG. 2. High costs of polyandry in *Crinia georgiana* where matings with two or more males reduced fertilization rates by approximately 30% (modified and redrawn from Byrne and Roberts, 1999). Bars on histogram are standard errors.

mates have been reported in many frog species where polyandry has not been reported (e.g., Howard, 1980; Wells, 1977, 2007). However, given some of the examples cited by Wells (2007) are now known to be polyandrous (e.g., *R. temporaria*, *B. bufo*, cf. Table I) they may require more critical evaluation. Given that the cost of polyandry is high in many mating systems, it seems sensible to expect that anurans might show similar patterns, and this should be looked for in other polyandrous anurans.

V. POLYANDRY AND ANURAN EVOLUTION

Much of the material that follows is deliberately speculative. We have established that polyandry occurs in several anuran species in eight different anuran families, and we can see groups where it occurs in many species (e.g., the Rhacophoridae). There are many types of behaviors that may generate polyandry, male scramble competition, and mating balls, for example, that have been interpreted in a context of monandrous not polyandrous mating systems. We cannot confidently include or comprehensively exclude polyandry in many anuran mating systems, but if it is more widespread than we have documented, its impacts are likely to be strong, as they have been in many other animals (e.g., Arnqvist and Rowe, 2005; Simmons, 2001). We offer some well-supported examples and some speculations on how polyandry may have shaped anuran evolution.

A. MATING TACTICS AND BODY SIZE

In many species with alternative mating tactics, male body size or age often set the tactics used to achieve paternity (Oliveira et al., 2008), but in others, the adoption of alternative tactics may be either state dependent (e.g., energy-depleted males may adopt satellite tactics, Lucas and Howard, 1995; Lucas et al., 1996) or context dependent, with males adopting satellite tactics if they are smaller than rivals (e.g., Arak, 1988).

In *C. georgiana*, matings involve 1–8 males with one male in conventional, inguinal amplexus, a second male amplexed in the same area but ventral (Roberts et al., 1999; Fig. 3), and with additional males arrayed around those two focal frogs. Matings involving two or more males occurred in all populations studied, with frequencies varying from 33% to 73% of all matings observed (Byrne, 2002; Roberts et al., 1999). In matings involving only singe males, pairing involved (i) apparent female choice among an array of calling males (13/22 matings); (ii) interception by satellite males (silent males) sitting adjacent to calling males (1/22); or (iii) interception of females by calling or searching males (8/22) (Byrne and Roberts, 2004).

In polyandrous matings, females (i) selected from calling males; (ii) were intercepted by satellites; or (iii) were intercepted by males who either called or searched. Then in each case, additional males joined the initially amplexed pair. Searching and interception were more likely at higher chorus densities (> 5 males m^{-2}) (Byrne and Roberts, 2004).

In low-density choruses (< 5 males m^{-2}), large males achieved dorsal amplexus, and ventral males were significantly smaller, but in high-density choruses, ventral and dorsal males (the presumed preferred positions based on male shares of paternity; Section IV.A) were similar in body size (Fig. 4).

In *C. georgiana*, there is very high variance in both male and female body size, higher than in any other anurans, and in many populations, an element of bimodality in male body size can be detected (Smith and Roberts, 2003a). Smith and Roberts (2003b,c) showed that females have preferences, in both field and laboratory situations, for males with high call rates and low first note duration, characteristically produced by smaller males, or relatively low call rates but high first note durations, characteristically produced by larger males, but the selective advantage in these preferences was not clear (Smith and Roberts, 2003b,c). The observed call preferences impose an element of disruptive selection on body size that may be reinforced by the relative success of large versus small males in polyandrous matings seen in low-density choruses (Byrne and Roberts, 2004) which are the prevailing breeding conditions (cf. Byrne, 2002; Smith

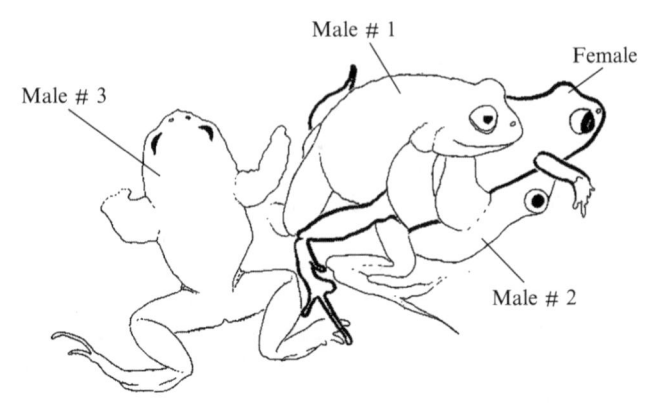

F<small>IG</small>. 3. Common amplexus positions in *Crinia georgiana*. Male #1 is in dorsal, inguinal (conventional) amplexus; male #2 is in a ventral position; and male #3 is positioned behind the multiply mated female. Female is outlined with a thick line and males with thin lines. Males were only found in position #1 in monandrous matings but in positions #1 and #2 in polyandrous matings. In polyandrous matings, additional males joined these basic pairings in many positions, for example, over the head, alongside or on back of the male in position #1, or hanging off the legs of the female. Drawn by D. Harms from an original photograph by M. Smith.

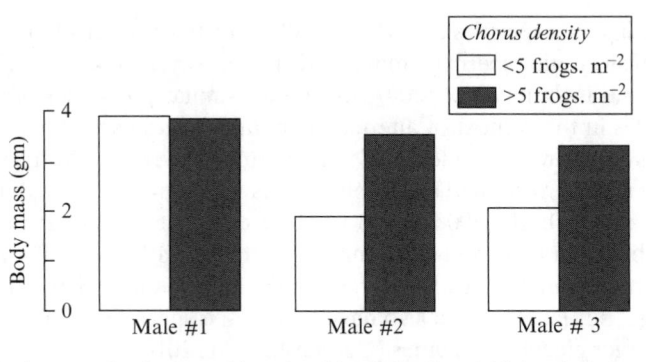

FIG. 4. Body mass of males in positions 1 and 2 (cf. Fig. 3) and third males in low- and high-density choruses (modified and redrawn from Byrne and Roberts, 2004).

et al., 2003). The causes of variation in body size are not clear. Initial egg yolk volume increases both offspring size at metamorphosis and survival to metamorphosis under both laboratory and field settings (Dziminski and Roberts, 2006; Dziminski et al., 2009b). Yolk volumes can vary widely within clutches, but eggs are also often of uniform size: all small, or all large (Dziminski and Roberts, 2006). Initial yolk volume may set a growth trajectory that results in small, or large body size. Patterns of pond persistence and the ability of tadpoles to disperse from natal ponds might also interact with initial yolk volumes to affect survival (Dziminski, 2005). However, size at metamorphosis might also be affected by conditions during larval development, with harsh conditions generating classic, plastic responses in tadpoles with acceleration of development traded off against small body size (Doughty, 2002; Doughty and Roberts, 2003). Smith and Roberts (2003a) showed that small size at metamorphosis could be readily compensated for if food availability was high, so predicting adult size is complicated. Smith et al. (2003) also showed that growth between breeding seasons could be substantial for smaller frogs (> 10 mm in both males and females, an almost 50% increase in snout-vent length). This might suggest that body size variation simply reflects annual growth patterns, but Smith and Roberts (2003a) recaptured very few males the next year (5 of 278 marked males) and marked frogs were not caught at adjacent choruses, suggesting poor annual survival and, therefore, very little opportunity for growth increments to explain variation in male body size. Small or large growth trajectories, or maturity and breeding at different ages (1 vs. 2 years old), might account for the variance in body size, making *C. georgiana* comparable to polyandrous, salmonid fish species where males use age-related, alternative mating tactics (e.g., Taborsky, 1994, 2008).

Fish using sneak tactics are often smaller but have relatively larger testes and faster swimming sperm (summarized in Taborsky, 2008). Byrne (2004) and Hettyey and Roberts (2006, 2007) looked for similar properties of small and large males in the context of alternative mating tactics used by *C. georgiana*. *C. georgiana* shows no evidence of a discontinuity in relative testis mass with body size (larger males had bigger but not relatively larger testes; Byrne, 2004; Hettyey and Roberts, 2006, 2007) nor any evidence that sperm properties differed between large and small males (Hettyey and Roberts, 2007). Larger males can presumably produce larger ejaculates, possibly giving them some advantage, but larger males also have less motile sperm, possibly trading off against larger ejaculate volumes (Dziminski et al., 2010a).

Although mating tactics used by small and large males can differ radically, particularly at high densities (Byrne and Roberts, 2004), there are few high-density nights in a breeding season (Byrne, 2002; Smith et al., 2003), so small and large body sizes, coupled with an element of bimodality in female preferences for calls from small and large males (Smith and Roberts, 2003b,c), may compensate to make both mating strategies equally fit (cf. Hettyey and Roberts, 2007).

The variation in body size in *C. georgiana* is intriguing, but understanding its evolution requires a detailed understanding of ejaculate size and properties in natural matings and the impact of male body size, time in amplexus, and position in amplexus on paternity rates. This is the focus of ongoing investigation.

B. Body Size Evolution and Frog Radiations

The variance in body size in *C. georgiana* was only matched by one other frog species in a study of 51 species by Smith and Roberts (2003a), suggesting the selection on variation in body size imposed by polyandry is strong. Body mass in *C. georgiana* is almost 5 times that reported for the second largest *Crinia* species (*C. tasmaniensis*, Byrne et al., 2002) and 10 times higher than its sister species, *C. glauerti* (Byrne et al., 2002; Read et al., 2001; Fig. 5), suggesting polyandry has imposed strong selection on body mass in *C. georgiana*. Most frogs in the family Myobatrachidae (*sensu* Frost et al., 2006) are small (15–30 mm; e.g., *Arenophryne, Assa, Crinia, Geocrinia, Metacrinia, Paracrinia, Pseudophryne, Uperoleia*, and *Spicospina* (snout-vent length data in appendix to Byrne et al., 2002), but females of *Myobatrachus* can be much larger (Tyler and Doughty, 2009). The shift in maximum body size in *C. georgiana* takes the body size into the bottom end of the range of larger body sizes seen in another major Australian frog family, the Limnodynastidae, the sister taxon to the Myobatrachidae (Byrne et al., 2002; Frost et al., 2006). Large body size in *C. georgiana* provides larger

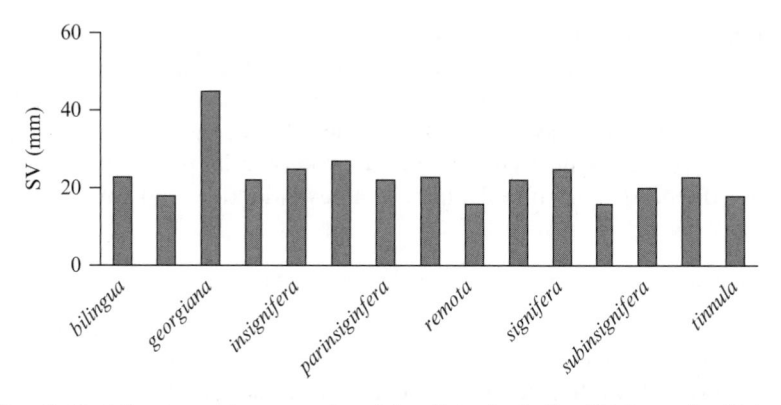

FIG. 5. Variation in maximum snout-vent length in Australian *Crinia* species. Data are taken from Byrne et al. (2002), Smith and Roberts (2003a), and various Australian field guides (Barker et al., 1995; Tyler et al., 2000) reflecting both field experience and specimens in Australian Museums.

males with a mating advantage in high-density choruses but might also be the raw material of an adaptive shift allowing radiations of frogs with larger body sizes—a step analogous to the generally larger size of species in the family Limnodynastidae, the sister taxon to the family Myobatrachidae (Frost et al., 2006).

The evolution of body size could be analyzed in other frog groups where polyandry is known, for example, in the Rhacophoridae, where there are extensive data sets on phylogenetic relationships and data on the occurrence of polyandry (e.g., Li et al., 2009; Table I), or ranids, where there are similarly good phylogenetic data and but much more limited evidence of polyandry (e.g., Che et al., 2007; Hillis and Wilcox, 2005). Intra- and intersexual selection (e.g., Monnett and Cherry, 2002) or ecological conditions might also affect body size evolution in anurans (e.g., Moen and Wiens, 2009), but polyandry presents an alternative to these models of size change between species that has not been investigated.

If polyandry leads to new radiations, we would expect the derived (modern) lineages to contain species that are all polyandrous. That may be the case in the rhachophorids. The Rhacophorid clades containing the genera *Rhacophorus*, *Polypedates*, and *Chiromantis* have high rates of polyandry (Table I), foam egg masses (Li et al., 2009), highly derived morphology of the reproductive tract (Grosjean et al., 2008), and Japanese and some African species at least have relatively high testis mass (Jennions and Passmore, 1993; Kusano et al., 1991). Loss of polyandry might also be expected if ecological conditions favoring maintenance of polyandry change. In *C. georgiana*, the occurrence of polyandry is dependent on the OSR, and the OSR varies night by night (Byrne and Roberts, 2004), though the ecological conditions predicting OSR variation are not clear (Section V.A). As Emlen and Oring (1977) noted when they introduced the OSR concept, OSR may vary with environmental conditions, so an initial quantum shift allowing a new radiation, promoted by polyandry, does not require the persistence of polyandry in a new adaptive landscape.

C. Sperm Competition and the Evolution of Ejaculates

A common, but not universal, pattern seen in many animal groups is that increasing risks of sperm competition favor the evolution of larger ejaculates, presumably reflected in large relative testis size, and ejaculate properties that improve performance when sperm are competing with other ejaculates (e.g., Byrne et al., 2002, 2003; Fitzpatrick et al., 2009).

1. Testis Mass

In anurans, several comparative data sets have analyzed variations in testis mass either in relation to the risk of sperm competition occurring or by contrasting species with simultaneous polyandry with those that have monandrous mating systems. The data were mostly analyzed without phylogenetic control and based on small numbers of species (Emerson, 1997; Jennions and Passmore, 1993; Kusano et al., 1991; Prado and Haddad, 2003). Byrne et al. (2003) analyzed testis size variation in two Australian frog groups, the Myobatrachids (covering the current families Myobatrachidae and Limnodynastidae, which are sister taxa; Frost et al., 2006) and the Hylidae (subfamily Pelodyradinae). They included the majority of known species in both groups and included correction for phylogenetic effects using CAIC (comparative analysis by independent contrasts, Purvis and Rambaut, 1995) and an array of alternative explanatory variables (e.g., egg size and number and egg deposition mode).

The smaller data sets, uncorrected for phylogenetic effects, generally show that species which have mating behaviors consistent with the occurrence of simultaneous polyandry also have relatively larger testes (Jennions and Passmore, 1993; Kusano et al., 1991; Prado and Haddad, 2003). Those data were preselected based on observed mating behaviors of outlier species, and with a larger sample of species with conventional mating behavior, the polyandrous species might fall within the range of variation seen in other species. This is exactly the pattern seen in Emerson's (1997) data sets for hylid species where two polyandrous species had relatively large testes (along with several where mating patterns were unknown), but there was also one polyandrous species with average sized testes. Emerson (1997) also found positive correlations between testis mass and egg number and testosterone levels, suggesting factors other than sperm competition can affect testis mass in frogs. Kusano et al. (1991) noted that rhachophorid frog species generally had relatively larger testis masses compared to other frog families with individual rhacophorid species known to have polyandrous mating behaviors even higher, but the same pattern was not evident in data reported by Jennions and Passmore (1993).

Byrne et al. (2002) measured the risk of sperm competition by spatial proximity of males, and known patterns of mating. For example, males calling from burrows, where only one male had ever been found, scored the lowest risk, but species where multiple-male/single-female groups had been observed scored the highest. Risk data were assessed from the literature on mating behaviors and chorus densities and supplemented with some unpublished observations. In addition to sperm competition risk, this study also assessed the relationship of testis mass (corrected for body size) to egg number, yolk diameter, capsule diameter, and site and form of egg deposition (e.g., aquatic, terrestrial, aquatic in foam, terrestrial in foam).

In myobatrachids, testis mass was predicted by the risk of sperm competition: higher risk was associated with larger testes (Fig. 6A). Testis mass was lower in foam nesters, but clutch and egg size did not affect relative testis mass. For hylids, no significant relationships were found (Fig. 6A). Less data on mating behavior and testes mass were available for hylids, but hylids also differ in many other ways, for example, many Australian hylid species have extremely complex calls which may reduce the potential for satellite or sneak behaviors (e.g., Doughty and Anstis, 2007; Smith and Roberts, 2003d; cf. Byrne et al., 2002).

Dziminski et al. (2010b) looked at intraspecific variation in testis and sperm properties in *C. georgiana* in relation to rates of polyandry estimated from field-collected egg masses. Such intraspecific comparisons eliminate many of the weaknesses associated with cross-species comparisons that are inevitably confounded by genetic differences between species as well as the selective pressure of interest (e.g., Garland and Adolph, 1994). Their analysis showed significant among population variation in testes size, the number of sperm stored in the testes, and in the proportion of stored sperm that were motile. Testis size, stored sperm, and percentage motile sperm were correlated positively with male density. Male density was a basic metric used to estimate risk of sperm competition in earlier cross-species comparisons, indicating a consistency both across and within species (Byrne et al., 2002, 2003; Dziminski et al., 2010b), and is also positively correlated with the degree of male bias in the OSR (Byrne and Roberts, 2004; cf. Fig. 1).

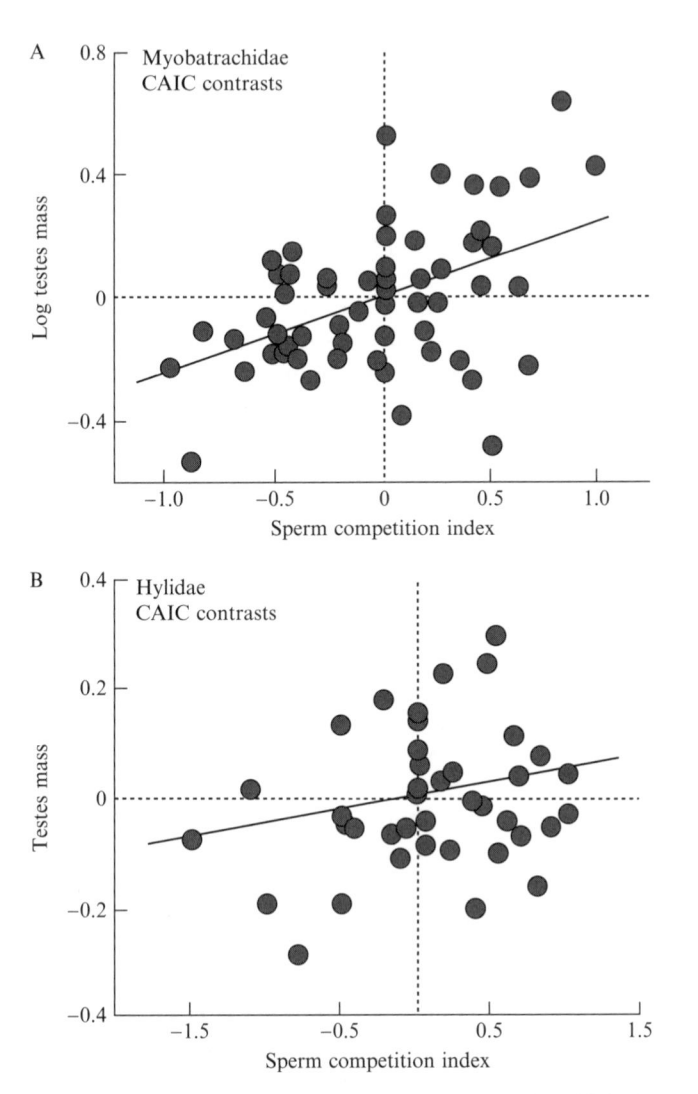

FIG. 6. Independent contrasts in testis mass and sperm competition risk in the Australian frogs families Myobatrachidae (A) and the Hylidae (B) (modified and redrawn from Byrne et al., 2002).

2. Sperm Morphology

Byrne et al. (2003) analyzed sperm length against sperm competition risk in myobatrachid frogs. There was a weak, but significant, effect of sperm competition risk on sperm head length, and a strong significant effect of sperm competition risk on sperm tail length, but several other factors (e.g., egg size, egg deposition mode) also had important impacts. Variation in sperm form is not clearly related to egg deposition mode in anurans with, for example, weak support for the proposition that the undulating membrane is lost in families with aquatic egg deposition (Garda et al., 2004). Sperm form is highly variable in frogs (e.g., Kuramoto, 1996; Scheltinga et al., 2002). For example, in rhacophorids, there are strong generic differences with species in the genus *Rhacophorus* having tightly coiled, large sperm quite different from other rhacophorid genera (e.g., *Polypedates*; Kuramoto, 1996), but these differences may also be related to motility in the viscous medium provided by foam nests in this group (cf. Muto and Kubota, 2009). In other genera (e.g., Scheltinga et al., 2002), sperm are simpler and shorter, but in both *Rhacophporus* and *Polypedates*, there are species exhibiting polyandry (Kuramoto, 1996).

The comparative analyses document contradictory outcomes—sperm competition may be selectively affecting testis size and sperm structure in some frog groups but not in others (cf. Byrne et al., 2002, 2003) just as in other animal groups. These data also show that despite relatively few overt examples of polyandrous mating systems, there are still strong relationships in some groups explained by risk of sperm competition, and in many groups, there are species with very high relative testis mass in which polyandry has not been reported (but cannot be excluded) (Byrne et al., 2002; Emerson, 1997). The challenge is to determine whether this reflects (i) reality or (ii) inadequate data on frog mating systems. For example, in both hylids and myobatrachids from Australia, if a testis mass of greater than 1% of total body mass was taken as an indicator of the potential for polyandry, then six species might show this form of mating behavior. If that ratio was reduced to 0.5%, the potential number of polyandrous species rises to 15 species (based on data reported by Byrne et al., 2002). In Emerson's (1997) data set, species known to have polyandrous mating (e.g., *A. callidryas*) did not always have particularly large testes, or even the largest testes in their genus, so relative testis mass alone may not be a sufficient indicator of polyandry.

3. Sperm Storage and Strategic Ejaculation

In many frog species, there are large sperm storage organs, the *vesicula seminalis*, formed as diverticulations of the Wolffian duct (Bhaduri, 1953; Gaup, 1904; Noble, 1931). Noble (1931) suggested the *vesicula seminalis* "...would seem to permit the use of a large amount of sperm in a short time...," almost anticipating strategic ejaculation models relating to sperm competition risk and intensity (Ball and Parker, 1996). The *vesicula seminalis* and other modifications of the Wolffian duct occur in many frogs (e.g., for extensive comparative data sets, see Bhaduri, 1953) and not only may be related to egg deposition mode (e.g., foam nesting) but also may be selectively associated with polyandrous mating systems as they occur in *R. temporaria* (Gaup, 1904) and in several rhacophorid species known to be polyandrous (e.g., Iwasawa and Michibata, 1972). The *vesicula seminalis* is known to be strongly secretory, though the exact nature of those secretions and whether or how they might affect sperm function are unknown (Mann et al., 1963). The distribution of the *vesicula seminalis* across frog families in relation to the occurrence of polyandry is a subject of current investigation. Structural modifications of the reproductive tract (coupled with relative testis mass) might give a further clue to the potential for polyandry in species with unknown mating systems—a way to define targets for further investigation of anuran polyandry.

D. CALL STRUCTURES AND POLYANDRY

Studies on sexual selection in frogs have had a strong emphasis on the function of male calls, both in interactions between males and their roles in allowing female choice among mates (e.g., Gerhardt and Huber, 2002; Ryan, 2001; Wells, 2007). We expect that mixed breeding systems, where matings may involve one male, or many, will impose two forms of selection on call structure. There will be conventional sexual selection pressures: intersexual selection for features indicating male quality or intrasexual selection for call properties that improve competitiveness over rival males, as many matings occur in low-density choruses where polyandry is less likely (Byrne and Roberts, 2004). There may also be novel pressures imposed by polyandry for call structures that minimize the chance of polyandrous matings occurring, for example, by minimizing the attraction of satellites or repelling males actively searching for females in choruses. We discuss these ideas in the context of field and experimental data on call function in *C. georgiana*, as this is the only polyandrous anuran species we are aware of with more than basic descriptions of call structure.

1. *Call Structures and Function in* C. georgiana

The call of *C. georgiana* consists of 1–11 pulsed notes, but the modal high number of notes is five, and males actively vary the number of notes per call (Gerhardt et al., 2000; Smith et al., 2003). The first notes of calls are longer than subsequent notes, but notes in single-note calls are the same duration as first notes in multiple-note calls (Ayre et al., 1984; Gerhardt et al., 2000). Males respond to even crude imitations of male calls by humans. Those responses were investigated experimentally by Gerhardt et al. (2000) who played simulated calls containing one, two, four, or eight notes. Less than 40% of males responded to playbacks of one-note calls, just under 50% responded to two notes, around 70% to four-note calls, and nearly 80% to eight-note calls. Males approximately matched note number when played two- and four-note stimuli, generally made two notes in response to single-note playbacks, and averaged about six notes to a stimulus with eight notes. Gerhardt et al. (2000) interpreted these data as showing that males produced calls at least as attractive as their rivals. The discrepancies to playbacks of one and eight notes may indicate an attempt to outsignal rivals at one note, or physiological limits in response to eight notes. Smith and Roberts (2003b) analyzed call structures of males involved in single-male matings and compared them with unmated males in the same mating aggregations—both in natural breeding choruses. They found successful males had longer first notes and called more slowly, or shorter first notes and called faster (though the latter effect was not quite significant). Importantly, neither the number of notes in a male's call, nor peak frequency, affected mating success. In laboratory trials using simulated calls in two choice discrimination trials, females showed similar preference patterns, except that they also exhibited a preference for modal frequencies (Smith and Roberts, 2003c). Despite the strong pattern of note matching in males, note number does not seem to be important to females. This result suggests the role of call matching outlined above is wrong: females are not using note number to discriminate among males, so there is no value in males varying note number to match or outsignal competitors. Males might therefore be signaling for other purposes. Males may lengthen calls (i) to repel satellites or searching males, but given that about half of all matings involve two or more males (Byrne, 2002; Dziminski et al., 2010b; Roberts et al., 1999), this must frequently be ineffective; (ii) to attract satellites as females prefer mating with multiple males (e.g., for the compatibility benefits discussed above) or because females can choose among males more readily and gain an exclusive mating often enough to trade-off against known costs of polyandry; (iii) because in acoustically complex choruses, discrimination tasks may be much more difficult (cf. Bee and Micheyl, 2008; Schwartz and Freeberg, 2008) and trailing notes may convey critical information about male quality (cf. Grafe, 1999; Gerhardt and Huber, 2002); or (iv) to attract related males who cooperate as can occur in bird leks (e.g., Reynolds et al., 2008). Selective mating based on relatedness has been demonstrated in anurans in the field, and this may be based on male call (e.g., Waldman et al., 1992), suggesting the possibility of a mechanism allowing kin associations. Contrarily, in the European tree frog, *Hyla arborea*, Knopp et al. (2008) found no evidence that silent, satellite males associated with calling males were more closely related than random. *C. georgiana* has a complex calling system, but neither is the variation in note number easily explained by conventional inter- or intrasexual selection arguments, nor is it clear how varying note number reduces the chance of polyandry, an obvious risk for males in terms of reduced fertilization success and paternity share.

Our understanding of the function of call complexity in anurans is rudimentary. A recent study on *P. pustulosus* emphasizes this point. There is a very large literature on the function of whines and additional chucks (up to seven) in the call of *P. pustulosus*, suggesting that more chucks are more attractive to females and elicit more calling activity from other males (Bernal et al., 2009). In the field, males generally only added one chuck and there was no strong evidence that more chucks actually improved attractiveness (Bernal et al., 2009). How call structure has evolved in relation to the novel selection pressures imposed by polyandrous matings clearly requires further investigation in *C. georgiana* and will benefit from comparative analyses of call structure and how call functions in other polyandrous species.

VI. Polyandry and Speciation

Much recent work on anuran speciation has focused on interactions between species leading to reinforcement or reproductive character displacement (e.g., Gerhardt and Brooks, 2009; Lemmon, 2009), or isolation and local differentiation that have identified evidence of local selection or drift as causes of difference between populations (e.g., Boul et al., 2007; Funk et al., 2009; Ohmer et al., 2009; Wang and Summers, 2010). In examples where sexual selection has been invoked as causing differences, the patterns of female preference are clear (e.g., Boul et al., 2007; Maan and Cummings, 2009), but there is no explanation why patterns of sexual selection should differ between populations. Sexual conflict caused by polyandry can lead to the evolution of local mate preferences and speciation (e.g., Martin and Hosken, 2003; Parker and Partridge, 1998; Ritchie, 2007) and may contribute to the evolution of differences between populations. Because the nature of signals used in species and mate recognition is well known in anurans (e.g., Gerhardt and Huber, 2002), polyandrous frogs may offer well-understood models to dissect the interplay between patterns of directional sexual selection, sexual conflict, and the history and geography of local populations (e.g., Carnaval and Bates, 2007; Hua and Wiens, 2009). In *C. georgiana*, there is geographic variation in levels of polyandry in the field (Byrne, 2002; Dziminski et al., 2010b) and associated geographic variation in sperm and testis properties (Dziminski et al., 2010b; Hettyey and Roberts, 2006, 2007). This species also has high costs of polyandry (Byrne and Roberts, 1999), raising the prospect of variation in levels of sexual conflict between populations leading to local mate recognition and preference as predicted by sexual conflict models of speciation. This argument could be tested by matching geographic variation in call structure to female preference functions and local rates of polyandry with higher divergence expected if polyandry is more common. However, not all sexual conflict models predict own population preference (e.g., Hayashi et al., 2007), nor do experimental data show that pattern (Rowe et al., 2003). It is difficult to derive exclusive predictions that differentiate sexual conflict from other models that also predict geographic variation in call and mate preference (e.g., Ritchie, 2007; Snook et al., 2009). Sexual conflict driven by polyandry is a mechanism that may initiate directional sexual selection and should be considered as a possible explanation for the evolution of local call differences that have been reported in some frogs (e.g., Boul et al., 2007).

VII. ANURAN POLYANDRY—OPPORTUNITIES

This chapter has focused on a large natural history literature on anurans, tempered by some strong quantitative experiments on a very limited number of frog species. Neither is anuran polyandry a rare event resulting from scramble competition among males, nor is it an occasional mistake; it is an evolved mating strategy. We have comparatively few hard data and necessarily have frequently been very speculative, but we have also emphasized the opportunities that anurans offer for an improved understanding of polyandrous mating systems and anuran evolution.

The available data on testis mass, modifications of sperm morphology, and the widespread occurrence of sperm storage organs, coupled with extensive behavioral observations, all point to the possibility that a large number of anuran species may be characterized as having mating systems with simultaneous polyandry. These predictions can be tested with data on patterns of paternity in natural egg masses comparable to the pioneering data reported by Laurila and Seppä (1998). Genetic work should not be done in isolation but must be combined with appropriate behavioral observations. For example, Laurila and Seppä (1998) speculated that sperm leakage accounted for their evidence of multiple paternity in *R. temporaria*, but subsequent work by Vietes et al. (2004) demonstrating clutch piracy allows a very different interpretation. Our understanding of anuran mating systems may be turned upside down with an appropriate mix of genetic and behavioral analyses of polyandry in anurans.

When we understand the distribution of polyandry in anurans across systematic boundaries, we will also be in a position to refute or support many of the speculations we have made about the impacts of polyandry on anuran behavior, physiology, and call and body size evolution. There are some groups, for example, the Rhacophoridae, and possibly the Phyllome-dusine hylids, with major lineages where a very high proportion, or possibly all species, exhibit simultaneous polyandry, suggesting basal evolution of the trait, and subsequent diversification. Some suggestions on generic splits in Rhacophorids (e.g., Kuramoto, 1996) may reflect variation in sperm form arising from selection imposed by polyandry, though we acknowledge egg deposition in foam may also affect sperm evolution in this group (cf. Byrne et al., 2003; Muto and Kubota, 2009; but see Kuramoto, 1996 for a counter argument).

There are several recent studies on geographic variation in call structure in anurans that produce strong evidence of local differentiation and invoke directional sexual selection, driven by female preference, to account for those differences (e.g., Boul et al., 2007; Funk et al., 2009). Sexual conflict arising from polyandry might be an equally plausible explanation for many of these examples as local mate preference, local mating systems, and idiosynchratic calls are both predictions that also flow from speciation driven by sexual conflict (cf. Martin and Hosken, 2003). Alternative mating systems at different geographic locations might also be expected under sexual conflict models. Briggs (2008) analyzed mating patterns in red-eyed treefrogs, *A. callidryas*, in Belize and found no evidence of polyandry contrary to D'Orgeix and Turner (1995) who worked in Panama—fitting those predictions. Sexual conflict is potentially a powerful force driving the evolution of mating systems and anurans offer some interesting options for analysis given the depth of understanding of call function and the emerging data on chemical communication (Belanger and Corkum, 2009).

The limited data on selective egg allocation by females, the impact of egg jelly on sperm swimming speed, and the possibility that the *vesicula seminalis* may add critical products to ejaculates affecting sperm performance, or conceivably egg survival or development, all indicate that the apparent advantages of using external fertilizers to test many ideas about the evolution of polyandry may be just that: apparent. Females may be using cryptic choice, and males may be influencing the performance of their own sperm, or the sperm of other males, negating many of the advantages of using external fertilizers to address problems such as compatibility advantages arising from polyandrous matings (Dziminski et al., 2008; Neff and Pitcher, 2005). We know remarkably little about ejaculate properties in anurans. Recent studies on compatibility in frogs have used testes crushes to obtain sperm, or relied on hormone injections to induce sperm release (e.g.,

Dziminski et al., 2008; Sherman et al., 2009a,b), but there are currently no critical studies showing how natural ejaculate properties compare with artificial sources of sperm. Wilson et al. (1998) demonstrated differences in several measures of sperm motility in *Xenopus laevis* where sperm were obtained in four ways: (1) from males in amplexus after injection of human chorionic gonadotrophin, (2) in amplexus naturally with no hormone manipulation, (3) by electroejaculation, and (4) by testes crushes after electroejaculation. The percentage of motile sperm was highest in testes crushes (despite the testes already having been electroejaculated) and from naturally amplexed males, but straight-line velocities were highest in sperm released naturally. Sperm collection procedures may have impacts on sperm properties that have not been accounted for in many of the experiments reported above and are crying out for novel approaches that approximate natural ejaculates. Clever application of condom-based techniques (e.g., Hettyey et al., 2009) illustrates one way of obtaining, at least, minimum estimates of natural ejaculate sizes, and potentially, the nature of material added to sperm by the *vesicula seminalis* and their impacts on sperm and eggs. Trudeau et al. (2010) demonstrated novel combinations of hormones that more consistently induce spawning in frogs indicating another route for improving the quality of ejaculates used in sperm competition and compatibility studies.

Anurans were at the forefront of the renaissance of studies on sexual selection in the late 1970s and early 1980s. As Halliday and Verrell (1988), Halliday and Tejedo (1995), and Halliday (1998) so prophetically observed, polyandry in anurans may be more common than we think. The studies we have reviewed emphasize the need to integrate natural history and critical field observation with paternity analyses and targeted experimental approaches. Our initial observation of polyandry in *C. georgiana* was made during a study on oxygen consumption in developing eggs of that species (Seymour and Roberts, 1995), which triggered an investigation of site quality and mating success. The latter was largely superseded when our first night of field work repeated an earlier observation of apparent polyandry in *C. georgiana* and started our work on sexual selection in this frog species (Roberts et al., 1999). We were naive and did not expect polyandry as an outcome, but having worked with such a comparatively well-known species, we are now acutely aware of how easily this behavior may have been overlooked in analyses of anuran behavior. The recent data on polyandry in *R. temporaria* and *B. bufo*, two very common and highly studied species, confirm that claim. Studies on sexual selection in anurans can no longer ignore the possibility that polyandry may be an integral component of the mating system. Anuran polyandry has the potential to usher in a new era in the analysis of evolution under sexual selection as it may give us insights into the conventional, for example, sperm and testis evolution, and the novel, for example, sexual conflict, speciation, and the impact on the evolution of call structures. Anuran polyandry is not new; Darwin (1871) reported observations of mating balls in toads consistent with modern reports of polyandry in this species, but anuran polyandry has been neglected and the time is ripe to generate new insights into both sexual selection theory and anuran evolution.

Acknowledgments

J. D. R. and P. G. B. acknowledge the support of the Australian Research Council, the University of Western Australia, the Australian National University, Monash University, and the University of Witwatersrand. We also acknowledge our numerous collaborators on studies on anuran polyandry and, in particular, in our work on *C. georgiana*: Roger Seymour, Martin Dziminski, Michael Smith, Paul Doughty, Attila Hettyey, Maxine Beveridge, Leigh Simmons, and Martin Whiting. Thanks also to Sharron Perks, Yi-Huey Che, and Yeong-Choy Kam for help with literature sources and field work in Taiwan. Thanks to the Centre of Excellence in Natural Resource Management, University of Western Australia, Albany, who hosted JDR in 2009 and 2010 while this chapter was written.

This chapter is dedicated to the memory of Benjamin Roberts whose studies on sexual selection were cut untimely short in 2007.

References

Andersson, M., 1994. Sexual Selection. Princeton University Press, Princeton.
Andersson, M., Simmons, L.W., 2006. Sexual selection and mate choice. Trends Ecol. Evol. 21, 296–302.
Arak, A., 1988. Callers and satellites in the natterjack toad: evolutionarily stable decision rules. Anim. Behav. 36, 416–432.
Arnqvist, G., Rowe, L., 2005. Sexual Conflict. Princeton University Press, Princeton.
Ayre, D.J., Coster, P., Bailey, W.J., Roberts, J.D., 1984. Calling tactics in *Crinia georgiana* (Anura: Myobatrachidae): alternation and variation in call duration. Aust. J. Zool. 32, 463–470.
Backwell, P.R.Y., Passmore, N.I., 1990. Polyandry in the leaf-folding frog *Afrixalus delicatus*. Herpetologica 46, 7–10.
Ball, M.A., Parker, G.A., 1996. Sperm competition games: external fertilisation and "adaptive" infertility. J. Theor. Biol. 180, 141–150.
Barker, S.J.F., Grigg, G.C., Tyler, M.J., 1995. A Field Guide to Australian Frogs. Surrey Beatty and Sons, Chipping Norton.
Bateman, A.J., 1948. Intrasexual selection in *Drosophila*. Heredity 2, 349–368.
Bee, M.A., Micheyl, C., 2008. The cocktail party problem: what is it? How can it be solved? And why should animal behaviorists study it? J. Comp. Psychol. 122, 235–251.
Belanger, R.M., Corkum, L.D., 2009. Review of aquatic sex pheromones and chemical communication in anurans. J. Herpetol. 43, 184–191.
Berger, L., Rybacki, M., 1992. Sperm competition in European water frogs. Alytes 10, 113–116.

Bernal, X.E., Akre, K.L., Baugh, A.T., Rand, A.S., Ryan, M.J., 2009. Female and male behavioral response to advertisement calls of graded complexity in tungara frogs, *Physalaemus pustulosus*. Behav. Ecol. Sociobiol. 63, 1269–1279.

Bhaduri, J.L., 1953. A study of the urogenital system of Salientia. P. Zool. Soc. Bengal 6, 1–111.

Birkhead, T.R., 1995. Sperm competition: evolutionary causes and consequences. Reprod. Fertil. Dev. 7, 755–775.

Birkhead, T., Møller, A.P. (Eds.), 1992. Sperm Competition in Birds: Evolutionary Causes and Consequences. Academic Press, London.

Birkhead, T., Møller, A.P. (Eds.), 1998. Sperm Competition and Sexual Selection. Academic Press, London.

Biswas, S., 2000. Notes on the breeding habits of *Chirixalus dudhwaensis* Ray 1992, from Uttar Pradesh, north India. Hamadryad 25, 200–203.

Boul, K.E., Funk, W.C., Darst, C.R., Cannatella, D.C., Ryan, M.J., 2007. Sexual selection drives speciation in an Amazonian frog. Proc. R. Soc. B Biol. Sci. 274, 399–406.

Bourne, G.R., 1993. Proximate costs and benefits of mate acquisition at leks of the frog *Ololygon rubra*. Anim. Behav. 45, 1051–1059.

Briggs, V.S., 2008. Mating patterns of red-eyed treefrogs, *Agalychnis callidryas* and *A. moreletii*. Ethology 114, 489–498.

Brockmann, H.J., 1990. Mating-behavior of horseshoe crabs, *Limulus polyphemus*. Behaviour 114, 206–220.

Brockmann, H.J., Colson, T., Potts, W., 1994. Sperm competition in horseshoe crabs (*Limulus polyphemus*). Behav. Ecol. Sociobiol. 35, 153–160.

Byrne, P.G., 2002. Climatic correlates of breeding, simultaneous polyandry and potential for sperm competition in the frog *Crinia georgiana*. J. Herpetol. 36, 125–129.

Byrne, P.G., 2004. Male sperm expenditure under sperm competition risk and intensity in quacking frogs. Behav. Ecol. 15, 857–863.

Byrne, P.G., Keogh, S., 2009. Extreme sequential polyandry insures against nest failure in a frog. Proc. R. Soc. B Biol. Sci. 276, 115–120.

Byrne, P.G., Roberts, J.D., 1999. Simultaneous mating with multiple males reduces fertilization success in the myobatrachid frog *Crinia georgiana*. Proc. R. Soc. B Biol. Sci. 266, 717–721.

Byrne, P.G., Roberts, J.D., 2000. Does multiple paternity improve fitness of the frog *Crinia georgiana*? Evolution 54, 968–973.

Byrne, P.G., Roberts, J.D., 2004. Intrasexual selection and group spawning in quacking frogs (*Crinia georgiana*). Behav. Ecol. 15, 872–882.

Byrne, P.G., Roberts, J.D., 2011. Sequential polyandry in anuran amphibians: evolutionary causes and consequences. Bio. Rev. (in review after revision).

Byrne, P.G., Whiting, M., 2008. Simultaneous polyandry increases fertilization success in an African foam-nesting treefrog. Anim. Behav. 76, 1157–1164.

Byrne, P.G., Whiting, M., 2011. Effects of simultaneous polyandry on offspring fitness in an African tree frog. Behav. Ecol. doi:10.1093.

Byrne, P.G., Roberts, J.D., Simmons, L.W., 2002. Sperm competition selects for increased testes mass in Australian frogs. J. Evol. Biol. 15, 347–355.

Byrne, P.G., Simmons, L.W., Roberts, J.D., 2003. Sperm competition and the evolution of gamete morphology in frogs. Proc. R. Soc. B Biol. Sci. 270, 2079–2086.

Carnaval, A.C., Bates, J.M., 2007. Amphibian DNA shows marked genetic structure and tracks Pleistocene climate changes in northeastern Brazil. Evolution 61, 2942–2957.

Chapman, T., 2008. The soup in my fly: evolution, form and function of seminal fluid proteins. PLoS Biol. 6, e179.

Che, J., Pang, J.F., Zhao, H., Wu, G.F., Zhao, E.M., Zhang, Y.P., 2007. Phylogeny of Raninae (Anura:Ranidae) inferred from mitochondrial and nuclear sequences. Mol. Phylogenet. Evol. 43, 1–13.

Chen, S.L., 1991. The reproductive behavior and ecology of emerald green tree frog (Rhacophorus smaragdinus). Masters Thesis, National Taiwan Normal University.

Clutton-Brock, T.H., Vincent, A.C.J., 1991. Sexual selection and the potential reproductive rates of males and females. Nature 351, 58–60.

Coe, M.J., 1967. Co-operation of three males in nest construction by *Chiromantis rufescens* Gunther (Amphibia: Rhacophoridae). Nature 214, 112–113.

Crump, M.L., Townsend, D.S., 1990. Random mating by size in a neotropical treefrog, *Hyla pseudopuma*. Herpetologica 46, 383–386.

D'Orgeix, C.A., Turner, B.J., 1995. Multiple paternity in the red-eyed tree frog *Agalychnis callidryas* (Cope). Mol. Ecol. 4, 505–508.

Darwin, C., 1871. The Descent of Man and Selection in Relation to Sex. John Murray, London.

Davies, N.B., Halliday, T.R., 1977. Optimal mate selection in the toad *Bufo bufo*. Nature 269, 56–58.

Davies, N.B., Halliday, T.R., 1979. Competitive mate searching in male common toads, *Bufo bufo*. Anim. Behav. 27, 1253–1267.

Davis, R.A., Roberts, J.D., 2005. Operational sex ratio and mating behaviour of the myobatrachid frog *Neobatrachus kunapalari*. J. R. Soc. West. Aust. 87, 97–99.

Demeter, L., Benko, Z., 2007. Male *Rana temporaria* in amplexus with a clutch. N. West. J. Zool. 3, 105–108.

Doughty, P., 2002. Coevolution of developmental plasticity and large egg size in *Crinia georgiana* tadpoles. Copeia 2002, 928–937.

Doughty, P., Anstis, M., 2007. A new species of rock-dwelling hylid frog (Anura: Hylidae) from the eastern Kimberley region of Western Australia. Rec. West. Aust. Mus. 23, 241–257.

Doughty, P., Roberts, J.D., 2003. Plasticity in age and size at metamorphosis of *Crinia georgiana* tadpoles: responses to variation in food levels and deteriorating conditions during development. Aust. J. Zool. 51, 271–284.

Drury, J.P., 2010. Immunity and mate choice. Anim. Behav. 79, 539–545.

Dziminski, M.A., 2005. The evolution of variable offspring provisioning. D. Phil. Thesis, University of Western Australia.

Dziminski, M.A., Roberts, J.D., 2006. Fitness consequences of maternal provisioning in quacking frogs (*Crinia georgiana*). J. Evol. Biol. 19, 144–155.

Dziminski, M.A., Roberts, J.D., Simmons, L.W., 2008. Fitness consequences of parental compatibility in the frog *Crinia georgiana*. Evolution 62, 879–886.

Dziminski, M.A., Roberts, J.D., Beveridge, M., Simmons, L.W., 2009a. Sperm competitiveness in frogs: slow and steady wins the race. Proc. R. Soc. B Biol. Sci. 276, 3955–3961.

Dziminski, M.A., Vercoe, P.E., Roberts, J.D., 2009b. Variable offspring provisioning: a direct test in the field. Funct. Ecol. 23, 164–171.

Dziminski, M.A., Roberts, J.D., Beveridge, M., Simmons, L.W., 2010a. Covariation between the strength of selection from sperm competition and ejaculate expenditure among populations of the frog, *Crinia georgiana*. Behav. Ecol. 21, 322–328.

Dziminski, M.A., Roberts, J.D., Simmons, L.W., 2010b. Sperm morphology, motility, and fertilization capacity in the myobatrachid frog *Crinia georgiana*. Reprod. Fertil. Dev. 22, 516–522.

Eberhard, W.G., 1996. Female Control: Sexual Selection by Cryptic Female Choice. Princeton University Press, Princeton.

Edwards, D., Mahony, M.J., Clulow, J., 2004. Effect of sperm concentration, medium osmolality and oocyte storage on artificial fertilisation success in a myobatrachid frog (*Limnodynastes tasmaniensis*). Reprod. Fertil. Dev. 16, 347–354.

Elmberg, J., 1990. Factors affecting male yearly mating success in the common frog, *Rana temporaria*. Behav. Ecol. Sociobiol. 28, 125–131.

Emerson, S.B., 1997. Testis size variation in frogs: testing the alternatives. Behav. Ecol. Sociobiol. 41, 227–235.

Emlen, S.T., Oring, L.W., 1977. Ecology, sexual selection, and evolution of mating systems. Science 197, 215–223.

Evans, J.P., Marshall, D.J., 2005. Male-by-female interactions influence fertilization success and mediate the benefits of polyandry in the sea urchin *Heliocidaris erythrogramma*. Evolution 59, 106–112.

Fairbairn, D.J., 1993. Costs of loading associated with mate-carrying in the waterstrider, *Aquarius remigis*. Behav. Ecol. 4, 224–231.

Feng, A.S., Narins, P.M., 1991. Unusual mating behavior of Malaysian treefrogs, *Polypedates leucomystax*. Naturwissenschaften 78, 362–365.

Fitzpatrick, J.L., Montgomerie, R., Desjardins, J.K., Stiver, K.A., Kolm, N., Balshine, S., 2009. Female promiscuity promotes the evolution of faster sperm in cichlid fishes. Proc. Natl. Acad. Sci. USA 106, 1128–1132.

Frost, D.R., Grant, T., Faivovich, J., Bain, R.H., Haas, A., Haddad, C.F.B., et al., 2006. The amphibian tree of life. B. Am. Mus. Nat. Hist. 297, 1–370.

Fukuyama, K., 1991. Spawning behavior and male mating tactics of a foam-nesting treefrog, *Rhacophorus schlegelii*. Anim. Behav. 42, 193–199.

Funk, W.C., Cannatella, D.C., Ryan, M.J., 2009. Genetic divergence is more tightly related to call variation than landscape features in the Amazonian frogs *Physalaemus petersi* and *P. freibergi*. J. Evol. Biol. 22, 1839–1853.

García-González, F., 2008. The relative nature of fertilization success: implications for the study of post-copulatory sexual selection. BMC Evol. Biol. 8, 140.

Garda, A.A., Costa, G.C., Colli, G.R., Báo, S.N., 2004. Spermatozoa of Pseudinae (Amphibia, Anura, Hylidae), with a test of the hypothesis that sperm ultrastructure correlates with reproductive modes in anurans. J. Morphol. 261, 196–205.

Garland, T., Adolph, S.C., 1994. Why not to do two species comparative studies: limitations on inferring adaptation. Physiol. Zool. 67, 797–828.

Garner, S.R., Bortoluzzi, R.N., Heath, D.D., Neff, B.D., 2010. Sexual conflict inhibits female mate choice for major histocompatibility complex dissimilarity in Chinook salmon. Proc. R. Soc. B Biol. Sci. 277, 885–894.

Gaup, E., 1904. Anatomie des Frosches. Friedrich Vieweg und Sohn, Braunschweig.

Gerhardt, H.C., Brooks, R., 2009. Experimental analysis of multivariate female choice in gray treefrogs (*Hyla versicolor*): evidence for directional and stabilizing selection. Evolution 63, 2504–2512.

Gerhardt, H.C., Huber, F., 2002. Acoustic Communication in Insects and Anurans. University of Chicago Press, Chicago.

Gerhardt, H.C., Roberts, J.D., Bee, M.A., Schwartz, J.J., 2000. Call matching in the quacking frog (*Crinia georgiana*). Behav. Ecol. Sociobiol. 48, 243–251.

Grafe, T.U., 1999. A function of synchronous chorusing and a novel female preference shift in an anuran. Proc. R. Soc. B Biol. Sci. 266, 2331–2336.

Griffith, S.C., Owen, I.P.F., Thuman, K.A., 2002. Extra pair paternity in birds: a review of interspecific variation and adaptive function. Mol. Ecol. 11, 2195–2212.

Grosjean, S.J., Delorme, M., Dubois, A., Ohler, A., 2008. Evolution of reproduction in the Rhacophoridae (Amphibia, Anura). J. Zool. Syst. Evol. Res 46, 169–176.

Gwynne, D.T., 1988. Courtship feeding and the fitness of female katydids (Orthoptera: Tetti-goniidae). Evolution 42, 545–555.

Halliday, T.R., 1998. Sperm competition in amphibians. In: Birkhead, T.R., Møller, A.P. (Eds.), Sperm Competition and Sexual Selection. Academic Press, London, pp. 465–502.

Halliday, T., Tejedo, M., 1995. Intrasexual selection and alternative mating behaviour. In: Heatwole, H., Sullivan, B. (Eds.), Amphibian Biology, Volume 2, Social Behavior. Surrey Beatty and Sons, Chipping-Norton, pp. 419–468.

Halliday, T.R., Verrell, P.A., 1988. Sperm competition in anurans. In: Smith, R.L. (Ed.), Sperm Competition and the Evolution of Animal Mating Systems. Academic Press, Orlando, pp. 487–508.

Hayashi, T.I., Vose, M., Gavrilets, S., 2007. Genetic differentiation by sexual conflict. Evolution 61, 516–528.

Hettyey, A., Roberts, J.D., 2006. Sperm traits of the quacking frog, *Crinia georgiana*: intra- and interpopulation variation in a species with a high risk of sperm competition. Behav. Ecol. Sociobiol. 59, 389–396.

Hettyey, A., Roberts, J.D., 2007. Sperm traits in the quacking frog (*Crinia georgiana*), a species with plastic alternative mating tactics. Behav. Ecol. Sociobiol. 61, 1303–1310.

Hettyey, A., Vagi, B., Hevizi, G., Torok, J., 2009. Changes in sperm stores, ejaculate size, fertilization success, and sexual motivation over repeated matings in the common toad, *Bufo bufo* (Anura: Bufonidae). Biol. J. Linn. Soc. 96, 361–371.

Hillis, D.M., Wilcox, T.P., 2005. Phylogeny of the New World true frogs (*Rana*). Mol. Phylogenet. Evol. 34, 299–314.

Hosken, D.J., Martin, O.Y., Wigby, S., Chapman, T., Hodgson, D.J., 2009. Sexual conflict and reproductive isolation in flies. Biol. Lett. 5, 697–699.

Howard, R.D., 1978a. The evolution of mating strategies in bull frogs *Rana catesbeiana*. Evolution 32, 850–871.

Howard, R.D., 1978b. The influence of male defended oviposition sites on early embryo mortality in bull frogs. Ecology 59, 789–798.

Howard, R.D., 1980. Mating-behavior and mating success in woodfrogs, *Rana sylvatica*. Anim. Behav. 28, 705–716.

Hua, X., Wiens, J.J., 2009. Latitudinal variation in speciation mechanisms in frogs. Evolution 64, 429–443.

Iwasawa, H., Michibata, H., 1972. Comparative morphology of sperm storage portion of the wolffian duct in Japanese anurans. Annot. Zool. Jpn. 45, 218–233.

Jennions, M.D., Passmore, N.I., 1993. Sperm competition in frogs: testis size and a 'sterile male' experiment on *Chiromantis xerampelina* (Rhacophoridae). Biol. J. Linn. Soc. 50, 211–220.

Jennions, M.D., Backwell, P.R.Y., Passmore, N.I., 1992. Breeding behavior of the African frog, *Chiromantis xerampelina*: multiple spawning and polyandry. Anim. Behav. 44, 1091–1100.

Jones, A.G., 2005. GERUD 2.0: a computer program for the reconstruction of parental genotypes from half-sib progeny arrays with known or unknown parents. Mol. Ecol. Notes 5, 708–711.

Kaminsky, S.K., 1997. *Bufo americanus* (American toad). Reproduction. Herpetol. Rev. 28, 84.

Karn, R.C., Clark, N.L., Nguyen, E.D., Swanson, W.J., 2008. Adaptive evolution in rodent seminal vesicle secretion proteins. Mol. Biol. Evol. 25, 2301–2310.

Knopp, T., Merilä, J., 2009. Multiple paternity in the moor frog, *Rana arvalis*. Amphibia-Reptilia 30, 515–521.

Knopp, T., Heimovirta, M., Kokko, H., Merilä, J., 2008. Do male moor frogs (*Rana arvalis*) lek with kin? Mol. Ecol. 17, 2522–2530.

Krupa, J.J., 1994. Breeding biology of the Great Plains toad in Oklahoma. J. Herpetol. 28, 217–224.

Kuramoto, M., 1996. Generic differentiation of sperm morphology in treefrogs from Japan and Taiwan. J. Herpetol. 30, 437–443.

Kusano, T., Toda, M., Fukuyama, K., 1991. Testes size and breeding systems in Japanese anurans with special reference to large testes in the treefrog, *Rhacophorus arboreus* (Amphibia, Rhacophoridae). Behav. Ecol. Sociobiol. 29, 27–31.

Lack, D., 1968. Ecological Adaptations for Breeding in Birds. Methuen & Co., London.

Laurila, A., Seppä, P., 1998. Multiple paternity in the common frog (*Rana temporaria*): genetic evidence from tadpole kin groups. Biol. J. Linn. Soc. 63, 221–232.

Lemmon, E.M., 2009. Diversification of conspecific signals in sympatry: geographic overlap drives multidimensional reproductive character displacement in frogs. Evolution 63, 1155–1170.

Li, J., Che, J., Murphy, R.W., Zhao, H., Zhao, E., Rao, D., et al., 2009. New insights to the molecular phylogenetics and generic assessment in the Rhacophoridae (Amphibia: Anura) based on five nuclear and three mitochondrial genes, with comments on the evolution of reproduction. Mol. Phylogenet. Evol. 53, 509–522.

Limerick, S., 1980. Courtship behavior and oviposition of the poison-arrow frog *Dendrobates pumilio*. Herpetologica 36, 69–71.

Lodé, T., Lesbarrères, D., 2004. Multiple paternity in *Rana dalmatina*, a monogamous territorial breeding anuran. Naturwissenschaften 91, 44–47.

Lodé, T., Holveck, M.J., Lesbarrères, D., Pagano, A., 2004. Sex-biased predation by polecats influences the mating system of frogs. Proc. R. Soc. B Biol. Sci. (Suppl.) 271, S399–S401.

Lodé, T., Holveck, M.J., Lesbarrères, D., 2005. Asynchronous arrival pattern, operational sex ratio and occurrence of multiple paternities in a territorial breeding anuran, *Rana dalmatina*. Biol. J. Linn. Soc. 86, 191–200.

Lucas, J.R., Howard, R.D., 1995. On alternative reproductive tactics in anurans: dynamic-games with density and frequency-dependence. Am. Nat. 146, 365–397.

Lucas, J.R., Howard, R.D., Palmer, J.G., 1996. Callers and satellites: chorus behaviour in anurans as a stochastic dynamic game. Anim. Behav. 51, 501–518.

Maan, M.E., Cummings, M.E., 2009. Sexual dimorphism and directional sexual selection on aposematic signals in a poison frog. Proc. Natl. Acad. Sci. USA 106, 19072–19077.

Mac Nally, R., 1981. On the reproductive energetics of chorusing males: energy depletion profiles, restoration and growth in two sympatric species of *Ranidella* (Anura). Oecologia 51, 181–188.

Mann, T., Lutwak-Mann, C., Hay, M.F., 1963. A note on the so-called seminal vesicles of the frog *Discoglossus pictus*. Acta Embryol. Morphol. Exp. 6, 21–25.

Marshall, D.J., Evans, J.P., 2005a. Context-dependent genetic benefits of polyandry in a marine hermaphrodite. Biol. Lett. 3, 685–688.

Marshall, D.J., Evans, J.P., 2005b. The benefits of polyandry in the free-spawning polychaete *Galeolaria caespitosa*. J. Evol. Biol. 18, 735–741.

Martin, O.Y., Hosken, D.J., 2003. The evolution of reproductive isolation through sexual conflict. Nature 423, 979–982.

Moen, D.S., Wiens, J.J., 2009. Phylogenetic evidence for competitively driven divergence: body-size evolution in Caribbean treefrogs (Hylidae: *Osteopilus*). Evolution 63, 195–214.

Monnett, J., Cherry, M.I., 2002. Sexual size dimorphism in anurans. Proc. R. Soc. B Biol. Sci. 269, 2301–2307.

Muto, K., Kubota, H.Y., 2009. A novel mechanism of sperm motility in a viscous environment: corkscrew-shaped spermatozoa cruise by spinning. Cell Motil. Cytoskeleton 66, 281–291.

Neff, B.D., Pitcher, T.E., 2002. Assessing the statistical power of genetic analyses to detect multiple mating in fishes. J. Fish Biol. 61, 739–750.

Neff, B.D., Pitcher, T.E., 2005. Genetic quality and sexual selection: an integrated framework for good genes and compatible genes. Mol. Ecol. 14, 19–38.

Neff, B.D., Pitcher, T.E., Repka, J., 2002. A Bayesian model for assessing the frequency of multiple mating in nature. J. Hered. 93, 406–414.

Noble, G.K., 1931. The Biology of the Amphibia. McGraw-Hill, New York.

Ohmer, M.E., Robertson, J.M., Zamudio, K.R., 2009. Discordance in body size, colour pattern, and advertisement call across genetically distinct populations in a neotropical anuran (*Dendropsophus ebraccatus*). Biol. J. Linn. Soc. 97, 298–313.

Oliveira, R.F., Taborsky, M., Brockmann, H.J. (Eds.), 2008. Alternative Reproductive Tactics: An Integrative Approach. Cambridge University Press, Cambridge.

Parker, G.A., 1970. Sperm competition and its evolutionary consequences in insects. Biol. Rev. Camb. Philos. Soc. 45, 525–567.

Parker, G.A., Partridge, L., 1998. Sexual conflict and speciation. Philos. Trans. R. Soc. B 353, 261–274.

Parker, G.A., Simmons, L.W., 1996. Parental investment and the control of sexual selection: predicting the direction of sexual competition. Proc. R. Soc. B Biol. Sci. 263, 315–321.

Prado, C.P.A., Haddad, C.F.B., 2003. Testes size in Leptodactylid frogs and occurrence of multimale spawning in the genus *Leptodactylus* in Brazil. J. Herpetol. 37, 354–362.

Prado, C.P.A., Toledo, L.F., Woehl, G., Castanho, L.M., 2006. *Phyllomedusa distincta* (Leaf frog). Multimale spawning. Herpetol. Rev. 37, 206–207.

Pröhl, H., 2002. Population differences in female resource abundance, adult sex ratio, and male mating success in *Dendrobates pumilio*. Behav. Ecol. 13, 175–181.

Purvis, A., Rambaut, A., 1995. Comparative-analysis by independent contrasts (CAIC)—An Apple-Macintosh application for analyzing comparative data. Comput. Appl. Biosci. 11, 247–251.

Read, K., Keogh, J.S., Scott, I.A.W., Roberts, J.D., Doughty, P., 2001. Molecular phylogeny of the Australian frog genera *Crinia* and *Geocrinia* and allied taxa (Anura: Myobatrachidae). Mol. Phylogenet. Evol. 21, 294–308.

Reyer, H.-U., Frei, G., Som, C., 1999. Cryptic female choice: frogs reduce clutch size when amplexed by undesired males. Proc. R. Soc. B Biol. Sci. 266, 2101–2107.

Reyer, H.-U., Niederer, B., Hettyey, A., 2003. Variation in fertilisation abilities between hemiclonal hybrid and sexual parental males of sympatric water frogs (*Rana lessonae, R. esculenta, R. ridibunda*). Behav. Ecol. Sociobiol. 54, 274–284.

Reynolds, S.M., Christman, M.C., Uy, J.A.C., Patricelli, G.L., Braun, M.J., Borgia, G., 2008. Lekking satin bowerbird males aggregate with relatives to mitigate aggression. Behav. Ecol. 20, 410–415.

Rice, W.R., Stewart, A.D., Morrow, E.H., Linder, J.E., Orteiza, N., Byrne, P.G., 2006. Assessing sexual conflict in the *Drosophila melanogaster* laboratory model system. Philos. Trans. R. Soc. B 361, 287–299.

Ritchie, M.G., 2007. Sexual selection and speciation. Annu. Rev. Ecol. Syst. 38, 79–102.

Roberts, W.E., 1994. Explosive breeding aggregations and parachuting in a neotropical frog, *Agalychnis saltator* (Hylidae). J. Herpetol. 28, 193–199.

Roberts, J.D., Standish, R.J., Byrne, P.G., Doughty, P., 1999. Synchronous polyandry and multiple paternity in the frog *Crinia georgiana* (Anura: Myobatrachidae). Anim. Behav. 57, 721–726.

Robertson, J.G.M., 1990. Female choice increases fertilization success in the Australian frog, *Uperoleia laevigata*. Anim. Behav. 39, 639–645.

Rosengrave, P., Gemmell, N.J., Metcalf, V., McBride, K., Montgomerie, R., 2008. A mechanism for cryptic female choice in chinook salmon. Behav. Ecol. 19, 1179–1185.

Rowe, L., 1992. Convenience polyandry in a water strider: foraging conflicts and female control of copulation frequency and guarding duration. Anim. Behav. 44, 189–202.

Rowe, L., Cameron, E., Day, T., 2003. Detecting sexually antagonistic coevolution with population crosses. Proc. R. Soc. B Biol. Sci. 270, 2009–2016.

Ryan, M.J., 1980. Female mate choice in a Neotropical frog. Science 209, 523–525.

Ryan, M.J., 1983. Sexual selection and communication in a Neotropical frog, *Physalaemus pustulosus*. Evolution 39, 261–272.

Ryan, M.J., 1985. The Túngara Frog. The University of Chicago Press, Chicago.

Ryan, M.J., 1998. Receiver biases, sexual selection and the evolution of sex differences. Science 281, 1999–2003.

Ryan, M.J. (Ed.), 2001. Anuran Communication. Smithsonian Institution Press, Washington.

Ryan, M.J., Tuttle, M.D., Taft, L.C., 1981. The costs and benefits of frog chorusing behavior. Behav. Ecol. Sociobiol. 8, 273–278.

Ryser, J., 1989. The breeding migration and mating system of a Swiss population of the common frog *Rana temporaria*. Amphibia-Reptilia 10, 13–21.

Salinas, F.V., 2006. Breeding behavior and colonization success of the Cuban treefrog *Osteopilus septentrionalis*. Herpetologica 62, 398–408.

Scheltinga, D.M., Jamieson, B.G.M., Bickford, D.P., Garda, A.A., Bao, S.N., McDonald, K.R., 2002. Morphology of the spermatozoa of the Microhylidae (Anura, Amphibia). Acta Zool. 83, 263–275.

Schwartz, J.J., Freeberg, T.M., 2008. Acoustic interaction in animal groups: signaling in noisy and social contexts—Introduction. J. Comp. Psychol. 122, 231–234.

Sever, D.M., Moriarty, E.C., Rania, L.C., Hamlett, W.C., 2001. Sperm storage in the oviduct of the internal fertilizing frog *Ascaphus truei*. J. Morphol. 248, 1–21.

Seymour, R.S., Bradford, D.F., 1995. Respiration of amphibian eggs. Physiol. Zool. 68, 1–25.

Seymour, R.S., Roberts, J.D., 1995. Oxygen-uptake by the aquatic eggs of the Australian frog *Crinia georgiana*. Physiol. Zool. 68, 206–222.

Seymour, R.S., Roberts, J.D., Mitchell, N.J., Blaylock, A.J., 2001. Influence of environmental oxygen on development and hatching of aquatic eggs of the Australian frog, *Crinia georgiana*. Physiol. Biochem. Zool. 73, 501–507.

Shapiro, D.Y., Marconato, A., Yoshikawa, T., 1994. Sperm economy in a coral reef fish *Thalassoma bifasciatum*. Ecology 75, 1334–1344.

Sherman, C.D.H., Uller, T., Wapstra, E., Olsson, M., 2008a. Within-population variation in ejaculate characteristics in a prolonged breeder, Peron's tree frog, *Litoria peronii*. Naturwissenschaften 95, 1055–1061.

Sherman, C.D.H., Wapstra, E., Uller, T., Olsson, M., 2008b. Male and female effects on fertilization success and offspring viability in the Peron's tree frog, Litoria peronii. Austral Ecol. 33, 348–352.

Sherman, C.D.H., Wapstra, E., Uller, T., Olsson, M., 2008c. Males with high genetic similarity to females sire more offspring in sperm competition in Peron's tree frog *Litoria peronii*. Proc. R. Soc. B 275, 971–978.

Sherman, C.D.H., Wapstra, E., Olsson, M., 2009a. Consistent male-male paternity differences across female genotypes. Biol. Lett. 5, 232–234.

Sherman, C.D.H., Wapstra, E., Olsson, M., 2009b. Consistent paternity skew through ontogeny in Peron's tree frog (*Litoria peronii*). PLoS ONE 4, e8252.

Sherman, C.D.H., Wapstra, E., Olsson, M., 2010. Sperm competition and offspring viability at hybridization in Australian tree frogs, *Litoria peronii* and *L. tyleri*. Heredity 104, 141–147l.

Shuster, S.M., 2008. The expression of crustacean mating strategies. In: Oliveira, R.F., Taborsky, M., Brockmann, H.J. (Eds.), Alternative Reproductive Tactics. Cambridge University Press, Cambridge, pp. 224–250.

Sih, A., Krupa, J.J., Travers, S.E., 1990. An experimental study on the effects of predation risk, and feeding regime on the mating behavior of the water strider, *Gerris remigis*. Am. Nat. 135, 284–290.

Simmons, L.W., 2001. Sperm Competition amd its Evolutionary Consequences in the Insects. Princeton University Press, Princeton.

Simmons, L.W., 2005. The evolution of polyandry: sperm competition, sperm selection, and offspring viability. Annu. Rev. Ecol. Evol. Syst. 36, 125–146.

Simmons, L.W., Roberts, J.D., Dziminski, M.A., 2009. Egg-jelly influences sperm motility in the externally fertilizing frog, *Crinia georgiana*. J. Evol. Biol. 22, 225–229.

Smith, M.J., 2001. Inter-sexual selection and the evolution of dramatic body size variation in the myobatrachid frog *Crinia georgiana*. D. Phil. Thesis, University of Western Australia.

Smith, M.J., Roberts, J.D., 2003a. No sexual dimorphism in the frog *Crinia georgiana* (Anura: Myobatrachidae): an examination of pre and post-maturational growth. J. Herpetol. 37, 132–137.

Smith, M.J., Roberts, J.D., 2003b. Call structure may affect mating success in the quacking frog *Crinia georgiana* (Anura: Myobatrachidae). Behav. Ecol. Sociobiol. 53, 221–226.

Smith, M.J., Roberts, J.D., 2003c. An experimental examination of female preference patterns for components of the male advertisement call in the quacking frog (*Crinia georgiana*). Behav. Ecol. Sociobiol. 55, 144–160.

Smith, M.J., Roberts, J.D., 2003d. Call repertoire of an Australian treefrog, *Litoria adelaidensis* (Anura, Hylidae). J. R. Soc. West. Aust. 86, 91–95.

Smith, M.J., Withers, P.C., Roberts, J.D., 2003. Reproductive energetics and behavior of an Australian myobatrachid frog *Crinia georgiana*. Copeia 2003, 248–254.

Snook, R.R., Chapman, T., Moore, P.J., Wedell, N., Crudgington, H.S., 2009. Interactions between the sexes: new perspectives on sexual selection and reproductive isolation. Evol. Ecol. 23, 71–91.

Stephenson, B., Verrell, P., 2003. Courtship and mating of the tailed frog (*Ascaphus truei*). J. Zool. 259, 15–22.

Sullivan, B.K., Ryan, M.J., Verrell, P.A., 1995. Female choice and mating system structure. In: Heatwole, H., Sullivan, B.K. (Eds.), Amphibian Biology, Volume 2, Social Behavior. Surrey Beatty and Sons, Chipping Norton, pp. 469–517.

Sztatecsny, M., Jehle, R., Burke, T., Hödl, W., 2006. Female polyandry under male harassment: the case of the common toad (*Bufo bufo*). J. Zool. 270, 517–522.

Taborsky, M., 1994. Sneakers, satellites, and helpers: parasitic and cooperative behavior in fish reproduction. Adv. Study Behav. 23, 1–100.

Taborsky, M., 1998. Sperm competition in fish: "bourgeois" males and parasitic spawning. Trends Ecol. Evol. 13, 222–227.

Taborsky, M., 2008. Alternative reproductive tactics in fish. In: Oliveira, R.F., Taborsky, M., Brockmann, H.J. (Eds.), Alternative Reproductive Tactics. Cambridge University Press, Cambridge, pp. 251–299.

Tejedo, M., 1993. Do male natterjack toads join larger breeding choruses to increase mating success? Copeia 1993, 75–80.

Thrall, P.H., Antonovics, J., Bever, J.D., 1997. Sexual transmission of disease: implications for disease heterogeneity and host mating system evolution. Am. Nat. 149, 485–506.

Trivers, R., 1972. Parental investment and sexual selection. In: Campbell, B. (Ed.), Sexual Selection and the Descent of Man 1871-1971. Aldine Press, Chicago, pp. 136–179.

Trudeau, V.L., Somoza, G.M., Natale, G.S., Pauli, B., Wignall, J., Jackman, P., et al., 2010. Hormonal induction of spawning in 4 species of frogs by coinjection with a gonadotropin-releasing hormone agonist and a dopamine antagonist. Reprod. Biol. Endocrinol. 8, 36.

Tyler, M.J., Doughty, P., 2009. Field Guide to Frogs of Western Australia. Western Australian Museum, Welshpool.

Tyler, M.J., Smith, L.A., Johnstone, R.E., 2000. Field Guide to frogs of Western Australia. Western Australian Museum, Perth.

Vieites, D.R., Nieto-Román, S., Barluenga, M., Palanca, A., Vences, M., Meyer, A., 2004. Post-mating clutch piracy in an amphibian. Nature 431, 305–308.

Wake, M.H., 1980. The reproductive biology of *Nectophrynoides malcolmi* (Amphibia: Bufonidae), with comments on the evolution of reproductive modes in the genus Nectophrynoides. Copeia 1980, 193–209.

Waldman, B., Rice, J.E., Honeycutt, R.L., 1992. Kin recognition and incest avoidance in toads. Am. Zool. 32, 18–30.

Walker, W.F., 1980. Sperm utilization strategies in nonsocial insects. Am. Nat. 115, 780–799.

Wang, I.J., Summers, K., 2010. Genetic structure is correlated with phenotypic divergence rather than geographic isolation in the highly polymorphic strawberry poison-dart frog. Mol. Ecol. 19, 447–458.

Wells, K.D., 1977. The social behavior of anuran amphibians. Anim. Behav. 25, 666–693.

Wells, K.D., 2007. The Ecology and Behavior of Amphibians. The University of Chicago Press, Chicago.

Wen, H.S., 2001. The reproductive ecology of Moltrecht's treefrog (Rhacoporus moltrechti) at Pu-Lo-Wan in Taroko National Park. Masters Thesis, National Dong Hwa University.

Wilson, B.A., Horst, G.V.D., Channing, A., 1998. Comparison of motility patterns of sperm aspirated from amplectant pairs of *Xenopus laevis*, by electro-ejaculation and from the testis. Herpetol. J. 8, 51–56.

Wogel, H., Abrunhosa, P.A., Pombal Jr., J.P., 2005. Breeding behaviour and mating success of *Phyllomedusa rohdei* (Anura, Hylidae) in south-eastern Brazil. J. Nat. Hist. 39, 2035–2045.

Yang, Y.J., 1987. The Reproductive Behavior of Rhacophorus taipeianus. Masters Thesis, National Taiwan University.

Yang, Y.R., 1998. A Field Guide to the Frogs and Toads of Taiwan. Chinese Photography Association, Taipei (in Chinese and English).

Yasui, Y., 1998. The genetic benefits of female multiple mating reconsidered. Trends Ecol. Evol. 13, 246–250.

Zamudio, K.R., Chan, L.M., 2008. Alternative reproductive tactics in amphibians. In: Oliveira, R.F., Taborsky, M., Brockmann, H.J. (Eds.), Alternative Reproductive Tactics. Cambridge University Press, Cambridge, pp. 300–331.

Zeh, J.A., 1997. Polyandry and enhanced reproductive success in the harlequin-beetle-riding pseudoscorpion. Behav. Ecol. Sociobiol. 40, 111–118.

Zeh, D.W., Smith, R.L., 1985. Paternal investment by terrestrial arthropods. Am. Zool. 25, 785–805.

Zhang, S.M., 1988. The reproductive behavior of Rhacophorus megacephalus. Masters Thesis, National Taiwan University.

The Role of Coloration in Mate Choice and Sexual Interactions in Butterflies

Darrell J. Kemp* and Ronald L. Rutowski†

*DEPARTMENT OF BIOLOGICAL SCIENCES, MACQUARIE UNIVERSITY,
SYDNEY, AUSTRALIA
†SCHOOL OF LIFE SCIENCES, ARIZONA STATE UNIVERSITY, TEMPE,
ARIZONA, USA

I. Introduction

Animal color patterns constitute a large and intriguing component of phenotypic diversity. Perhaps most interesting from an evolutionary perspective is the diversity of conspicuous color badges or colored structures thought to act as sexual signals. Studies of these traits, including the famously iridescent peacock's train (Loyau et al., 2007), and the orange, black, and iridescent spots of guppies (Endler, 1983; Endler and Houde, 1995), have informed our understanding of intraspecific signaling, speciation, and the evolution of exaggerated secondary sexual signals. By using model organisms in target groups such as birds, fishes, and lizards, such work has demonstrated how information regarding phenotypic and/or genetic quality may be encoded in various types of color ornaments (Blount et al., 2003; Grether et al., 2005; Hill and Montgomerie, 1994; Keyser and Hill, 1999). This work offers an explanation for the adaptive value of color signals in mate assessment, and has delivered significant insights into the actions and outcomes of sexual selection.

Curiously, until recent times, attempts to address these issues have rarely used butterflies as subjects. This is surprising on several fronts. First, as noted, butterflies display highly diverse color patterns borne from various combinations of pigments and reflective nanoscale surface structures (e.g., Prum et al., 2006). Few groups rival the sheer diversity of visual signals seen across the day-flying Lepidoptera, and butterfly wings exhibit among the brightest, most chromatic and optically complex colors seen in nature (Prum et al., 2006; Vukusic and Sambles, 2003). Second, butterflies are

55

0065-3454/11 $35.00
DOI: 10.1016/B978-0-12-380896-7.00002-2

well suited to behavioral, physiological, morphological, and genetic investigations. Features of their life history offer novel opportunities for testing ideas about the connections between the mechanisms of color production, the causes of variation in coloration, and the potential information value of color signals. Many species are easily reared in captivity, with relatively rapid generation times ($\sim$ 3–5 weeks), which offers excellent opportunities for manipulative and genetic studies of color signal development. Quantitative genetics, a necessary tool for the *in vivo* examination of the map between genotype and phenotype, is therefore eminently possible with this system (e.g., Beldade et al., 2002; Kemp and Rutowski, 2007). Their compartmentalized (holometabolous) life cycle also permits controlled examinations of how and when resources are acquired and allocated to coloration, and how individual differences in these processes may be signaled through wing coloration (Kemp, 2007; Kemp and Rutowski, 2007; Talloen et al., 2004). Behaviorally, butterflies are suited to experimentation and observation both in the field and the lab, and because their colors are housed in dead, metabolically divorced cuticular wing material, they are amenable to precise manipulations using straightforward techniques (e.g., Kemp, 2007; Lederhouse and Scriber, 1996; Silberglied and Taylor, 1978; Stride, 1957, 1958).

In this chapter, we review recent efforts to understand visual signaling that have taken greater advantage of the variety of empirical opportunities afforded by the Lepidoptera. The field has been advanced considerably by work in several groups (e.g., Costanzo and Monteiro, 2007; Fordyce et al., 2002; Jiggins et al., 2001; Knuttel and Fiedler 2001; Robertson and Monteiro 2005), but we focus here on the functional, behavioral, developmental, and quantitative genetic studies in two exemplar genera of the subfamily Coliadinae: *Colias* and *Eurema*. This butterfly subfamily has a rich legacy of research into color function and evolution (e.g., Gerould, 1923; Ghiradella, 1974; Ghiradella et al., 1972; Rutowski, 1977; Silberglied and Taylor, 1973; Silberglied and Taylor, 1978; Watt, 1964) and exemplifies the potential that butterflies present for understanding the evolution of color-based sexual signaling in nature.

Further, because the field of color signal evolution is large and fast moving, we wish to limit our focus to female mating biases and the evolution of exaggerated male-limited signals. This is the same focus as used by Darwin (1874) in his presentation of sexual selection theory (see Section III), and we wish to update the debate regarding Darwin's assertion that female choice drives color exaggeration in butterflies (a debate best summarized over two decades ago by Silberglied, 1984). Separate from this, there is also the increasingly popular possibility that mate choice imposed by males may also potentially select for female phenotypic traits (e.g.,

Bateman and Fleming, 2006). However, at least in insects, the current view is that male mate choice is more likely to select for female traits subject to existing vectors of natural selection, such as body size (Bonduriansky, 2001), rather than display traits such as ornamental wing coloration. Recent modeling efforts indicate further difficulties with the evolution of male mate choice under scenarios when mates are encountered sequentially (Barry and Kokko 2010). Because butterflies are well suited to studying male mate choice, they offer opportunities to test these viewpoints. Kemp and Macedonia (2007), for example, investigated the consequences of a clear, color-based male mating bias to the reproductive biology of differentially attractive conspecific females but found no signature of male choice. Although we treat the issue no further here, excellent additional progress in understanding male choice and its potential influence on female coloration is given by the work of Ellers and Boggs (2002, 2003, 2004a,b), Fordyce et al. (2002), Jiggins et al. (2001), Knuttel and Fiedler (2001), and Sweeney et al. (2003).

II. Coloration as a Signal Element

A. Coloration, Condition, and Honesty

The color patterns seen on the external surfaces of animals may have evolved, either wholly or partly, due to their function as visual signals. In some cases, the signals may have defensive function, such as the "warning" colors of noxious or dangerous species (e.g., the coral snake; Brodie, 1993), and the false "eyespots" best seen in larval and adult Lepidoptera (Kodandaramaiah et al., 2009). In other cases, the color patterns may advertise species identity, mate identity, or mate quality. Such signals may have also evolved as secondary sexual characters and are often famously exaggerated, such as the stunning iridescent blue and green train of the peacock. These traits may signal mate attractiveness (in the purely "Fisherian" sense; Fisher, 1930), or they may provide clues to the bearer's physical or physiological condition, his abilities as a forager or caring parent, the quality of his territory, or the quality or potential compatibility of his genome.

Many sexual signals are described as highly "exaggerated." Exaggeration in this sense is really equivalent to the extent to which their expression causes a departure from the viability-selected optimum phenotype (Bonduriansky, 2007a; Bonduriansky and Rowe, 2005), that is, the phenotype most conducive to survival and offspring production. By definition, therefore, such exaggerated signals exact viability costs upon their bearers.

Indeed, the theory of honest signaling (Zahavi, 1975) proposes that the very reason such signals are evolutionary stable is because they are costly to express and, therefore, contain "honest" information regarding the ability of their bearer to withstand or pay such costs. Viability costs could arise because signaling is nutritionally or physiologically demanding or because it increases the risks of predation (Lyytinen et al., 2004) or social harassment (Martin and Forsman, 1999). Alternatively, as Maynard Smith and Harper (2003) discuss, the signals may be just plain difficult to achieve or construct, such that only strong and healthy individuals can achieve the greatest levels of expression (see also the arguments of Fitzpatrick, 1998). In either case, not all signalers should be able to display with the same intensity, which means that signal expression can be reliably used as a proxy for mate quality. This insight from the theory of honest signaling has provided a consistent framework for understanding and fruitfully studying the types of signal traits thought to evolve as components of mate signaling systems.

A key prediction from honest signaling theory is that the expression of directionally selected sexual traits, such as sexual ornaments, should covary tightly with phenotypic condition. This is the phenomenon known as "condition-dependence" (Andersson, 1994; Johnstone, 1995; Rowe and Houle, 1996). Strictly defined, this is a form of developmental plasticity whereby investment into discrete aspects of the phenotype varies according to the total pool of available resources (i.e., condition; Rowe and Houle, 1996). Sexually selected traits are expected to be especially condition-dependent compared to naturally selected traits because their close relationship to fitness means that individuals of increasingly higher condition will incur lower marginal costs per unit elaboration of these traits (Grafen, 1990). Perhaps due to the apparent simplicity of this prediction, considerable effort has gone into testing it across a range of animals and traits, including many color-based sexual signals (e.g., Johnsen et al., 2003; Lim and Li, 2007; Masello et al., 2008; Siitari et al., 2007). However, as pointed out by Tomkins et al. (2004) and Cotton et al. (2004a,b), properly defining condition and testing for condition-dependence demand great care. Many studies have fallen short of convincingly demonstrating it for their focal (putatively sexual) traits. In particular, researchers often failed to appreciate that condition is likely to affect most aspects of organismal growth, development, and function (West-Eberhard, 2003), and the key prediction for costly sexually selected traits is for *heightened* condition-dependent variation, relative to nonsexual metric or somatic traits (Cotton et al., 2004b; indeed, the distinction between sexual and nonsexual traits may not be clear-cut). More recent efforts at examining this prediction have therefore emphasized a comparison among sexual and nonsexual traits in their relationship to underlying variation in condition (e.g., Bondurianksy, 2007a; Bondurianksy and Rowe, 2005; Cotton et al., 2004a; Kemp, 2008a; Kemp and Rutowski, 2007).

From the perspective of signal information content, the presence of condition-dependence means that the level of signal expression, such as the brightness of a color badge, could be used by a receiver to gain insights into (at least) the bearer's phenotypic condition. If such phenotypic information is relevant to female reproductive fitness—for example, if she gained access to a higher-quality territory or a more nutritious ejaculate— then selection would favor female choice for high-signaling males. Moreover, because "condition" is effectively shorthand for the total pool of resources available for conversion to fitness and encompasses both present and future reproductive potential, achieving high levels of condition will call upon the ability to acquire, appropriate, and conserve nutrients, energy, and other essential resources; the ability to avoid or repel predators and pathogens; and the ability to withstand myriad other environmental stressors and challenges (Tomkins et al., 2004). This suggests that phenotypic condition should depend upon a large proportion of the functional genome and that females could also use condition-dependent signals as a source of information on underlying genetic quality (Hunt et al., 2004; see below). However, these ideas predict that such a signaling system will remain evolutionarily stable only if low-condition/low genetic quality individuals are unable to "cheat," which predicts in turn that signal traits should be highly developmentally and physiologically integrated (Badyaev, 2004; Rowe and Houle, 1996).

B. THE SIGNALING OF GENETIC QUALITY

Empirically testing the theory of honest signaling, particularly as it pertains to genetic quality, continues to pose challenges for the field of behavioral and evolutionary ecology. Phenotypic condition-dependence has proven relatively simple to demonstrate in many signaling systems, but few researchers have investigated whether there is an underlying genetic basis to condition and/or condition-dependent trait expression (Cotton et al., 2004b). Such knowledge is ultimately necessary to appraise what type of information is revealed by the signal and, hence, to fully understand the evolution of the signaling system. However, getting to the bottom of these issues demands a quantitative genetic approach, ideally coupled with realistic environmental manipulations that impinge upon the ability to acquire condition (see below). Such designs and manipulations require known pedigrees and large sample sizes and are obviously very difficult to achieve in many systems.

One approach to investigating the potential genetic basis to a condition-dependent display is to search for genotype-by-environment interactions (GEIs) in the expression of the signal trait (Hunt et al., 2004; Kokko and Heubel, 2008). Simply, a GEI refers to a developmental outcome in which the phenotype that results from a particular genotype is a function of the environment under which the organism developed (or in which the gene(s) of interest were expressed). Alternatively, this phenomenon can be viewed as a specific type of "phenotypic plasticity," wherein the relationship between phenotype and environment in which it develops is expressed as the "norm of reaction." A significant GEI can arise for several reasons, including among-environment differences in the rank order of genotypes (equating to a "crossing over" of reaction norms) or differences in the spread of genotypes among environments (equating to differences in genetic variance among environments).

In studies of sexual signaling, the GEI of special interest is that relating to genetic variance for the acquisition of phenotypic "condition," which is, in turn, signaled by the ornament. Thus, individuals of high genetic quality, that is, in possession of "good genes," are able to attain high condition regardless of their developmental environment, whereas low genetic quality individuals can only do so in favorable environments. This situation would generate significant GEIs relating to both overall phenotypic condition as well as ornamental trait expression of a nature in which genetic variance for both condition and trait expression increases under stress. As noted for the purely phenotypic study of condition-dependence (Cotton et al., 2004a,b), the crucial evidence is not just significant GEIs but those of a larger magnitude than seen in nonsexual traits and homologous (nonsexually functional) traits in the opposite sex.

Empirically, GEIs for sexual signal expression can be revealed by rearing or housing full- or half-sibling families under a range of differently challenging environments. The best known empirical example of this is given by the work of David et al. (2000) on stalk-eyed flies. Females of this species prefer to mate with males that have their eyes spanned further apart, and male eyes are located on laterally protruding stalks. David et al. (2000) reared full sibling families under three environments of decreasing nutritional quality, and assayed eye span and wing length (a nonsexual trait) in the subsequent adult males and females. Their results are perhaps the clearest demonstration of genetically mediated condition-dependence in the contemporary literature. Whereas males of all families achieved highly exaggerated eye spans in the best environment, and many did so in the mid-quality environment, only several families were able to maintain this high level of trait expression in the most suboptimal environment (and some families suffered markedly). The result is therefore an increasing "fanning" of family means for ornament expression (i.e., an increase in genetic and phenotypic variance) across environments of decreasing nutritional quality. Importantly, this result held even when male eye span was adjusted for body size, which rules out a simple mechanistic explanation based upon scaling. The same pattern was also not evident for female eye span, or for either male or female forewing length. On average, therefore, male eye span exhibits the greatest degree of phenotypic condition-dependence, but this effect is modulated by genes. Given environmental variation, female choice for exaggerated male eye span would deliver mates in high phenotypic condition and (on average; Kokko and Heubel, 2008) in possession of higher-quality genomes. Whether the exaggerated coloration seen in many male butterflies could function in this way is unknown but well worthy of empirical investigation (see also the commentary of Kemp and Rutowski, 2007, as below). It also has to be considered that the presence of environmental variation, or GEIs, has the potential to in fact erode the genetic information content of the signal, and to constrain the benefits to choosiness in females (see, e.g., Greenfield and Rodriguez 2004). Full treatment of the different views on GEIs in relation to sexual selection is given by Kokko and Heubel (2008).

C. Potential Sexual Signaling Function of Butterfly Color

Much recent effort in testing the signal content of color-based sexual ornaments has focused on vertebrate models, such as birds and fishes. Many of these species have well-characterized mating systems, social systems, and ecological niches, and much is often known about their sensory physiology, and that of major competitors and predators (e.g., Endler, 1991; Endler and Mielke, 2005). This information is, at present, lacking for most of the more than 20,000 described species of butterflies. However, detailed empirical work in several species has provided a solid platform for investigating the full use of wing coloration during social and sexual interactions in this group (e.g., Brakefield, 1996; Kemp, 2007; Kunte, 2009; Oliver et al., 2009; Vane-Wright and Boppre, 1993).

The wing coloration of day-flying Lepidoptera functions primarily for thermoregulation, protection (including crypsis and aposematism), and intraspecific communication (Lederhouse and Scriber, 1996; Vane-Wright and Boppre, 1993). Dorsal and ventral surfaces frequently differ, often markedly so, and sexual dimorphism, genetic polymorphism, and seasonal polyphenism are commonplace (Silberglied, 1984). Above all, the many cases of sexual dimorphism in this group present a strong signature of sexual selection in that the males exhibit the more visually striking color patterns (Rutowski, 1997; Silberglied, 1984). Sometimes, as in the case of many Nymphalids and Pierids, the dorsal surfaces of male wings are adorned with bright and/or iridescent color pattern elements that are completely absent in the opposite sex. These colors are sometimes obviously presented to females via highly ritualized aerial courtship routines, which support the idea that they evolved as mating signals. There is good evidence across many species that such color patterns are used by females to recognize potential mates. As we outline below, several studies also demonstrate female discrimination based on the expression of the male color signals, which suggests that the function of these traits transcends the mere announcement of species and/or sexual identity (Kemp, 2007, 2008b; Papke et al., 2007).

In trying to understand the evolution of color-based signaling, it is important to appraise what kind of information may be encoded within the standing levels of signal variation. In butterflies, males donate not only sperm to females but also a package of nutrients comprising a structure known as a spermatophore and accessory gland secretions. Radiolabeling experiments have revealed that these male-derived nutrients are incorporated into egg production and that females use them for somatic maintenance (Boggs and Gilbert, 1979; Boggs and Watt, 1981). Females of some species are also thought to forage for matings in order to supplement their lifetime resource budget (Kaitala and Wiklund, 1994; Karlsson, 1998). Moreover, at least in *Colias eurytheme*, we know that females can receive differential fitness benefits from mating with different members of the population (Rutowski et al., 1987). This raises the possibility that evolution may have favored females that discriminate among potential mates to receive direct benefits. However, it is not known whether such choice occurs in butterflies, let alone whether it is based upon wing coloration. The only known attempt to investigate this empirically (that we are aware of) produced negative results (Kemp et al., 2008). Aside from direct benefits, there is also the possibility that female butterflies could obtain indirect benefits from mating with more strikingly colored males. This encompasses the possibility that such females could generate more attractive and/or viable offspring due to receiving "good" or "complementary" genes from their partner. These possibilities are treated at length later in this chapter.

III.   BUTTERFLY COLOR: IS IT A SEXUAL SIGNAL?

As one of nature's most colorful animal groups, butterflies have been called upon in the study of visual-based mating preferences, and such preferences have been successfully demonstrated across a range of species (e.g., Ellers and Boggs, 2003; Fordyce et al., 2002; Robertson and Monteiro,

2005; Silberglied and Taylor, 1978; Stride, 1957, 1958; Sweeney et al., 2003). Data have steadily accumulated in support of the idea that wing coloration is used (at least) to recognize potential mates, but until recently, few experimenters have set out to isolate behavioral responses to intraspecific signal variation. Most manipulations have therefore amounted to the entire removal or substitution of specific color pattern elements, rather than graded manipulations of color element size, brightness, hue, or chromaticity. As a consequence, it has remained largely unclear whether the expression of butterfly wing colors may serve to indicate phenotypic and/or genetic mate quality, as appears to be the case in other well-studied animal groups. A second interesting (but slightly unfortunate) point is that manipulations in butterflies have tended to target relatively inconspicuous (e.g., Fordyce et al., 2002; Wiernasz, 1995) or sexually monomorphic (e.g., Robertson and Monteiro, 2005) color pattern elements. Theory predicts that mate-quality indicators should evolve to be highly exaggerated, that is, to depart significantly from the optimum phenotype for viability and that production and/or maintenance costs should lead to their sex limitation (thereby leading to the evolution of sexual dimorphism; Bonduriansky, 2007a,b; Bonduriansky and Chenoweth, 2009). Third, many more studies have addressed male mate choice rather than female mate choice in butterflies, mainly because the former is far easier to measure and manipulate (Silberglied, 1984). But, as Darwin (1874) observed, where sex dimorphism occurs in butterflies, it is nearly always the males which exhibit the more obviously striking color pattern. Theory also indicates that male choice is unlikely to strongly select for arbitrary or maladaptive advertisement traits such as wing coloration (Bonduriansky, 2001). This suggests that, at least in terms of understanding the evolution of exaggerated wing patterns in butterflies, inadequate attention has been given to the study of female mate choice. In turn, these issues may be collectively responsible for butterflies, as a group, rarely featuring in the theoretically grounded literature on how and why exaggerated sexual traits evolve in nature.

More recent efforts have, however, sought to examine the signal relevance of visually exaggerated, male-limited color patches. In this section, we outline this work by focusing on empirical progress in two exemplar species: *C. eurytheme* and *Eurema hecabe*.

A. CASE #1: *COLIAS EURYTHEME*

The orange sulfur butterfly, *Colias eurytheme*, is a common and widespread North American species that has been used extensively in studies of physiology, life history, genetics, and behavior. As suggested by its common name, the wings of both sexes of *C. eurytheme* are predominately orange

FIG. 1. Dorsal wing coloration in the orange sulfur butterfly, *Colias eurytheme*. Males are shown above females, and the images indicate the appearance of wings in the human-visible spectral range (left) and the ultraviolet (right). Only the males exhibit the bright and iridescent wing coloration, which functions during mate choice in this species.

(males), or yellowish orange (females). The dorsal wing surface of both sexes has a band of black around the distal margin, and in males, the orange color is overlain by a bright and iridescent ultraviolet (UV) reflectance (Fig. 1), which is thought to be the primary sexual signal. The history of the study of this species illustrates nicely how interest in the role of color in mate choice in butterflies has developed, how the approaches to these questions have evolved, and the strengths and weaknesses of butterflies as a system for addressing these questions.

1. Hybridization and Mate Choice in Colias

Interest in mate choice in *C. eurytheme* quickly followed the observation that this species naturally hybridizes with its close relative *C. philodice* where the two species occur sympatrically. Hybridization was first described in the 1930s, and was then followed by work on the occurrence and consequence of interspecific matings (e.g., Hovanitz, 1949). These investigations were especially motivated by the fact that hybrids produced viable offspring but yet introgression between the two species was never complete. In areas of sympatry, hybrids occurred but always at a lower frequency than the parental phenotypes, which was proposed to be a result of female preference for conspecific mates. However, Hovanitz (1949) reported on the occurrence of interspecific matings in the field, and reported little evidence of female preference for conspecific mates.

Field investigation of these phenomena was facilitated by the occurrence of these species in fields of commercially grown alfalfa (*Medicago sativa*), a perfectly acceptable larval host for both. This connection with alfalfa cultivation not only expanded the range of sympatry but also produced dense populations of both species due to abundant larval foodplant. In the 1960s and early 1970s, Taylor (1972) took advantage of the opportunity presented by sympatric populations of exceptional density in cultivated alfalfa fields in south central and southeastern Arizona. His work suggested that females do in fact prefer intraspecific mates and that interspecific matings only resulted from males mating with freshly emerged females before their wings had hardened and they could effectively reject heterospecific suitors.

2. UV Iridescence and Species Recognition in Colias

Additional interest in this system was stimulated by Silberglied and Taylor's (1973) observation that males of *C. eurytheme* but not *C. philodice* have brilliant iridescent UV coloration on their dorsal wing surfaces (Fig. 1). This interspecific difference in male coloration was proposed to be an important cue in species recognition by females. This idea was tested by Silberglied and Taylor (1978) in a series of impressive experiments that explored the role of color in female mate selection in these species. Their experiments also took advantage of the hugely dense populations that were available in Arizona. At the right time in the summer, they were able to collect thousands of pupae to obtain males, but equally as important, virgin females. Females in these species mate more than once but after the initial mating are unreceptive for days before mating again (Rutowski and Gilchrist, 1986). Efficient studies of mate choice depend upon a good supply of virgin females who are certain to be receptive.

Silberglied and Taylor (1978) conducted two major experiments in which manipulated males were presented to virgin females in a large flight cage. In the first, they used color markers to manipulate male color across a wide range of the spectrum visible to humans. The markers also obliterated UV reflectance. The results indicated that coloration in the human-visible range of the spectrum was not important in species identification. The second experiment presented females with males whose dorsal wing surfaces were covered with transplanted dorsal wing surfaces of other conspecific, heterospecific, and hybrid males. In these manipulations, they only transplanted the nonblack regions of wing, which presented various combinations of diffuse yellow, orange, and iridescent UV. The results indicated that

C. eurytheme females preferred males in possession of dorsal UV reflectance, which provided the first evidence that a male-specific color character might have evolved in the context of female mate preference. However, there was a potential confound in their wing transplant study. Silberglied and Taylor suspected that a male chemical signal used by females in mate choice (Grula et al., 1978) might be arising from special scales found in the black margins of the dorsal wing surface. This is why their transplants involved only the nonblack areas of the dorsal wing surface. As it turned out, there is a chemical signal that stimulates virgin females to assume a receptive posture, but it arises from an area on the ventral forewing and spreads out over all wing surfaces, especially the dorsal hindwing and forewing (Rutowski, 1980). These areas were included in Silberglied and Taylor's (1978) wing transplants, an observation which weakens their conclusions regarding the role of color in mate selection by females.

3. Intraspecific Mate Choice in Colias

Silberglied and Taylor's work focused on interspecific and not intrasexual variation in coloration, and utilized dramatic manipulations of male color. In contrast, sexual selection as a hypothesis for male coloration focuses on female preferences acting on existing phenotypic variation among conspecific males. This variation, and its consequences for male mating success, has been the key issue in several studies since Silberglied and Taylor's pioneering work. Rutowski (1985) tested for female mate preferences in *C. eurytheme* by presenting virgin females to free-flying conspecific males in the field and noting the form and outcome of the ensuing courtships. Like many butterflies, females of this species can reject males via two characteristic methods: first, by assuming postures that prevent males from coupling, and second, by ascending high into the air which is apparently used as a signal of unreceptivity (Rutowski, 1978). Although color was not assessed quantitatively in this study, the presented virgin females were found to mate preferentially with young males in the middle of the size range. UV reflectance declines with age due to wing wear and scale loss (Kemp, 2006a), which was suggested as the proximate cue used in mate assessment by females (Rutowski, 1985).

A similar experimental design was used by Papke et al. (2007) to address the relative roles of chemical and visual signals in the mating success of male *C. eurytheme*. The results showed that out of a number of color and pheromonal parameters measured, bright UV coloration was the best predictor of whether or not a male would be accepted by a female in mating.

In sum, there is substantial evidence that females in *C. eurytheme* attend to male coloration in the UV and prefer males with bright signals. However, there are two caveats to this conclusion in this species. First, there have still been no studies in which manipulations have produced male color that varies in the way that it does in nature, and examined the effect of these manipulations on male attractiveness. Second, it is not clear whether variation in male coloration leads to variation in male mating success in the field. In one study, a comparison of male coloration between naturally occurring copulating males versus their unattached counterparts found no differences between the two groups (Kemp, 2006b). However, this study was necessarily conducted at the height of the breeding season, and in alfalfa fields when the butterflies were at high population density. This high density of breeding animals means that many of the copulating females may have been freshly emerged adults, and such females are constrained in their ability to exercise precopulatory mate choice (Taylor, 1972). Ideally, work on this species would seek to investigate mating patterns under conditions of lower population density, or among females that have the confirmed ability to reject courting males (such as nonvirgin females).

B. CASE #2: *EUREMA HECABE*

Known as the large or common grass yellow, *E. hecabe* is a small, slow-moving coliadine butterfly that is widely distributed throughout the Indo-Pacific. Like *Colias eurytheme*, it is a well-studied species, having been called upon for investigations of seasonal development, reproduction and polyphenism (Jones, 1987a,b, 1992), reproductive strategies (Hiroki and Kato, 1996; Hiroki and Obara, 1997; Hiroki et al., 1998), and host-seeking behavior (Hirota and Kato, 2001, 2004), among other things. Recently *E. hecabe* has also emerged as a model system for studying host-endosymbiont dynamics (Hiroki, 2002; Narita et al., 2007a,b,c), based principally upon the discovery that it harbors (and is reproductively manipulated by) the bacterial endosymbiont *Wolbachia* (Werren, 2008). As we discuss below, part of the reason for *E. hecabe*'s popularity as a study species across many different empirical contexts is because of its small size, ease of use in behavioral trials, and ease of large-scale culturing in the laboratory.

The wing coloration of this species is similar to the general pattern of *C. eurytheme* (as described above), in that the wings of both sexes are predominantly yellow/orange (yellow in *Eurema*, orange in *Colias*) and are framed by a margin of black on their dorsal surface. Males also have bright UV iridescence across most of the yellow areas of their dorsal wings. *E. hecabe* differs from *C. eurytheme* (and almost all other butterflies) in that females possess these markings as well, albeit only on the proximal half of their dorsal forewings, and which are only about half as bright as the homologous male UV (Kemp, 2008a). Females also have slightly less chromatic yellow, slightly brighter black margins, and greater suffusion

of black into the yellow regions, which collectively results in them possessing a less striking color pattern than that of their male counterparts. Again,
this is also true for *C. eurytheme*, and for many other Coliadine species,
which is consistent with the notion that wing coloration (i.e., intrawing
signal contrast) is generally under stronger selection in males.

The similarity of the *E. hecabe* color scheme to that of *C. eurytheme* has
allowed the former species to be used (at least) to validate earlier findings in
the latter (i.e., Papke et al., 2007; Rutowski, 1985; Silberglied and Taylor,
1978). However, due to its smaller size, *E. hecabe* has proven considerably
more versatile as a behavioral subject. This is best evidenced by the work of
Kemp (2008b), in which he performed a series of experiments designed to
evaluate whether *E. hecabe* females prefer the UV-brightest males. As we
describe below, Kemp's (2008b) program was conceived to exploit the full
spectrum of empirical opportunities offered by this system, and coupled
manipulations of ambient light and butterfly wing color, in small and large
enclosures, with nonmanipulative observational studies of mating patterns
in the wild. Such a coupling is desirable because it combines the benefits of
"*in vitro*" observation of natural behavioral patterns with the power of
experimental manipulation to isolate causality among candidate variables.
Regrettably, however, this combination of empirical approaches is not
realistically achievable in many systems.

Kemp's (2008b) first experiment involved a manipulation of ambient
light. Because the trait of primary interest consists of light reflected in the
UV range, its visual expression will be directly determined by the intensity
of UV in the illumination spectrum. As anyone who has been afflicted with
sunburn can attest, unfiltered sunlight contains adequate UV light (although it is interesting to note that atmospheric scattering causes a reduction in the relative intensity of shorter wavelengths reaching the earth's
surface—which is why sunlight appears yellowish). Kemp's (2008b) experiment was established by releasing virgin male and female *E. hecabe* into
two replicate 1-m^3 cages, one of which was covered by UV-absorbing plastic
film (the "UV-minus" arena) and the other which was covered by a non-
colored "neutral density" film (the "control" arena). He then monitored
the rate at which matings occurred in each cage, substituting each observed
copulating pair with a fresh virgin male and female. As predicted, if UV
patterning plays a crucial role during mating interactions, copulations accumulated six times faster on average in the control arena (Fig. 2A). Ultimately, however, this experiment only tells us that having UV illumination
is important, which could apply for many reasons, not the least of which are
changes in male and/or female behavior under a highly visually altered
environment.

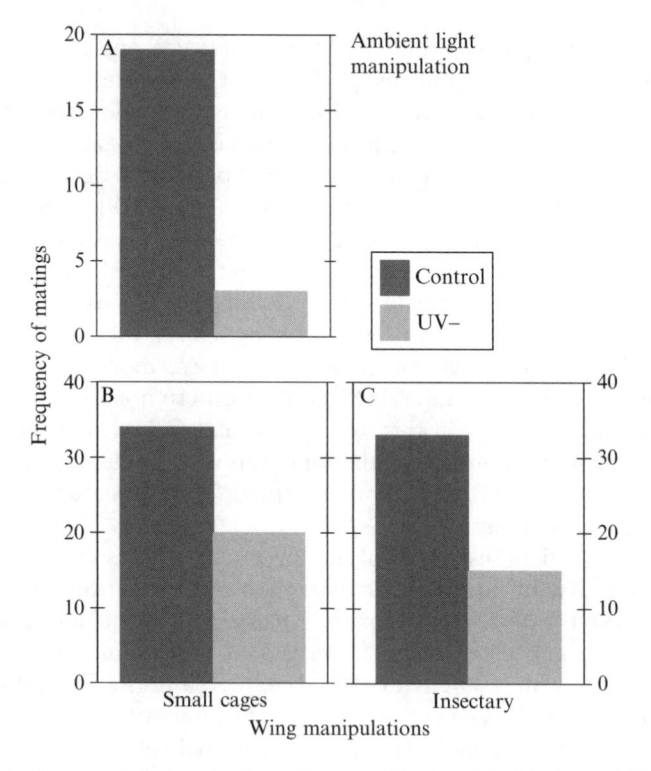

FIG. 2. Results of experiments conducted into the behavioral significance of UV coloration in *Eurema hecabe*. (A) The frequency of matings between virgin individuals housed under full spectrum (dark column) versus UV-minus (light column) illumination. (B, C) The frequency of matings achieved by visually unaltered ("control"; dark columns) versus UV-dulled ("UV–"; light columns) males in mating experiments conducted in (B) 1-m³ cages and (C) an outdoor insectary.

In order to isolate the relevance of male UV wing markings, Kemp (2008b) then established two further experiments, one in the 1-m³ cages and one in a large (6 × 5 × 4 m) outdoor insectary. In both cases, the enclosures were covered with open-weave mesh, such that the ambient light spectrum was virtually unchanged from that of natural sunlight. The manipulative element consisted of a UV-absorbing solution painted onto male wings (which consisted of the plant flavonoid rutin dissolved in ethanol, as used earlier by Robertson and Monteiro, 2005). In the UV-minus treatment group, this solution was applied to the male dorsal surfaces, thus effectively halving the brightness of reflected UV, while members of the control group were painted on their otherwise UV-absorbing ventral surfaces. Both groups were then released in equal numbers into the enclosures, together with an equivalent number of virgin females, and copulations were monitored. The results, indicated by Fig. 2B–C, were clear and consistent: copulations were significantly more likely to involve males from the control group, in both experiments, and in almost precisely the same ratio. Coupled with this, there was also evidence in both experiments that control males achieved copulations with larger females (Fig. 3A–B). While not specifically predicted *a priori*, this result is nevertheless also consistent with a situation where UV-brighter males are more attractive, in that they were able to mate with more reproductively valuable females. Because the male UV-signal was dulled (rather than removed completely), these results indicate that females prefer to mate with males that have more brightly colored wings. Importantly, as Kemp (2008b) was careful to point out, the range of color manipulation used in this experiment also falls within the naturally occurring range of brightness variation in this species; hence, the observed effect is unlikely to represent a mere artifact of an unnatural or extreme experimental manipulation.

Manipulative demonstration of mating preferences is crucial for determining causality, but questions inevitably remain regarding whether and how such results transfer to the animal's natural ecological context. Following the earlier approaches with *C. eurytheme* (as outlined above; Kemp, 2006b; Papke et al., 2007; Rutowski, 1985), Kemp (2008b) attempted to bridge this gap for *E. hecabe* by examining the phenotypic characteristics of individuals found in copula at a high-density field mating site in Cairns, Australia. The results presented an intriguing mix of contradiction and corroboration in relation to the experimental findings. First, and most intriguingly, comparison of 161 copulating males with 188 free-flying males indicated that in-copula individuals were older and actually possessed significantly *less bright* markings than their free-flying counterparts. The most parsimonious explanatory model of male "status" (in-copula vs. free-flying) was one containing UV brightness as the sole predictor variable. Second, and this time consistent with the experimental findings, among the males that were copulating, male UV brightness was correlated (along with their body size) with the size of their mate (Fig. 3C). Thus, males that were larger and in possession of brighter UV wing markings tended to copulate with larger females (male size and UV brightness were orthogonal factors).

How can this intriguing set of results be reconciled? As described for *C. eurytheme* (above), one possibility is that a contrast between in-copula versus free-flying males may not truly represent a random sample of "attractive" versus "unattractive" males. The roles of individual males in such a "snapshot" of mating activity may bear little relationship to their lifetime mating success (hence, attractiveness; Kemp, 2006b). Second, it is also

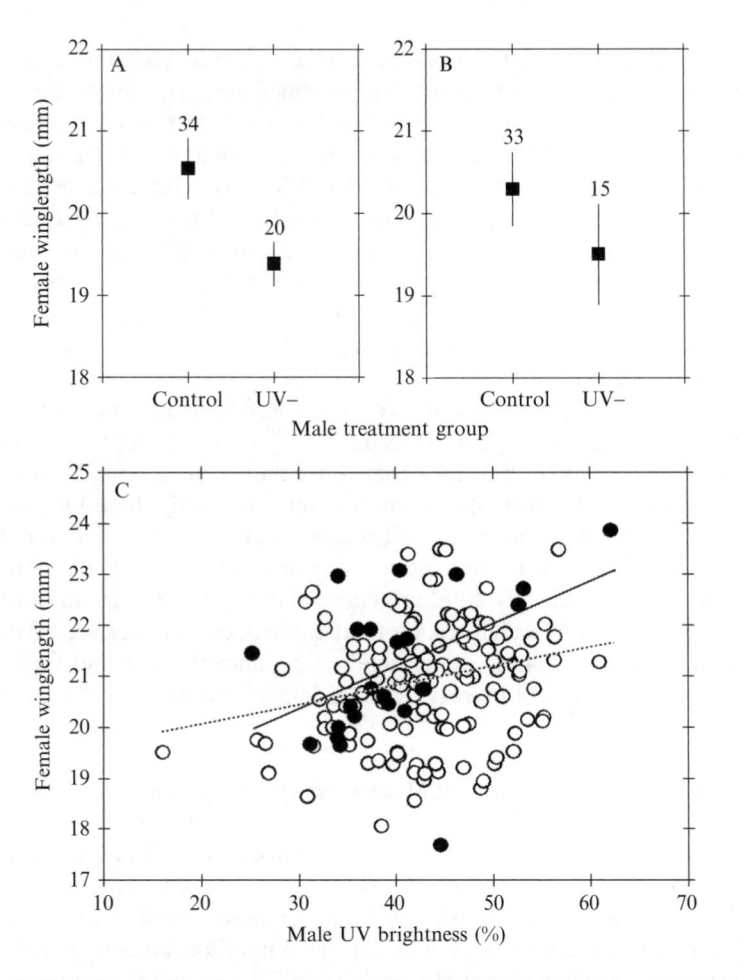

Fig. 3. Experimentally and naturally observed relationships between the putative attractiveness of male *Eurema hecabe* (the brightness of their dorsal wing UV markings) and the body size of their female mating partner. (A, B) The average size difference between females that mated with visually unaltered ("control") versus UV-dulled (UV−) males in mating experiments conducted in 1-m³ cages (panel A) and an outdoor insectary (panel B). (C) Covariance between the UV brightness of field sampled in-copula males (*x*-axis) and the size of their female partner (*y*-axis). The open circles and dashed line represents the entire sample of copulating pairs, captured from a high-density mating site in tropical Australia, while the closed circles and solid line represents the subset of females that were confirmed to be nonvirgins at the time of this mating. The stronger relationship in the latter sample is consistent with the presence of nonchoosy females in the former sample. Reproduced from Kemp (2008b) with the permission of Oxford University Press.

salient to note that due to the practicality of accessing workable numbers of copulating butterflies over a reasonable timeframe, studies of this nature can only realistically be conducted at high-density mating sites. These sites may or may not accurately represent the ecological context under which courtship and mating usually takes place. Moreover, because the densities are high, and activity is centered upon localized breeding sites, males at these sites are able to profitably locate virgin adult females as they have just emerged from their pupae. As noted earlier for *C. eurytheme*, newly emerged females are unable to reject male advances (Taylor, 1972), which means that precopulatory female mate selection is circumvented. The situation therefore effectively becomes one of scramble competition for matings. Mindful of this possibility, Kemp (2008b) dissected the female members of sampled copulating pairs in order to determine their mating history, which he then used as a basis for definitively identifying nonpupal mating females. Tantalizingly, an analysis including only these females indicated considerably stronger covariance between male UV brightness and female body size. This more closely corroborates the experimental findings and suggests that male UV coloration does play a role in the aerial courtships of free-flying butterflies. The lack of close corroboration between field and lab-manipulative results is nevertheless a significant issue and may stand testimony to the true complexity of mating signal evolution in this group.

IV.   Butterfly Color: Mechanisms and Production Costs

If we accept that the conspicuous wing markings of *Colias* and *Eurema*, and similar color traits in other butterflies (e.g., *Hypolimnas bolina*; Kemp, 2007), do indeed function for mate attractiveness, which appears most likely, the crucial question then becomes: Why? Do females benefit from receiving information signaled by the trait? Does such information transcend the mere signaling of species and/or sexual identity? Specifically, what information is signaled by the color trait, and how is such information encoded during development? As outlined earlier, these questions are best tackled using the explicit context of honest signaling theory (Zahavi, 1975), which predicts that signal exaggeration is costly and/or difficult for the average individual to achieve. One approach to testing this prediction is to attempt to measure the production costs directly, or via examination of the environmental, phenotypic and genetic basis of color signal variation (which we treat in Section V). Another popular approach is to examine the underlying mechanisms of color signal production, and then use such information to fuel *a priori* arguments for why certain color signals should be costly to express. However, this approach has been seriously criticized

(Griffith et al., 2006), primarily on the basis of its overly simplified application, and an almost exclusive focus on a single color mechanism (namely, carotenoid pigment-based coloration; as reviewed by Griffith et al., 2006).

Here we provide an overview of butterfly color-production mechanisms, along with what is known about their potential nutritional, physiological, and developmental costs. While mindful of the limitations of *a priori* cost-based argumentation (as outlined by Griffith et al., 2006), we feel that an understanding of these mechanisms is important for a holistic appraisal of signal function and evolution. Given that color is a product of light interacting with morphological structures and chemical pigments, selection acting upon color characteristics will lead to changes in those underlying structures and chemicals. Efforts to understand the evolution of color-based signaling, the paths it can and might be likely to take, and the sources and causes of variation in color signals must therefore be informed by an understanding of the structures and chemicals involved. From a more practical perspective, an understanding of color mechanisms may also guide more effective attempts to manipulate butterfly wing coloration in behavioral experiments (as in Section III).

In butterflies, all color signals are produced by the modification and reflection of incident light. There are no known cases of bioluminescence in this taxon, and while some pigments are known to fluoresce in the visible wavelengths when stimulated by light (Rawson, 1968), there is limited evidence that fluorescence contributes to visible or functional aspects of butterfly coloration (although see Vukusic and Hooper, 2005). The largest color signaling surfaces in butterflies are the wings, and the colors that contribute to the patterns on the wings are a result of properties of the scales and their distribution on the wings. Each scale acts like a pixel in a digitized image contributing one point of color to the image. In what follows, we will discuss the mechanisms known to contribute to the color of an individual scale and then take up how scales work together to create pattern. Finally, as noted above, we will assess the potential of the various mechanisms to provide a proximate basis for encoding in the resulting coloration information about the sender, that is, to produce a potentially honest signal.

A. Scales and Color Production

Butterfly scales are flattened hairs that are attached by their proximal end to the surface of the wing integument. Scales can vary dramatically in form, but a typical scale is about 200 μm long and 100 μm wide. They are arranged in a shingle-like array with each scale resting at an angle of 10–20° relative to the surface of the wing integument. Two distinct classes of scales, known as "cover" and "ground" scales are recognized, with the former situated externally to the former. Sometimes the cover scales are transparent, and may manipulate the colored light reflected off underlying ground scales (e.g., Vukusic et al., 1999; Yoshioka and Kinoshita, 2004). In other cases, the cover scales are most heavily endowed with color-producing structures and pigments (Fig. 4A), and contribute most to the wing's appearance. Across butterflies, the various scale surfaces and underlying wing membrane are enormously varied in their structural and optical characteristics (e.g., Ghiradella 2010; Prum et al., 2006; Stavenga et al., 2010) and in their contribution to the appearance of the wing (Stavenga et al., 2006).

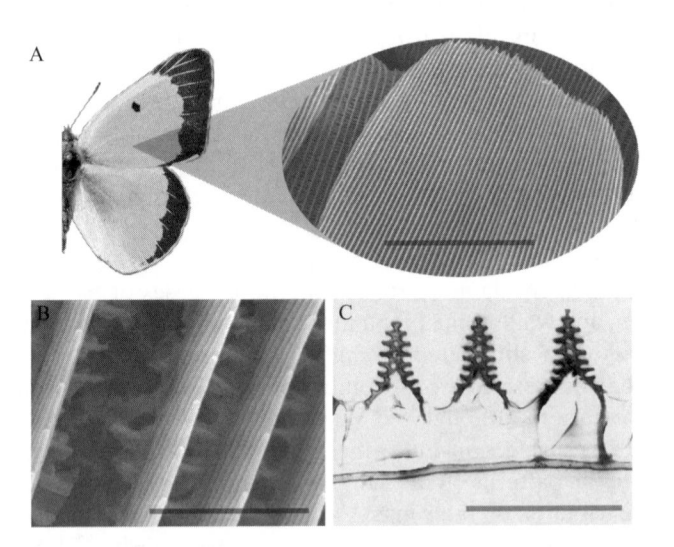

FIG. 4. Male wing coloration and wing scale morphology in the orange sulfur butterfly, *Colias eurytheme*. (A) The male dorsal wing photographed in "human-visible" light. The lighter wing areas appear yellowish orange to the human observer, but also reflect bright and iridescent ultraviolet (UV) over a restricted range of viewing angles. The inset in (panel A) shows a 1000× magnification Scanning Electron Micrograph (SEM) of a single scale from this region of wing. Far from being smooth, the upper surface of a lepidopteran wing scale is seen to feature a series of longitudinal ridges running its full length. (B) A higher magnification (18,000×) SEM of the male *Colias* wing scale showing the ridges and the underlying scale ultrastructure in more detail. The globular structures below the ridges are granules of pteridine pigment, responsible for both broadband scattering of light and absorption of short wavelengths. (C) An 18,000× magnification Transmission Electron Micrograph (TEM) of a cross-section through a male *Colias* wing scale, clearly indicating the vertical ridges and the horizontally oriented lamellae borne down each of their sides. These are the structural elements responsible for producing the brilliant, limited-view UV reflectance in this species. A similar structural architecture generates the iridescent UV of male *Eurema hecabe*, and the iridescent or metallic coloration of many other butterflies. The embedded scale bars represent 30 μm (panel A), 1.6 μm (panel B), and 1.5 μm (panel C). Reproduced from Kemp et al. (2006) with the permission of John Wiley and Sons.

Each scale is formed during the later stages of the pupal instar from a single cell that secretes an outer shell of cuticle (Ghiradella, 1974, 1984, 1994). This balloon-like shell collapses and forms a flat scale with a lower sheet of cuticle which is intact and flat, and an upper surface which can have a complex architecture of ridges, holes, flat areas, supportive cross members, and other structures. It is these upper surface structures that usually make the major contributions to the light reflected from the scale, although the lower scale membrane may have optical function as well (e.g., Stavenga et al., 2006; Vukusic and Hooper, 2005).

B. PIGMENTS AND BUTTERFLY COLORATION

Scales may contain pigments that selectively absorb certain wavelengths of light that would otherwise be scattered or reflected from the scale, thus generating color. Several major classes of pigments have been extracted from the wings of butterflies (Nijhout, 1991). These pigments differ in their properties in ways described below that might affect the information content of the color signals they produce.

Pterins absorb in the short wavelength region of the spectrum, and contribute to the reflection of what humans perceive as reds, oranges, and whites. Interestingly, pterins are reported to be the most nitrogen-rich pigments known, and so in species whose growth and development is routinely limited, pterin deposition in the scale may be limited, and so coloration might be indicative of the quality of the individual. This has been proposed specifically for the whites in the Family Pieridae who feed on crucifers, which are nitrogen poor (Morehouse and Rutowski, 2010a,b). An alternative view is that pteridines are by-products of routine metabolic processes and therefore unlikely to be particular costly in their acquisition and expression.

Melanins are the pigments often involved in the production of blacks and browns. What are the potential costs of melanin deposition? As a derivative of the common amino acid tyrosine, melanins have been proposed by some to be cheap to produce (e.g., Badyaev and Hill, 2000). However, melanin plays the role of encapsulating foreign materials in the insect immune response, which means that investments of melanin into wing coloring may compete with requirements for immunocompetence (Stoehr, 2006). A recent study with a moth revealed a negative correlation between melanin deposition in the wings and the strength of the immune response (Mikkola and Rantala, 2010); however, the coloration of this animal is a naturally selected cryptic color. In the case of sexual signals, high expression of black may be indicative of the individual's ability to invest in coloration while maintaining a responsive immune system (but see also Stoehr, 2010).

Flavonoids also absorb short wavelengths and so contribute to yellows and other longer wavelength colors, especially in the lycaenid butterflies (blues and hairstreaks). Like carotenoids in birds, these pigments cannot be synthesized by butterflies and must be obtained in the larval diet (Knuttel and Fiedler, 2001). As such, they could serve as a signal of success at acquiring larval resources. Flavonoids are also reported to have antioxidant properties (Rice-Evans et al., 1995) that might bolster their potential as a cue to signaler health and quality.

The last major class of butterfly pigments is the ommochrome, which is a compound derived from the common amino acid tryptophan (Linzen, 1974). This substrate is believed to be relatively common, albeit highly variable among different host plants (Linzen, 1974), which suggests no major or universal production costs to generating this class of signal. However, ommochrome-based wing colors in butterflies have not been thoroughly investigated for their potential to encode salient mate-quality information.

The exact placement of pigments in the scale structure is not well known except for the pterins. Pterins are deposited in granules or beads that are suspended from the structures that make up the upper surface of the scale (Giraldo and Stavenga, 2007; Morehouse et al., 2007). Recent work has demonstrated that these beads also contribute to the broadband scattering from the scale surface (Morehouse et al., 2007; Stavenga et al., 2004). High levels of pterin deposited in the scale then have the effect of making the wings more chromatic as a result of more UV absorption and more scattered light in the longer wavelengths. No other pigment is known to be deposited in packages whose physical structure contributes to color production over and above the absorption of light by the contained pigments.

C. SURFACE STRUCTURES AND BUTTERFLY COLORATION

Incident light interacts with physical structures on a surface, such as that of a scale, and these interactions can result in the reflection of some wavelengths and not others, thereby producing color. In general, these photonic interactions depend on the size and arrangement of the structures and on a difference in refractive index between the cuticle that makes up the structures and the surrounding medium (typically air). There are several broad categories of structures that function as photonic mechanisms to produce colorful reflections with different sorts of properties (Ingram and Parker, 2008).

General nano- and microstructures on scales: Particles and structures on the scale whose dimensions are of similar magnitude to light wavelengths may diffusely scatter incident light, thereby producing noniridescent reflection. Because the intensity of the scattered light is proportional to the inverse of the cube of the wavelength, light scattered by an array of similarly sized particles tends to be most intense in the short wavelengths. However, because the dimensions of small structures on a butterfly scale are usually highly variable, the spectrum of scattered light is often very achromatic. In fact, butterfly scales without pigment typically appear white to human eyes (Rutowski et al., 2005, 2007).

Diffraction gratings: When there are closely spaced and periodic micro-ribs or other ridges on the scale surface, each ridge can act as a scatterer and splits the incident light into its component wavelengths (e.g., Vukusic et al., 1999). This produces a reflection with a dominant hue that varies according to the angle of viewing (such as seen on the surface of a CD or DVD disk).

Thin film layers: Incident light will be reflected from both the upper and lower surface of a thin film. The beam reflected from the lower surface passes back through the film and subsequently combines with the upper surface reflection in ways that can be constructive or destructive, depending on wavelength. This produces reflection that varies in hue and intensity with angle of viewing, that is, an iridescent color. The structures that produce thin film iridescence in butterfly scales typically consist of multilayers of cuticle and air (Ghiradella et al., 1972; Ingram and Parker, 2008; Vukusic and Sambles, 2003). Constructive interference is the mechanism responsible for production of the iridescent UV in *C. eurytheme* and *E. hecabe* and is illustrated in detail for the former species in Fig. 4.

Photonic crystals: Some scales are made of materials that have highly ordered, periodic, and three-dimensional structures that permit some wavelengths to pass and not others (e.g., Michielsen and Stavenga, 2008; Poladian et al., 2009). These structures, by virtue of their three-dimensional optical functionality (i.e., their ability to manipulate the flow of light in three dimensions), are of significant interest for their ability to inspire future technologies (Vukusic and Sambles, 2003).

From an honest signal perspective, there are conflicting views concerning the potential costs and/or developmental challenges involved with producing the physical structures responsible for generating structural coloration. One view holds that the production of these structures may rely heavily on self-assembly organization principles, and that once the conditions for self-assembly are established they proceed with the organism incurring little cost other than the building materials (Ghiradella, 1989; Michielsen and Stavenga, 2008; Prum et al., 2009). This viewpoint has been used to predict little variation (across and within individuals) in the surface layer nanostructures, and therefore little phenotypic variation in the structurally produced color signal (e.g., Endler 1983, pp. 184). However, this "invariant self-assembly" viewpoint is overly simplistic in not considering how a concerted process of self-assembly may magnify important physiological processes, for example, the developmental/nutritional challenges involved with constructing an appropriate starting condition for self-assembly to occur. Self-assembly *per se* is not a sufficient condition to conclude that these signals will always be phenotypically and genetically invariant. An alternative view is that for these structures to produce a maximally bright and/or chromatic signal, they need to be built with great precision and consistency, which is potentially costly and/or difficult for an individual to achieve (Kemp and Rutowski, 2007). This view predicts high levels of phenotypic variation and condition-dependence in these color signals (Rowe and Houle, 1996). As we discuss in Section IV.D, evidence obtained in butterflies is accumulating in support of these predictions (e.g., Kemp, 2006a, 2008a; Kemp and Rutowski, 2007), although further work is needed to properly address this question.

D. MULTIPLE CONTRIBUTORS TO COLOR ON A SINGLE SCALE

The color produced by butterfly wing scales is typically a product of one or, more typically, several of these individual mechanisms. For example, the reflectance spectrum of the scale of a male sulfur butterfly begins with the broadband scattering of light off the underlying scale ultrastructure and granules of pteridine pigments (Rutowski et al., 2005). The short wavelengths of scattered light are, in turn, absorbed by these pigments, so that only the yellow, orange, and red wavelengths leave the scale surface. However, projecting above the scattering structures and pigment granules is a complex array of ridges (of 1–2 μm height) from which lamellae extend horizontally (Fig. 4B–C). These lamellae act as a thin film multilayer that produces an iridescent and highly limited-view UV reflection. The result is a bimodal reflection curve that has a diffuse peak in the red–yellow and a strong but highly directional peak in the UV. The involvement of multiple mechanisms can have important consequence for the signal and the information it might contain. In this case, the pteridine pigments absorb short-wave light that would otherwise be scattered diffusely off the scale ultrastructure, such that the only UV contained in the signal is that from the array of lamellar layers on the scale. Because the lamellar-generated UV is highly directional (i.e., only visible over a limited range of above-wing viewing angles), the presence of such UV-absorbing pigment ensures that the wing is entirely UV-dark when viewed from orientations unsuitable for seeing the lamellar UV. In this sense, the underlying pigment amplifies the limited-view nature of the structurally produced UV. The UV component of the wing color signal therefore only displays information about the quality of the construction of the complex lamellae (Rutowski et al., 2005), such as the density and/or arrangement of structural reflectors (e.g., Kemp et al., 2006).

E. MULTIPLE SCALES ACTING TOGETHER

Although the mechanisms of color production by individual scales have been studied in detail, far less is known about how scales work together to produce color signals. These effects have the potential to significantly influence the quality and potential information content of the signals. For example, in *Morpho* butterflies, the male's iridescent blue scales produce an intense signal visible over a relatively broad range of above-wing viewing angles. These scales are overlain by clear scales that, via diffraction, broaden the angle over which the iridescence is visible. This effect is presumed to enhance the perception of the signal by intended receivers (Yoshioka and Kinoshita 2004). As another example, in *Pieris rapae* (the cabbage white), overlapping layers of scales lead to brighter reflectance than would occur if the scales did not overlap (Stavenga et al., 2006). These kinds of optical interactions between scales and their potential consequences for color signal production, perception, and evolution remain understudied.

V. BUTTERFLY COLOR: WHAT DOES IT ACTUALLY SIGNAL?

As noted earlier, appraising the physiological and developmental basis of color production may provide clues into its costs, and henceforth the potential honesty and information content of the resulting visual signal. However, that a particular form of coloration is theoretically costly to express does not necessarily predispose it as an evolutionarily stable sexual signal, nor does it exclude alternative mechanisms from attaining costly levels of exaggeration (Griffith et al., 2006). Benefits-based models of sexual selection predict that natural selection will favor signaling systems in which salient, fitness-enhancing information is conveyed, which in butterflies may be the quality or compatibility of a male's genome, and/or his ability to provide direct benefits such as a nutritious ejaculate. While all of these things may be difficult to appraise (let alone to anticipate for species with vastly different ecologies), valuable insights can be gained by examining the environmental, phenotypic, and genetic correlates of color signal variation. Such data are only now accumulating for butterfly coloration (e.g., Talloen et al., 2004); here we outline what is known for one of our two focal species, *C. eurytheme*.

As outlined in Section III, female *C. eurytheme* prefer males bearing bright dorsal UV markings. Brightness and other reflectance characteristics of this trait vary with adult age (Kemp, 2006a), larval nutrient acquisition (Kemp and Rutowski, 2007), and thermal stress experienced during the pupal stage (Kemp and Rutowski, 2007). Younger males have brighter UV markings, as do individuals that experienced a more nutritious larval diet and a more thermally stable period of pupal development. Hence, UV brightness in this species contains information on a male's phenotypic condition, as well as providing a window into his prior developmental "experiences." Notably, the coincident pigment-based color of male wings—the yellowish orange—also varies according to age and larval nutrition, but the magnitude of variation (and therefore the potential signal information content) is much less than that exhibited by the structurally generated UV (Kemp, 2006a; Kemp and Rutowski, 2007). This is an important point because putative sexual traits are not only simply expected to be condition-dependent, but relatively more so in comparison with traits less strongly subject to sexual selection (Cotton et al., 2004b).

The phenotypic quality information encoded within the wing colors of male *C. eurytheme* is potentially salient because (as noted earlier), male-derived nutrients are known to contribute to female fitness traits (Boggs and Gilbert, 1979). Selection should favor—if at all possible—female choosiness for males capable of donating viable and nutritious ejaculates. This could be achieved through choosing UV-bright mates (to the extent that such males experienced high-quality juvenile environments). However, whether this is the ultimate reason why females have evolved such preferences stands to be demonstrated. In follow-up work, Kemp et al. (2008) addressed this possibility by mating virgin females with free-flying males in two separate experiments and then assaying male coloration, ejaculate size, and the fitness traits of their female mates. Intriguingly, there was no relationship between male coloration and the mass of their ejaculate, and only weak covariance between male coloration and female fecundity, fertility, and longevity. Given that any benefits of choice need to be balanced against any costs to being choosy (e.g., Kaitala and Wiklund, 1995), these results suggest that females are not likely to gain meaningful direct benefits from choosing mates based on their dorsal UV coloration.

There is also the possibility that bright coloration may signal indirect benefits (i.e., genetic viability). Because the dorsal UV of a *C. eurytheme* male depends upon an array of nanoscale surface structures, this component of male coloration could signal viability through its ability to magnify physiological and/or developmental processes (Fitzpatrick, 1998). This hypothesis proposes that males of higher genetic quality (i.e., possessing a more adapted or more internally harmonious genome) may be able to build the necessary fine-scale structures with greater precision, especially in the face of environmental stress. Kemp and Rutowski (2007) tested two predictions of this hypothesis in *C. eurytheme*, both of which are based on the fact that the adult phenotype (including wing structures) is constructed over several days during metamorphosis. First, they predicted that more viable individuals should be able to maintain bright UV expression even when subjected to limitations in the building blocks of the adult phenotype. The second prediction was that more viable individuals should be able to achieve greater architectural precision in their nanostructures even when faced with physiological stress (i.e., a highly variable thermal environment). Based on the theory formalized in Section II.B, these predictions were evaluated according to the presence of GEIs; specifically, a GEI of the nature of which genetic variation is magnified under environmental stress.

By rearing family groups in different nutritional environments, and subjecting them to heat and cold shocks during metamorphosis, Kemp and Rutowski (2007) were able to appraise the GEIs as a formal test of whether some families (i.e., some genetic combinations) withstood stress better than others, and whether this was signaled via their wing coloration. As we note above, in both manipulations, heightened stress reduced the expression of male UV, and color traits were also strongly heritable. However, GEIs were uniformly absent, weak, and/or not of the predicted nature. Genetic variance in UV brightness, for example, which is the key sexual parameter (Papke et al., 2007), actually decreased significantly in the stressful environment. This result argues against the viability indicator hypothesis in this species, at least in terms of the signaling of good genes for mitigating poor juvenile environments. However, there are other ways in which the expression of UV coloration, which is highly heritable, could be genetically correlated with viability. The fact that UV expression is strongly condition-dependent means that any genetic basis to the acquisition of condition, under natural conditions, would be signaled by the male's adult wing coloration (as well as his overall body size, the main vector of condition; Kemp 2008a). In this way, male UV could function as a revealing indicator of good genes for things like the ability to choose quality microhabitats and nutritious plant foliage, the ability to avoid predation or resist infection, and/or the ability to avoid or withstand stressful environments. This insight, and its suggested lines of enquiry, has been developed only through work in the butterfly system, as far as we are aware. However, effective tests of this idea will require the quantitative genetics of condition-dependence to be assayed under the most natural conditions possible. This is likely to prove challenging, although it may be achievable using large seminatural outdoor enclosures.

VI. DISCUSSION AND FUTURE DIRECTIONS

In this chapter, we have provided a selective review of the production, signaling function and information content of butterfly wing coloration. This presents, in some sense, an update of the past reviews of Silberglied (1984), and later Vane-Wright and Boppre (1993), Rutowski (1997), and Wiklund (2003), although we also acknowledge the progress being made on areas of butterfly coloration outside our present review (e.g., Ellers and Boggs 2002, 2003, 2004a,b; Fordyce et al., 2002; Jiggins et al., 2001; Knuttel and Fiedler (2001); Sweeney et al., 2003). Our review is also an attempt to float butterflies to the mainstream as an alternative, but presently under-utilized, candidate system for advancing our understanding of sexual selection and the evolution of color-based mate-quality indicators.

As noted earlier, color-based visual signaling in butterflies has provided valuable insights into evolutionary phenomena such as speciation (Chamberlain et al., 2009; Mavarez et al., 2006), reinforcement (Kronforst et al., 2007), and aposematism and mimicry (Kapan, 2001; Kunte, 2009), to name a few. In sexual signal terms, we have long understood the wing patterns of males and sometimes females to function during courtship for the recognition of potential mates (Fordyce et al., 2002; Nielsen and Watt, 2000; Robertson and Monteiro, 2005; Rutowski, 1977; Silberglied and Taylor, 1978; Stride, 1957, 1958; Sweeney et al., 2003; Wiernasz and Kingsolver, 1992). Studies such as those in *Colias* (Papke et al., 2007, Rutowski 1985), *Eurema* (Kemp 2008b), and *Hypolimnas* (Kemp 2007) illustrate that female choice can also target the qualitative aspects of color signal expression, a finding which then opens the door for the examination of male-limited butterfly colors as potentially informative sexual signals. As Sections II–V outline, male coloration in several of these species is condition-dependent. The pattern of relative condition-dependence across different wing pattern elements agrees with theoretical predictions (Cotton et al., 2004b; Rowe and Houle, 1996; Tomkins et al., 2004) based on their relative importance as components of male attractiveness. The particularly high level of condition-dependence in iridescent coloration (Kemp 2006a, 2008a; Kemp and Rutowski, 2007) supports the theory that structurally colored signals are not simply invariant products of some self-assembly process. In addition, male wing color traits show high levels of additive genetic variation, which is expected for sexually selected traits (Rowe and Houle, 1996) and which could allow for the signaling of indirect benefits. The one existing test of this hypothesis, based on the key prediction for genetically mediated condition-dependence, found no support for the signaling of indirect benefits (Kemp and Rutowski, 2007). However, condition was assayed under very restrictive and unrealistic laboratory conditions, which may have prevented or devalued the expression of genes that would normally greatly influence condition in the wild. Butterflies, by virtue of their tractability for seminatural environments, offer excellent opportunities for more realistic assays of condition-dependent trait expression, and for gathering much-needed data on the quantitative genetics of this parameter (Cotton et al., 2004a).

Despite the potential utility of this system, the few examples outlined here (Section IV; also see Kemp, 2007) represent most of what is known about the signal relevance of qualitative aspects of wing color expression, such as the brightness, hue, and/or relative size of certain color elements (although also see Breuker and Brakefield, 2002; Robertson and Monteiro, 2005). Without such information it is difficult to chart the limits to butterflies as a system for understanding the broader evolution of sexual signaling. Given their suitability for lab-based breeding experiments, developmental manipulations, and quantitative genetics, butterflies seem well placed to evaluate sexual selection models, such as sensory drive (Endler and Basolo, 1998), chase away (Holland and Rice, 1998), viability indicator (Møller and Alatalo, 1999), and genic capture (Rowe and Houle, 1996). The novel spread of color-production mechanisms in this group (Prum et al., 2006; Vukusic and Sambles, 2003) could also provide insights into how selection can generate mechanistic (as well as visual) diversity in animal coloration.

We suggest that students of sexual signaling in butterflies should seek to demonstrate convincingly, first and foremost, that individuals are sensitive to qualitative variation in the color signals of conspecifics. Behavioral experimentation to examine this question should ideally use wing color manipulations of a nature that targets the primary vector of signal exaggeration. For some species this will mean graded manipulations of signal brightness or chromaticity (e.g., Kemp, 2007, 2008b), for others it may mean manipulating the size or occurrence of particular elements of the wing pattern. In all cases, the extent of these qualitative manipulations should fall within the bounds of naturally occurring signal variation. Appropriate controls should be used in order to avoid the pitfalls of prior efforts (e.g., Silberglied and Taylor, 1978). Finally, conclusions reached using lab- or insectary-based experimentation should be validated against data obtained in more natural field-based settings. This has been achieved in studies of some species (e.g., *Hypolimnas bolina*; Kemp, 2007), but has proven challenging in others (as we have outlined for *Colias* and *Eurema* in Section IV). Part of this challenge stems from the highly dispersed, cryptic, and ephemeral nature of butterfly copulations, a well-maligned fact among lepidopteran biologists (see, e.g., Silberglied, 1984; Rutowski, 1997).

Given that data support the existence of female preferences for male coloration, well-designed breeding experiments could be used to reveal what information (if any) is encoded within the expression of the male color signal. These efforts should focus, in the first instance, on evaluating the honest color-based prediction of heightened condition-dependence (*sensu*. Zahavi, 1975; Rowe and Houle, 1996). This will demand well-designed experiments that avoid the empirical and logical limitations of past work (summarized by Cotton et al., 2004a,b). As outlined earlier, in the case of *C. eurytheme*, the UV component of male wing coloration is more generally and strongly affected by phenotypic stress—and henceforth more strongly condition-dependent—than its accompanying pigment-generated yellowish orange (Kemp and Rutowski, 2007). This agrees well with theory. This pattern is also true of *E. hecabe* (Kemp, 2008a), and further work on this species has indicated that most of the naturally occurring variation in phenotypic condition (and condition-dependent wing coloration) can be approximated by limiting individual's access to high-quality larval nutrition (Kemp, 2008a). If the same is true across many butterfly species, then quantifying and manipulating condition may be easier to achieve than in many other systems.

Along with questions relating to visually exaggerated male coloration, the butterfly study system also seems well placed to deepen our understanding of sexual dimorphism. Various authors have noted that differences between the sexes are pervasive in the group, and attributed such differences to the operation of sexual selection (e.g., Rutowski, 1997). While prior empirical efforts have set their sights on the evolution of sexual dimorphism in butterflies *per se*, again we wish to emphasize the potential to illuminate more general theories of the concept. Recent theory has cast the evolution of sex dimorphism in the context of intralocus sexual conflict (Bonduriansky, 2007a,b; Bonduriansky and Chenoweth, 2009) and implicated epigenetics and condition-dependence as key brokers of phenotypic divergence between the sexes. Research using butterfly models may not only illuminate these processes, but has broader potential for testing and refining this developing body of theory. An excellent lead in this regard is given by the exploitation of butterfly wing patterns to understand the workings of phenotypic evolution and evolutionary development (e.g., Beldade et al., 2002).

Finally, although we have focused throughout on intraspecific approaches to examining behavior, morphology, development, and genetics, we also appreciate that phylogenetically controlled comparative studies will provide a highly informative and complementary empirical approach. Indeed, the comparative method has been fruitfully applied to the study of the evolution of sexual color signals in sulphur butterflies (Brunton 1998;

Brunton and Majerus, 1995; Kemp et al., 2005). Whereas examining intra-specific color variation can furnish direct insights into signal function, expression costs, and information content, examination of interspecific patterns of wing color variation has the potential to guide our understanding of how and when particular signals and signaling systems evolve. Ideally, and ultimately, researchers will draw upon both levels of analysis in appraising the color signals of butterflies, and in using this system as a model for the broader study of sexual signal evolution.

Acknowledgments

We thank Leigh Simmons and two anonymous reviewers for thorough, constructive, and thought-provoking comments. Peter Vukusic provided the electron micrographs featured in Fig. 4. Work outlined in this chapter was supported by the Maytag Postdoctoral Fellowship, Australian Research Council Grant DP0557190 (D. J. K.), and US National Science Federation grant IBN 0316120 (R. L. R.).

References

Andersson, M.B., 1994. Sexual Selection. Princeton University Press, Princeton, New Jersey.

Badyaev, A., 2004. Developmental perspective on the evolution of sexual ornaments. Evol. Ecol. Res. 6, 975–991.

Badyaev, A.V., Hill, G.E., 2000. Evolution of sexual dichromatism: contribution of carotenoid-versus melanin-based plumage coloration. Biol. J. Linn. Soc. 69, 153–172.

Barry, K.L., Kokko, H., 2010. Male mate choice: why sequential choice can make its evolution difficult. Anim. Behav. 80, 163–169.

Bateman, P.W., Fleming, P.A., 2006. Males are selective too: mating, but not courtship, with sequential females influences choosiness in male field crickets (*Gryllus bimaculatus*). Behav. Ecol. Sociobiol. 59, 577–581.

Beldade, P., Koops, K., Brakefield, P.M., 2002. Developmental constraints versus flexibility in morphological evolution. Nature 416, 844–847.

Blount, J.D., Metcalfe, N.B., Birkhead, T.R., Surai, P.F., 2003. Carotenoid modulation of immune function and sexual attractiveness in zebra finches. Science 300, 125–127.

Boggs, C.L., Gilbert, L.E., 1979. Male contribution to egg production in butterflies—evidence for transfer of nutrients at mating. Science 206, 83–84.

Boggs, C.L., Watt, W.B., 1981. Population structure of pierid butterflies IV. Genetic and physiological investment in offspring by male *Colias*. Oecologia 50, 320–324.

Bonduriansky, R., 2001. The evolution of male mate choice in insects: a synthesis of ideas and evidence. Biol. Rev. 76, 305–339.

Bonduriansky, R., 2007a. The evolution of condition-dependent sexual dimorphism. Am. Nat. 169, 9–19.

Bonduriansky, R., 2007b. The genetic architecture of sexual dimorphism: the potential roles of genomic imprinting and condition-dependence. In: Fairbairn, D.J., Blanckenhorn, W.U., Szekely, T. (Eds.), Sex, size and Gender Roles: Evolutionary Studies of Sexual Size Dimorphism. Oxford University Press, Oxford, pp. 176–185.

Bonduriansky, R., Chenoweth, S.F., 2009. Intralocus sexual conflict. Trends Ecol. Evol. 24, 280–288.

Bonduriansky, R., Rowe, L., 2005. Sexual selection, genetic architecture, and the condition-dependence of body shape in the sexually dimorphic fly *Prochyliza xanthostoma* (Piophilidae). Evolution 59, 138–151.

Brakefield, P.M., 1996. Seasonal polyphenism in butterflies and natural selection. Trends Ecol. Evol. 11, 275–277.

Breuker, C.J., Brakefield, P.M., 2002. Female choice depends on size but not symmetry of dorsal eyespots in the butterfly *Bicyclus anynana*. Proc. R. Soc. Lond. Ser. B 269, 1233–1239.

Brodie, E.D., 1993. Differential avoidance of coral snake banded patterns by free-ranging avian predators in Costa Rica. Evolution 47, 227–235.

Brunton, C.F.A., 1998. The evolution of ultraviolet patterns in European *Colias* butterflies (Lepidoptera: Pieridae): a phylogeny using mitochondrial DNA. Heredity 80, 611–616.

Brunton, C.F.A., Majerus, M.E.N., 1995. Ultraviolet colors in butterflies: intra- or inter-specific communication? Proc. R. Soc. Lond. B 260, 199–204.

Chamberlain, N.L., Hill, R.I., Kapan, D.D., Gilbert, L.E., Kronforst, M.R., 2009. Polymorphic butterfly reveals the missing link in ecological speciation. Science 326, 847–850.

Costanzo, K., Monteiro, A., 2007. The use of chemical and visual cues in female choice in the butterfly *Bicyclus anynana*. Proc. R. Soc. Lond. B 274, 845–851.

Cotton, S., Fowler, K., Pomiankowski, A., 2004a. Condition-dependence of sexual ornament size and variation in the stalk-eyed fly *Cyrtodiopsis dalmanni* (Diptera: Diopsidae). Evolution 58, 1038–1046.

Cotton, S., Fowler, K., Pomiankowski, A., 2004b. Do sexual ornaments demonstrate heightened condition-dependent expression as predicted by the handicap hypothesis? Proc. R. Soc. Lond. B 271, 771–783.

Darwin, C., 1874. The Descent of Man and Selection in Relation to Sex. John Murray and Sons, London.

David, P., Bjorksten, T., Fowler, K., Pomiankowski, A., 2000. Condition-dependent signalling of genetic variation in stalk-eyed flies. Nature 406, 186–188.

Ellers, J., Boggs, C.L., 2002. The evolution of wing color in *Colias* butterflies: heritability, sex linkage, and population divergence. Evolution 56, 836–840.

Ellers, J., Boggs, C.L., 2003. The evolution of wing color: male mate choice opposes adaptive wing color divergence in *Colias* butterflies. Evolution 57, 1100–1106.

Ellers, J., Boggs, C.L., 2004a. Evolutionary genetics of dorsal wing color in *Colias* butterflies. J. Evol. Biol. 17, 752–758.

Ellers, J., Boggs, C.L., 2004b. Functional ecological implications of intraspecific differences in wing melanization in *Colias* butterflies. Biol. J. Linn. Soc. 82, 79–87.

Endler, J.A., 1983. Natural and sexual selection on color patterns in poeciliid fishes. Environ. Biol. Fish. 9, 173–190.

Endler, J.A., 1991. Variation in the appearance of guppy color patterns to guppies and their predators under different visual conditions. Vis. Res. 31, 587–608.

Endler, J.A., Basolo, A.L., 1998. Sensory ecology, receiver biases and sexual selection. Trends Ecol. Evol. 13, 415–420.

Endler, J.A., Houde, A.E., 1995. Geographic variation in female preferences for male traits in *Poecilia reticulata*. Evolution 49, 456–468.

Endler, J.A., Mielke, P.W., 2005. Comparing entire color patterns as birds see them. Biol. J. Linn. Soc. 86, 405–431.

Fisher, R.A., 1930. The Genetical Theory of Natural Selection. Clarendon Press, Oxford.

Fitzpatrick, S., 1998. Color schemes for birds: structural coloration and signals of quality in feathers. Ann. Zool. Fenn. 35, 67–77.

Fordyce, J.A., Nice, C.C., Forister, M.L., Shapiro, A.M., 2002. The significance of wing pattern diversity in the Lycaenidae: mate discrimination by two recently diverged species. J. Evol. Biol. 15, 871–879.

Gerould, J.H., 1923. Inheritance of white wing color, a sex-limited (sex-controlled) variation in yellow pierid butterflies. Genetics 8, 495–551.

Ghiradella, H., 1974. Development of ultraviolet-reflecting butterfly scales: how to make an interference filter. J. Morphol. 142, 395–410.

Ghiradella, H., 1984. Structure of iridescent Lepidopteran scales: variations on several themes. Ann. Entomol. Soc. Am. 77, 637–645.

Ghiradella, H., 1989. Structure and development of iridescent butterfly scales—lattices and laminae. J. Morphol. 202, 69–88.

Ghiradella, H., 1994. Structure of butterfly scales: patterning in an insect cuticle. Microsc. Res. Tech. 27, 429–438.

Ghiradella, H., 2010. Insect cuticular surface modifications: scales and other structural formations. In: Advances in Insect Physiology: Insect Integument and Color, vol. 38. Academic Press Ltd/Elsevier Science Ltd, London, pp. 135–180.

Ghiradella, H., Aneshansley, D., Eisner, T., Silberglied, R.E., Hinton, H.E., 1972. Ultraviolet reflection of a male butterfly: interference color caused by thin-layer elaboration of wing scales. Science 178, 1214–1217.

Giraldo, M.A., Stavenga, D.G., 2007. Sexual dichroism and pigment localisation in the wing scales of *Pieris rapae* butterflies. Proc. R. Soc. Lond. B 274, 97–102.

Grafen, A., 1990. Biological signals as handicaps. J. Theor. Biol. 144, 517–546.

Greenfield, M.D., Rodriguez, R.L., 2004. Genotype-environment interaction and the reliability of mating signals. Anim. Behav. 68, 1461–1468.

Grether, G.F., Cummings, M.E., Hudon, J., 2005. Countergradient variation in the sexual coloration of guppies (*Poecilia reticulata*): drosopterin synthesis balances carotenoid availability. Evolution 59, 175–188.

Griffith, S.C., Parker, T.H., Olson, V.A., 2006. Melanin-versus carotenoid-based sexual signals: is the difference really so black and red? Anim. Behav. 71, 749–763.

Grula, J.W., McChesney, J.D., Taylor, O.R., 1978. Aphrodisiac pheromones of the sulphur butterflies *Colias eurytheme* and *C. philodice* (Lepidoptera, Pieridae). J. Chem. Ecol. 6, 241–256.

Hill, G.E., Montgomerie, R., 1994. Plumage color signals nutritional condition in the house finch. Proc. R. Soc. Lond. B 258, 47–52.

Hiroki, M., 2002. Feminisation of genetic males by a symbiotic bacterium in a butterfly, *Eurema hecabe* (Lepidoptera: Pieridae). Naturwissenschaften 89, 167–170.

Hiroki, M., Kato, Y., 1996. Age-related sexual receptivity change in virgin females of a butterfly, *Eurema hecabe*. Appl. Entomol. Zool. 31, 455–458.

Hiroki, M., Obara, Y., 1997. Delayed mating and its cost to female reproduction in the butterfly, *Eurema hecabe*. J. Ethol. 15, 79–85.

Hiroki, M., Obara, Y., Kato, Y., 1998. Changes in age-related reproductive tactics in the female of the butterfly, *Eurema hecabe*. Naturwissenschaften 85, 551–552.

Hirota, T., Kato, Y., 2001. Influence of visual stimuli on host location in the butterfly, *Eurema hecabe*. Entomol. Exp. Appl. 101, 199–206.

Hirota, T., Kato, Y., 2004. Color discrimination on orientation of female *Eurema hecabe* (Lepidoptera: Pieridae). Appl. Entomol. Zool. 39, 229–233.

Holland, B., Rice, W.R., 1998. Chase-away sexual selection: antagonistic seduction versus resistance. Evolution 52, 1–7.

Hovanitz, W., 1949. Interspecific matings between *Colias eurytheme* and *Colias philodice* in wild populations. Evolution 3, 170–173.

Hunt, J., Bussiere, L.F., Jennions, M.D., Brooks, R., 2004. What is genetic quality? Trends Ecol. Evol. 19, 329–333.

Ingram, A.L., Parker, A.R., 2008. A review of the diversity and evolution of photonic structures in butterflies, incorporating the work of John Huxley (the Natural History Museum, London from 1961–1990). Philos. Trans R. Soc. Lond. B 363, 2465–2480.

Jiggins, C.D., Naisbit, R.E., Coe, R.L., Mallet, J., 2001. Reproductive isolation caused by color pattern mimicry. Nature 411, 302–305.

Johnsen, A., Delhey, K., Andersson, S., Kempenaers, B., 2003. Plumage color in nesting blue tits: sexual dichromatism, condition dependence and genetic effects. Proc. R. Soc. Lond. B 270, 1263–1270.

Johnstone, R.A., 1995. Sexual selection, honest advertisement and the handicap principle— reviewing the evidence. Biol. Rev. Camb. Philos. Soc. 70, 1–65.

Jones, R.E., 1987a. Reproductive strategies for the seasonal tropics. Insect Sci. Applic. 8, 515–521.

Jones, R.E., 1987b. Temperature, development and survival in monophagous and polyphagous tropical pierid butterflies. Aust. J. Zool. 35, 235.

Jones, R.E., 1992. Phenotypic variation in Australian *Eurema* species. Aust. J. Zool. 40, 371–383.

Kaitala, A., Wiklund, C., 1994. Polyandrous female butterflies forage for matings. Behav. Ecol. Sociobiol. 35, 385–388.

Kaitala, A., Wiklund, C., 1995. Female mate choice and mating costs in the polyandrous butterfly *Pieris napi* (Lepidoptera: Pieridae). J. Insect Behav. 8, 355–363.

Kapan, D.D., 2001. Three-butterfly system provides a field test of mullerian mimicry. Nature 409, 338–340.

Karlsson, B., 1998. Nuptial gifts, resource budgets, and reproductive output in a polyandrous butterfly. Ecology 79, 2931–2940.

Kemp, D.J., 2006a. Heightened phenotypic variation and age-based fading of ultraviolet butterfly wing coloration. Evol. Ecol. Res. 8, 515–527.

Kemp, D.J., 2006b. Ultraviolet ornamentation and male mating success in a high density assemblage of the butterfly *Colias eurytheme*. J. Insect Behav. 19, 669–684.

Kemp, D.J., 2007. Female butterflies prefer males bearing bright iridescent ornamentation. Proc. R. Soc. Lond. B 274, 1043–1047.

Kemp, D.J., 2008a. Resource-mediated condition dependence in sexually dichromatic butterfly wing coloration. Evolution 62, 2346–2358.

Kemp, D.J., 2008b. Female mating biases for bright ultraviolet iridescence in the butterfly *Eurema hecabe* (Pieridae). Behav. Ecol. 19, 1–8.

Kemp, D.J., Macedonia, J.M., 2007. Male mating bias and its potential reproductive consequence in the butterfly *Colias eurytheme*. Behav. Ecol. Sociobiol. 61, 415–422.

Kemp, D.J., Rutowski, R.L., 2007. Condition dependence, quantitative genetics, and the potential signal content of iridescent ultraviolet butterfly coloration. Evolution 61, 168–183.

Kemp, D.J., Rutowski, R.L., Mendoza, M., 2005. Color pattern evolution in butterflies: a phylogenetic analysis of structural ultraviolet and melanic markings in North American sulphurs. Evol. Ecol. Res. 7, 133–141.

Kemp, D.J., Vukusic, P., Rutowski, R.L., 2006. Stress mediated covariance between nanostructural architecture and ultraviolet butterfly coloration. Funct. Ecol. 20, 282–289.

Kemp, D.J., Macedonia, J.M., Ball, T.S., Rutowski, R.L., 2008. Potential direct fitness consequences of ornament-based mate choice in a butterfly. Behav. Ecol. Sociobiol. 62, 1017–1026.

Keyser, A.J., Hill, G.E., 1999. Condition-dependent variation in the blue-ultraviolet coloration of a structurally based plumage ornament. Proc. R. Soc. Lond. B 266, 771–777.

Knuttel, H., Fiedler, K., 2001. Host-plant-derived variation in ultraviolet wing patterns influence mate selection by male butterflies. J. Exp. Biol. 204, 2447–2459.

Kodandaramaiah, U., Vallin, A., Wiklund, C., 2009. Fixed eyespot display in a butterfly thwarts attacking birds. Anim. Behav. 77, 1415–1419.

Kokko, H., Heubel, K., 2008. Condition-dependence, genotype-by-environment interactions and the lek paradox. Genetica 132, 209–216.

Kronforst, M.R., Young, L.G., Gilbert, L.E., 2007. Reinforcement of mate preference among hybridizing Heliconius butterflies. J. Evol. Biol. 20, 278–285.

Kunte, K., 2009. The diversity and evolution of Batesian mimicry in Papilio swallowtail butterflies. Evolution 63, 2707–2716.

Lederhouse, R.C., Scriber, J.M., 1996. Intrasexual selection constrains the evolution of the dorsal color pattern of male black swallowtail butterflies, Papilio polyxenes. Evolution 50, 717–722.

Lim, M.L.M., Li, D.Q., 2007. Effects of age and feeding history on structure-based UV ornaments of a jumping spider (Araneae: Salticidae). Proc. R. Soc. Lond. B 274, 569–575.

Linzen, B., 1974. The tryptophan-ommochrome pathway in insects. Adv. Insect Physiol. 10, 117–246.

Loyau, A., Gomez, D., Moureau, B.T., Thery, M., Hart, N.S., Saint Jalme, M., et al., 2007. Iridescent structurally based coloration of eyespots correlates with mating success in the peacock. Behav. Ecol. 18, 1123–1131.

Lyytinen, A., Lindstrom, L., Mappes, J., 2004. Ultraviolet reflection and predation risk in diurnal and nocturnal Lepidoptera. Behav. Ecol. 15, 982–987.

Martin, J., Forsman, A., 1999. Social costs and development of nuptial coloration in male Psammodromus algirus lizards: an experiment. Behav. Ecol. 10, 396–400.

Masello, J.F., Lubjuhn, T., Quillfeldt, P., 2008. Is the structural and psittacofulvin-based coloration of wild burrowing parrots Cyanoliseus patagonus condition dependent? J. Avian Biol. 39, 653–662.

Mavarez, J., Salazar, C.A., Bermingham, E., Salcedo, C., Jiggins, C.D., Linares, M., 2006. Speciation by hybridization in Heliconius butterflies. Nature 441, 868–871.

Maynard Smith, J., Harper, D., 2003. Animal Signals. Oxford University Press, Oxford.

Michielsen, K., Stavenga, D.G., 2008. Gyroid cuticular structures in butterfly wing scales: biological photonic crystals. J. R. Soc. Interface 5, 85–94.

Mikkola, K., Rantala, M.J., 2010. Immune defence, a possible non-visual selective factor behind industrial melanism in moths (Lepidoptera). Biol. J. Linn. Soc. 99, 831–838.

Møller, A.P., Alatalo, R.V., 1999. Good-genes effects in sexual selection. Proc. R. Soc. Lond. B 266, 85–91.

Morehouse, N.I., Rutowski, R.L., 2010a. Developmental responses to variable diet composition in the cabbage white butterfly, Pieris rapae: the role of nitrogen, carbohydrates and genotype. Oikos 119, 636–645.

Morehouse, N.I., Rutowski, R.L., 2010b. In the eyes of beholders: female choice and predation risk associated with an exaggerated male butterfly color. Am. Nat. 176, 768–784.

Morehouse, N.I., Vukusic, P., Rutowski, R.L., 2007. Pterin pigment granules are responsible for both broadband light scattering and wavelength selective absorption in the wing scales of pierid butterflies. Proc. R. Soc. Lond. B 274, 359–366.

Narita, S., Kageyama, D., Nomura, M., Fukatsu, T., 2007a. Unexpected mechanism of symbiont-induced reversal of insect sex: Feminizing Wolbachia continuously acts on the butterfly Eurema hecabe during larval development. Appl. Environ. Microbiol. 73, 4332–4341.

Narita, S., Nomura, M., Kageyama, D., 2007b. A natural population of the butterfly *Eurema hecabe* with *Wolbachia*-induced female-biased sex ratio not by feminization. Genome 50, 365–372.

Narita, S., Nomura, M., Kageyama, D., 2007c. Naturally occurring single and double infection with *Wolbachia* strains in the butterfly *Eurema hecabe*: transmission efficiencies and population density dynamics of each *Wolbachia* strain. FEMS Microbiol. Ecol. 61, 235–245.

Nielsen, M.G., Watt, W.B., 2000. Interference competition and sexual selection promote polymorphism in *Colias* (Lepidoptera, Pieridae). Funct. Ecol. 14, 718–730.

Nijhout, H.F., 1991. The Development and Evolution of Butterfly Wing Patterns. Smithsonian Institution Press, Washington, DC.

Oliver, J.C., Robertson, K.A., Monteiro, A., 2009. Accommodating natural and sexual selection in butterfly wing pattern evolution. Proc. R. Soc. B 276, 2369–2375.

Papke, R.S., Kemp, D.J., Rutowski, R.L., 2007. Multimodal signalling: structural ultraviolet reflectance predicts male mating success better than pheromones in the butterfly *Colias eurytheme* L. (Pieridae). Anim. Behav. 73, 47–54.

Poladian, L., Wickham, S.K., Lee, K., Large, M.C.J., 2009. Iridescence from photonic crystals and its suppression in butterfly scales. J. R. Soc. Interface 6, S233–S242.

Prum, R.O., Quinn, T., Torres, R.H., 2006. Anatomically diverse butterfly scales all produce structural colors by coherent scattering. J. Exp. Biol. 209, 748–765.

Prum, R.O., Dufresne, E.R., Quinn, T., Waters, K., 2009. Development of color-producing keratin nanostructures in avian feather barbs. J. R. Soc. Interface 6, S253–S265.

Rawson, G.W., 1968. Study of fluorescent pigments in Lepidoptera by means of paper partition chromatography. J. Lepidopterists' Soc. 22, 27–40.

Rice-Evans, C.A., Miller, N.J., Bolwell, P.G., Bramley, P.M., Pridham, J.B., 1995. The relative antioxidant activities of plant-derived polyphenolic flavonoids. Free Radic. Res. 22, 375–383.

Robertson, K.A., Monteiro, A., 2005. Female *Bicyclus anynana* butterflies choose males on the basis of their dorsal UV-reflective eyespot pupils. Proc. R. Soc. Lond. B 272, 1541–1546.

Rowe, L., Houle, D., 1996. The lek paradox and the capture of genetic variance by condition dependent traits. Proc. R. Soc. Lond. B 263, 1415–1421.

Rutowski, R.L., 1977. Use of visual cues in sexual and species discrimination by males of small sulfur butterfly *Eurema lisa* (Lepidoptera, Pieridae). J. Comp. Physiol. 115, 61.

Rutowski, R.L., 1978. The form and function of ascending flights in *Colias* butterflies. Behav. Ecol. Sociobiol. 3, 163–172.

Rutowski, R.L., 1980. Male scent-producing structures in *Colias* butterflies: function, localization, and adaptive features. J. Chem. Ecol. 6, 13–26.

Rutowski, R.L., 1985. Evidence for mate choice in a sulphur butterfly (*Colias eurytheme*). Z. Tierpsychol. 70, 103–114.

Rutowski, R.L., 1997. Sexual dimorphism, mating systems and ecology in butterflies. In: Choe, J.C., Crespi, B.J. (Eds.), The Evolution of Mating Systems in Insects and Arachnids. Cambridge University Press, Cambridge, pp. 257–272.

Rutowski, R.L., Gilchrist, G.W., 1986. Copulation in *Colias eurytheme* (Lepidoptera: Pieridae): patterns and frequency. J. Zool. 209, 115–124.

Rutowski, R.L., Gilchrist, G.W., Terkanian, B., 1987. Female butterflies mated with recently mated males show reduced reproductive output. Behav. Ecol. Sociobiol. 20, 319–322.

Rutowski, R.L., Macedonia, J.M., Morehouse, N., Taylor-Taft, L., 2005. Pterin pigments amplify iridescent ultraviolet signal in males of the orange sulfur butterfly, *Colias eurytheme*. Proc. R. Soc. Lond. B 272, 2329–2335.

Rutowski, R.L., Macedonia, J.M., Kemp, D.J., Taylor-Taft, L., 2007. Diversity in structural ultraviolet coloration among female sulphur butterflies (Coliadinae, Pieridae). Arthropod Struct. Dev. 36, 280–290.

Siitari, H., Alatalo, R.V., Halme, P., Buchanan, K.L., Kilpimaa, J., 2007. Color signals in the black grouse (*Tetrao tetrix*): signal properties and their condition dependency. Am. Nat. 169, S81–S92.

Silberglied, R.E., 1984. Visual communication and sexual selection among butterflies. In: Vane-Wright, R.I., Ackery, P.R. (Eds.), The Biology of Butterflies. Academic Press, London, pp. 207–223.

Silberglied, R.E., Taylor, O.R., 1973. Ultraviolet differences between sulfur butterflies, *Colias eurytheme* and *C. philodice*, and a possible isolating mechanism. Nature 241, 406–408.

Silberglied, R.E., Taylor, O.R., 1978. Ultraviolet reflection and its behavioral role in the courtship of the sulphur butterflies *Colias eurytheme* and *C. philodice* (Lepidoptera, Pieridae). Behav. Ecol. Sociobiol. 3, 203–243.

Stavenga, D.G., Stowe, S., Siebke, K., Zeil, J., Arikawa, K., 2004. Butterfly wing colors: scale beads make pierid wings brighter. Proc. R. Soc. Lond. B 271, 1577–1584.

Stavenga, D.G., Giraldo, M.A., Hoenders, B.J., 2006. Reflectance and transmittance of light scattering scales stacked on the wings of pierid butterflies. Opt. Express 14, 4880–4890.

Stavenga, D.G., Giraldo, M.A., Leertouwer, H.L., 2010. Butterfly wing colors: glass scales of *Graphium sarpedon* cause polarized iridescence and enhance blue/green pigment coloration of the wing membrane. J. Exp. Biol. 213, 1731–1739.

Stoehr, A.M., 2006. Costly melanin ornaments: the importance of taxon? Funct. Ecol. 20, 276–281.

Stoehr, A.M., 2010. Responses of disparate phenotypically-plastic, melanin-based traits to common cues: limits to the benefits of adaptive plasticity? Evol. Ecol. 24, 287–298.

Stride, G.O., 1957. Investigations into the courtship behaviour of the male of *Hypolimnas misippus* L., (Lepidoptera, Nymphalidae), with special reference to the role of visual stimuli. Anim. Behav. 5, 153–167.

Stride, G.O., 1958. Further studies on the courtship behaviour of African mimetic butterflies. Anim. Behav. 6, 224–230.

Sweeney, A., Jiggins, C., Johnsen, S., 2003. Polarized light as a butterfly mating signal. Nature 423, 31–32.

Talloen, W., Van Dyck, H., Lens, L., 2004. The cost of melanization: butterfly wing coloration under environmental stress. Evolution 58, 360–366.

Taylor, O.R., 1972. Reproductive isolation in *Colias eurytheme* and *C. philodice*: random vs. non-random mating. Evolution 26, 344–356.

Tomkins, J.L., Radwan, J., Kotiaho, J., Tregenza, T., 2004. Genic capture and resolving the lek paradox. Trends Ecol. Evol. 19, 323–328.

Vane-Wright, R.I., Boppre, M., 1993. Visual and chemical signalling in butterflies: functional and phylogenetic perspectives. Philos. Trans R. Soc. Lond. B 340, 197–205.

Vukusic, P., Hooper, I., 2005. Directionally controlled fluorescence emission in butterflies. Science 310, 1151.

Vukusic, P., Sambles, J.R., 2003. Photonic structures in biology. Nature 424, 852–855.

Vukusic, P., Sambles, J.R., Lawrence, C.R., Wootton, R.J., 1999. Quantified interference and diffraction in single *Morpho* butterfly scales. Proc. R. Soc. Lond. B 266, 1403–1411.

Watt, W.B., 1964. Pteridine components of wing pigmentation in the butterfly *Colias eurytheme*. Nature 201, 1326–1327.

Werren, J.H., 2008. *Wolbachia*: master manipulators of invertebrate biology. Nat. Rev. Microbiol. 6, 741–751.

West-Eberhard, M.J., 2003. Developmental Plasticity and Evolution. Oxford University Press, Oxford.

Wiernasz, D.C., 1995. Male choice on the basis of female melanin pattern in *Pieris* butterflies. Anim. Behav. 49, 45–51.

Wiernasz, D.C., Kingsolver, J.G., 1992. Wing melanin pattern mediates species recognition in *Pieris occidentalis*. Anim. Behav. 43, 89–94.

Wiklund, C., 2003. Sexual selection and the evolution of butterfly mating systems. In: Boggs, C.L., Watt, W.B., Ehrlich, P.R. (Eds.), Butterflies: Ecology and Evolution Taking Flight. University of Chicago Press, Chicago, pp. 67–90.

Yoshioka, S., Kinoshita, S., 2004. Wavelength-selective and anisotropic light-diffusing scale on the wing of the *Morpho* butterfly. Proc. R. Soc. Lond. B 271, 581–587.

Zahavi, A., 1975. Mate selection—a selection for a handicap. J. Theor. Biol. 53, 205–214.

Hormone-Behavior Interrelationships of Birds in Response to Weather

John C. Wingfield and Marilyn Ramenofsky

DEPARTMENT OF NEUROBIOLOGY, PHYSIOLOGY AND BEHAVIOR,
UNIVERSITY OF CALIFORNIA, DAVIS, CALIFORNIA, USA

In Nature there are unexpected storms and in life unpredicted vicissitudes.
Wu Cheng-En, "Journey to the West" (ca. sixteenth century China)
I've lived in a good climate, and it bores the hell out of me. I like weather rather than climate.

John Steinbeck, "Travels With Charlie" (1962)

I. Introduction

The world is an inherently unpredictable place with periods of routine tranquility punctuated by perturbations of weather, upheavals of social relations, reduced food supply, predation risk, and disease. Such perturbations are often linked and the occurrence of one frequently triggers others. Weather is a major source of perturbations that affects all life on earth, and in the face of global climate change, it is likely that storms, droughts, and periods of heat and cold will reach new extremes and occur with greater frequency. Therefore, mechanisms underlying behavioral responses to weather perturbations are important and relevant to basic biology, conservation, and biomedical research. However, investigating the effects of inclement weather on animals in their natural habitat is difficult because these perturbations are by nature unpredictable, at least in the long term. For these reasons, any field study on the effects of weather must be opportunistic and usually requires dedicated fieldwork under unpleasant conditions. In many cases, field biologists head for home and shelter once the weather turns bad. This is understandable because almost always the field research being conducted is disrupted by the perturbation. Nonetheless, some stalwart biologists braved the storms and discovered a rich suite of

93

0065-3454/11 $35.00
DOI: 10.1016/B978-0-12-380896-7.00003-4

behavioral and hormonal traits by which organisms cope with weather (Gessamen and Worthen, 1982; Elkins, 1983; Wingfield and Ramenofsky, 1997, 1999; Wingfield and Romero, 2001). This in turn led to laboratory experiments to explore mechanisms further. Here, we summarize what is known about behavioral and hormonal responses to weather events, mostly in birds, and how coping mechanisms provide flexibility to deal with an increasingly capricious environment in which global climate change and human disturbance provide further challenges (e.g., Travis, 2003). But first, it is important to consider some definitions and an emerging theoretical framework.

A. THE UNPREDICTABLE AND LABILE PERTURBATION FACTORS: DEFINITIONS
    AND THEORETICAL FRAMEWORK

Climate includes overall environmental conditions that, on average, can be expected over the year. These climatic conditions are predictable, and organisms can prepare for future changes allowing breeding, molt, and migrations. In contrast, weather encompasses actual environmental conditions at any time and these may deviate dramatically from the predicted "climate" for that locality for many days at a time. Although organisms prepare for predictable changes of climate, they must also be able to respond in a facultative way to unpredictable weather conditions, or other environmental perturbations, often on short notice (Jacobs and Wingfield, 2000; Wingfield, 2008; Wingfield and Jacobs, 1999).

It is important to bear in mind that exposure to unpredictable conditions in the environment is generally stressful which is not equivalent to the demands of predictable changes that occur during the course of a day, high tide, low tide, or the seasons. Yet, at the same time there are extremes of a continuum of daily and seasonal energy demand that can contribute to the "wear and tear" on an organism over time. It is common to consider climates with long cold winters or hot summers as "stressful," but nonetheless they are predictable and organisms anticipate the phenology of a particular climate including its specific demands. How often do we see references to "the stress of reproduction" or "the stress of migration"? These statements are misleading because life-history stages occur on predictable schedules and necessary preparations are anticipated. They are energetically demanding but not stressful *per se* (see Wingfield and Ramenofsky, 1997, 1999; Wingfield et al., 1998).

Organisms respond to environmental change in two fundamentally different ways. Typically, vertebrates show changes in morphology, physiology, and behavior in ANTICIPATION of the predictable changes so that they can respond appropriately to the changing seasons (Wingfield, 2003).

An example of this would be the development of the reproductive system before the breeding season so that individuals are able to begin breeding as soon as environmental conditions are favorable. By contrast, organisms must respond to unpredictable changes in the environment, only DURING or AFTER the perturbation as there is no way of predicting the actual onset (Wingfield, 2003). It is possible that an individual can detect the onset of a perturbation, such as an approaching storm and changes in barometric pressure and temperature, but this would be a brief period of minutes or at most a few hours whereas anticipatory preparations before predictable changes in environment are initiated days or weeks ahead. This concept of two major types of responses to environmental change, anticipatory, and facultative, is probably applicable to many organisms, including plants, invertebrates, and vertebrates.

Behavioral and physiological responses to predictable and unpredictable events of the environment are essential to maximize fitness (e.g., Wingfield, 2003; Wingfield and Ramenofsky, 1997, 1999). Proximate environmental factors affecting the life cycle of vertebrates have been classified into functional groups according to whether they have predictive value (for anticipating events in the daily and seasonal routines), or are unpredictable events (modifying factors). Social interactions can also influence responses of individuals to the physical environment (see Wingfield, 1980, 1983, 2006; Wingfield and Kenagy, 1991). Unpredictable events (modifying factors or more appropriately perturbation factors) are frequently disruptive to daily and seasonal routines and have the potential to be stressful. A potentially confusing aspect is that some environmental factors can act as predictive information *and* as perturbation factors depending upon circumstances. Weather can act in these ways. For example, a cold spring can slow down reproductive development, or a warm spring may have the opposite effect resulting in more rapid recrudescence of the gonad and onset of breeding (e.g., Wingfield, 1980, 1983; Wingfield and Kenagy, 1991). Such an action would serve as local predictive information regulating reproductive maturity. However, a severe storm with cold weather, heavy winds, or prolonged precipitation can disrupt breeding and other life-history stages. In this case, weather is acting as a perturbation factor (Wingfield and Ramenofsky, 1999; Wingfield et al., 1998). Clearly, the ways in which organisms respond to weather as local predictive information anticipating a future event, or as a perturbation factor requiring physiological and behavioral responses during and/or immediately after the event will involve very different neural, neuroendocrine, and endocrine control mechanisms.

Perturbation factors can be classified further to provide a framework to understand how they may influence how an individual copes (Fig. 1). Many perturbation factors are labile, that is, they are often short lived occurring

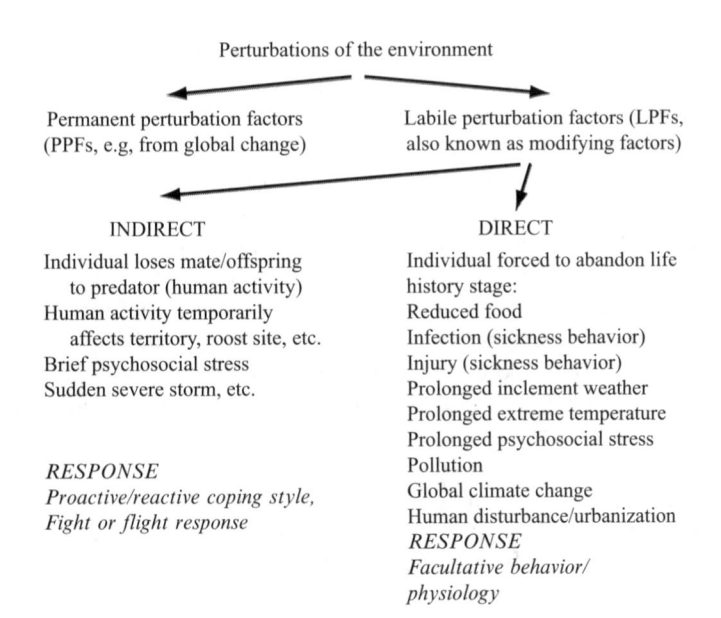

FIG. 1. Perturbations of the environment may be long-term (permanent) or they may be short-lived ("labile"). Permanent perturbations acting at population scales result in selection for individuals that can acclimate to the change. Labile perturbation factors result in physiological and behavioral responses that allow individuals to cope with the temporary disruption. There are two types of labile perturbation factors: indirect and direct. Responses to these factors are given in italics. Expanded from Wingfield et al. (1998) and Wingfield and Ramenofsky (1999).

over minutes to hours. Although they require temporary disruption of the predictable life cycle, they do not result in marked alteration in phenology. However, in other instances, perturbations of the environment may become long-lived or even permanent (Jacobs and Wingfield, 2000). For example, a severe perturbation that changes the habitat for several years or permanently will result in selection for genotypes that can acclimate to such changes and eventually continue their daily and seasonal routines in the new conditions. Massive mortality may result in those individuals that are unable to acclimatize. Some examples in the literature are listed in Gessamen and Worthen (1982) including such events as urbanization, clear-cutting forests, and introduction of invasive species that modify the habitat in many ways. There may also be widespread mortality to labile perturbation factors (LPFs; e.g., Gessamen and Worthen, 1982) selecting for mechanisms by which organisms cope. The distinction here is that permanent perturbation factors favor individuals that are able to adjust to a different habitat, whereas LPFs favor individuals that are able to cope temporarily and then return to normal life-history stages in the same habitat.

LPFs are of two types, direct and indirect (Wingfield, 1988; Wingfield et al., 1998; Fig. 1). Indirect LPFs typically are short lived such as loss of a mate or offspring through predation, a sudden storm (e.g., downpour, sudden wind) that can alter social and reproductive status, or affect territory quality but do not affect the individual directly in terms of injury and access to resources. Direct LPFs have generally longer-term effects on an individual that directly impair its ability to continue daily and seasonal routines. Examples include reduced food supply, injury or parasite infection, pollution, and human disturbance. These direct LPFs often result in the individual being redirected into emergency physiology and behavior to cope with the perturbation (Fig. 1). In general, many individuals are able to respond to direct LPFs appropriately but some cannot suggesting there must be strong selection for individuals that can adjust their life cycles accordingly and survive. It should also be borne in mind that perturbations do not always fall automatically into direct or indirect categories and there is much overlap including the types of responses. Physiological and behavioral responses to perturbations are thus customized to fit the circumstances and frequently involve combinations of different emergency life-history substages (Fig. 2).

1. The Emergency Life-History Stage

Environmental perturbations occur in all habitats but at varying intensities and frequencies. Further, perturbations have presented a problem for organisms for as long as there has been life on Earth indicating that selection for coping mechanisms is ancient. However, even though no organism is entirely insulated from such events, there is still little information on hormonal responses of free-living animals, particularly vertebrates, to actual perturbations. As mentioned above, this is in part because such studies cannot be planned and investigators need to be opportunistic. Nonetheless, examples in birds and other vertebrates now indicate some common physiological and behavioral ways that organisms cope.

There are four major substages of the emergency life-history stage (Fig. 2) including the well-known "fight-or-flight" response (Axelrod and Reisine, 1984; Sapolsky et al., 2000), proactive/reactive coping styles (e.g., Koolhaas et al., 1999; Korte et al., 2005), sickness behavior and

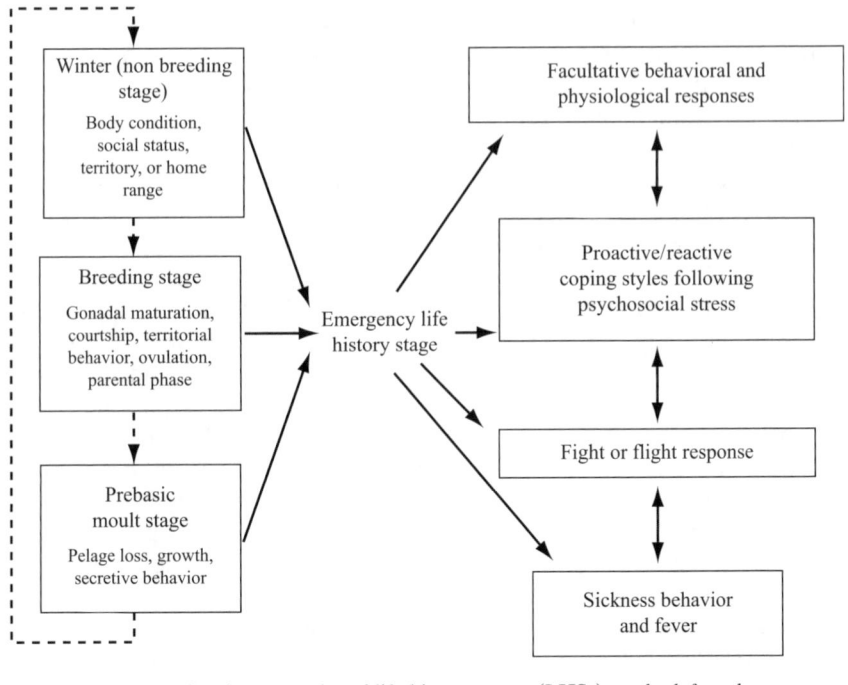

Fig. 2. Scheme showing examples of life history stages (LHSs) on the left and emergency life history stage on the right. In, for example, a nonmigratory bird, LHSs include breeding, nonbreeding, and molt stages. Each has a unique set of substages. The progression of LHSs is one way with each cycle taking a year. The temporal progression of normal LHSs is regulated by the predictable annual cycle of seasons and environmental factors such as day length, temperature, and others. Superimposed upon this predictable life cycle are unpredictable events such as severe storms, predator pressure, human disturbance, etc. These "labile perturbation factors" have the potential to trigger the emergency life history stage (ELHS) which redirect the individual away from the normal LHSs into survival mode. Once the perturbation passes, the individual can then return to an LHS appropriate for that time of year. The ELHS has three characteristic components: The "fight or flight response" is typical of very rapid responses to, for example, sudden attack by a predator. If the perturbation is an infection, or wounding following an attack by a predator, then sickness behavior and fever may result. Responses to other less acute LPFs such as a severe storm trigger facultative behavioral and physiological responses (see Jacobs and Wingfield, 2000; Wingfield and Romero, 2000). From Wingfield (2003) courtesy of Elsevier Press and the Association for the Study of Animal Behavior.

fever (Hart, 1988; Owen-Ashley et al., 2006), and facultative behavioral and physiological responses (Wingfield and Ramenofsky, 1997, 1999; Wingfield et al., 1998). Typical coping responses to indirect LPFs include the fight-or-flight response and/or proactive and reactive coping styles (Fig. 1, see also below, e.g., Korte et al., 2005). Proactive coping styles generally involve aggression and active behavioral responses to novel events, including social challenges, whereas reactive responses to the same events involve behavioral immobility and low rates of aggression (e.g., Coppens et al., 2010; Koolhaas et al., 1999; Korte et al., 2005; Sih et al., 2004). Extensive evidence suggests that there is a genetic basis to proactive versus reactive coping styles (Drent et al., 2003) and their hormonal and neural bases (Koolhaas et al., 1999, 2007; van Hierden et al., 2002), and also a strong environmental component because many individuals show both strategies to varying degrees that may change over time (Coppens et al., 2010; Koolhaas et al., 2007; Øverli et al., 2007). Relationships of coping styles to responses to weather and climate events remain virtually unexplored.

These major components can occur singly or in various combinations to customize the response of the individual to unique circumstances of habitat configuration, social status, body condition, and health (Fig. 3). In essence,

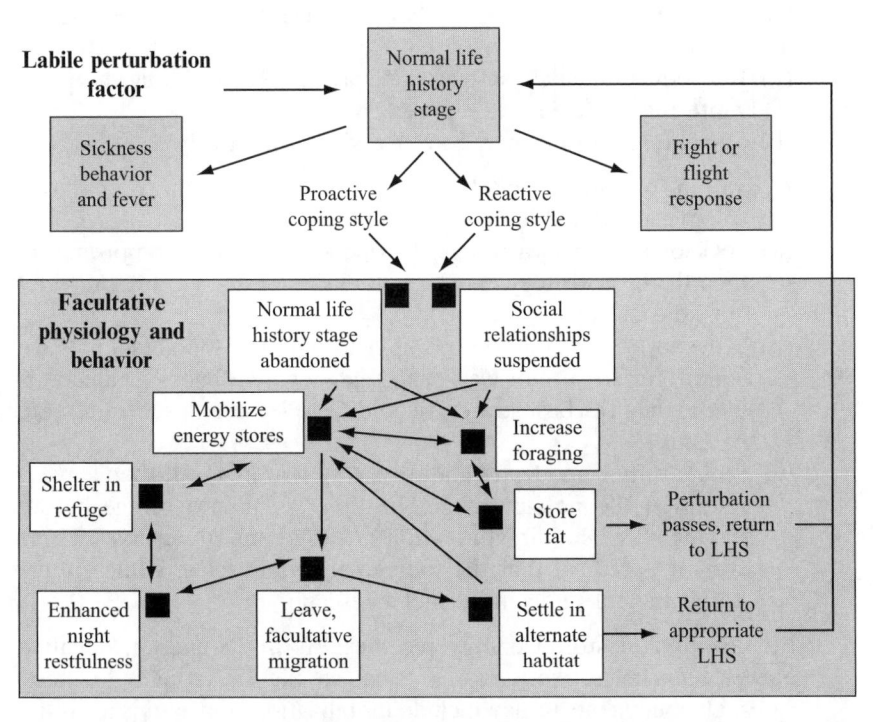

FIG. 3. Possible interrelationships of substages of the emergency life history stage. These can be expressed in many combinations depending upon the type of perturbation and condition of the individual responding. Note the connectivity of substages in facultative physiology and behavior.

these combinations allow many different ways in which an individual can cope with an unpredictable environment. Further, because each individual does not experience either the predictable or unpredictable environments in exactly the same way as another (even its neighbor), these systems can explain interindividual variation in responses to a capricious world.

Climate events, including changes in phenology accompanying global warming, affect the predictable life cycle. The short-term effects of weather generally act as direct LPFs although short violent weather events such as thunderstorms and wind squalls may act as indirect LPFs. As such, most weather events have the potential to act through facultative changes in physiology and behavior and will be the focus from here on. Note, however, that these facultative physiology and behavior mechanisms can be influenced markedly by other components of the emergency life-history stage (Fig. 3). There are several clearly definable events that make up facultative physiological and behavioral responses to direct LPFs summarized by Wingfield and Ramenofsky (1997, 1999) and Wingfield et al. (1998).

1. Deactivation of territorial behavior/disintegration of social hierarchies:
    (a) Reproduction and associated behavior, seasonal migration, or wintering strategies are suppressed.
    (b) Social relationships may be suspended temporarily.

2. Activation of emergency behavior (includes certain preparative physiology as outlined in Sapolsky et al., 2000):
    (a) Seek or remain in a refuge. If food supply is not compromised, then the best strategy may be to find shelter and endure or "ride-out" the LPF.
    (b) Move away from the source of perturbation. If food resources are compromised in any way such that negative energy balance is likely, then the best strategy would be to leave and seek alternate habitat.
    (c) Seek a refuge and try to endure the LPF at first, but then leave if conditions do not improve. The time spent in a refuge before leaving may be a direct function of stored energy reserves. However, it is critical that the individual should leave while energy stores are still sufficient to fuel an escape.

3. Mobilization of stored energy reserves: As in 2b and 2c, negative energy balance is likely, stores of fat should be tapped. In many cases, gluconeogenesis may include mobilization of proteins as well.

4. Settlement in alternate habitat or return to the original site—termination of the emergency life-history stage:

(a) If the individual remains in its original habitat, then the normal life-history stage can be assumed immediately after the LPF has abated.

(b) If the individual leaves, then suitable habitat should be identified, and the individual can then settle and resume the normal sequence of life-history stages.

(c) In many cases, the individual may return to its original habitat once the LPF has passed.

(d) Recovery following an emergency life-history stage may be a critical component of the whole process.

Evidence to date indicates that behavioral and physiological components of the emergency life-history stage are similar, perhaps identical, at all times of year, regardless of the life-history stage, gender, and age of the organism (Jacobs, 1996). Moreover, it is also possible that the mechanisms by which this stage is initiated, maintained, and terminated may be the same throughout the life cycle of the individual. Many hormones have been identified in classical responses to stress in vertebrates, and because many aspects of the emergency life-history stage are superficially similar to stress, it is tempting to draw parallels. However, the evidence is now convincing that the emergency life-history stage involves a suite of mechanisms by which individuals *avoid stress* thus enhancing survival and potentially life-time reproductive success (Sapolsky et al., 2000; Wingfield et al., 1998).

B. HORMONAL ACTIONS IN RESPONSE TO LABILE PERTURBATION FACTORS

In vertebrates, both responses to predictable and unpredictable environmental change are regulated by the nervous and endocrine systems. The autonomic nervous system and adrenal medulla, along with cytokines of the immune system and neuropeptides (e.g., corticotropin-releasing hormone, CRH) associated with the hypothalamo-pituitary-adrenal cortex (HPA) axis, adrenocorticotropin (ACTH), and glucocorticosteroids regulate the facultative physiology and behavior components of the emergency life-history stage (e.g., Axelrod and Reisine, 1984; Dhabhar, 2002; Sapolsky et al., 2000; Wingfield, 1994), although it is certain that other endocrine secretions may also be involved. Hypothalamo-pituitary (glycoprotein and polypeptide hormone families) axes interacting with the gonads, thyroid, and other peripheral endocrine glands and processes regulate many of the anticipatory changes for diel and seasonal rhythms. This is not an exclusive division, there is much cross-talk and some systems are active in both responses triggering different actions depending upon receptor type activated in the target cell (e.g., mineralocorticoid receptor (MR) and glucocorticoid receptor (GR); Sapolsky et al., 2000; Korte et al., 2005; Romero et al., 2009). Glucocorticoid actions—both basal and stress-induced—are central to how individuals cope with direct LPFs. Sapolsky et al. (2000) have reviewed the mammalian literature providing a framework to understand the complex actions of the HPA axis. CRH regulates the HPA axis, and the glucocorticosteroids such as corticosterone that are secreted as a result. CRH also regulates the pituitary-thyroid axis, and its secretory products thyroxine (T4) and tri-iodothyronine (T3). Both axes are important in development as well as daily and seasonal regulation of metabolic processes. The involvement of CRH in the stress response across vertebrates is also widely known (Crespi and Denver, 2005).

Here, we will focus on the HPA axis and its actions on the responses to weather acting as direct LPFs. This response is common to most vertebrates and there are remarkably comparable parallel responses of very different organisms such as fish and mammals to those perturbations. One thing we do not know well is the natural history of responses to perturbations, yet this is critical for understanding how populations can be maintained in the face of environmental challenges.

It is well known that diverse obnoxious agents (stressors including inclement weather) activate the HPA axis resulting in elevation of glucocorticosteroid secretion. The actions of glucocorticosteroids during this so-called "stress-response" attracted attention at first because of the many similarities to events of the emergency life-history stage. Owing to constraints of space, we will focus primarily on the actions of glucocorticosteroids. Wingfield (1994) suggested that there may be two distinct suites of responses to glucocorticosteroids during a stress response. By far, the most studied are chronic effects induced by many days or even weeks of exposure to continual high circulating levels of glucocorticosteroids resulting from prolonged exposure to stress. These effects include failure of reproductive function, increased susceptibility to disease owing to suppression of the immune system, neuronal cell damage, particularly in the hippocampus, severe protein loss for gluconeogenesis, disruption of the arachidonic acid cascade, and inhibition of growth and metamorphosis (e.g., Axelrod and Reisine, 1984; Munck et al., 1984; Sapolsky, 1987, 2002; Sapolsky et al., 2000). Clearly, these effects have great significance for medicine and agriculture, but it is difficult to imagine how any one of these states would be adaptive for an organism because death would be imminent in any of these states. Thus, it is unlikely that chronic effects of prolonged high circulating levels of glucocorticosteroids have much to contribute to understanding the mechanisms of coping (Wingfield et al., 1998). Nonetheless, severe environmental perturbations occasionally result in massive mortality in natural populations (see Gessamen and Worthen, 1982; Wingfield et al., 1998), but this suggests strong selection for mechanisms by which such deleterious states are avoided in survivors. Therefore, the short-term effects of elevated glucocorticosteroids (over minutes to hours) may be highly adaptive in avoiding a severe, chronically stressed state. These short-term effects have been summarized extensively in Wingfield (1994, 2003), Wingfield et al. (1998), and Sapolsky et al. (2000).

One of the hallmarks of an emergency life-history stage is that individuals redirect their activities from those typical of the normal life-history stage for that time of year. For example, abandonment of breeding territories and offspring in response to LPF-like environmental events appears maladaptive at first because reproductive success becomes zero. However, temporary suspension of breeding activity may actually increase lifetime reproductive success by allowing an individual to survive the perturbation in the best condition possible so it can breed again at the earliest opportunity. Glucocorticoids secreted at higher concentrations in blood have the potential to temporarily suppress sexual and territorial behavior and trigger facultative physiology and behavior such as mobilization of energy resources (particularly fats and proteins) in preparation for coping with the perturbation (e.g., Sapolsky et al., 2000). Behavioral changes include seeking shelter or moving away from the perturbation, increased night restfulness to save energy, and finally recovery once the perturbation passes (see Wingfield, 2003, Wingfield and Ramenofsky, 1997, 1999; Wingfield et al., 1998). Taken together, these facultative physiological and behavioral responses regulated by hormones of the HPA axis potentiate avoidance of a chronic stressed state so that the individual can resume the cycle of normal life-history stages in the predictable life cycle.

C. THE CONCEPT OF ALLOSTASIS

A framework for modeling LPF intensity and frequency in relation to life-history stages of the predictable life cycle has long been difficult to conceptualize. A different approach is needed that is applicable to all seasons, but also takes into account individual differences in territory quality, social status, parasite load, old injuries, and other factors. Currently, the burgeoning deleterious effects of anthropogenic activity resulting in pollution, urbanization, habitat degradation, and climate change add further demands on free-living organisms and underscore an urgent need to understand how environmental perturbations may affect the predictable life cycle. In the past 20 years, concepts have been developing that may help provide such a framework with wide relevance to organisms in their natural environment (e.g., Korte et al., 2005; McEwen and Wingfield, 2003, 2010) and to the control mechanisms underlying individual differences (see also Williams, 2008).

1. Homeostasis in a Changing World and Physiological State Levels

It is surprisingly difficult to separate energetically demanding aspects of life-history stages in the normal life cycle from additional demands imposed by unpredictable events including stress. This is further complicated because secretion of glucocorticoids increases in response to both demands (e.g., Landys et al., 2006; Romero, 2002). Moreover, the term stress is arbitrarily used to describe life-cycle processes that do not involve environmental perturbations, for example, the "stress" of reproduction, migration, winter, and other life-history stages. This led to the concept of three state levels (Landys et al., 2006; Wingfield, 2003) involving: (A) the physiological state required to simply maintain life, basic homeostasis; (B) the change in physiological state, homeostatic set points, during daily and annual routines of the predictable life cycle; and (C) facultative adjustments of physiology to adapt to perturbations of the environment in addition to the predictable life cycle. Thus, high energetic demand life-history stages such as reproduction or migration could affect sensitivity to perturbations, but how does an organism integrate these otherwise different processes?

2. Allostasis and Energy Demand in Relation to the Individual

Allostasis, stability through change (McEwen, 2000; Schulkin, 2003; Sterling and Eyer, 1988), presents a framework to integrate metabolic demands of the predictable life cycle with those resulting from unpredictable perturbations. Perhaps what is most useful is that allostasis allows for a continuum of responses that includes anticipation of environmental change so that a life-history stage is developed before the environment changes, whereas classical homeostasis results in adjustments of physiology and behavior after the environment has changed or as it changes via acclimation. Changes in response to the unpredictable become part of this continuum and by definition must happen after the fact. It is well known that homeostatic mechanisms change over the life cycle, but the allostasis framework includes homeostatic processes of both the unpredictable components that are potentially stressful, and the demands of anticipatory switches in life-history stages.

It should also be borne in mind that no individual experiences the environment in exactly the same way as another, even though they may live side by side. Territories differ in quality and physical attributes, social status, parasite load, and old injuries can differ across individuals. Moreover, one territory may contain more predators or pathogens or have reduced food supply. Thus, as a concept, allostasis extends beyond classical acclimation allowing integration of all the experiences of an individual as a continuum from the predictable life cycle to the unpredictable and potential for stress instead of considering each as separate issues. This framework will be critical for understanding the complex behavioral and physiological responses to perturbations such as weather and the hormonal controls.

3. Allostatic Load and Allostatic Overload

Evidence to date suggests a common physiological pathway by which diverse environmental information regulating the life cycle is transduced into hormone secretion pathways that then regulate the response (Wingfield et al., 1998). This common physiological pathway is based on a simple energetic theme, E, that also represents a common currency for allostatic load—the cumulative demands of daily/seasonal routines, parasites, social status, habitat quality, and other factors (McEwen and Wingfield, 2003; Fig. 4). The term for general energetic requirements (E) of organisms during their life cycle includes, for convenience, all potential requirements for nutrition in general, although essential components of nutrition could also be modeled separately.

The energy required for basic homeostasis, existence energy, is represented by E_e (Fig. 4). Additional energy required for the individual to go about its daily routines to find, process, and assimilate food under ideal conditions is E_i. The amount of energy (in food) available in the environment is E_g (McEwen and Wingfield, 2003). These components obviously will change in relation to seasons and other factors. For example, we would expect E_g to rise in spring and summer and subsequently decline through autumn and winter when primary productivity is low (Fig. 4). Energy required for basic homeostasis (existence energy, E_e) would be lowest in summer when ambient temperatures are highest, and thus E_i (energy for daily routines under ideal conditions) will vary in parallel with E_e. Then the sum of E_e plus E_i is the basic energetic demand (allostatic load) required for basic daily and seasonal routines of the individual (McEwen and Wingfield, 2003). Superimposed on this daily routine are additional demands imposed by the energy required to reproduce, molt, or migrate. The additional E required to fuel this higher allostatic load must remain below E_g if positive energy balance is to be maintained. Similarly, a perturbation (such as a storm) will also increase energetic demand in addition to $E_e + E_i$. This is E_o and represents the energy required to find food, process it, and assimilate nutrients under nonideal conditions (Fig. 4). As long as the sum of $E_e + E_i + E_o$ does not exceed E_g, then the individual can tolerate higher allostatic load, at least temporarily (Korte et al., 2005; McEwen and Wingfield, 2003; Wingfield, 2004).

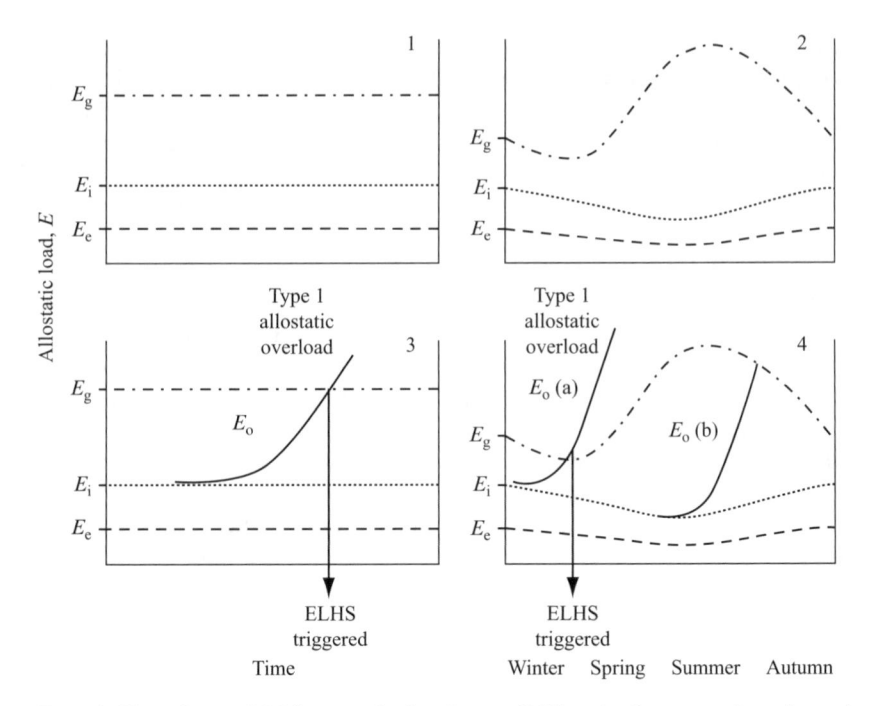

FIG. 4. The effects of labile perturbation factors (LPFs—the frequency, intensity and durations of storms, predators, human disturbance, and other factors) on allostatic load (E—energy levels) in free-living organisms. E_e is the existence energy simply to sustain life and E_i is the energy required to go about daily routines such as foraging and maintaining a territory. In panel 1, E_g is held constant, but as environmental conditions deteriorate, the energy required to go out, obtain food, process, and assimilate it increases and a new line, E_o, can be inserted (panel 3). As the LPF persists (panel 3), then E_o increases until $E_e + E_i + E_o > E_g$. At this point, the individual goes into negative energy balance, (allostatic overload type I) and an emergency life-history stage (ELHS) is triggered. At this point, secretion of glucocorticosteroids increases dramatically thus driving the transition to an ELHS (see Wingfield et al., 1998, 2000). In panel 2, a more realistic scenario based on seasons is presented in which E_e and E_i decrease in summer because of higher ambient temperatures and increase in winter. E_g tends to increase in spring due to primary productivity in the environment and then decreases through autumn and winter. If we then insert an LPF, E_o (a), in winter allostatic overload, is achieved very quickly and an ELHS is triggered. However, if the same LPF occurs in summer, E_o (b), then allostatic overload is not reached and the individual can maintain its normal life-history stage throughout this perturbation (panel 4). In this case, the same LPF would result in the same rise in E_o, but an ELHS would be triggered in one case but not the other. In this way, the energy model can explain individual differences in coping with the environment but keeps the potential mechanisms working within a common framework. Note also that when in negative energy balance, the triggering of an ELHS is designed to reduce allostatic load ($E_e + E_i + E_o$) so that the individual can regain positive energy balance and survive the LPF in the best condition possible. If allostatic load is so high that even an ELHS cannot reduce it sufficiently to gain positive energy balance, then chronic stress will ensue. From McEwen and Wingfield (2003), courtesy of Elsevier Press.

Allostatic load therefore increases further as a direct function of $E_e + E_i + E_o$ and if it exceeds E_g, then type 1 allostatic overload develops which means that the individual is in negative energy balance (Fig. 4). At this point, the individual becomes dependent on supplementing E_g with endogenous reserves. The amount of those reserves determines whether the individual can seek a shelter to endure the perturbation, or whether it should leave so that allostatic load is reduced below a level for E_g in alternate habitat. In either event, the facultative physiological and behavioral strategies of the emergency life-history stage are triggered to allow the individual to cope. This will include abandonment of the normal life-history stage with further savings on energy demand. Examples are abandonment of a nest and interruption of reproductive function.

Type 2 allostatic overload is a function of long-term (sometimes permanent) perturbations as might result from human disturbance and global climate change. In this scenario, energetic demand (E_o) resulting from nonideal conditions increases and remains high but below the amount of energy available as food in the environment (E_g). This type of allostatic load is a long-term or permanent increase in $E_e + E_i + E_o$ and likely will have deleterious effects unless individuals are able to adjust their life cycles accordingly (McEwen and Wingfield, 2003). Increased intensity and frequency of storms as a result of global warming may thus have serious consequences in the form of allostatic overload types 1 and 2 in the future.

Mediators of allostasis include many hormones and neural inputs (see McEwen, 2006; McEwen and Wingfield, 2010; Romero et al., 2009; Schulkin, 2003). Major hormones associated with increasing allostatic load are the glucocorticoids that orchestrate the physiological and behavioral adjustments that parallel increasing allostatic load and particularly allostatic overload. Type 1 allostatic overload stimulates further elevation of plasma glucocorticoid levels, and an emergency life-history stage is then triggered. Facultative physiological and behavioral strategies as well as interruption of the normal life-history stage for that time of year reduce allostatic load below E_g and glucocorticoid levels subsequently decline (Korte et al., 2005; McEwen and Wingfield, 2003; Wingfield, 2004). An important concept here is that circulating levels of glucocorticoids should parallel allostatic load and the point at which they go above a threshold at negative energy balance, an emergency life-history stage is triggered. There is mounting evidence that circulating glucocorticoid levels do indeed parallel energetic demand (McEwen and Wingfield, 2003; Sapolsky et al., 2000; Wingfield and Kitaysky, 2002; Wingfield and Ramenofsky, 1999; Wingfield et al., 1998). Such a framework will be essential to interpret how weather events may interact with the predictable life cycle, and climate, to result in diverse behavioral responses varying with intensity of the event, time of year, life-history stage, and condition/experience of the individual.

II. BEHAVIORAL AND GLUCOCORTICOID RESPONSES TO WEATHER AND CLIMATE EVENTS

Using a framework provided by the concepts of allostasis and physiological state levels, we can interpret effects of increasing allostatic load resulting from rising intensity and frequency of short-term weather events such as storms and floods or other longer-term climatic events, for example, droughts and monsoons resulting from El Niño Southern Oscillation events. These will increase E_o, sometimes simultaneously with decreasing E_g, the food available in the environment. E_o must also be integrated with other contributors to allostatic load such as reproductive effort. Next, we summarize effects of weather on hormones and behavior of free-living birds. Over the past 30 years, a number of field investigations that serendipitously collected data on weather events in diverse circumstances indicate that common underlying themes may indeed be present. First, the natural history of the responses of individuals and populations to specific weather events is considered, and second, we use the allostasis framework to explain the behavioral and physiological responses, and particularly any trends and patterns that emerge. These findings have important implications for understanding future responses of individuals and populations to global change.

A. WEATHER AND THE BREEDING SEASON

Breeding birds, indeed vertebrates in general, incur considerable energetic costs to breed successfully thus making them particularly vulnerable to weather events. Spring weather can be particularly devastating. Late snowfall can result in total loss of broods. Conversely, hotter weather can result in more rapid growth of insect food such as caterpillars so that availability of food after fledging is reduced (e.g., Perrins, 1979). Heavy rains occurring during postfledging can increase mortality as can cool weather and rain during the nestling period because caterpillars are less active and harder to find (Perrins, 1979). The number of spiders caught by captive great tits, *Parus major*, increased with ambient temperatures from 2 to 13 °C compared with immobile prey such as insect pupae. The data suggest that mobility of prey with increasing temperature is an important factor in foraging success (Avery and Krebs, 1984). Link these effects of weather with increased numbers of predators, and survival can be affected even more (Perrins, 1979). Clearly, the cumulative effects of multiple contributors to allostatic load must be borne in mind.

In American kestrels, *Falco sparverius*, inclement weather affected hunting success for small mammals. Kestrel nestlings exposed to inclement weather were smaller and lighter at fledging than nestlings reared during good weather (Dawson and Bortolotti, 2000). Similar effects of rainfall and lower temperature were seen in breeding black kites, *Milvus nigrans*, (Hiraldo et al., 1990) suggesting that weather affects availability of food above an assumed threshold of abundance that allows breeding. Rainfall significantly decreased frequency of prey capture attempts and success in black kites, whereas higher temperatures increased foraging success. Further, provisioning rates to nestlings decreased during rainy weather (Sergio, 2003). There was also a relationship between weather conditions over the year and female black kite condition prior to laying. This may have been mediated through the ability of males to hunt successfully and provision their mates (Sergio, 2003). In European sparrow hawks, *Accipiter nisus*, cold wet weather in the early spring period, February to April, led to reduced numbers of breeding birds than expected from the previous year's breeding success (Newton, 1986). When weather was warm and dry during March and April, egg laying was earlier, clutch sizes larger, and breeding success greater than in years when the same period was cold and wet (Newton, 1986).

In a Scottish population of hen harriers, *Circus cyaneus*, brooding time of chicks by females increased in cold weather. Provisioning rates of male harriers were negatively related to temperature and rainfall. This was also accompanied by an increase in chick mortality rates (Redpath et al., 2002), and fledging of hen harriers was positively related to summer temperatures. In contrast in a southern population of harriers in Spain, the opposite effect was observed with fledging rates that were negatively related to summer temperature (Redpath et al., 2002). The authors point out that although effects of temperature and precipitation on reproductive productivity may be strong at different latitudes, the mechanisms involved may be very different, that is, cold spells versus warmth may trigger different physiological responses. Note also that the timing and distance of dispersal of recently fledged European buzzards, *Buteo buteo*, are affected by weather variables such as minimum temperature and wind direction in autumn and winter (Walls et al., 2005).

In golden eagles, *Aquila chrysaetos*, hatching dates were negatively affected by severity of the preceding winter in southern Idaho (Steenhof et al., 1997) apparently because of reduced numbers of prey—jackrabbits, *Lepus californicus*. Eggs of these eagles hatched earlier and more pairs nested when the abundance of jackrabbits was greater, whereas fewer eagles nested when the numbers of jackrabbits were reduced after severe winters. Additionally, the frequency of hot days in spring reduced fledging success and brood size suggesting multiple effects of weather throughout the breeding period (Steenhof et al., 1997).

Alpine swifts, *Apus melba*, like many other avian species that forage for flying insects exclusively on the wing, may be unable to feed their young during inclement weather and numbers of flying insects are reduced. During a week-long period of inclement weather in Switzerland, nestlings showed up to an 18 °C reduction in body temperature and a reduction of pectoral muscle size presumably to provide energy during a prolonged fasting period (Bize et al., 2007).

Rotenberry and Wiens (1991) investigated the effects of extreme precipitation years on the breeding of Brewer's sparrows, *Spizella breweri*, and Sage sparrows, *Amphispiza belli*, in a semiarid shrub-steppe habitat in central Oregon. Both species had greater reproductive productivity in the wetter year. Brewer's sparrows apparently were able to assess potentially favorable conditions and increase clutch size. In contrast, Sage sparrows showed higher hatching rates in the wet year likely a proximate consequence of conditions during incubation.

Wilson (1975) first proposed the principle of stringency in which time and energy budgets may have evolved to allow sudden increased episodes of foraging when food supplies are poor or when unpredictable weather events such as rain, wind, and snow reduce the food supply. This may be particularly important in aerial insectivores in which unpredictable weather may affect food supply especially when feeding young (Ettinger and King, 1980). Periods of "loafing" behavior may provide a buffer against episodes of "stringency" that could lead to loss of body condition and/or reduced reproductive success. In other words, some species raise the number of young they likely can feed during periods of stringency, and thus may appear to be loafing during periods of good weather. Further evidence for the stringency hypothesis comes from Foster (1974) who provides evidence that many tropical species do not raise the number of young they possibly could because rainfall and other unpredictable events may decrease foraging time and the amount of food available.

It should also be pointed out that these behavioral responses to weather have an important role in resilience to climate change (Sergio, 2003). Breeding seasons of many vertebrate species in mid-latitudes are occurring earlier probably as a result of earlier spring (e.g., Saether et al., 2000). Physiological responses to weather, particularly hormonal, can mediate many behavioral responses described above. Examples from investigations of free-living birds are given next.

Reproduction, particularly raising young to independence, can increase allostatic load considerably. For example, in male white-crowned sparrows, *Zonotrichia leucophrys pugetensis*, baseline corticosterone levels increase normally during the nesting season and decline thereafter (Wingfield et al., 1983; Fig. 5). However, in May 1980, a severe and prolonged storm resulted in abandonment of nests and territories. Circulating levels of corticosterone were greatly elevated at this time compared with males sampled in a year with no storm (Wingfield and Farner, 1978; Wingfield et al., 1983; Fig. 5). Later in the season, after the severe storm had passed and birds were renesting, plasma levels of corticosterone had returned to normal for that

FIG. 5. The Puget Sound subspecies of white-crowned sparrow, *Zonotrichia leucophrys pugetensis*, (B) nests on or near the ground in open areas near forest edge (A). In May 1980, there were periods of inclement weather resulting in blown-down trees (C) near breeding habitat. Breeding *Z. l. pugetensis* abandoned breeding territories and even formed small flocks during this period. Corticosterone levels in free-living birds were greatly elevated over those in birds captured in 1979 when there were no severe storms (bar and line graph). Note that during the second parental phase (after the storms had passed), plasma levels of corticosterone had decreased and were identical to those at the same time in 1979. From Wingfield et al. (1983). All photos by J. C. Wingfield. Courtesy of Allen Press and the American Ornithologist's Union.

time of year (Fig. 5). During the storm, subcutaneous fat deposits were virtually depleted but returned to normal after the storm had passed and when renesting was initiated. It should also be noted that during the storm of 1980, male white-crowned sparrows had normal levels of luteinizing hormone and testosterone, hormones that regulate reproductive function (Fig. 6), thus supporting the hypothesis that corticosterone may be acting directly to suppress expression of reproductive behavior rather than indirectly through decreased secretion of sex steroids. Further research is needed to determine the mechanisms and locus of corticosterone action including when renesting occurs.

Using the allostasis concept as a framework, we can suggest that reproduction entails additional energetic costs over and above E_e and E_i. These costs are represented by the line E_y that includes the added energy required to produce young and raise them to independence (Fig. 7). In many ways, it

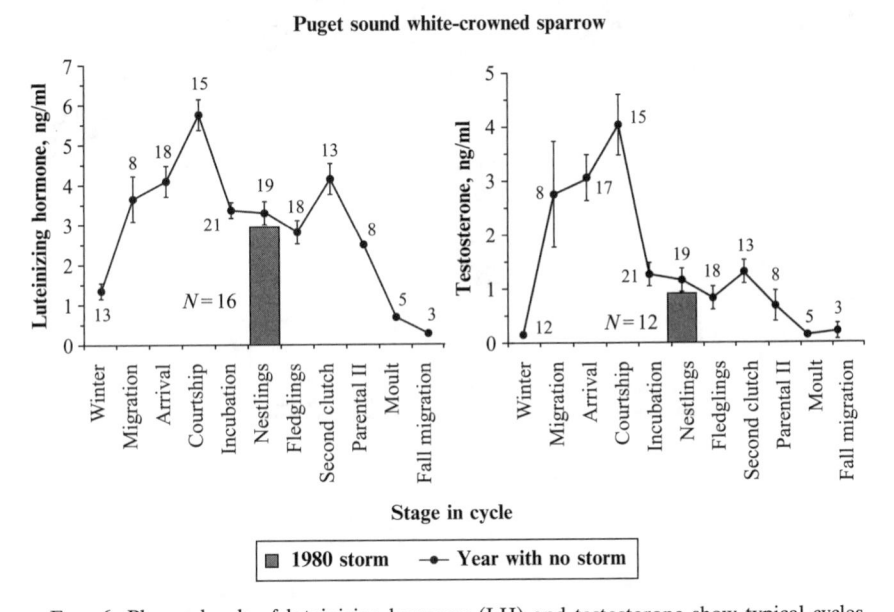

Puget sound white-crowned sparrow

FIG. 6. Plasma levels of luteinizing hormone (LH) and testosterone show typical cycles during the breeding season for socially monogamous birds such as the Puget Sound white-crowned sparrow, *Zonotrichia leucophrys pugetensis*, (lines). LH levels tend to peak at each sexual phase for each brood and are lower during the parental phases. Testosterone levels peak early in the season when establishing territories and remain lower thereafter. During the severe storms of 1980 (see Fig. 5), plasma levels of LH and testosterone were identical to those of 1979 (no severe storms). From Wingfield and Farner, 1978; Wingfield et al., 1983. Courtesy of Alan Press and the American Ornithologist's Union.

has parallels to E_o, but E_y is always part of the predictable life cycle. We can assume that the cost of E_y must remain below E_g. However, as E_y increases, then susceptibility to storms and other LPFs that result in an increase in E_o becomes greater (Fig. 7, upper panel). The outcome is the same if we model this as a decrease in E_g (see Wingfield, 2004).

Other examples of global warming trends suggest that inclement weather events might exacerbate the above scenario. In the Santa Catalina Mountains of SE Arizona (32°N), springtime temperatures (especially minimum temperatures) have risen about 2–3 °C in recent decades (Decker and Conway, 2009). As a result, many birds begin breeding earlier making them vulnerable to late spring storms. In late May 2008, a very late spring snow storm resulted in nest abandonment by 68% of red-faced warblers, *Cardellina rubrifrons*, breeding between 2300 and 2700 m elevation (Decker and Conway, 2009). Global warming can result in birds and other organisms breeding earlier, but the frequency of severe storms could increase vulnerability to weather. Here, there are clearly two issues. First, the onset of breeding is occurring earlier, and second, sensitivity to severe storms and/or the frequency of storms could have changed. Will selection favor further coping mechanisms or are they already at the limit?

Other investigations of weather events and the breeding season in birds have not been consistent in the relationship of circulating corticosterone levels and reproductive function (Wingfield, 1984). The allostasis concept may provide a framework to understand this (Fig. 7), particularly the interplay of predictive information regulating onset of breeding and responses to perturbations during breeding.

Looking again at Fig. 7, E_y, the extra energy and nutrients required to incubate eggs, then raise young to fledging and independence increases steadily as the season progresses. Fledging occurs while E_g is still sufficient to fuel increasing allostatic load (Fig. 7, top panel). A further perturbation, E_o, will increase allostatic load even faster or sooner (red lines), and when it exceeds E_g (allostatic overload type 1), the adult abandons the nest and young. However, a perturbation would take longer to reach allostatic overload early in the parental phase (left hand E_o) than an identical perturbation later (right hand E_o). Timing of when a perturbation occurs in the parental phase is critical and storms later in the parental phase can be particularly disruptive to breeding because E_o increases may exceed E_g very quickly. However, conditions early in the breeding season are usually more severe than later in spring and summer, such as lower E_g in early spring and higher $E_e + E_i$ as a result of lower temperature and more energy needed to forage. Then E_y, the extra energy and nutrients required to raise young to fledging will increase allostatic load immediately even without further E_o (lower panel of Fig. 7). In this scenario, delayed onset of

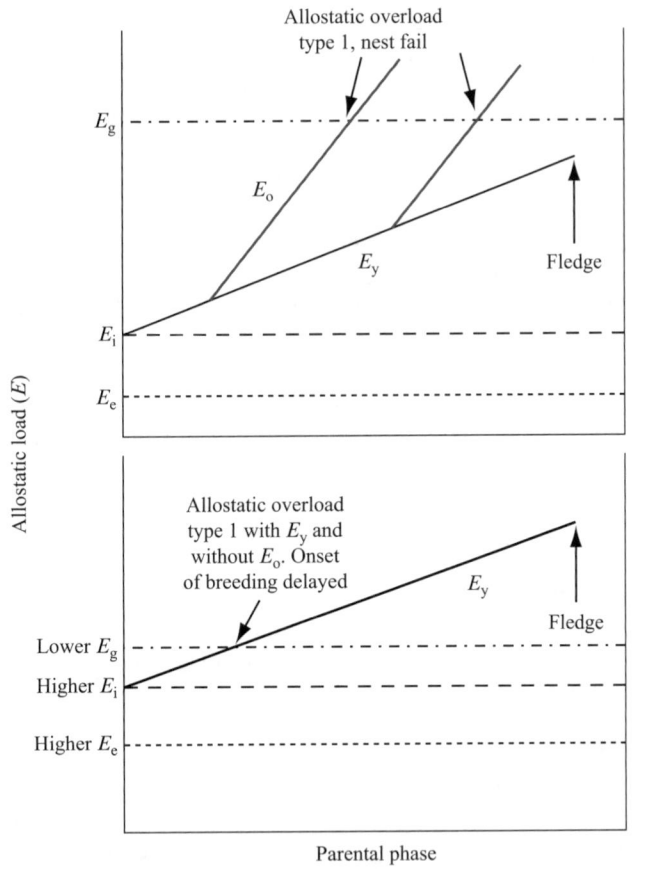

FIG. 7. E_y, the extra energy and nutrients required to incubate eggs, then raise young to fledging and independence increases steadily as the season progresses. Fledging occurs while E_g is still sufficient to fuel increasing allostatic load (top panel). A further perturbation, E_o, will increase allostatic load even faster (red lines), and when it exceeds E_g, (allostatic overload type I) the nest and young will be abandoned. However, a perturbation would take longer to reach allostatic overload early in the parental phase (left hand E_o) than an identical perturbation later (right hand E_o). Timing of the parental phase is thus critical to ensure E_g is sufficient to permit growth and fledging of offspring. Storms during the parental phase can be particularly disruptive to breeding because E_o increases may exceed E_g quickly. Conditions early in the breeding season are usually more severe than later in spring and summer (such as lower E_g in early spring and higher $E_e + E_i$ as a result of lower temperature and more energy needed to forage). Then E_y, the extra energy and nutrients required to raise young to fledging, will increase allostatic load immediately even without further E_o (lower panel). In this scenario, delayed onset of breeding (until E_g increases and $E_e + E_i$ decrease) will occur but not necessarily because of allostatic overload type 1, but because local conditions are not conducive to onset of breeding. However, if breeding does commence, then these individuals would be more susceptible to storms early in the season. Thus corticosteroids may or may not be involved at this time. (For interpretation of the references to color in this figure legend, the reader is referred to the Web version of this chapter.)

breeding (until E_g increases and $E_e + E_i$ decrease) will occur but not necessarily because of allostatic overload type 1, but because local conditions are not conducive to onset of breeding. Here, we can predict that glucocorticoids may not be involved in delay of nesting onset as other neuroendocrine mechanisms could be operating. If breeding does commence then these individuals would be more susceptible to storms early in the season. Thus, here the prediction would be that glucocorticosteroids are involved at this time. The following field examples of storms and reproduction provide some support for these hypotheses.

Observations of free-living song sparrows, *Melospiza melodia*, responding to severe storms before and after onset of breeding are particularly informative concerning the scenarios suggested in Fig. 7. A late snow storm (200–300 mm) on April 6, 1982 in the Dutchess Country region of New York was accompanied by subfreezing temperatures for 6 days. In contrast, there was no snow cover and temperatures remained above freezing the same time in 1981 (Fig. 8). During this period, gonadal recrudescence just prior to onset of nesting is occurring in eastern song sparrows, *M. m. melodia* (Fig. 8). In 1982, the snow storm was accompanied by significantly lower plasma levels of LH and testosterone in males and females versus the same time the previous year (no storm, Wingfield, 1985a,b; Fig. 9). Further, in females, ovarian follicle diameter was smaller during the storm in 1982 (Fig. 9) consistent with the prediction that gonadal development should be delayed in severe weather. There were no differences in circulating corticosterone levels between years and inconsistent effects of the storm on subcutaneous fat score and body weight (Fig. 10, Wingfield, 1985a,b). This again is consistent with the predictions of Fig. 7 that a storm early in the breeding season may be a response to phenological conditions regulating gonadal recrudescence and onset of nesting and not necessarily increased allostatic load *per se*. Indeed, experimentally induced low temperatures can decrease the rate of gonadal development and high temperatures can increase recrudescence (e.g., Perfito et al., 2006; Silverin et al., 2008; Wingfield et al., 1997, 2003). Plasma concentrations of corticosterone are not affected as long as food availability remains sufficient.

Inclement weather late in the season during the parental phase, however, may, be more disruptive as shown for white-crowned sparrows (Wingfield et al., 1983; Fig. 5). In the same population of song sparrows in Dutchess County, New York, prolonged rain storms over a period of 10 days in May and June 1982 resulted in severe flooding although temperatures were not different between years (Wingfield, 1985a,b; Fig. 11). These storms resulted in song sparrows abandoning nests with eggs and young and moving to higher ground while the floods persisted. Later in June, the storms abated, floods receded, and song sparrows returned to the same territories, often

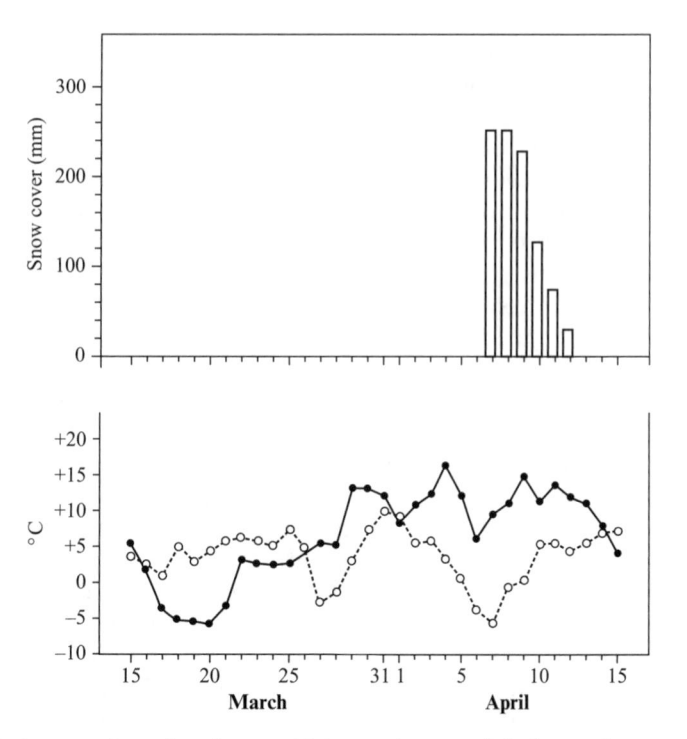

FIG. 8. A comparison of environmental temperature, precipitation, and snow cover for March and April, 1981 (solid squares and circles) and 1982 (open squares and circles) in Dutchess County, New York. From Wingfield (1985a). Courtesy of Wiley-Blackwell Press and the Zoological Society of London.

with the same mate and renested (Wingfield, 1985a,b). As seen in white-crowned sparrows (Fig. 6), there were no differences in plasma levels of reproductive hormones in either males or females (Fig. 12). However, males did have higher blood concentrations of corticosterone during the storm than during the same time in 1981 (Fig. 13) consistent with the predictions from Fig. 7 that storms may be more disruptive to breeding during the parental phase when E_y is increasing rapidly resulting in greater sensitivity to storms and rising E_o on top of E_y. Note, however, that females showed no increase in plasma corticosterone concentrations during the storm period of 1982. The reasons for such a gender difference remain known.

Sex differences in baseline plasma levels of glucocorticoids, as well as stressed levels (measured after 30–60 min of capture, handling, and re-straint stress), are widespread and may represent sex differences in parental investment (e.g., Bókony et al., 2009; Wingfield et al., 1995a,b) as well as population differences in energetic demand of the life cycle (Hau et al.,

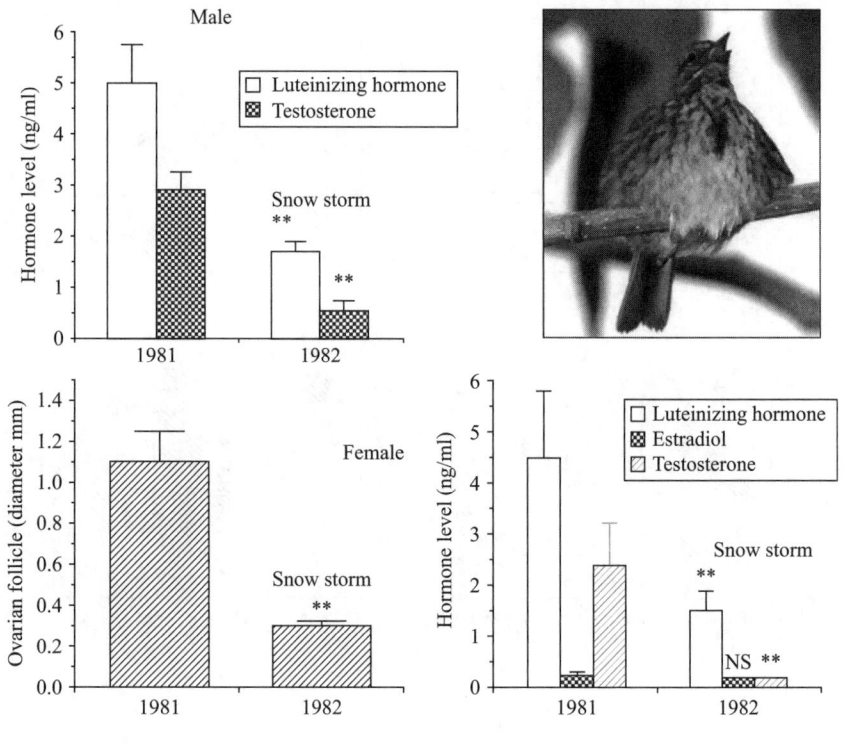

Fig. 9. Effects of a spring snow storm in 1982 on gonadal development and plasma levels of luteinizing hormone (LH), testosterone, and estradiol in male and female song sparrows, *Melospiza melodia*. Comparisons are made with the same time in 1981 when weather was much warmer with no snow cover. In males, both LH and testosterone levels were significantly lower during the snow storm in 1982 compared to males in 1981. Similarly in females, plasma levels of LH and testosterone, but not estradiol, were also lower during the snow storm in 1982 compared with 1981. Further, the diameter of ovarian follicles was significantly less in 1982. From Wingfield (1985a,b). Photo by J. C. Wingfield. Courtesy of Wiley-Blackwell Press and the Zoological Society of London.

2010) but are beyond the scope of this review. A summary of baseline and stress plasma levels of corticosterone in arctic birds (sampled at Barrow, Alaska, on the Arctic Ocean coast, Table I) during the parental phase of breeding and in relation to inclement weather revealed no sex differences (unlike early in the season) and no correlations with weather (temperature, precipitation, Romero et al., 2000). This may be an adaptation of birds breeding in severe environments that may be resistant to bad weather as the nesting season is so short that delay in onset of nesting is not an option. Consistent with

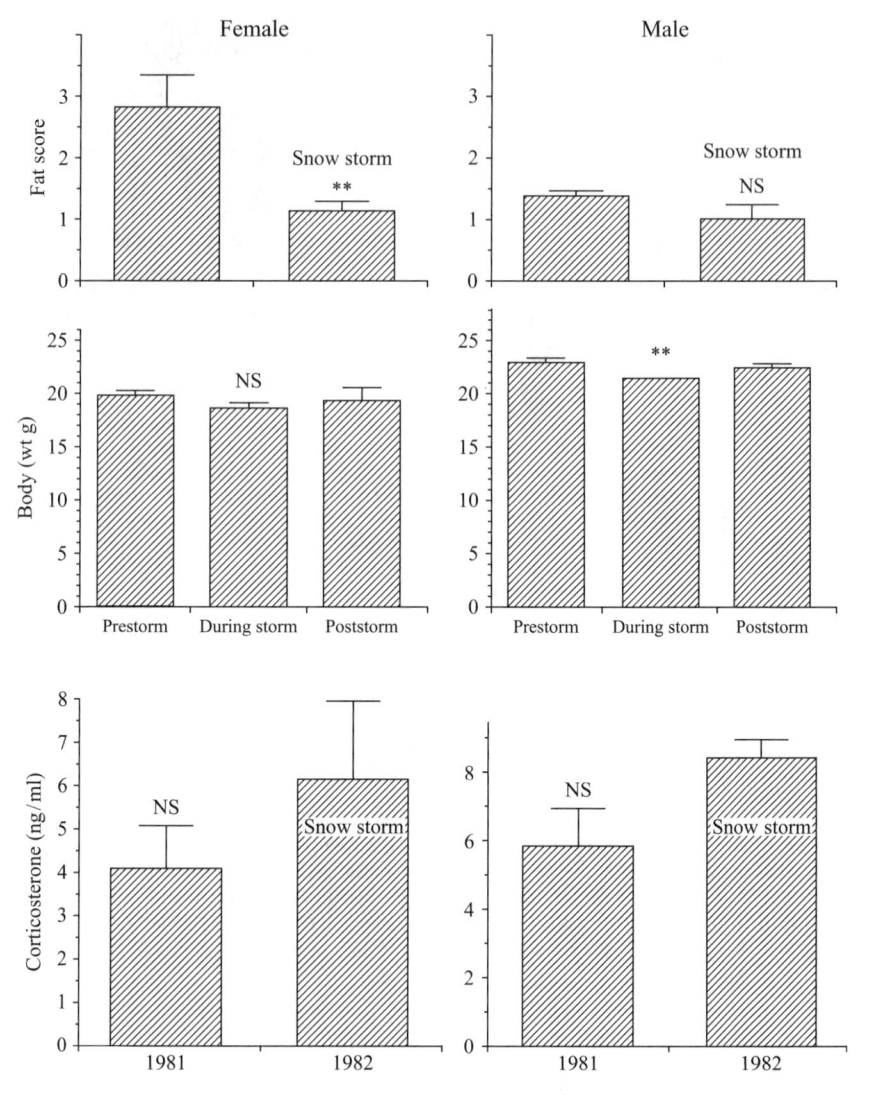

FIG. 10. Effects of a spring snow storm in 1982 on subcutaneous fat score (top panel), body weight (middle panel), and plasma levels of corticosterone in female and male song sparrows (*Melospiza melodia*) in Dutchess County, New York. Comparisons are made with the same time (early April) in 1981 when the weather was warmer with no snow cover. Fat score was lower during the snow storm in females but not males compared with the same time in 1981. Although females showed no changes in body weight before during and after the storm in 1982, males had significantly lower weight during the storm. Comparing baseline plasma levels of corticosterone during the snow storm in 1982 versus fine weather at the same time in 1981 revealed no significant differences. From Wingfield (1985a,b). Courtesy of Wiley-Blackwell Press and the Zoological Society of London.

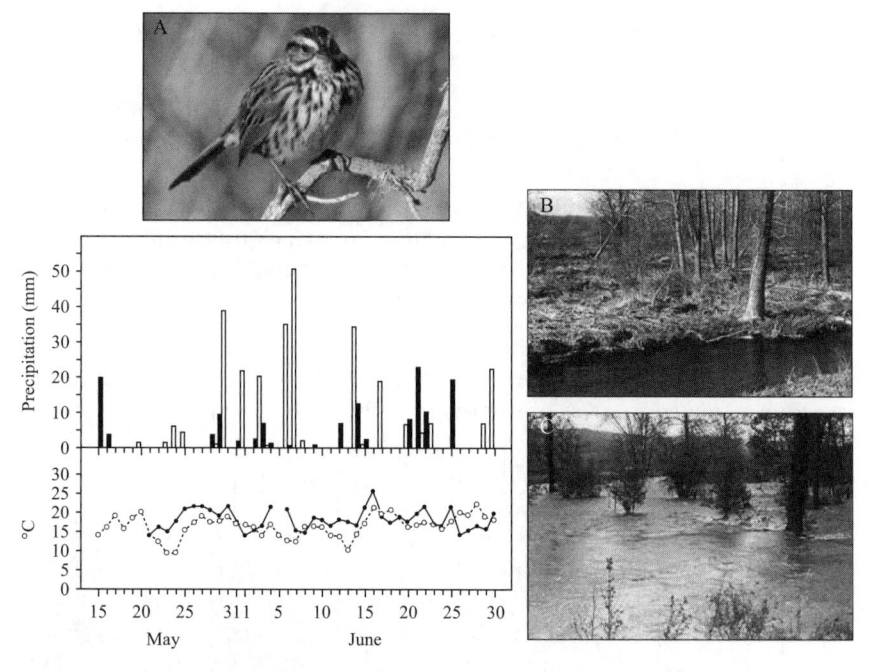

FIG. 11. Comparisons of environmental temperature and precipitation for May and June, 1981 (black squares and circles) and 1982 (open squares and circles) in Dutchess County, New York. Panel a: the song sparrow, *Melospiza melodia*. Panel b: Ham Creek, Dutchess County, in late April 1982. Song sparrows were beginning to nest or were incubating at this site. Panel c: late May 1982, the same site on Ham Creek after several days of continual rain. Birds abandoned nests and territories and moved to higher ground (in the distance of panel c) until flood waters receded later in June. From Wingfield (1985a). All photos by J. C. Wingfield. Courtesy of Wiley-Blackwell Press and the Zoological Society of London.

this suggestion are the more significant effects of inclement weather on both baseline and stressed plasma concentrations of corticosterone in arctic birds during the postbreeding molt (Table I, Romero et al., 2000).

There is no question that inclement weather can have delaying (i.e., onset of breeding) and disruptive effects on reproductive function. Potential mechanisms are emerging and are probably complex. The allostatic load model may help us to make predictions on whether glucocorticoids are involved (Fig. 7), but much more research is needed on free-living populations. Other examples come from song sparrows in western Washington State where populations breed in low, coastal, habitats as well as at higher elevations in the Cascade Mountains. Cool spring weather (e.g., in May) may be more severe resulting in elevated corticosterone at higher versus

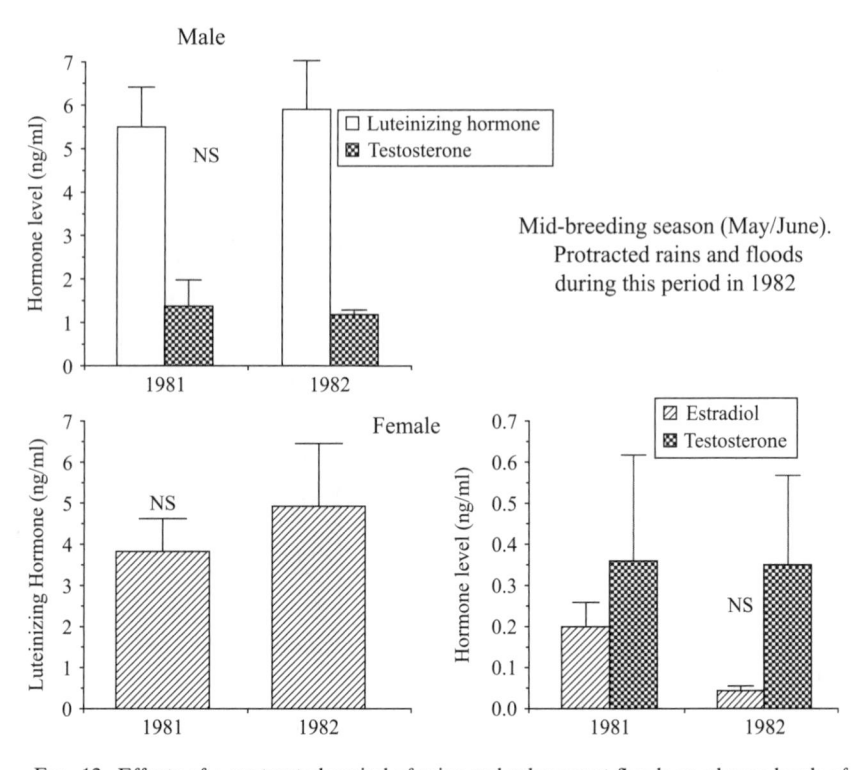

Fig. 12. Effects of a protracted period of rains and subsequent floods on plasma levels of luteinizing hormone (LH), testosterone, and estradiol in male and female song sparrows (*Melospiza melodia*) in Dutchess County, New York, in 1982. Comparisons are made with song sparrows sampled at the same time of year and location, and similar reproductive status in 1981 (when there were no protracted periods of rain or floods). In contrast to the effects of a snow storm earlier in the breeding season, there were no significant differences in any reproductive hormone plasma levels between years. From Wingfield (1985a,b). Courtesy of Wiley-Blackwell Press and the Zoological Society of London.

lower elevation sites (Fig. 14). As is typical of socially monogamous songbirds, baseline plasma levels of corticosterone, and stress-induced levels, decrease during the parental phase of dusky flycatchers, *Empidonax oberholseri*, breeding at an alpine site in the Sierra Nevada of California (Pereyra and Wingfield, 2003). Further, individuals with less fat and weighing less had higher baseline and stress-induced corticosterone levels. During incubation, baseline levels of corticosterone increased dramatically in relation to longer periods of precipitation prior to sample. Those birds experiencing 4–5 days of precipitation had higher corticosterone levels than those experiencing less precipitation.

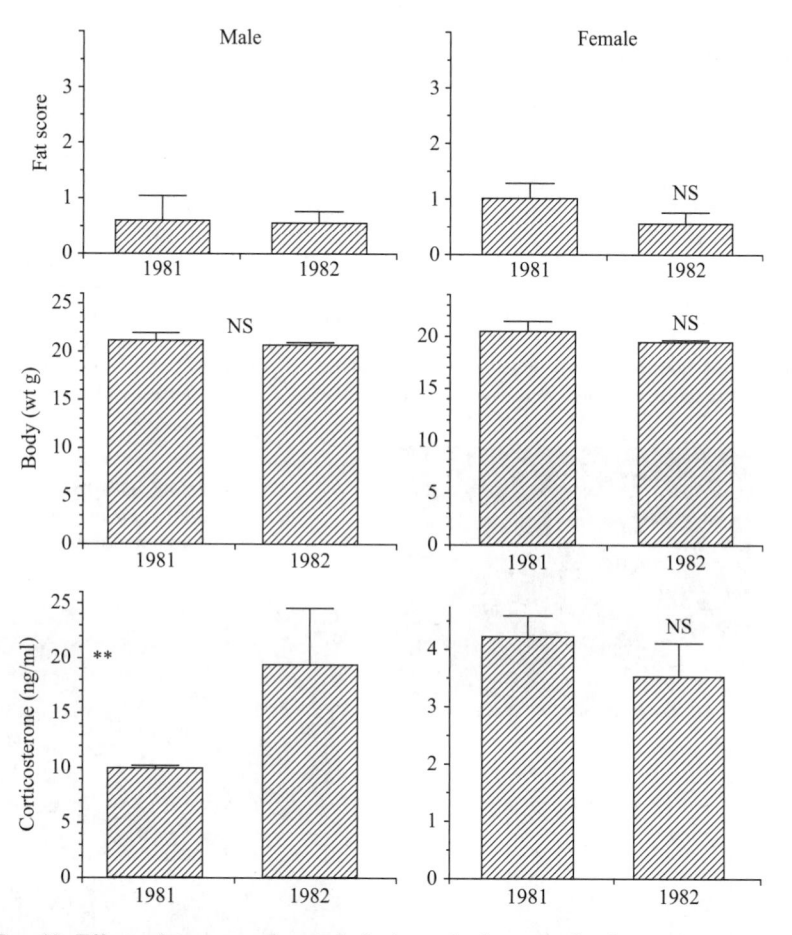

Fig. 13. Effects of a protracted period of rains and subsequent floods on subcutaneous fat score (tope panel), body weight (middle panel), and plasma levels of corticosterone in male and female song sparrows (*Melospiza melodia*) in Dutchess County, New York, in 1982. Comparisons are made with song sparrows sampled at the same time of year and location, and similar reproductive status in 1981 (when there were no protracted periods of rain or floods). There were no significant differences in fat score and body mass between years in either males or females. However, plasma levels of corticosterone were significantly higher in males during the rains and floods of 1982. Females showed no differences in circulating corticosterone. From Wingfield (1985a,b). Courtesy of Wiley-Blackwell Press and the Zoological Society of London.

In contrast, harlequin ducks, *Histrionicus histrionicus*, breeding along rivers in the Olympic Mountains of western Washington State, USA, generally show an increase in baseline and stress-induced plasma corticosterone as the breeding season progresses. However, high river flow following

TABLE I
CORTICOSTERONE LEVELS IN RELATION TO WEATHER AT BARROW

	Breeding		Molt	
	Baseline	Stress	Baseline	Stress
Lapland Longspur	No	Yes 37–39%	Yes 47–53%	Yes 41–73%
Snow Bunting	No	No	Yes 19%	Yes 25–30%
Common Redpoll Adult	No	No	Yes 35–59%	Yes 36–60%
Juvenile			Yes 44–88%	Yes 48–58%

Correlations of baseline (i.e., blood levels sampled within 3 min of capture) and stress levels (after 30–60 min of capture, handling, and restraint stress) with weather in arctic-breeding birds: snow buntings, *Plectrophenax nivalis*, Lapland longspurs, *Calcarius lapponicus*, and common redpolls, *Carduelis flammea*. From Romero et al. (2000). Courtesy of Elsevier Press.

Male song sparrow
Melospiza melodia morphna
early season (May)

FIG. 14. Effects of cool spring weather and elevation on plasma levels of corticosterone in male song sparrows, *Melospiza melodia morphna*, (panel a) during the early breeding season in western Washington State in 1987 and 1982. Panel b shows typical low elevation habitat (0–10 m) close to water in the Puget Sound region. Panel c shows higher elevation habitat (500–1000 m) near the Pack Forest Experimental Station near Mt. Ranier. Cold spring temperatures in 1988 were accompanied by higher corticosterone levels versus 1987 at the higher elevation sites. Corticosterone levels were lower at the same time at the low elevation sites on Whidbey Island in Puget Sound. J. C. Wingfield, unpublished. All photos by J. C. Wingfield.

extended periods of precipitation had no effect, but both baseline and stress-induced corticosterone levels were negatively correlated with body condition in females (Perfito et al., 2002).

It is hoped that the investigations summarized above will encourage field investigators to take advantage of weather events to record behavioral responses of birds (and other animals) as well as collect samples for endocrine measurements. In a changing world, such information is vital.

B. HEAT, DROUGHT, AND DESERT BIRDS

Many organisms frequenting lower latitudes are exposed to periods of extreme heat often accompanied by drought. These conditions can be disruptive to the life cycle, particularly breeding seasons. We usually associate exposure to heat and drought with deserts, but such conditions can also be occasionally located in other regions where an individual finds itself exposed to direct sunlight, for example, open nesting birds, or to unusually hot, dry weather. However, some species are adapted to xeric conditions and adjust their life cycles according to short, often unpredictable, rainy seasons (e.g., Miller, 1963; Perfito et al., 2006, 2007; Tieleman et al., 2002; Tielemann, 2002; Williams and Tieleman, 2001). Birds adjust to predictable changing climatic conditions of desert environments by an integration of behavior and physiology. Small birds may completely cease all foraging during the hottest part of the day and seek refugia where exposure to extreme heat is lowest (Wolf, 2000). Use of microhabitats can greatly ameliorate potentially disruptive effects of weather. Verdins, *Auriparus flaviceps*, may reduce metabolic rate up to 50% by frequenting a microhabitat protected from wind and exposed to solar radiation. However, avoiding solar radiation and wind may decrease evaporative water loss fourfold (Wolf and Walsberg, 1996). Clearly, microhabitat selection is important for balancing water and energy budgets. Verdins and black tailed gnatcatchers, *Polioptila melanura*, in the Sonoran Desert repeatedly used thermal refugia during the hottest part of the day. In the sun and shade, temperatures exceeded 43 °C, but in knot holes and clefts in the bark of trees such as Palo Verde, temperature was cooler (Wolf et al., 1996). Birds repeatedly frequented these clefts.

Other behavioral responses enhancing heat-dissipating mechanisms include seeking a refuge with shelter. If no shelter for extreme heat is available, then behavioral traits such as fluffed back and crown feathers allow circulation of air (rather than trap air in cold environments), panting, exposing the edges of wings, legs, periodic wetting of plumage and other areas of the body, and even defecating on legs in some vultures, all contribute to dissipation of heat (see Calder and King, 1974; Drent, 1972; Gill, 1995; Welty and Baptista, 1988).

Enclosed nests of cactus wrens, *Campylorhynchus brunneicapillus*, of the Sonoran Desert have insulation for retaining heat during cold weather but also may shield the occupant from direct sun in hot weather. Further, orientation of the nest opening is frequently away from prevailing winds at cooler times of the year and in line with prevailing winds in hotter weather (Ricklefs and Reed-Hainsworth, 1969). As ambient temperatures in the Sonoran Desert increase, cactus wrens seek relatively cooler habitats. Above a threshold temperature, additional behavioral changes such as decreased activity may facilitate temperature regulation in extreme heat (Ricklefs and Hainsworth, 1968).

The mechanisms by which components of the life cycle such as reproduction are regulated by hormones in arid and semiarid regions remain unclear. Again, we should be careful to separate mechanisms involved in the predictable life cycles where individuals are able to anticipate onset of the hot dry season and adjust accordingly, versus unpredicted hot and dry weather, or habitat modification after a hurricane or human exploitation where individuals suddenly find themselves exposed to heat. In relation to the predictable life cycle, two, not necessarily mutually exclusive, hypotheses to explain environmental control of reproductive function in relation to rainy seasons and drought can be proposed based on the allostatic load models of Fig. 7. First, rain and associated cues such as food and green grass may act as local predictive information to regulate gonadal maturation and onset of nesting (Perfito et al., 2008; Vleck and Priedkalns, 1985). Wet conditions stimulate breeding, and dry conditions inhibit breeding via unknown pathways (Perfito et al., 2008; Vleck and Priedkalns, 1985). From Fig. 7, E_y increases as the eggs are incubated and young raised. Second, it is possible that occasional droughts and periods of extreme heat could act as direct LPFs leading to disruption of life cycles, particularly breeding, through elevation of E_o in addition to E_y (Fig. 7). Such disruptions are likely to be mediated by completely different pathways involving increased allostatic load and potential activation of the emergency life-history stage.

In a songbird breeding during the monsoons of the Sonoran Desert of southeastern Arizona, the rufous-winged sparrow, *Aimophila carpalis*, song control regions in the telencephalon of the brain were larger in volume and singing behavior increased markedly after the monsoon rains began (Strand et al., 2007). This is coincident with onset of nesting. The monsoons usually begin in July and thus the effects on song control nuclei occur while photoperiod is decreasing. Birds respond to day length, but rainfall cues are also important (Deviche et al., 2006; Small et al., 2007).

Cain and Lien (1985) proposed a mechanism by which the dry season or drought may inhibit reproductive function in birds. They found that water restriction of bobwhite quail, *Colinus virginianus*, resulted in elevated levels of corticosterone. Treatment of quail with doses of corticosterone that mimicked circulating levels generated by the stress of water restriction resulted in decreased weights of testes, ovaries, and oviducts accompanied by reductions of sperm and egg production (Cain and Lien, 1985). These authors claim that inhibition of reproduction by drought may be mediated through stress-induced increases of circulating corticosterone that then suppress reproductive function. Despite this attractive hypothesis, there are few data from free-living organisms to support the idea. Sapolsky (1987) reported that plasma levels of testosterone were reduced in adult male olive baboons, *Papio anubis*, during a severe drought in East Africa in 1984. Investigations of the reproductive biology and circulating levels of hormones in free-living populations of the white-browed sparrow weaver, *Plocepasser mahali*, in the Luangwa valley of Zambia (Wingfield et al., 1991) spanned a prolonged dry season in which nesting was delayed compared with a year when the dry season ended earlier. Blood samples were collected from August 1986 through April 1988 spanning two complete breeding seasons. The dry season (May to October) of 1987 was longer (by almost 2 months) than the previous year, and the period September to December 1987 was also approximately 5 °C hotter than the same period in 1986. Correlated with this longer than usual dry season was an almost complete failure to initiate breeding during the period August to December 1987 (Table II). Breeding only began in earnest once the major rainy period began in January and February. These data agree with many other reports

TABLE II

REPRODUCTIVE SUCCESS OF WHITE-BROWED SPARROW WEAVERS, *Plocepasser mahali*, AT NYAMALUMA CAMP, ZAMBIA

	1986/1987	1987/1988
Total number of birds	153	125
Number of groups	30	30
Group size (and range)	5.1 (2–9)	4.2 (2–9)
Number of clutch initiations	45	41
Number of clutch initiations (August to December)	12	3
Number of clutch initiations (January to April)	31	38
Clutch attempts per group	1.47 ± 0.24	1.36 ± 0.17
Number of successful clutches	18 (40%)	11 (26.8%)
Percent of groups that did not lay	20	17
Number of young	21	15
Number of young per group	0.7 ± 0.16	0.15 ± 0.13
Percent of groups producing no young	57	63

From Wingfield et al. (1991) and J. C. Wingfield, R. E. Hegner and D. Lewis, unpublished.

showing an inhibitory effect of drought on breeding in birds and other vertebrates (e.g., Brown and Britton, 1980; Dittami, 1986, 1987; Lack, 1950; Marshall, 1963; Sapolsky, 1987). However, the hormonal correlates and mechanisms underlying adjustments of breeding in relation to drought are enigmatic.

White-browed sparrow weavers in the Luangwa Valley are highly social and breed cooperatively in groups of 2–11 birds (Lewis, 1982). Typically, there were two periods of breeding (clutch initiations). The first occurred in September to November followed by a breeding hiatus in December and January. A second surge of breeding occurred in February to April (Lewis, 1982; Fig. 15). Although the total number of clutch initiations in each

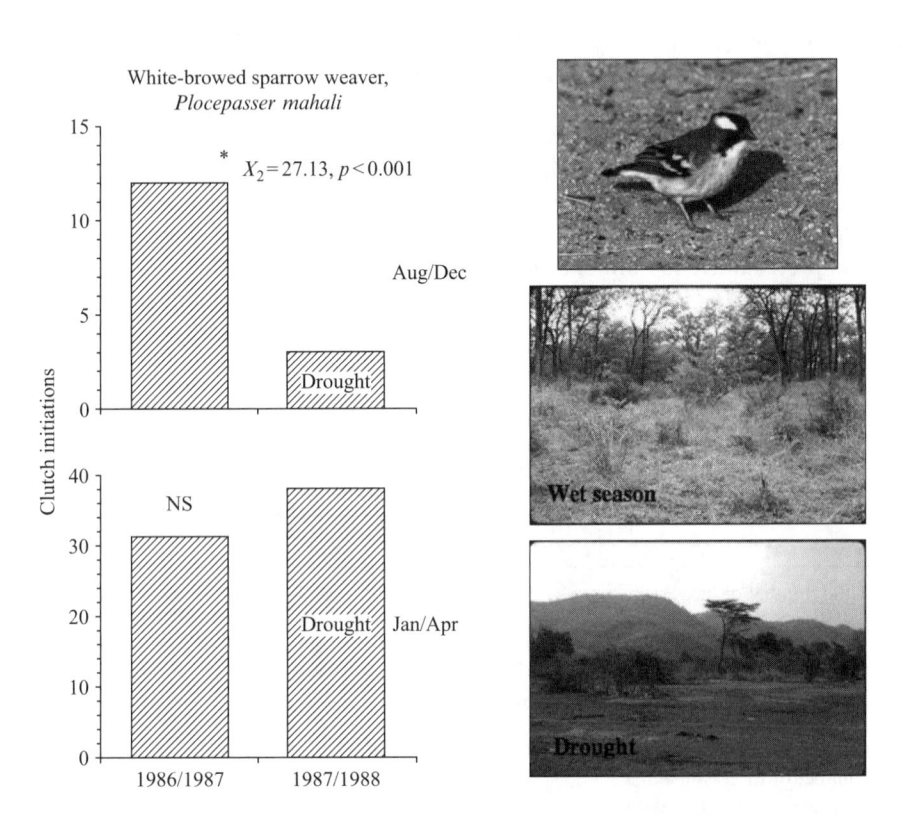

FIG. 15. Timing of clutch initiations in white-browed sparrow weavers, *Plocepasser mahali*, in the Luangwa Valley of Zambia was delayed during the drought of 1986/1987 compared with the wetter season in 1987/1988 (left hand panels). The right hand panels show a white-browed sparrow weaver and vegetation in the Mopane forest of the Luangwa Valley during the wet and dry seasons. From J. C. Wingfield, Dale. M. Lewis and Robert E. Hegner, unpublished.

breeding season was the same, there were roughly four times as many clutches initiated during the first part of the season in 1986 than after the drought in 1987 (Fig. 15, Table II). This was compensated for when the rains came in February 1988. However, the number of successful clutches (i.e., those resulting in fledged young), the total number of young produced, and the number of young per group were all greatly reduced in 1987/1988 after the drought (Table II). Whether this was due to reduced ability of the adults to raise young, or whether the rains, once they arrived in 1988, did not allow sufficient recovery of trophic resources from the drought period is unclear.

Plasma levels of estradiol were mostly below the sensitivity of the assay system (< 0.03 ng/ml, data not presented), and plasma levels of progesterone did not change significantly throughout the period (data not presented, see also Wingfield et al., 1991). In males, plasma levels of LH increased during each breeding period and were low in the middle of the dry season (June to September, Wingfield et al., 1991). There were no differences in LH level in drought and normal years (Fig. 16). In contrast, plasma testosterone increased during January and February in 1987, but not during the breeding season after the drought (Fig. 16). In females, LH did not show the same pattern as in males but were generally high during breeding and lowest in July (middle of the nonbreeding—dry—season; Wingfield et al., 1991). Testosterone levels were high during the breeding season of 1986/1987 and lower after the drought in 1987/1988 (Fig. 16), although these levels were lower than in males.

In males, body mass was lowest toward the end of the dry season and highest during breeding in both years (Wingfield et al., 1991). There were no differences in body mass between normal and drought years. Fat score varied more erratically, but again no differences were observed between drought and normal years (Wingfield et al., 1991, Fig. 16). Plasma levels of corticosterone tended to be lowest in August and slightly elevated during breeding (Wingfield et al., 1991). In females, body mass again tended to be lowest toward the end of the dry season, but there was no effect of drought (Wingfield et al., 1991, Fig. 16). Fat score was lowest in July and increased during breeding at the same levels in both years (Wingfield et al., 1991). There were no effects of drought on plasma levels of corticosterone in either sex (Fig. 16).

It is important to bear in mind that the white-browed sparrow weavers in the Luangwa Valley had access to water throughout the drought period. The Luangwa River was within a kilometer of all study groups, and there were several leaking faucets around the camp that were used regularly for drinking and bathing by our study population. Thus, delay of breeding must be due to other factors associated with resources for breeding. Further experimental work could now resolve this issue especially in relation to

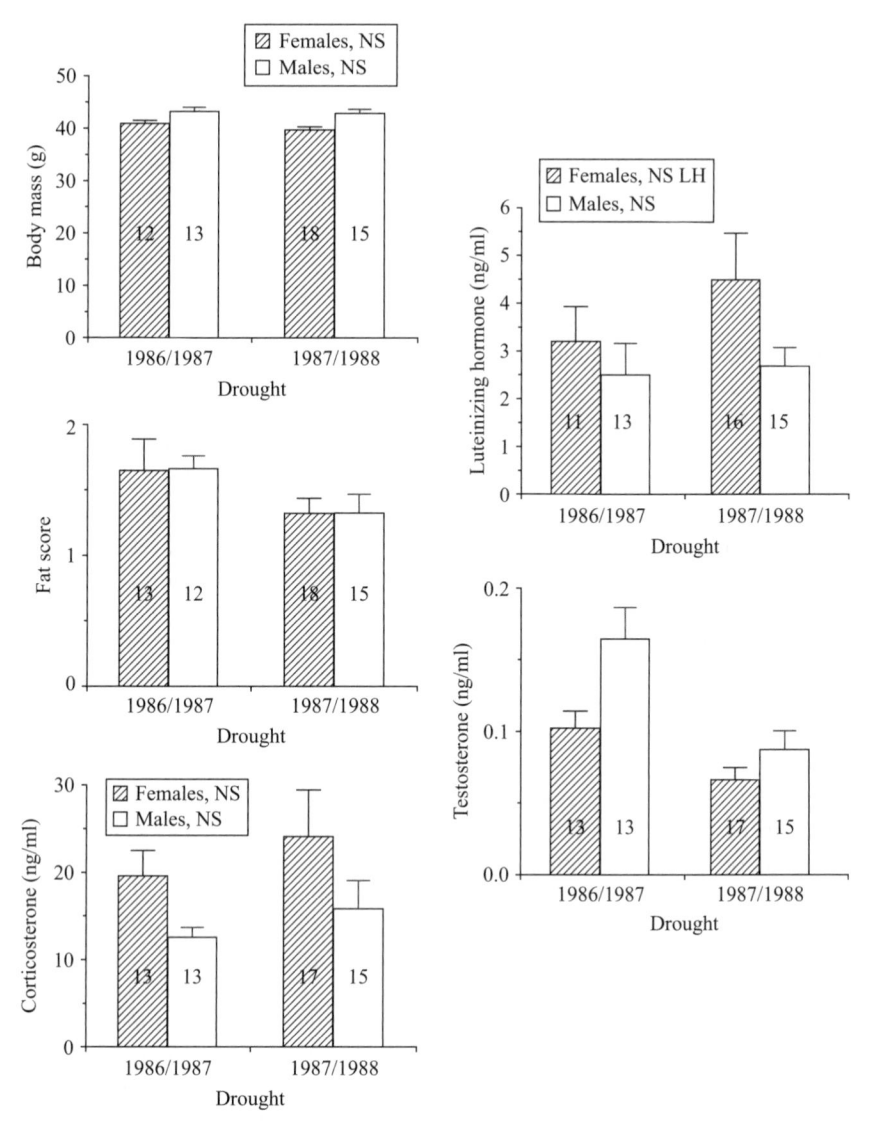

FIG. 16. Right hand panels: plasma levels of luteinizing hormone and testosterone in male and female white-browed sparrow weavers, *Plocepasser mahali*, in a drought year (1987/1988) and a wet year (1986/1987). Left hand panels: body weight, fat score, and plasma levels of corticosterone, luteinizing hormone and testosterone in male and female white-browed sparrow weavers, *Plocepasser mahali*, in a drought year (1987/1988) and a wet year (1987/1988). From J. C. Wingfield, Dale. M. Lewis and Robert E. Hegner, unpublished.

allostatic load and the contributions of E_y and E_o. It is likely that many species adapted for life in arid and semiarid habitats are not stressed by dry conditions *per se*, that is, allostatic load may not be higher because of their behavioral and physiological adaptations (e.g., Miller, 1963, see also Tielemann, 2002; Tieleman et al., 2002). Thus droughts (unless they are extremely severe) are unlikely to stress these species. We feel that Cain and Lien's (1985) mechanism for drought inhibition of breeding due to stress may be restricted to exceptionally severe and prolonged droughts, or to those species that are not adapted to semiarid environments in which E_o increases rapidly contributing to allostatic load and potential overload (Fig. 7). Thus for most arid land species, it is likely that rainfall and associated cues accelerate gonadal maturation and/or stimulate breeding behavior, and that any inhibitory component probably does not involve the classical stress-induced suppression of the hypothalamo-pituitary-gonad axis.

It is also important to balance social factors with environmental changes such as rainfall when determining the effects on behavioral and hormonal responses to acute stress. In the cooperative (plural) breeding superb starling, *Lamprotornis superbus*, baseline (i.e., with 1–3 min of capture) and maximal stress-induced corticosterone levels varied in relation to pre-breeding rainfall, but in different ways depending upon status (Rubenstein, 2007). Birds that became helpers had higher circulating corticosterone (baseline and stress-induced maxima) in drier years, whereas birds that did not breed or became breeders showed no such relationships. These results suggest that environmental conditions may influence social interactions and eventual reproductive status (Rubenstein, 2007).

The zebra finch, *Taenopygia guttata*, is a classical opportunistic migrant and breeder in arid regions of the Australian continent (e.g., Zann et al., 1995). Perfito et al. (2006) water restricted zebra finches for 11 weeks; these individuals showed a decrease in LH levels compared with controls given free access to water. Testis volume also tended to decrease although this was not consistent. Exposure of these birds to *ad libitum* water resulted in elevation of LH levels. There were no differences in immunoreactive-gonadotropin-releasing hormone-I (ir-GnRH-1, a brain peptide that stimulates reproductive function through the hypothalamo-pituitary-gonad axis) or ir-GnRH-II in the hypothalamus suggesting that as predicted, the GnRH system remains in a near state of readiness to breed in these opportunistic species. Conditions conducive to breeding then can rapidly release GnRH and LH rather than having to wait for a period of full reproductive development. Perfito et al. (2007) compared two free-living populations of zebra finches in Australia, one in the unpredictable rainfall area of central Australia and another in a more predictable, seasonal habitat in southern

Australia. Reproductive state tended to be closer to onset of nesting in the opportunistic population whereas in the more seasonal habitat, variation in reproductive development was greater. There was no evidence that elevated glucocorticoids were associated with inhibition of breeding, rather cues associated with conditions conducive to breeding stimulated (released an inhibition?) breeding. Birds taken into captive conditions with food and water *ad libitum* were able to activate their reproductive systems rapidly. In a Lesser Sundas population, day length *per se* may not influence reproductive development, instead increased foraging time during a longer day may be important. Taken together, these observations implicate the role of food availability, or alternatively, behavior associated with it (Perfito et al., 2008; Vleck and Priedkalns, 1985).

These data are consistent with effects of water on a semiaquatic population of song sparrows in western Washington State (Wingfield et al., submitted-b). This population of song sparrows tends to live at high density close to water. In an unusually dry spring, males were still territorial but responded less strongly to a simulated territorial intrusion. Captive males and females that had access to open water baths showed greater photoperiodically induced gonadal growth than controls with no access to open water. All had access to drinking water through a glass tube. Body weights and fat scores were not affected by treatment.

Birds of the Sonoran Desert in southwestern United States breed during periods of restricted or no access to water compared with species breeding in suburban and riparian habitats (e.g., Vleck, 1993). Using a standardized acute stressor of capture, handling, and restraint to follow the pattern of increase in circulating corticosterone levels, it was found that desert birds such as black-throated sparrow, *Amphispiza bilineata*, cactus wrens, and curve-billed thrasher, *Toxostoma curvirostra*, all suppressed their adrenocortical responses to stress during the summer breeding season compared to the much cooler winter. Species inhabiting more mesic habitats, such as the Inca dove, *Scardafella inca*, and Abert's towhee, *Piplo aberti*, did not modulate the adrenocortical response to acute stress (Wingfield et al., 1992). Baseline corticosterone levels (i.e., before stress effects are manifest) generally did not differ between seasons. However, in the summer of 1990, there was a period of extreme heat in which temperatures reached 44 °C and greater in Tucson (normally July maximum temperatures are 36–40 °C). In Phoenix, temperatures in July 1990 reached 50 °C. Inca doves and Abert's towhees sampled during the period of extreme heat showed no change in baseline corticosterone level except for a slight elevation in male towhees that was still well below those levels generated by capture stress (Fig. 17). However, in black-throated sparrows sampled in open desert during the period of extreme heat, baseline corticosterone

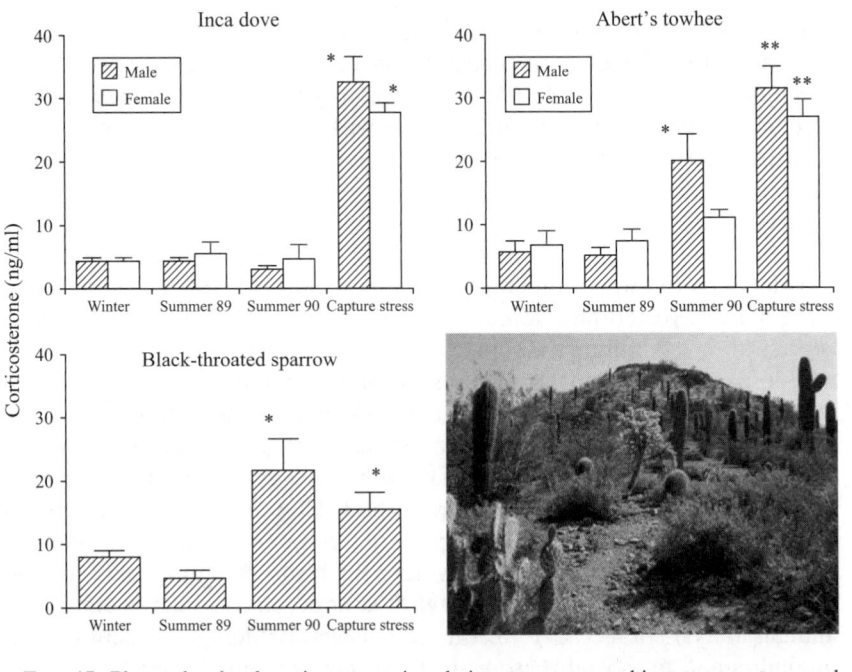

FIG. 17. Plasma levels of corticosterone in relation to season, ambient temperature, and capture stress in the Inca Dove, *Scardafella inca*; Abert's Towhee, *Pipilo aberti*, and black-throated sparrow, *Amphispiza bilineata*. All birds were sampled on breeding grounds in mesic (Inca dove and Abert's towhee) versus xeric (black-throated sparrow) habitat in the Sonoran Zone of southeastern Arizona, USA. The lower right hand panel shows typical Sonoran Desert. There were no differences in baseline corticosterone levels from winter to summer in any species. During a period of extreme heat in summer 1990, birds in mesic habitat of suburbs and riparian habitat showed little change in baseline corticosterone versus levels reached during exposure to capture, handling, and restraint stress (top panels). However, black-throated sparrows breeding in the desert habitat showed marked increase in baseline corticosterone levels during the extreme heat of June 1990. Because these levels were similar to those induced by capture stress, this suggests that the extreme heat may have been stressful. From Wingfield et al., 1992). Photo by J. C. Wingfield. Courtesy of Wiley Press.

levels had increased to levels comparable with those generated by capture stress (Wingfield et al., 1992, Fig. 17). It is possible that birds in suburban and riparian habitats with extensive shade plants and access to water were able to withstand the heat better than black-throated sparrows in open desert.

Dry seasons and heat that follow a predictable cycle probably are not accompanied by elevated corticosterone levels in arid zone birds. Onset of breeding is probably triggered by rainfall or some other environmental factor associated with the rainy season. However, unpredictable episodes of extreme heat, even for a normally arid region, may trigger an emergency life stage with high levels of corticosterone, especially in those species with greatest exposure to direct sun and least opportunity for shade. Future research during periods of extreme heat will shed further light on adaptations of desert birds.

C. COLD

Weather with lower temperatures can be challenging for ectothermic and endothermic vertebrates alike. Small birds are particularly vulnerable; species that do not migrate to escape the cold must use microhabitats and/or physiological mechanisms such as torpor to endure. Reinertsen (1983) reviews the physiological and behavioral adaptations for small birds surviving the night in arctic and subarctic regions. Thermoregulatory responses to cold involve the use of microhabitats such as a cavity in a tree, a well-insulated nest, or cavity beneath snow. However, others seem not to seek shelter although even branches in trees may offer some form of protection. Huddling is commonly seen in birds and mammals in cold regions and at high altitude, although it is important to bear in mind that animals may huddle for a variety of reasons including protection from predators and for social reasons. In both small mammals and birds, there are significant energetic advantages to huddling when ambient temperature drops well below the thermo-neutral zone. These advantages can be even greater if huddling occurs in a shelter (Vickery and Millar, 1984). Small passerines such as the bushtit, *Psaltriparus minimus*, (about 5.5 g) may show slight hypothermia at colder temperatures but also will huddle in tight masses especially during the night. This reduces metabolism by about 20% compared with isolated birds and may be an important energy savings during periods of reduced food availability and/or inclement weather (Chaplin, 1982).

In black-tailed gnatcatchers, *Polioptila melanura*, a small 5 g songbird, roosting may occur communally in the co-opted domed nest of a verdin, *Auriparus flaviceps*, just over 2 m above the ground. The black-tailed gnatcatcher normally does not flock, but 15–16 birds were observed roosting in this nest (Walsberg, 1990). Temperature inside the nest was elevated over ambient levels. Oxygen and CO_2 concentrations in the nest were not affected sufficiently to likely affect respiration in these roosting birds. Further, the author notes that the roost site was not used every night perhaps suggesting the use of alternate roost sites. After the nest was accidentally disturbed, the birds left immediately and never returned suggesting high sensitivity to the possibility of predation (Walsberg, 1990). The sociable weaver, *Philetairus socius*, builds a huge communal nest but with separate cavities occupied by an individual pair and young. In the winter, these enormous nests are used as roost sites with social roosting reducing heat loss and the costs of enduring cold winter nights (White et al., 1975).

Meservey and Kraus (1976) review and summarize earlier literature suggesting that cliff, barn, bank, *Riparia riparia*, and tree swallows, *Tachycineta bicolor*, usually perch several centimeters apart, but during inclement and cold weather they perch closer, frequently in contact to conserve energy. In some cases, different species may be in contact in mixed aggregations. Many avian species, big and small, huddle in flocks to cope with cold stress (e.g., du Plessis and Williams, 1994), thus maintaining body temperature at a reduced energetic cost. By huddling, surface area exposed to severe conditions is reduced and each individual gains by collective heat production (e.g., Chaplin, 1982; du Plessis and Williams, 1994; Smith, 1972). Further, those at the center of the huddle should benefit most, but not always if the huddle becomes sufficiently large to crush individuals.

Huddling of green woodhoopoes, *Phoeniculus purpureus*, during inclement weather can reduce nighttime energy expenditure by about 30% (du Plessis and Williams, 1994). Circadian rhythms of metabolism help reduce costs when roosting at night, but huddling augments this (Boix-Hinzen and Lovegrove, 1998). In gray partridges, *Perdix perdix*, held at − 30 °C, resting metabolic rate was 6–24% lower in birds allowed to huddle versus lone birds (Putaala et al., 1995). Further, metabolic rate was lowest in larger groups. Acorn woodpeckers, *Melanerpes formicivorus*, excavate nesting and roosting cavities in the larger limbs of oak trees, *Quercus* sp. These cavities cool more slowly than the surrounding air, and even when ambient temperature was 0 °C, air in unoccupied cavities was on average 4.3 °C warmer (du Plessis et al., 1994). Although these woodpeckers do not huddle *per se*, the more birds in a cavity, the greater the temperature leading to higher energetic savings overnight. This also accords with the finding that woodpeckers that live in larger groups survive overwinter better than smaller groups (du Plessis et al., 1994).

Brenner (1965) exposed single, paired, and groups of four European starlings, *Sturnus vulgaris*, to temperature ranges of 24–30 and 2–4 °C in captivity. Metabolic rates appeared to be lower in grouped birds when roosting and higher in birds at the lower temperature range. Flocking behavior at roost sites may be essential for this species during inclement weather (Brenner, 1965). Weatherhead et al. (1985) made observations of tree swallows, barn swallows, cliff swallows, and bank swallows during inclement weather (rain, snow and winds, low ambient temperatures) in the spring of 1983 by Lake Manitoba in Canada. They also review other literature on the subject (see also Gessamen and Worthen, 1982). Tree swallows were seen clustering in the evenings close to natural cavities in which they entered communally. Overnight, many individuals died (body weights considerably below normal) and were found dead both in roosts stacked in piles or lying on the ground outside the roost. The gastrointestinal tracts of these birds were also empty suggesting starvation. In one example, they observed tree swallows clustering on perches in a tree touching one another along the branch. In some cases, birds perched on top of those on the twig resulting in an even denser cluster. In another example, barn swallows clustered in an old open cup nest in a garage, head first into the nest, and at least 2 deep. Those on the outside attempted to force their way deeper into the cluster and were vocalizing almost constantly. Other nests were available, but these birds clustered at a single nest. Similar clusters occurred in other buildings with nests, and the next day, many dead swallows were found either in nests or on the ground beneath (Weatherhead et al., 1985). Cliff swallows were found dead beneath overhanging roofs but it was unclear whether they had been clustered the night before because none of their old nests were intact. Sealy (1966) reports finding bank swallows clustered in their nest cavities excavated in earth banks. Many of these birds died in nest clusters during inclement spring weather. Weatherhead et al. (1985) speculate whether a trade-off may exist for clustering in enclosed spaces during inclement weather. Energy saved by clustering may be more than offset in some cases by the problems associated with being buried under other birds, potentially impairing respiration in the process. The swallows studied by Weatherhead et al. (1985) do flock but only form such concentrated clusters during highly inclement weather. Thus optimal position in such clusters would be to be surrounded by other warm bodies but not trapped or crushed under others. Those on the periphery may not conserve enough heat and thus failure to compete may also be a factor emphasizing that position in a huddle is likely influenced by dominance status (e.g., Calf et al., 2002). Bronze manikins, *Lonchura cucullata*, in South Africa huddle in communal nests during cold nights in winter. These flocks tend to have linear dominance hierarchies with dominant birds holding the central location in a huddle (Calf et al., 2002). Social dominance is clearly an important factor and should be included in allostatic load models. However, being dominant does not always result in lower allostatic load and in some cases may even increase it. A meta-analysis of birds and mammals showed that allostatic load of maintaining dominance status was correlated with higher glucocorticoid levels rather than status *per se* (Goymann and Wingfield, 2004).

Cold stress has been shown to decrease "social distance" in several avian species including huddling behavior in communal roosts (see also Grubb, 1973; Smith, 1972). Beal (1978) exposed 10 male house sparrows in captivity to night time temperatures ranging from 0 to 10 °C. These birds clumped closer together at night at lower temperatures providing experimental support for the hypothesis. Smith (1972) found that bushtits tend to clump together along a branch in a roost tree at night compared to warmer nights. This also suggests that huddling lowers heat loss by individuals. White-backed mousebirds, *Colius colius*, live in arid regions of southern Africa and appear to be obligate huddlers. This behavior can result in metabolic rates 40% below predicted values for isolated birds (McKechnie and Lovegrove, 2001).

Songbirds generally have similar lower critical temperatures regardless of whether they winter in the arctic, mid-latitude, or in the tropics (Steen, 1958). Thus they must increase metabolic rate to maintain body temperature most of the time. Some, but by no means all, species may lower body temperature at night or during the worst weather (Steen, 1958). Many fluff out their plumage (ball up) to reduce heat loss and increase insulation (see below). This may allow songbirds wintering in cold regions to survive the night at 50–70% of the daytime metabolism (Steen, 1958). Postural adjustments in small birds are important—fluffing of contour feathers to trap warm air, retraction of extremities, and the placement of the head (with bare eyes and bill as potential sources of heat loss) under a wing or beneath feathers on the back (e.g., Calder and King, 1994; Gill, 1995; Reinertsen, 1983; Welty and Baptista, 1988). An almost spherical roosting shape may be adopted to minimize the surface area to volume ratio (Irving, 1972). In small birds, changes in peripheral circulation may have little effect beneath feathers, although counter current mechanisms in the feet and tarsi may be important (Dawson and Hudson, 1970).

Andreev (1999) points out the diversity in how birds wintering in extreme cold utilize energy sources. Some such as ptarmigan, *Lagopus lagopus*, use widespread browse of willow shrubs (*Salix* sp.) but this tends to be a low energy source (Andreev, 1991a). Others may store food items individually and segregate by sex into different habitats (e.g., Andreev, 1991b). In all cases, wintering birds tend to minimize energy utilization. This includes shortening of foraging time under extremely low ambient temperatures (Andreev, 1999). Using the allostatic load model, this would mean minimizing heat loss, E_e, and decreasing E_i.

Territorial aggression in extreme cold is not prevalent, and social behavior (flocking) may serve to minimize foraging time by reducing risk of predation. Reduced territorial aggression and relaxed dominance–subordinance relations may be highly important when dealing with severe weather and disruption of normal life-history stages (Andreev, 1999). This is another component of the facultative behavioral and physiological responses to LPFs There are many examples of normally territorial birds flocking in response to LPFs, another facultative behavioral response in the ELHS. Sociality may help for huddling to reduce heat loss, reduce the risk of predation, and help individuals locate food sources. However, once a shelter or food source is found, aggression may increase again for access to resources, if limited.

Individual energy reserves during episodes of extreme cold are critical, and energy use should be minimized (Andreev, 1999). In contrast, migrants show no such minimization of energy use if breeding begins under unstable weather conditions of the high arctic and alpine tundras. In such conditions, the young must grow under in the face of unpredictably fluctuating availability of food. Clearly, E_g, food available in the environment, E_e and E_i must be monitored closely (Fig. 7) to keep allostatic load at a minimum. Even when breeding in the Arctic, incubation on arctic permafrost can potentially increase allostatic load versus nests in areas with no permafrost (Andreev, 1999). In some species, the insulating layer at the base of the nest must be fluffed regularly to maximize insulation properties, for example, nest fluffing behavior of Lapland longspurs (J. C. Wingfield and K. Hunt, unpublished observations).

Comparing southern and northern populations of pied flycatchers, *Ficedula hypoleuca*, in Finland, Eeva et al. (2002) showed that northern birds lay smaller clutches and carry more fat reserves than do birds in southern populations, and they have higher fledging success when the weather turns cold and rainy (Eeva et al., 2002). Clutch size reduction is consistent with the stringency hypothesis (Wilson, 1975, see above). Development of homeothermy in nestling passerines of many species also includes huddling behavior to reduce heat loss (Marsh, 1980).

Shorebirds on beaches, estuaries, and mud flats have problems finding food when temperature drops and prey moves deeper into substrate or high winds prevent foraging (Evans, 1976). Shorebirds lay down fat reserves for winter survival, but during periods of inclement weather when food intake is not sufficient for daily energetic needs, they may have to draw upon protein reserves from muscles as well (Davidson and Evans, 1982). The oxygen (energy) consumption of fat as a tissue was one-tenth that of liver and muscle providing "cheap" energy storage but could affect predictions of BMR among individuals of varying fat content (Scott and Evans, 1992). Many redshanks, *Tringa totanus*, and oystercatchers, *Haematopus ostralegus*, died during a period of severe weather in January and February 1979 in Scotland. Analysis of carcasses showed that they had used virtually all their fat and protein reserves from their pectoralis muscles (Davidson and Evans, 1982). During another sudden period of exceptionally low temperatures in January 1982, these birds were able to mobilize fat quickly, but as these stores became depleted, they apparently could not mobilize protein fast enough and died (Davidson and Evans, 1982). Average fat content of yellow buntings, *Emberiza citrinella*, at a roost in England during winter was closely correlated with mean temperature expected that day. Curiously, it was not correlated with actual temperatures experienced suggesting that winter fattening may be photoperiodically controlled (Evans, 1969).

Grouse and other species burrow into snow to escape extreme cold (Formozov, 1946; Korhonen, 1980, 1981; Pruitt, 2005). Temperatures in such burrows may be above $-10\,°C$ compared to -30 to $-45\,°C$ outside the burrow. Many species, including small songbirds, also burrow to find seeds and other food items. Snow burrows for willow grouse in Finland reliably kept temperatures above the lower critical temperature for overnight survival (Hannon et al., 1998; Stokkan, 1992). CO_2 did not accumulate in the burrow, and snow density did not appear to be important (Korhonen, 1980). Willow ptarmigan, white-tailed ptarmigan, *Lagopus leucurus*, and rock ptarmigan, *L. mutus*, make winter roosts in snow by digging a tunnel into a snow bank, sometimes several birds together. In the coldest months, they can remain in snow burrows all night and spend up to 80% of the day if weather remains inclement, that is, snow and wind (Braun et al., 1983; Holder and Montgomerie, 1993). Ptarmigan also develop increased insulation from feathers on the body and feet in winter, and low ambient temperatures have a minimal effect on energy budget (Hannon et al., 1998). Further, large pectoralis muscles of ptarmigan shiver in bursts to produce heat efficiently (Hannon et al., 1998) and they collect and store food in the crop for extra nutrition during the long polar night (Stokkan, 1992).

Small songbirds are able to withstand periods of cold weather and wind chill in winter by metabolic acclimatization including increased thermoregulation through shivering thermogenesis (Dawson et al., 1992). Fatty acid catabolism by muscle is the primary energy source, and associated enzyme activity is also elevated (e.g., beta-hydroxyacyl Co-A dehydrogenase and phosphofructokinase). Thyroid hormones, but not corticosterone, may be involved in increased thermoregulatory capacity in winter in American goldfinches, *Carduelis tristis* (Dawson et al., 1992). Other behavioral correlates of thermoregulation during cold weather include puffing of plumage to enhance insulation and movement to shelters/refuges where wind chill and heat loss are reduced. In red knots, *Calidris canutus*, in captivity, plasma levels of the biologically active thyroid hormone, T3, were highest during the winter months when temperatures lowest. Circulating levels of the other thyroid hormone, T4, considered a precursor of T3, was highest during molt and subsequent weight gain. Further, T4 levels were correlated with molt intensity among individuals.

Thermosensitivity of the hypothalamus in conscious willow ptarmigan has been measured using implanted perfusion thermodes (Mercer and Simon, 1987). This allowed hypothalamic temperature (T_{hy}) to be clamped for periods of 20 min at different levels between 28 and 43 °C, while the ptarmigan were exposed to either cold (-10 °C) or warm ($+25$ °C) ambient conditions. At -10 °C, warming of the hypothalamus inhibited shivering followed by a decrease in body temperature. However, hypothalamic cooling to less than 34 °C also resulted in a drop of body temperature possibly due to inhibition of shivering. However, hypothalamic cooling to between 34 and 36 °C facilitated shivering resulting in an increase in body temperature. At ambient temperatures of $+25$ °C, warming of the hypothalamus increased panting behavior (to lose heat) while hypothalamic cooling to 38 °C inhibited panting. These data suggest that willow ptarmigan, like mammals, possess a type of specific cold thermosensor in the hypothalamic region (Mercer and Simon, 1987).

The high Arctic ptarmigan in Svalbard (77–80°N) store fat at up to 30% of body mass as a further buffer against extreme cold and severe storms in winter that may reduce foraging time. Reduced activity patterns and lower daily energy budgets emphasize the underlying ability of these birds to withstand severe weather (Stokkan, 1992). Hazel grouse usually roost in snow burrows, but when there is no snow, they prefer spruce (*Picea* sp.) trees with the greatest vertical cover to provide insulation and shelter from wind (Swenson and Olssen, 1991).

Songbirds such as redpolls, *Carduelis flammea*, and Siberian tits, *Parus cinctus*, use snow burrows and tree holes in the winter of northern Finland. This behavior is thought to protect against severe cold as well as wind (Novikov, 1972; Sulkava, 1969). Both types of cavities warmed to constant temperature within 30 min of occupancy. Siberian tits preferred tree holes even though the temperature in snow burrows was always warmer. This may be because closed snow burrows accumulated CO_2 or may become damp and birds had to leave within an hour or so. These strategies may be much more widespread in small birds of the northern forests and tundra.

Johnson (1954) reports common redpolls feeding on snow-covered ground to eat seeds. In extreme cold, they retract their feet and cover them with contour feathers. They then use primaries of wings and rectrices of the tail for support and to move about the surface—"drag and roll" to support themselves. Obstructions to air flow often produce a snow-free area to leeward that is important for birds to find food such as seeds and also grit for proper functioning of the gizzard (Pruitt, 2005). Heavy accumulation of snow on trees (*qali*) may force tree foraging species, for example, Pine grosbeaks, *Pinicola enucleator*, chickadees (*Poecile* sp.) and red crossbills, *Loxia curvirostra*, to forage in wind exposed areas where *qali* is blown off (Korhonen, 1980, 1981; Pruitt, 2005). In contrast, some species (particularly chickadees) will shelter under accumulations of *qali* on trees to reduce heat loss. In northern maritime climates, snow cover may be intermittent during the winter (Formozov, 1946; Novikov, 1972, Pruitt, 2005), thus requiring movement among patches of forest where snow accumulation varies. This could be a challenge for small species to survive periods of extreme cold and wind if refuges are not available.

Great bustards, *Otis tarda*, show facultative migration away from severe weather conditions in winter. Deep snow cover was found to be a much stronger trigger of facultative migration than low environmental temperature. Available food apparently does not affect this migration and thus other factors besides covered food supply may also be important (Streich et al., 2006).

In Antarctic regions, king penguin chicks, *Aptenodytes patagonicus*, huddling in winter result in savings of energy that can lengthen the voluntary winter fast up to 84 days compared with only 44 days in summer (Barré, 1984). Studying emperor penguins, *A. forsteri*, during breeding, which occurs in winter in Antarctica, Gilbert et al. (2006) found that periods of huddling by individual birds were short and of variable duration (1–2 h). This was apparently not because of differential access to huddles. Individuals appear to have equal access to huddles and can save energy to successfully incubate eggs and brood young. Core temperatures of breeding male emperor penguins were stable in incubating birds but may drop up to 1 °C in birds that had lost an egg. It appears that energy savings in huddling penguins are mostly through reduced metabolic rate (and activity) and avoidance of exposure to ambient temperatures for long periods (Gilbert et al., 2007).

Not all winter conditions are challenging for wintering birds. Steen (1958) and Hendricks (2009) reviewed literature of birds using snow as a source of water, as well as to hide food, forage (for chilled arthropods etc.), and to bathe. There are few reports of snow bathing, but many species are likely to do this. They tend to bathe as in water, flipping snow over the back and head with feathers raised. This has been observed in five orders from Arctic species to temperate species in the north. Most prefer uncompacted snow although there are some exceptions (Steen, 1958). Snow buntings, *Plectrophenax nivalis*, have been observed rubbing their heads and backs against snow in Barrow, Alaska (J. C. Wingfield, unpublished). This may be a mechanism to erode brown and buff portions of feathers to obtain nuptial plumage (see also Welty and Baptista, 1988). Many seabirds breeding at high latitude may bathe in snow to remove dirt and vomited oil (e.g., in snow petrels, *Pagodroma nivea*, in Antarctica, J. C. Wingfield and F. Angelier, unpublished observations).

Unpredictable foraging conditions due to weather can increase secretions of glucocorticoids. Mountain chickadees, *Poecile gambeli*, cope with limited and unpredictable food supplies over the winter period. For over 90 days, captive birds were maintained on a limited (food restricted) and unpredictable (time for access varied) food source (Pravosudov et al., 2001). Food restricted birds had higher baseline corticosterone than controls on *ad libitum* food. There were no differences in their responses to acute stress (capture). However, females responded more quickly and reached higher levels than males. These data suggest that free-living birds, resident in a winter area with unpredictable food supplies, should have higher baseline corticosterone for long periods (Pravosudov et al., 2001). This could have implications for long-term deleterious effects of high corticosterone consistent with the field data on weather effects in other species.

In another study, long-term (90 days) intermediate elevation of corticosterone with subcutaneous implants into mountain chickadees resulted in greater food consumption, higher food caching activity, and great efficiency of caching than controls (Pravosudov, 2003, 2005). They also showed enhanced spatial memory performance than controls. Corticosterone treatment (using noninvasive ingestion of meal worms injected with corticosterone) increased food retrieval from stored sites but had no effect on caching behavior compared with controls (Saldanha et al., 2000). The number of retrieved seeds eaten and storage sites visited also did not differ from controls suggesting a complicated effect of corticosterone on appetite and/or activity. Pravosudov (2005) concludes that moderate chronic elevation of corticosterone may enhance performance in unpredictable environments and by facilitating foraging, food caching, and cache retrieval.

Another example from a very different ecological context shows that plasma corticosterone levels increased in captive red knots, *C. canutus*, when food was provided on an irregular time schedule versus controls fed at the same time each day. Irregular timing of food availability may result from bad weather conditions on mud flats, and increased corticosterone may facilitate increased foraging and fat accumulation as well as memory of potentially good feeding sites (Reneerkens et al., 2002a,b).

Baseline and maximum levels of corticosterone in mountain chickadees were the same on long and short days (Pravosudov et al., 2002). However, birds on long days reached maximum corticosterone levels more quickly (5–20 min) than on short days, and females responded faster than males (Pravosudov et al., 2002). The data suggest that while photoperiod does affect the adrenocortical response to stress, changes in baseline corticosterone and effects on spatial memory and foraging are regulated by other environmental factors. Subordinate birds surprisingly cached less food, were less efficient in cache retrieval, and had reduced spatial memory ability compared with dominants (Pravosudov et al., 2003). Whether this is because subordinates are potentially chronically stressed, allostatic overload type 2, remains to be determined. Curiously dominant birds had higher maximum corticosterone levels (stress series) than subordinates although the overall pattern of response was the same in both groups. Subordinates did not have higher baseline corticosterone than dominants (Pravosudov et al., 2003), and so the complete picture is uncertain at this point.

Insectivorous species such as American pipits, *Anthus spinoletta*, in alpine areas use arthropod food sources from the alpine vegetation (Hendricks, 2009). There is also an aeolian source of arthropods—the fallout on snow fields (see Edwards, 1987; Edwards and Banko, 1976) that is used to varying degrees. This may be particularly useful during bad weather when arthropods on vegetation are less active and harder to find.

D. HETEROTHERMY

Nocturnal hypothermia is also an important mechanism to reduce energetic costs of long winter nights or cooler temperatures at other times of year. Reinertsen (1983) defines hypothermia as body temperature a few degrees (1–8 °C) below normal (normothermia for a resting bird), whereas torpor involves much greater reduction of body temperature with concomitant reduction in metabolic rate and heart rate with almost no response to external stimuli (see also Geiser, 2010). Hibernation is defined by Reinertsen (1983) as a prolonged state of torpor throughout a long winter of 6 months or more. Torpor frequently is only overnight with the organisms active during the day. Birds express all these traits to varying degrees in response to weather. The ability to decrease metabolic rate and enter a hypothermic state is essential for some mammals and birds to endure severe environmental conditions. It is important to bear in mind that it appears to be a regulated decrease in metabolic rate that then results in lower body temperature not the other way round (Storey, 2001).

Hypothermic responses are widespread in many taxa of birds, mostly nonpasseriformes, ranging from 3 to 6500 g and in those that experience minimum body temperatures varying continuously from 4 to 38 °C. McKechnie and Lovegrove (2002) point out differences of torpor versus rest-phase hypothermia, although the distinction between them is unclear. Entry into hypothermic states is regulated by a combination of ecological and physiological factors in response to temperature and perhaps other weather variables. To more precisely define and thus investigate torpor in mammals and birds, it is important first to determine the normothermic body temperature for each individual and then define torpor as when body temperature drops below that level. Depth and duration of torpor bouts can then be determined accurately (Barclay et al., 2001). It is possible that heterothermy evolved because of variations in body size. For example, small-bodied animals lose heat more readily than large animals, and dietary

issues such as food not being available during cold periods are also important (Geiser, 1998). It is thought that endothermy and torpor apparently
evolved independently in birds and mammals.

The poorwill, *Phalaenoptilus nuttallii*, is able to enter torpor as well as
tolerate high day time temperatures. In winter, periods of torpor may
extend for several days and resemble hibernation as in other vertebrates
(Csada and Brigham, 1992). This is perhaps not true hibernation in the
sense of Wang and Wolowyk (1988). Birds may even enter torpor when
nesting under certain conditions including inclement weather (Kissner and
Brigham, 1993). The lowest body temperature recorded for any bird was in
a torpid poorwill (5 °C). This species can enter torpor on a regular daily
basis after foraging at dusk, not just in relation to weather perturbations.
Torpor appears to be used most frequently on a daily and a facultative basis
in spring when cold and wet conditions are more prevalent (see also Ligon,
1970). Torpor in birds and mammals may be seasonal as in hibernation and
estivation, or non-seasonally facultative nocturnal as in hypothermia and
daily torpor. Depending on the duration and degree of torpor, energy
savings of 10–88% can be achieved (Wang and Wolowyk, 1988).

Torpor bouts in tropical birds may be more widespread than previously
thought. In the freckled nightjar, *Caprimulgus tristigma*, of South Africa, there
was wide variation in the extent and duration of torpor being most pronounced during the winter months when flying insects are less common
(McKechnie et al., 2007). Many nightjars such as whip-poor-wills, *Caprimulgus vociferous*, forage at night especially under moon light. Thus weather
could influence foraging of these birds on dark cloudy nights. Common night-
hawks, *Chordeiles minor*, are less affected because they forage more during
the day. In poorwills, ability to enter torpor may also influence when or if they
forage on cloudy nights for example (Brigham and Barclay, 1992). In owlet-
nightjars, *Aegotheles cristatus*, birds entered torpor during the coldest months
of the year in New South Wales, Australia, with each bout lasting about 4 h
(Brigham et al., 2000). Torpor was most common when ambient temperature
dropped below 3.9 °C and some birds showed multiple bouts of torpor. The
tawny frogmouth, *Podargus strigoides*, a large caprimulgid of Australia,
showed a reduction of body temperature as low as 29 °C during the coldest
months of the year during the night and the first part of the day (Körtner et al.,
2001). Torpor bouts lasted up to 7 h. These data suggest that large as well as
small birds use torpor to save energy during colder weather.

Black-capped chickadees, *Poecile atricapilla*, resident in central Alaska
are exposed to extreme low temperatures in winter compared with populations at lower latitudes such as western Washington State. Sharbaugh
(2001) exposed captive black-capped chickadees to temperatures as low
as − 30 °C. Fat stores were higher in winter but standard metabolic rate did
not vary with season (summer vs. winter), but birds went into nocturnal

hypothermia (to 33.9 ± 1.3 °C from 41 °C). However, Grossman and West (1977) found no nocturnal hypothermia in this population. On the other hand, in Scandinavia, willow tits, *Parus montanus*, do experience nocturnal hypothermia in a more maritime, but sub-arctic (63°N) habitat (Reinertsen and Haftorn, 1983). Sharbaugh (2001) also showed that lesser degrees of hypothermia were used at temperatures of 25 °C.

The Puerto Rican tody, *Todus mexicanus*, is a small (5–7 g) nonpasserine with an average body temperature of 36.7 ± 1.2 °C as compared with other small birds (40–41 °C). These birds are also able to show heterothermy (27.9–42.9 °C) between ambient temperatures of 15–40 °C (Merola-Zwartjes and Ligon, 2000). Body temperatures may drop up to 11 °C, characteristic of torpor, during cold nights in the breeding season, but only in females. Torpor was not recorded in males (Merola-Zwartjes and Ligon, 2000) for reasons still unclear.

Torpor is apparently widespread in hummingbirds but in the rufous hummingbird, *Selasphorus rufus*, incidence of torpor varies with season (Hiebert, 1993). Use of torpor was highest in autumn and lower in spring and summer, perhaps reflecting different energetic circumstances related to migration, breeding and molt. However, torpor can be used at any time of year perhaps providing maximum flexibility in relation to weather conditions. Experimental manipulations in rufous hummingbirds showed that during migration, and especially when sugar concentration of nectar was lower, torpor use increased as did excreted corticosterone levels in cloacal fluid in the evening prior to a torpor bout (Hiebert et al., 2000a). During molt, torpor bouts were less frequent and there was no correlation with corticosterone levels in cloacal fluid. Experimental administration of corticosterone in nectar (Hiebert et al., 2000b) increased use of torpor and depressed food intake (Hiebert et al., 2004).

Much more research is needed to tease apart the potentially fascinating mechanisms underlying the use of torpor in birds, but in mammals a hormone derived from adipose tissue, leptin, is involved in the induction of torpor (Gavrilova et al., 1999; see also Nelson, 2004), as well as ghrelin (Gluck et al., 2006). Such actions in birds remain to be investigated partly because the actions of leptin and ghrelin in birds are still unclear.

E. SNOW AND GROUND FEEDING BIRDS

Many avian species wintering at mid- to high-latitudes forage strictly on the ground even when snow covers food resources. Others migrate to avoid snow, but many remain despite extensive snow cover during the winter months. Larger species easily dig to find covered food, whereas for small passerines access to food requires much more energetically expensive digging in deep snow. In some cases ground feeding birds abandon winter home ranges and facultatively migrate when snow and ice conditions become too severe (Wingfield and Ramenofsky, 1997). These movements are called irruptive migrations and may cover few hundred meters to thousands of kilometers. During these irruptive migrations (also called facultative dispersal) birds seek refugia to provide shelter and trophic resources sufficient to survive the rest of the winter. Many utilize "feeders" at human habitations enabling them to remain in wintering areas where they could not have survived without human assistance. Nonetheless, some small ground-feeding birds are able to persist in otherwise severe conditions. How do they do this and when do conditions become too severe triggering an emergency life-history stage?

Investigations of wintering populations of Dark-eyed Juncos, *Junco hyemalis*, and white-throated Sparrows, *Zonotrichia albicollis*, in the mid-Hudson Valley of New York State (Wingfield and Ramenofsky, 1997) showed that these birds feed almost exclusively on the ground despite snow depths up to 40 cm. Flocks of both species prefer to forage in open forest and along the scrub edges of fields and glades. Further, when overall snow depth exceeded 1–2 cm, these birds foraged in micro-habitats such as bare patches of ground, or beneath the conifer canopy and scrub vegetation at the edges of glades and fields where depth of snow was much less than in open forest or fields. These micro-habitats are well known in the Taiga of Siberia and many birds and mammals depend on them for feeding in winter (e.g., Formozov, 1946; Pruitt, 1970). These "snow shadows" under trees and bare round spots under vegetation harbor berries, *Vaccinum* sp., and mosses and leaves that shelter arthropods—important food items for hazel grouse, *Bonasa bonasia*, Siberian Jay, *Perisoreus infaustus*, Eurasian Jay, *Garrulus glandarius*, titmice, *Parus* sp., nuthatches, *Sitta* sp., Emberizids and finches (Formozov, 1946; Wingfield and Ramenofsky, 1997). Pruitt (1970, 1978, 2005) uses an inland Inuit term, "qamaniq" to describe open or shallow depressions in snow cover beneath vegetation, and Wingfield and Ramenofsky (1997; Fig. 18) adopted this term because it describes these micro-habitats employed by ground-feeding birds precisely. Snow also clings to the branches of coniferous trees or scrub and is called "qali" in the Inuit parlance employed by Pruitt (1970; "kukhta" by Formozov, 1946). *Qali* is important also because it provides insulation, reduces ice formation, and attenuates wind speed in the *qamaniq* (Formozov, 1946).

Temperature measurements at localities in the wintering range of dark-eyed juncos and white-throated sparrows (Fig. 19) revealed that the *qamaniq* was 7–10 °C warmer than all other locations (Wingfield and Ramenofsky, 1997). When sunny on otherwise cold winter days temperature may be up to 18 °C in *qamaniq* whereas ambient air temperature outside was − 2 °C.

Microhabitat such as *qamaniq* are not only a reliable source of food despite deep snow in open areas, but also potential refuges during winter storms. However, high winds can blow snow into the *qamaniq* and *qali* falls

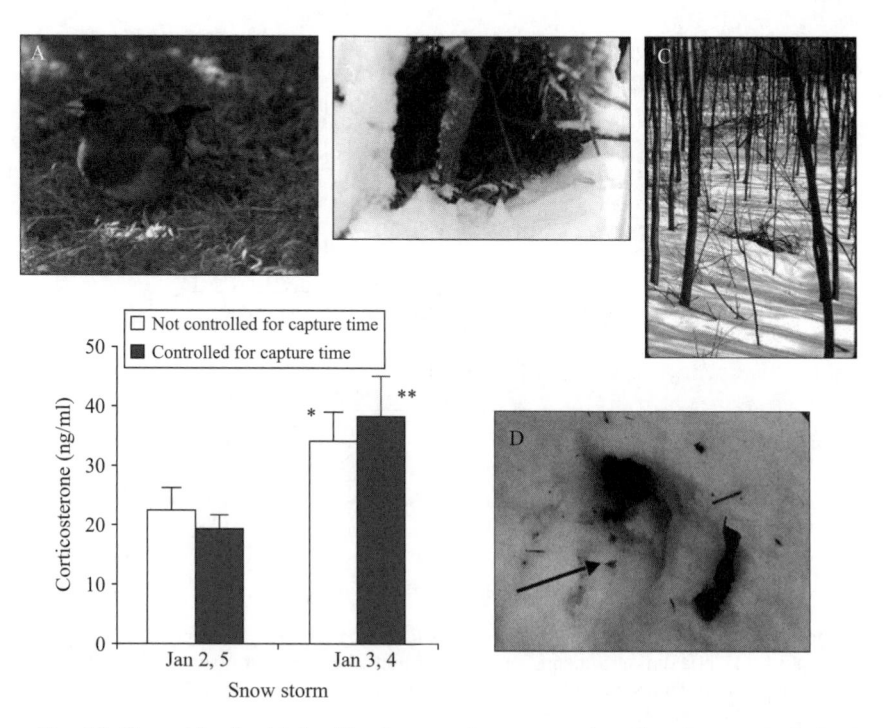

Fig. 18. Ground feeding birds utilize features of snow cover that allow them to obtain food in otherwise severe conditions. They find food in *qamaniq* (snow free areas under vegetation—panel b) compared with panel c where snow depth is deeper. Panel d shows seeds uncovered in shallow snow cover in *qamaniq*. Plasma levels of corticosterone in Dark-eyed Juncos, *Junco hyemalis*, (panel a) sampled before, during, and after a snow storm (lower left panel) that triggered an emergency life-history stage (abandonment of home range). Bars are means and vertical lines the standard errors. Note that plasma corticosterone levels are significantly higher regardless of whether data are controlled for capture time (note that corticosterone levels tend to increase as a result of capture stress and thus capture time must be measured carefully). From Rogers et al. (1993), with permission of the American Ornithologist's Union; Wingfield and Ramenofsky (1997), with permission of Ardea; Silverin and Wingfield (2010), with permission of Elsevier Ltd. All photos by J. C. Wingfield. Courtesy of Ardea and the Netherlands Ornithologist's Union.

from covering vegetation increasing snow depth further (Formozov, 1946; Wingfield and Ramenofsky, 1997; Fig. 20). As a result, energetic demands of digging for food when the *qamaniq* is filled ($E_e + E_i + E_o$) may exceed the energy likely to be gained from food (E_g). Allostatic overload type 1 that results (Fig. 7) will trigger a facultative behavioral and physiological pattern, irruptive migration, to alternate refugia and sources of food. Indeed, after a severe storm in the mid-Hudson Valley that filled up the *qamaniq* so that it no longer provided a refuge with food, white-throated

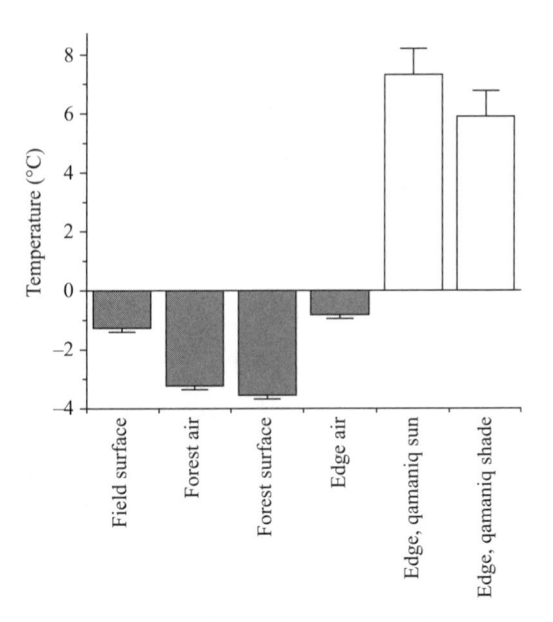

Fig. 19. Mean temperatures at different sites along a 2 km transect near Millbrook, New York (42°N). Bars are means and vertical lines the standard errors. $N = 10$ for each mean. See text for details. From Wingfield and Ramenofsky (1997). Courtesy of Ardea and the Netherlands Ornithologist's Union.

sparrows and dark-eyed juncos abandoned their home ranges when the average snow depth exceeded 5 cm in the *qamaniq* (Wingfield and Ramenofsky, 1997; Fig. 20). Both juncos and sparrows abandoned the forest edge and were found along roadsides where snow plows had uncovered strips of vegetation and potential food (Fig. 21). Although many moved only a few hundred meters to feeders in local homeowner's gardens, others may have moved several hundred kilometers south if no local refuges were available.

Allostatic overload type 1 resulting from wind-blown snow filling in the *qamaniq* was followed by abandonment of the winter home ranges of dark-eyed juncos and white-throated sparrows. This begs the question of whether plasma levels of corticosterone were also elevated thus triggering an emergency life-history stage. Rogers et al. (1993) showed that dark-eyed juncos wintering in Tennessee had higher plasma levels of corticosterone during a snow storm than before or after (Fig. 18). Note that corticosterone levels were highest when the juncos were actually on the move and had left their home range (Rogers et al., 1993); they were lower when they had occupied a refuge after the storm.

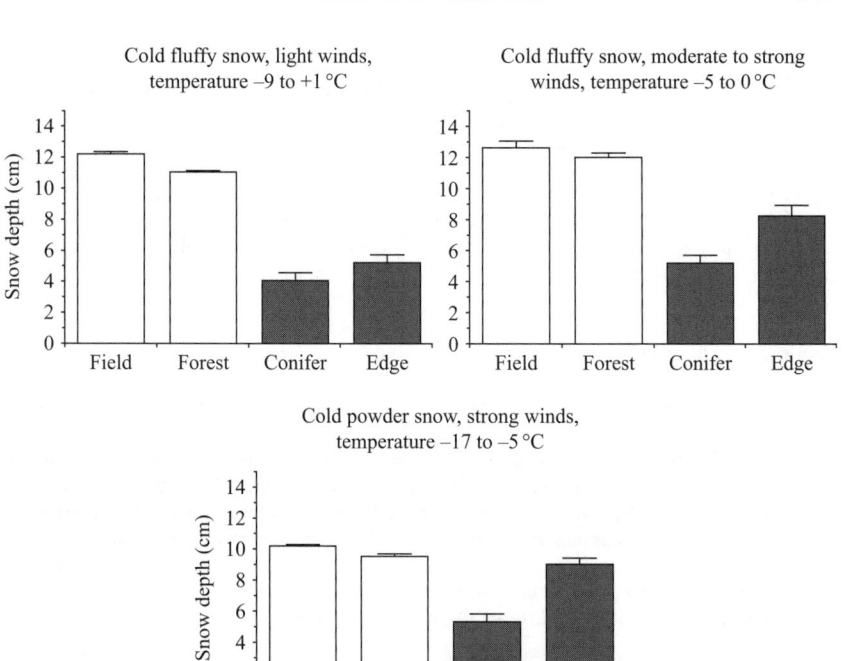

FIG. 20. Snow depths at four localities during three storms (increase of intensity from the top down—see text for full description) along a 2 km transect near Millbrook, New York (42°N). Bars are means and vertical lines the standard errors. $N = 20$ for each locality. From Wingfield and Ramenofsky (1997). Courtesy of Ardea and the Netherlands Ornithologist's Union.

Other field studies support these findings. Severe weather in the central Great Plains of North America can have serious consequences for ground-feeding birds during the nonbreeding season. Harris' sparrows, *Zonotrichia querula*, winter in this region in flocks that feed almost exclusively on the ground. These flocks have a rigid dominance hierarchy with subordinate birds having less black feathering around the face and upper breast than dominant birds (Fig. 22). When snow storms occur, competition for food in patches increases with dominants gaining more access to food. As a result, subordinate birds showed higher circulating levels of corticosterone than dominants suggesting greater allostatic load from being forced to the periphery of the flock and possibly foraging in less productive patches (Rohwer and Wingfield, 1981, Fig. 22). In this case, Harris' sparrows did not leave their home range but instead chose to "ride-out" the storm (i.e., a "take it" strategy). Additionally, behavioral strategies can act to reduce

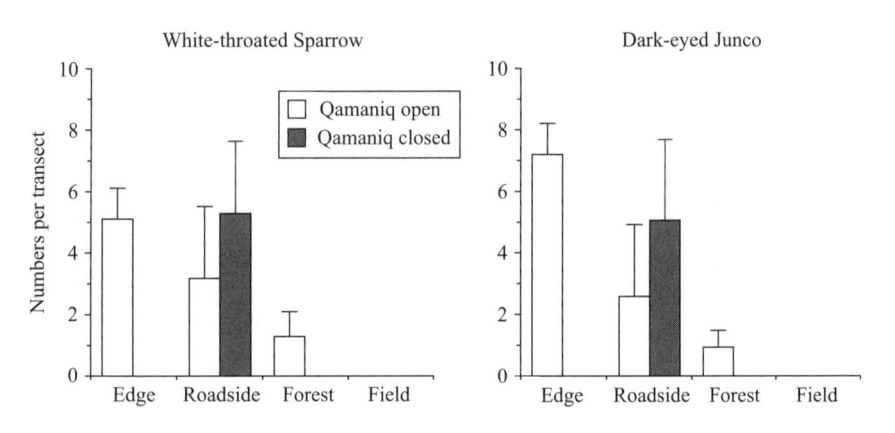

Fɪɢ. 21. Distribution of Dark-eyed Juncos, *Junco hyemalis*, (right panel) and White-throated Sparrows, *Zonotrichia albicollis*, (left panel) at localities along a 2 km transect near Millbrook, New York (42°N). Censuses were conducted when the *qamaniq* was open (mean snow depth in the *qamaniq* was less than 5 cm) and closed (mean snow depth greater than 5 cm in the *qamaniq*). Bars are means and vertical lines the standard errors. $N = 10$ censuses when *qamaniq* was open and 7 when *qamaniq* closed. From Wingfield and Ramenofsky (1997). Courtesy of Ardea and the Netherlands Ornithologist's Union.

potential elevations of E_i. Dark-eyed Juncos during winter will form large flocks when food resources become patchy with snow and ice cover. Flock formation increases foraging efficiency and predator detection, but dominance status precludes limited access for subdominants that include generally females and juveniles. If conditions allow, subdominants avoid conflict by waiting for dominants to become sated and then move in to feed resulting in corticosterone levels comparable across these age and sex classes (Ramenofsky et al., 1992).

European blackbirds, *Turdus merula*, wintering in southern Germany feed on berries and domestic fruit in orchards when snow falls and covers other foods. When conditions deteriorate and competition for limited fruit increases resulting in allostatic overload type 1, the subordinate first year birds of both sexes migrate south thus avoiding conflict with more dominant adults. At this time, first year European blackbirds of both sexes had elevated plasma levels of corticosterone compared to adults (Schwabl et al., 1985, Fig. 23) consistent with triggering facultative behavioral and physiological responses. In this example the home range was abandoned but individuals only moved as far as they needed to find alternate shelter and food. These field studies of responses to severe weather in wintering birds indicate that mechanisms underlying allostatic overload type 1 may be the same despite what appear to be spectacular differences in irruptive-type behavior.

Harris Sparrow, *Zonotrichia querula*

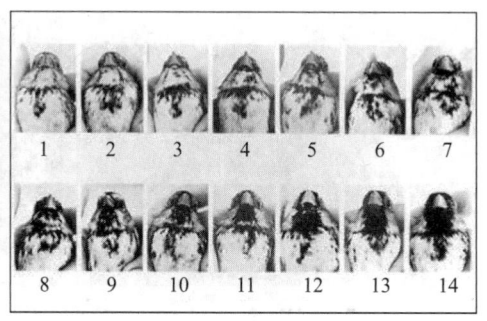

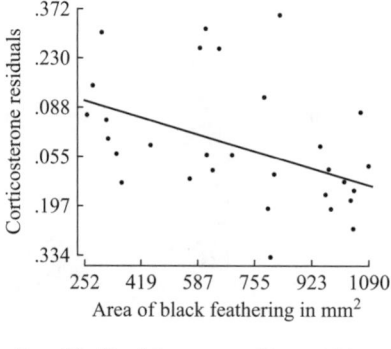

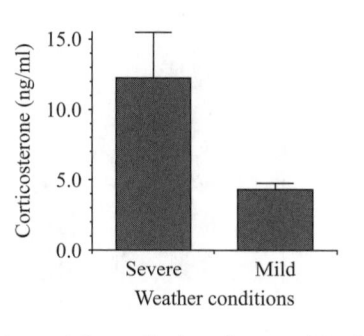

Fig. 22. Harris' sparrows, *Zonotrichia querula*, (upper left panel) winter in ground-feeding flocks in the central Great Plains of the USA. These flocks have rigid dominance hierarchies delineated by the amount of black feathering around the face and upper breast (upper right panel, number is the most subordinate and number 14 the most dominant). During severe weather (snow), overall plasma levels of corticosterone were higher than in less severe winter weather (lower right panel), and dominants tended to have lower baseline levels of corticosterone than subordinates (lower left panel). From Rohwer and Wingfield (1981) courtesy of Springer-Verlag. Photo in upper left panel by J. C. Wingfield.

F. Arrival of Migrant Birds in Arctic and Alpine Habitats

Most avian species that breed in the Arctic spend the winter well below the Arctic Circle (Pielou, 1994; Piersma, 1994). As they migrate north in spring, they must arrive on the tundra breeding grounds as early as possible to establish a breeding territory and begin nesting (Hahn et al., 1995; O'Reilly and Wingfield, 1995). However, early arrival in the Arctic presents problems because of the capricious arctic weather (Hahn et al., 1995; O'Reilly and Wingfield, 1995) that is notoriously unpredictable. Annual spring snow melt can vary by up to a month in arctic and alpine habitats affecting when birds can begin breeding (Martin and Wiebe, 2004). Then further storms and snow depth may also be a problem. Ground

European Blackbird, *Turdus merula*

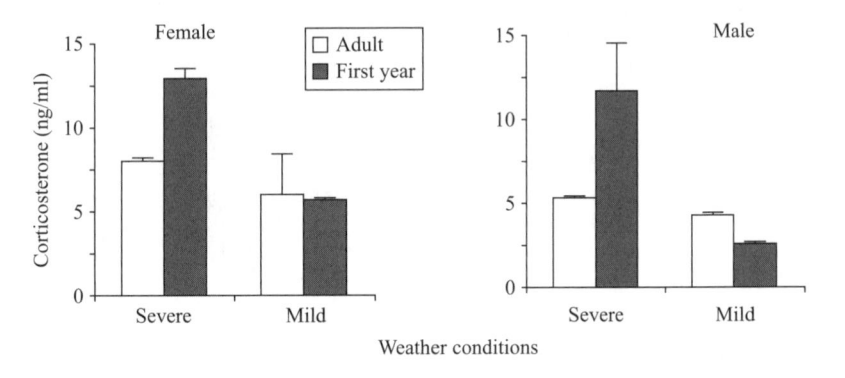

FIG. 23. European blackbirds, *Turdus merula*, (female upper left panel, male upper right-panel) wintering in southern Germany sometimes must endure severe weather including snow that covers food resources. Competition for food following snow increases allostatic load to an extent that the less dominant juveniles of both sexes abandon home ranges and migrate further south to less severe conditions. These juveniles have higher baseline levels of corticosterone than adults that do not leave. From Schwabl et al. (1985). Photos by J. C. Wingfield. Courtesy of Springer-Verlag.

temperatures can vary from below freezing to 45 °C or more in direct sun (see also Wingfield et al., 2004). In alpine zones, breeding generally occurs when conditions are suitable, and this usually means after snow melt and higher temperatures and when severe storms are less likely (Martin and Wiebe, 2004). However, late storms can delay breeding in some years and reduce the possibility for renesting should they lose the first clutch. Usually, reproductive success tends to be reduced in years when conditions result in late onset of nesting. Because variation in extremes occurs with increased climate variability, alpine and arctic-breeding species may be especially vulnerable to inclement weather during breeding (Martin and Wiebe, 2004).

The problems facing arctic and alpine breeding birds fall into four categories (after Martin and Wiebe, 2004; Wingfield et al., 2004):

1. Migrant birds arrive in spring when conditions are still severe compared with wintering grounds far to the south.
2. Food supply is unpredictable early in the season.
3. The breeding season in arctic and alpine regions is brief and individuals must initiate nesting immediately despite severe conditions.
4. Even when nesting has begun, they must "resist" acute stressors such as inclement weather throughout the breeding season.

Although the arrival dates of many migrants are consistent from year to year, arctic and alpine weather and snow cover can vary substantially; snow cover can be complete on arrival of migrants in 1 year, or patchy in another. Further, snow cover along the migratory route may have no relation to snow conditions on the breeding grounds. For example, in 2002, snow cover south of the Brooks Range of Alaska was 100% when songbirds were migrating through, whereas north of the Brooks Range there was no snow illustrating how migrants may be unable to predict snow cover conditions until they arrive on the breeding grounds. However, after arrival, snow storms can occur at any time requiring individuals to seek microhabitats for shelter (Martin and Wiebe, 2004; Wingfield et al., 2004).

Depth of snow cover determines which areas open up first and where migrant birds will settle (Hahn et al., 1995). Ridges scoured free of snow by winds have reduced snow depth to a few centimeters. In valleys, snow depth may reach several meters especially in areas with taller vegetation. Nonetheless, as spring progresses, the increasing angle of the sun's incident radiation can melt snow very rapidly. As patches of ground become snow-free, the darker surfaces absorb radiant energy resulting in higher temperatures at ground level compared with the open-air. Indeed temperatures at ground level in the sun can be as high as 30–60 °C (Wingfield et al., 2004). Alternatively, if clouds, intervening mountains, or low angles of the sun late in the day reduce insolation, then temperatures drop rapidly to below freezing (Wingfield et al., 2004). Thus daily cycles of temperature at ground level can fluctuate widely, but the ground can become snow-free extremely rapidly providing microhabitat for migrant birds. Moreover, accumulation of snow on these bare patches during late spring storms is greatly reduced compared to existing snow pack (Hahn et al., 1995).

Another problem for migrant birds in arctic and alpine habitats is high wind speed. This in conjunction with low temperature results in extreme wind chill factors. As a result, access to food and movement between patches of food is restricted leading to potential competition. However, wind speed can be greatly attenuated by over 90% close to the ground in vegetation. Thus, local patches of ground that emerge from snow cover first are warmer than air and also provide shelter from wind, resulting in greatly reduced wind chill (Wingfield et al., 2004). Migrant songbirds arriving in arctic and alpine habitats may only be exposed to severe weather conditions when they move from one microhabitat to another over snow-covered areas. Nonetheless, late spring snow storms with high wind speeds may force songbirds into fewer patches of microhabitat that in turn increases density and competition for food (Wingfield et al., 2004).

The stochastic nature of conditions in arctic and alpine habitats when migrants arrive in spring as well as during the nesting season suggest that the potential for stress and increased circulating levels of glucocorticoids is high. In the mountain white-crowned sparrow, *Zonotrichia leucophrys oriantha*, breeding in alpine meadows of the Sierra Nevada of California, inclement weather, especially snow fall, can result in temporary abandonment of the territory in early spring (Breuner and Hahn, 2003). Birds retreat down the mountain to refugia in more temperate zones and then return when the inclement weather passes. Implants of corticosterone into males in early spring delayed return to their alpine territories following an abandonment event compared with controls. Corticosterone treatment did not induce abandonment of the territory in fair weather but did increase activity in and around the territory. Further, the adrenocortical response to stress, assayed via corticosterone in plasma samples at capture and up to an hour after, was inversely related to body condition (Breuner and Hahn, 2003).

In Gambel's white-crowned sparrow, *Z. l. gambelii*, the response to stress in males actually increased on arrival in arctic-breeding grounds (Romero et al., 1997) and then declined as the nesting phase progressed (Holberton and Wingfield, 2003). In contrast, a nonmigratory subspecies of white-crowned sparrow, *Z. l. nuttalli*, breeding along the central coast of California, did not show an increase of the adrenocortical response to stress (Wingfield et al., 2004). Similar elevation of the adrenocortical response to capture stress on arrival from spring migration, or at the beginning of the nesting season, has now been demonstrated in other songbirds nesting at the northern edge of their range. Examples are the bush warbler, *Cettia diphone*, in Hokkaido, Japan (Wingfield et al., 1995a), the snow bunting and Lapland longspur arriving at the northern edge of their range at Thule, Greenland (77°N, J. C. Wingfield et al., unpublished), and arriving red knots at Alert, Ellesmere Island, Canada (82°N, Reneerkens et al., 2002a,b). Mechanisms for this upregulation of the adrenocortical response to acute stress include decreased sensitivity to glucocorticosteroid negative feedback (Astheimer et al., 1994) and enhanced sensitivity of adrenal cortex to ACTH (Romero and Wingfield, 1998).

Circulating glucocorticosteroid levels should be interpreted as a function of the extent to which they are bound to a carrier protein, corticosteroid-binding globulin (CBG), and are largely biologically inactivated because they are unable to enter target cells and interact with receptors that mediate biological actions (Breuner and Orchinik, 2001, 2002). There was also an increase in CBG levels at arrival from spring migration in male Gambel's White-crowned Sparrows that could buffer stress-induced increases in corticosterone. Therefore, free (unbound) corticosterone, potentially available to enter cells and interact with receptors, was reduced (Breuner et al., 2003; Romero and Wingfield, 1999). In the mid-latitude breeding *Z. l. pugetensis* that does not increase responsiveness to stress in early spring, (J. C. Wingfield, unpublished), lower binding capacity of CBG may actually result in higher free levels of corticosterone at baseline and after 30 min of capture stress compared to *Z. l. gambelii* (Breuner et al., 2003). Calculation of free corticosterone levels in blood, to give an estimated level of potentially biologically active steroid (Breuner et al., 2003), showed that during the nesting phase, free levels of corticosterone in *Z. l. gambelii* were lower than in male *Z. l. pugetensis* (Breuner et al., 2003). These data are consistent with the hypothesis that the adrenocortical response to stress, at least in terms of the free level of hormone generated in response to a LPF, is actually reduced at higher latitudes. It has been suggested that this buffering action of CBG may allow flexibility of metabolic and behavioral responses to LPFs at different times of the year.

If changes in CBG occur seasonally, then synthesis and release of this carrier protein by the liver must be regulated. To mimic the effects of a storm that covers food resources, food was restricted in captive male *Z. l. gambelii*. This treatment increased plasma corticosterone levels for 2 h but had no immediate effect on CBG binding capacity. Only after 22 h of food restriction did CBG levels decline resulting in an increase of free corticosterone levels in blood (Lynn et al., 2003).

In birds as in mammals, there are two genomic receptors for glucocorticosteroids, the high affinity MR activated at basal levels of hormone and the low affinity GR activated at higher "stress" levels of hormone. A similar system appears to operate in songbirds (Breuner and Orchinik, 2001; Breuner et al., 2003). The binding capacity of GR-like receptors was similar in liver and brain of both *Z. l. gambelii* (arctic breeding) and *Z. l. pugetensis* (mid-latitude breeding). Using mean levels of free corticosterone and GR-like receptor capacity, a measure of receptor occupancy during stress can be calculated. Although the binding capacity of GR-like receptors did not vary between taxa, there were potentially more GR-like receptors occupied by corticosterone 30 min postcapture in both liver and brain of *Z. l. pugetensis* (Breuner et al., 2003). These data strengthen the argument that CBG can buffer sensitivity to LPFs in *Z. l. gambelii*, arriving on the arctic-breeding grounds in spring. These studies also suggest that there is a flexible control system for migrant songbirds to respond rapidly and adaptively to unpredictable weather that in turn allows them to begin nesting as soon as possible.

Even after spring conditions conducive to onset of breeding have begun, severe snow storms with high winds and below freezing temperatures can occur at any time. In one example on the North Slope of Alaska, Lapland longspurs, *Calcarius lapponicus*, had begun incubation when a multiday snow storm covered nests (Astheimer et al., 1995; Fig. 24). Females excavate holes in the snow so that they can then leave temporarily to find food while also being attentive to the nest. Because snow cover decreases efficiency of feeding, females tend to use stored fat to allow them to incubate while feeding less. However, after 3 days, fat stores are probably close to depletion and females abandoned their nests forming wide-ranging foraging flocks. At

FIG. 24. Lapland longspurs, *Calcarius lapponicus*, (panel a) breed throughout Arctic tundra regions. They nest on the ground (panel b), but when sever snow storms occur, nests are frequently buried and females excavate holes through which they can leave to forage and then return to incubate (panel c). However, if snow cover persists for more than 3 days, then the combination of high allostatic load of feeding in snow cover while also trying to incubate coupled with low E_g results in eventual abandonment of the nest and foraging over a wide area (panel d). At this time, the adrenocortical response to capture stress was greatly enhanced in birds after abandonment of the nest (storm) compared to incubating birds before the storm (lower left panel). From Astheimer et al. (1995) courtesy of Elsevier. Photos by Lee B. Astheimer, Bill Buttemer, and J. C. Wingfield.

this time, the adrenocortical response to capture, handling, and restraint was greatly increased compared to birds sampled before the storm (Astheimer et al., 1995; Fig. 24). In this case, female Lapland longspurs were able to resist allostatic overload type 1 for a few days using fat stores (see also Goymann and Wingfield, 2004; Wingfield, 2004) to substitute for reduced E_g. However, such substitution is restricted by the amount of fat that can be stored, and the most prolonged and severe storms may still result in an emergency life-history stage and termination of nesting.

G. Antarctic Penguins

It is widely known that many species of birds may fast "voluntarily" during breeding and migration, or because inclement weather or other unfavorable environmental conditions may prevent normal access to food. This is particularly well known in penguins breeding in Antarctic regions. In general, larger birds do not undergo periods of torpor during fasting but rather reduce their locomotor activity and resting metabolic rates (Cherel et al., 1988). During these fasts, body weight decreases (mostly from utilization of fat) in three phases: phase I is a period of rapid physiological change where lipids are mobilized and protein catabolism is decreased; phase II is a stable period where lipids are metabolized steadily but locomotor activity is reduced; and phase III is a critical period where proteins begin to be catabolized although some reserves of fat remain. The last phase is usually followed by changes in behavior to favor refeeding and cessation of the fast. Emperor and king penguins remain on land or ice for several weeks while completely replacing their plumage. Thus they are vulnerable to cold weather and storms while utilizing endogenous reserves of fat and protein for energy and plumage production (Groscolas and Cherel, 1992). These responses could be even more significant given that the insulating properties of their plumage are compromised while molting. So, they must stay out of the ocean while not feeding (Adams and Brown, 1990). During this time, they may lose up to 45% of body weight and 50% of body protein. Hormone studies suggest that the thyroid hormone T4 increased at the onset of molt whereas metabolite T3 increased during molt and may be involved in energy expenditure while fasting. Insulin levels did not change throughout molt or the postmolt period when animals return to the sea. Although corticosterone and glucagon levels remained stable throughout the period of molt and fasting, both hormones increased dramatically postmolt as the birds returned to the ocean (Groscolas and Cherel, 1992).

Some seabird chicks, for example, king penguins, may also fast throughout the sub-Antarctic winter because the parents are unable to find sufficient food and bring it back to the breeding colony during the winter months (Cherel and Le Maho, 1985; Cherel et al., 1987). The ability to fast while breeding is also found in other large avian species such as geese (*Anser* sp.) when nesting birds may fast for up to 2.5 months (Geleon, 1981) showing almost complete anorexia (Mrosovsky and Sherry, 1980) and the three phases of fasting and protein sparing (Le Maho et al., 1981). In king penguin chicks, the phase of fasting is accompanied by a two- to threefold reduction in the magnitude of the adrenocortical response to capture stress (Corbel et al., 2009).

Although fasting large birds do not become torpid, they can show slight decreases in core temperature (Cherel et al., 1988), which may result in some energy savings. Further, behavioral changes such as huddling in severe weather can, for example, in emperor penguins, reduce energy expenditure close to basal metabolic rate (Le Maho et al., 1976). Solitary emperor penguins that are unable to huddle in severe cold of the Antarctic winter lose weight twice as rapidly during phase 2 than penguins that are able to huddle with others (Le Maho, 1983). Additionally, Emperor penguins, and other species, reduce locomotor activity to a minimum to further reduce energetic costs. On average, during severe weather, Emperor penguins move less than 30 m a day (Le Maho, 1983). Similar reductions in locomotion and grouping behavior have been observed in high-latitude rock ptarmigan in winter (Stokkan et al., 1986). Phase 2 of fasting in emperor penguins was accompanied by greatly reduced locomotor activity and an almost nonexistent escape response to capture. However, when phase 3 was reached, there was an 8–15-fold increase in spontaneous locomotor activity and a robust escape response during attempts at capture (Robin et al., 1998). This was accompanied by increases in plasma levels of corticosterone and uric acid and a decrease in plasma beta-hydroxybutyrate. Robin et al. (1998) suggest that these metabolic changes may trigger a refeeding signal hence increased locomotor activity. These behavioral changes are in complete contrast to increased locomotor activity in white-crowned sparrows and dark-eyed juncos deprived of food (Astheimer et al., 1992; Ketterson and King, 1977; Ramenofsky et al., 2008a,b). The latter scenario has been suggested to be similar to phase 3 in larger avian species (Cherel et al., 1988).

Corticosterone is thought to increase foraging activity, or at least play a permissive role in regulation of food intake, in response to food shortage or stress in general (e.g., Angelier et al., 2007a,b, 2008; Astheimer et al., 1992; Kitaysky et al., 2003; Ramenofsky et al., 2008a,b). It may also trigger refeeding signals and abandonment of the egg or chick in penguins in phase 3 of fasting (Groscolas and Robin, 2001; Groscolas et al., 2008) and may avoid potential lethal effects of prolonged fasting in phase 3. Plasma levels of corticosterone were elevated but stable during fasting and incubation compared to arrival from a feeding trip in Adélie penguins (McQueen et al., 1999; Vleck and Vleck, 2002).

Corticosterone is normally further elevated in Adélie penguins in phase III of fasting (just before they need to leave for the ocean). But, in 2001, a large iceberg stopped movement of ice in the Ross Sea, and birds were likely lighter than normal because they had to travel further on ice to find food and then return. Corticosterone levels were highest in departing birds rather than in returning birds consistent with the self-preservation hypothesis (Cockrem et al., 2006). In Adélie penguins sampled in Adélie Land, East Antarctica, earlier retreat of sea ice does not seem to pose a threat because they are able to adjust at sea foraging and distance from the colony to open water is reduced (Beaulieu et al., 2010). Plasma levels of corticosterone did not differ between years of early versus later retreat of sea ice. This is unlike a study by Cockrem et al. (2006) which showed that transit time was affected by sea ice conditions in birds sampled on Ross Island (further west).

H. WIND AND RAIN

Whereas weather events including extremes of temperature and precipitation can have profound influences on the behavior and physiology of free-living birds, when combined with wind, severe conditions can be exaggerated even further. High winds are frequently deleterious for foraging in many land birds, but the opposite may be true for seabirds that rely on wind for dynamic soaring to forage. The latter species may be unable to fly in calm winds (Warham, 1996). There is a considerable literature on the effects of wind, frequently in combination with rain, but few studies have been conducted on mechanisms of coping behavior in this type of weather.

Individuals in winter foraging flocks of *Zonotrichia leucophrys* and *Z. atricapilla* in western Oregon favored microhabitats when possible (DeWoskin, 1980). Differences in wind speed, temperature, and solar radiation were sufficient to increase metabolic rate by as much as 20% in open flat field areas compared with more sheltered habitats such as a hedge row. Spatial orientation was not random. Birds frequently would face into the wind to reduce resistance to air flow when other foraging activities allowed (DeWoskin, 1980).

Violent movements of higher and smaller branches in wind are a problem for canopy feeding birds (Grubb, 1975). Low temperature and high wind velocity affected foraging heights of forest birds in winter regardless of tree species selected and whether birds foraged in the canopy, in lower shrubs or near the tree trunk. Multiple observations of canopy feeding passerines show that during low wind speeds, birds move directly from the canopy of one tree to the next (J. C. Wingfield, unpublished observations, Fig. 25). However, during high winds, violent movements of twigs and branches are avoided by birds leaving the canopy at the base where movement of twigs and branches is minimal (Fig. 26), flying directly to the next tree, and entering the canopy from the base and the lee side (Fig. 25). Indeed, measurements of movements of trees at the canopy and the mid- and low story of three species of trees show considerable decrease in lateral movement lower in the tree. Further, wind speed tends to be highest at the upper story of the canopy and attenuated markedly at lower levels (Fig. 26). These

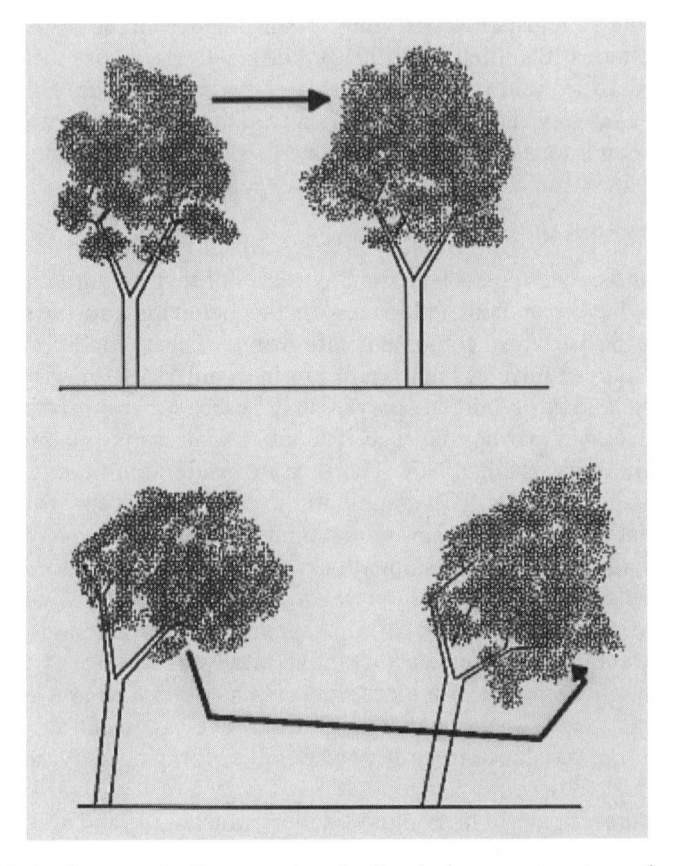

Fig. 25. Small canopy feeding passerines fly directly from one tree to another in calm conditions (upper panel). As wind speed increases, these birds leave from the bottom of the canopy and enter the next tree also at the bottom of the canopy and on the lee side (lower panel). J. C. Wingfield, unpublished observations from numerous field investigations in North America, Europe, and New Zealand.

data suggest that in high winds, the lower story of trees is a less violent place (in terms of branch and twig movements) with wind chill lower as well. However, foraging conditions may be less rich in the lower stories.

Carolina chickadees (*Poecile carolinensis*) and tufted titmice (*Baeolophus bicolor*) foraging in winter in small woodlots reduced the height of foraging in the forest canopy in relation to increasing wind speed (Dolby and Grubb, 1999). These and other species such as male downy woodpeckers (*Picoides pubescens*) and white-breasted nuthatches (*Sitta carolinensis*) also moved away from the windward edge of woodlots as wind speeds increased and temperatures declined (Dolby and Grubb, 1999). The combined effects of wind and low temperature may have important effects of bark foraging birds in small, fragmented, woodlots. Similar results were obtained in golden-crowned kinglets, *Regulus satrapa*, and chestnut-backed chickadees foraging in wind and rain in western Washington State (Fig. 27) as well as in four canopy species feeding in southern beech forests of New Zealand (Fig. 28). In a different scenario, house sparrows given equal protection from predators will frequent feeders with the most shelter, or reduced energetic cost, due to wind and cold (Grubb and Greenwald, 1982).

In another case of birds utilizing protective formations within the habitat, solitary saw whet owls, *Aegolius acadicus*, were found roosting under boughs of deciduous trees laden with fallen big-leaf maple, *Acer macrophyllum*, leaves providing roofing shelter from rain and wind during winter in forests of western Washington State, USA (M. Ramenofsky and J. C. Wingfield, personal observation).

Wind and temperature are main weather variables affecting foraging of shorebirds (Evans, 1976). Wind blows birds around making it more difficult to maintain a position for prey capture. Foraging efficiency and prey capture rates decrease in black-bellied plovers, *Pluvialis squatorola*, and heat losses tend to be greater. Wind disturbs the water surface making it more difficult to locate prey (Evans, 1976) or dries exposed substrate driving prey deeper or back into water. Interaction of wind and tide can exacerbate wave action dramatically disturbing the substrate and reducing feeding efficiency (Evans, 1976). As a result, individuals may be forced to feed at the tide line where competition with others becomes greater (Evans, 1976).

Conversely, low wind speeds may be deleterious for foraging in some seabird species. Dunn (1973) correlated fishing success of common terns, *Sterna hirundo*, and Sandwich terns, *S. sandvicensis*, with water surface conditions and wind speed. Calm conditions reduced fishing success probably because they had to work harder to hover and locate fish. Very windy conditions may obscure visual location of fish because the water surface may be disturbed. In hunting ospreys, *Pandion haliaetus,* if sunlight and

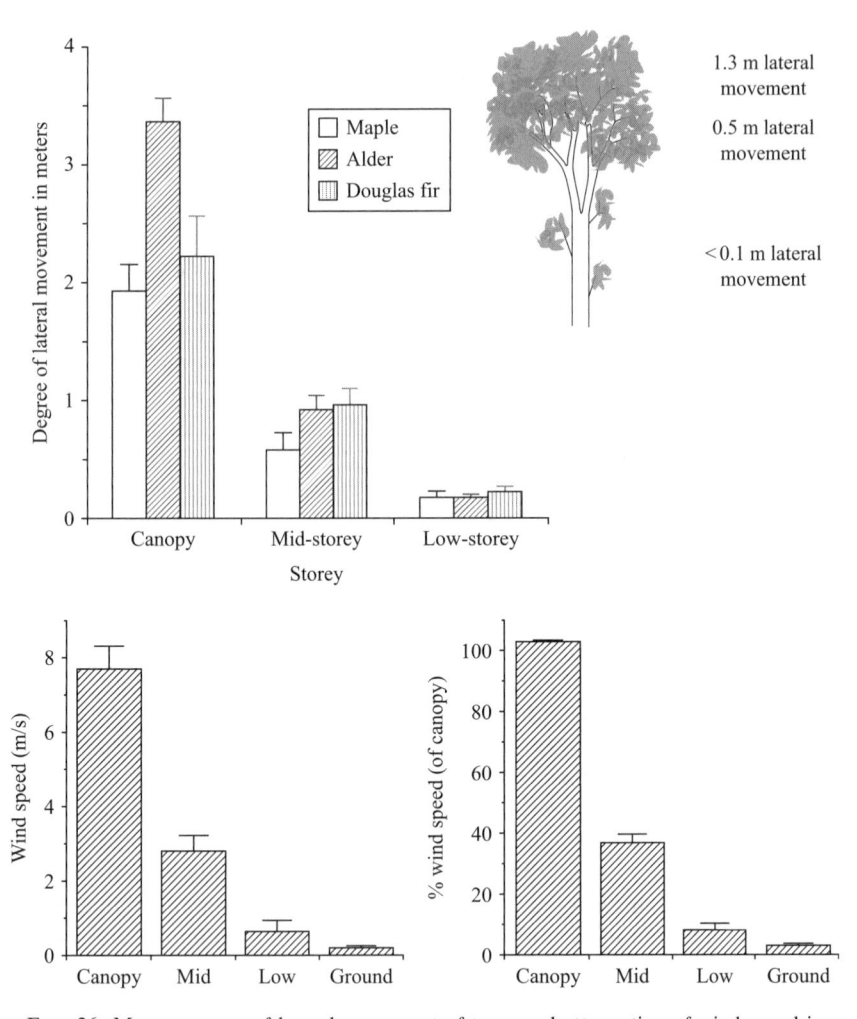

Fig. 26. Measurements of lateral movement of trees and attenuation of wind speed in a mixed forest in Western Washington State, USA. Top right hand panel shows the average lateral movement in wind decreases from the canopy to the base (upper story to mid- and low story). The upper left hand panel shows lateral movement measured for three species of trees (big-leaf maple, red alder and Douglas fir). Lateral movement was measured in 5 m/s and higher winds. All three species showed similar decrease in lateral movement with height. The lower two panels show attenuation of winds speeds from the high to low story (in meters per second, lower left panel and as percent of wind speed at the high story canopy). From J. C. Wingfield, unpublished observations. (For interpretation of the references to color in this figure legend, the reader is referred to the Web version of this chapter.)

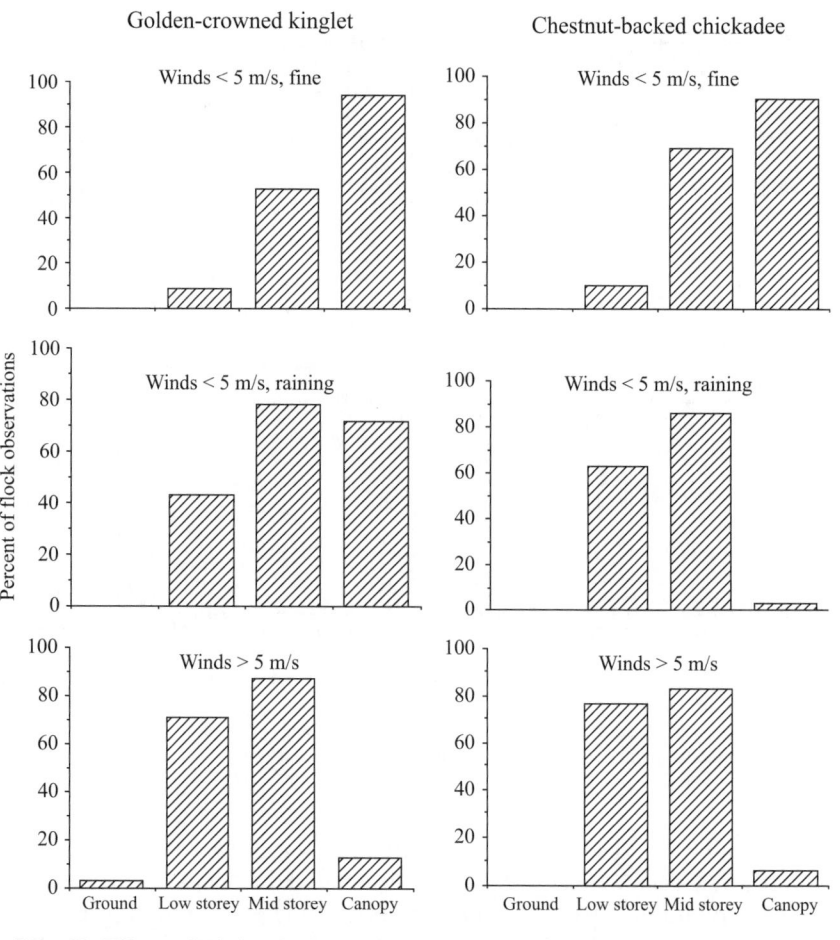

FIG. 27. Effects of wind and rain on the height of foraging in mixed forests in western Washington State, USA. Flocks of golden-crowned kinglets and chestnut-backed chickadees (N = at least 8) were scored as being in the upper, mid- or lower story (or a combination of stories) in winds less than 5 m/s (upper panels), less than 5 m/s but also raining (mid panels), and in winds greater than 5 m/s (lower panels). In both species, there was a tendency to foraging more in the upper story at low wind speeds and move down to the lower story (and in some cases, the ground) at higher wind speeds and in rain. From J. C. Wingfield, unpublished observations.

water disturbance (ripples) were held constant, then increasing wind speed had no effect on rates of attempted and successful captures of fish or the rates of hovering and percentage of successful dives. However, cloudy weather and wind-induced rippling of the water surface reduced capture

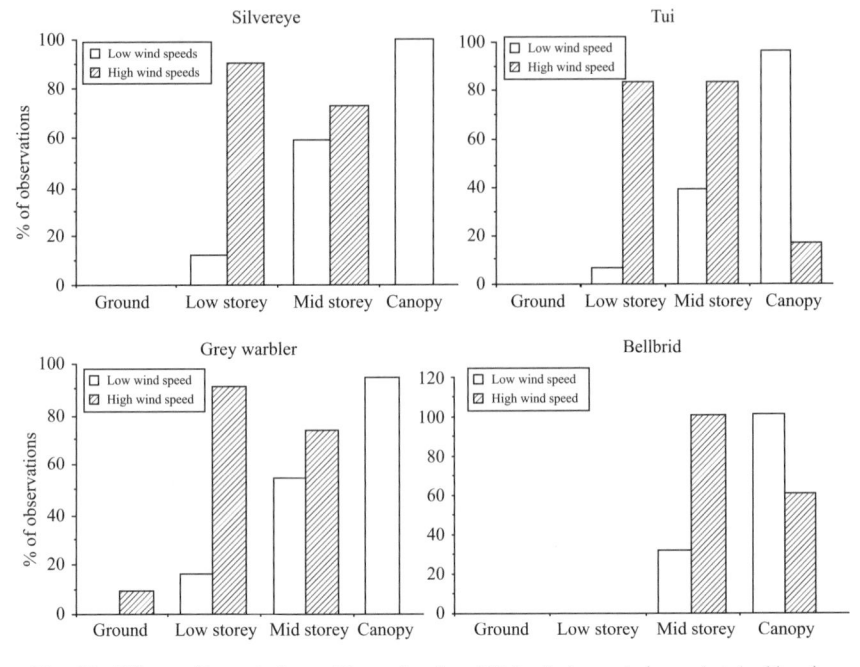

FIG. 28. Effects of low wind speed (open bars) and high wind speeds (cross-hatched bars) on percent of flocks observed in the high, mid-, or low stories of forests in New Zealand. In all species, there was a tendency for birds to move to lower stories (and sometimes the ground) at high wind speeds. From J. C. Wingfield, unpublished observations.

rates possibly because of lower visibility of fish underwater (Grubb, 1977). Moreover, Machmer and Ydenberg (1990) found that wind speed and water surface conditions were the most important factors decreasing foraging success of ospreys. Cloud cover, sunlight, and precipitation did not affect fishing success but could contribute to water surface conditions (Flemming and Smith, 1990). All these factors will contribute to allostatic load as well as affecting E_g, the amount of food available for a foraging individual.

An example in a totally different habitat, the open ocean, illustrates further how the allostatic load framework provides a potential common pathway for understanding how diverse environmental conditions can contribute to triggering an emergency life-history stage in response to weather events. Most seabirds thrive in severe weather typical of many mid- and high-latitude oceans. Indeed, calm weather may result in an inability to forage properly because it requires too much energy to hover searching for fish without favorable winds to sustain lift (e.g., Dunn, 1973). Calm conditions result in some of the larger albatrosses (*Diomedea* sp.) being unable to fly at all. In these cases, what to humans would be pleasant calm weather is a labile perturbation factor for oceanic birds. Nonetheless, truly severe gales with up to hurricane force winds can have debilitative effects on foraging seabirds (e.g., Elkins, 1983). Seabird "wrecks" occur in which hundreds to thousands of individuals may be blown inland or wash up on beaches in a moribund state. In such examples, those seabirds that are able to respond to severe weather by leaving the area or finding a refuge such as on an island would be the ones selected for the best coping mechanism.

Seabirds of the southern oceans are almost entirely pelagic returning to land only to breed (Warham, 1996). The common diving petrel, *Pelecanoides urinatrix*, exposed to very severe weather conditions can retreat to oceanic islands to shelter. These diving petrels tolerate high winds and mountainous seas, as do many seabirds in this region, as they feed on krill swarms near the sea surface. In June 1991 a severe storm with high winds, low temperatures, snow, and near zero visibility led to a reduction of feeding efficiency (Veit and Hunt, 1991), that is, an increase in E_o and a decrease in E_g. Body mass of birds captured during the storm was lower than those captured during calm weather, and plasma levels of corticosterone were higher (Smith et al., 1994, Fig. 29). During the storm, diving petrels were observed flying toward Annekov Island—a breeding locality where burrows presumably provide shelter. In New Zealand, numbers of common diving petrels aggregate in sheltered bays and the lee side of breeding islands (Richdale, 1945). These refuge seeking responses to severe weather conditions are remarkably similar to those of ground-feeding passerines described above, and the responses of corticosterone secretion appear identical.

In barn swallows, *Hirundo rustica*, plasma corticosterone levels of free-living parents feeding young increased when mean daytime temperature declined and thus insect availability, that is, flying insects, also decreased (Jenni-Eiermann et al., 2008). Body condition of parents also deteriorated. Low temperatures had a negative effect on weights of nestlings (Jenni-Eiermann et al., 2008). Similar results were found during inclement weather in colonies of breeding cliff swallows, *Petrochelidon pyrrhonota*, when flying insect numbers declined precipitously and corticosterone levels increased (Raouf et al., 2006, Fig. 30). Further, this was exacerbated in colonies that had high infestation of blood sucking parasites versus colonies that had been experimentally fumigated (Raouf et al., 2006). Swallows with very high or very low corticosterone levels also had lower annual survival rates than birds with intermediate levels (Brown et al., 2005a), and those with higher levels that did survive tended to switch to other colonies (Brown et al., 2005b). Weather conditions had no effects on fecal corticosterone metabolite levels in adult blue tits or pied flycatchers. However, in

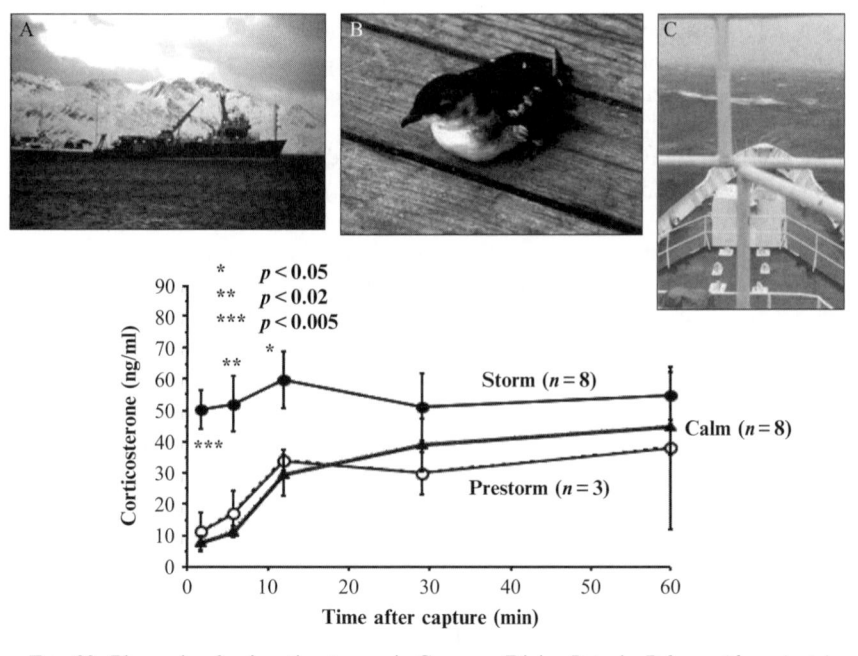

FIG. 29. Plasma levels of corticosterone in Common Diving Petrels, *Pelecanoides urinatrix*, (panel b) during calm weather (panel a), just prior to, and during (panel c) a severe storm off the South Georgia Islands. Bars are means and vertical lines the standard errors (lower panel). Drawn from data in Smith et al. (1994); courtesy of University of Chicago Press. Photos by Professor Troy Smith with permission.

nestlings of both species, fecal corticosterone metabolite levels increased with decreasing temperature. This effect was not found in blue tit nestlings in a colder year suggesting that sensitivity to ambient temperature may change from one year to the next dependent upon other, as yet unknown, factors (Lobato et al., 2008).

I. More on Seabirds, Island Birds, Weather, and El Niño Southern Oscillation Events

Seabirds worldwide are affected by ocean conditions both in terms of food available and how far they must travel from land-based breeding sites and in terms of weather conditions that determine how hard they have to work to get food. One major climatic event is the El Niño Southern Oscillation event (ENSO, Enfield, 2001; Trenberth, 1997). El Niño conditions prevail when a warm water layer develops originating from the Pacific Ocean and overlays

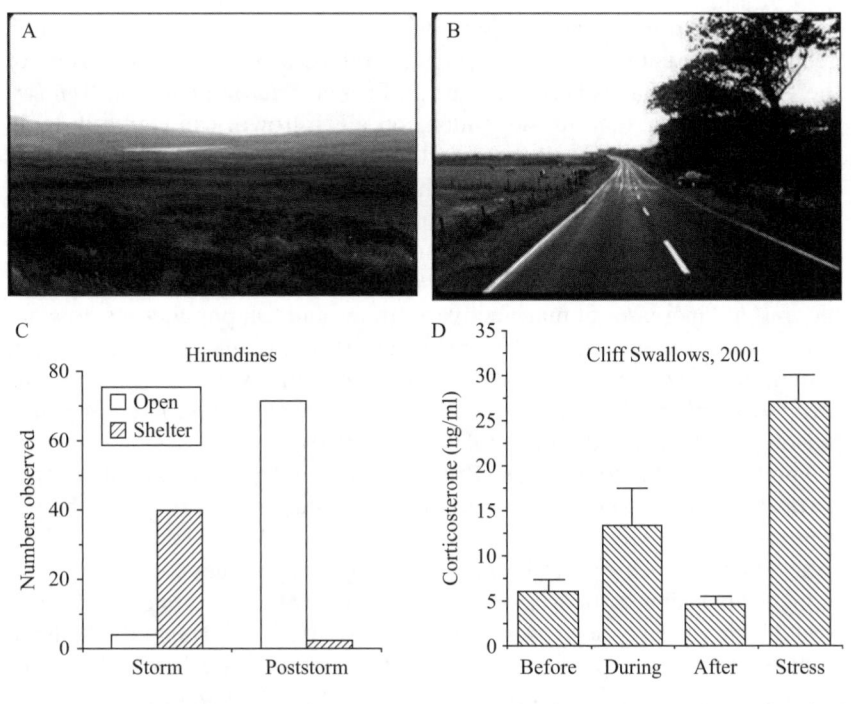

FIG. 30. Swallows (Hirundines) feed exclusively on flying insects. Panel a shows a swath of Scottish moorland that many Hirundines use to catch flying midges and other insects. When inclement weather prevails, flying insect numbers drop to almost zero in such exposed areas and Hirundines are forced to congregate in sheltered areas on the lee side of copses (panel b) and similar shelter. Sometimes 50 plus birds may be competing for flying insects in a sheltered only 100×50 m (panel c). In panel d, plasma levels of corticosterone were higher in cliff swallows during inclement weather, but not as high as in response to the acute stress of capture, handling, and restraint (from Raouf et al., 2006). Photos by J. C. Wingfield. Courtesy of the Animal Behaviour Society and Elsevier Press.

cold water of the Humboldt current off the west coast of South America. In some years, it is so large, 5000 km or more across the eastern Pacific Ocean, that it affects oceans and land masses globally (Ropelewski and Halpert, 1987). In the Galapagos Islands, an ENSO event typically results in heavy and prolonged rains for over a year compared with a wet season of about a month in February in years when La Niña conditions prevail.

Extensive rainfall during an ENSO event is followed by prodigious productivity of plant growth and arthropods so that land birds such as Galapagos finches can breed several months longer than in a dry year (Gibbs and Grant, 1987; Wilson et al., 2007). Conversely in the ocean, warming during an ENSO event blocks the upwelling of nutrients with the cold Humboldt

Current, and primary productivity declines markedly. Algal growth then declines to virtually zero, the food chain collapses and the subtidal zone of the Galapagos Islands becomes barren. Fish and marine iguanas, *Amblyrhynchus cristatus*, that are dependent on algal growth can starve in large numbers during ENSO events (e.g., Laurie, 1989; Newton, 1998; Wikelski and Trillmich, 1997). Many seabirds that feed on fish and marine life close to shore also lose body condition and usually fail to breed. When La Niña conditions return, the upwelling of the Humboldt Current resumes, sea temperatures drop, and upwelling of nutrients surge followed by rich algal blooms and increases of marine invertebrates and fish populations. Inshore seabirds have sufficient food to breed successfully, but on land, drought conditions prevail with reduced primary productivity and a decline in arthropod numbers. Most terrestrial species now have a restricted breeding season (e.g., Grant and Grant, 1980; Lack, 1950).

The brood value hypothesis (Bókony et al., 2009) predicts that adrenocortical responses to climatic conditions and acute stressors will be higher when conditions preclude successful reproduction. Moreover, higher energetic demands during periods of reduced trophic resources could also result in higher baseline corticosterone levels (Hau et al., 2010). In seabirds, this would be in the El Niño year, and in land birds, this would be in the La Niña year. Baseline and capture stress-induced maximal plasma levels of corticosterone were affected in breeding birds of inshore Galapagos Island habitats. In Galapagos penguins, *Spheniscus mendiculus*, and flightless cormorants, *Phalacrocorax harrisi*, corticosterone titers in blood were higher in the El Niño year compared to La Niña conditions. Offshore feeding seabirds such as great frigate birds, *Fregatta minor*, and red-footed boobies, *Sula sula*, showed no effects of ENSO on baseline or plasma levels of corticosterone (Wingfield et al., submitted). Land birds such as Galapagos finches, *Geospiza* sp., doves, *Zenaida galapagoensis*, and mockingbirds, *Nesomimus parvulus*, showed few differences in adrenocortical responses to acute stress with the ENSO event with the exception of two small species (< 18 g) that revealed, contrary to predictions, increases in baseline corticosterone and stress responses in the El Niño year (Wingfield et al., submitted-a,-b). Smaller species may be more susceptible to inclement weather during El Niño years than larger species. It is important to point out that modulation of adrenocortical responses to stress with climatic conditions should address ecological conditions as well as body condition and breeding status.

In superb starlings, *Lamprotornis superbus*, of East Africa, spring rainfall correlated with baseline and maximum stress concentrations of corticosterone, with levels being highest in driest years. Dominant and subordinate animals responded differently with subordinates having higher levels of corticosterone (Rubenstein, 2007). Tropical birds generally show similar corticosterone responses to stress as do mid- and high-latitude species, although future sampling in relation to seasonal and weather events such as ENSO may show differences not apparent at present (Martin and Rubenstein, 2008).

Investigations of a nesting blue-footed booby, *Sula nebouxi*, colony on Isla Isabel, Pacific coast of Sinaloa, Mexico, revealed zero reproductive success during the ENSO event of 1993. Approximately 20% of pairs in the colony attempted to breed and some hatched chicks. However, because there was insufficient food to feed adults and their chicks, all the latter died by day 18 of age (Wingfield et al., 1999; Fig. 31). In contrast, La Niña conditions prevailed in 1994, and most pairs in the colony bred successfully. Baseline plasma levels of corticosterone in male and female blue-footed boobies were similar in 1993 and 1994, and further, the responses to capture, handling, and restraint were identical in El Niño and La Niña years (Wingfield et al., 1999, Fig. 31). Circulating testosterone levels were slightly lower in males and females in the El Niño year as expected, given that most birds did not initiate nesting. In blue-footed boobies, and other seabirds, brood reduction is a typical response to adverse breeding conditions. Adults cease to feed chicks if food supply is reduced and rather invest available food in self-preservation. This would also reduce $E_e + E_i$ when E_g is also reduced thus providing a buffer against possible perturbations, E_o.

El Niño events that change sea surface temperatures and food distribution can have dramatic effects determining the distribution of many seabirds such as petrels and whether some populations breed or not that year (Warham, 1996). In the common murre, *Uria aalge*, and the black-legged kittiwake, *Rissa tridactyla*, food abundance around breeding islands in the Gulf of Alaska predicts baseline corticosterone levels in breeding adults. Plasma corticosterone was lower when food abundance was high (Kitaysky et al., 1999, 2007, 2010). This is in turn affects corticosterone titers of developing chicks, and ultimately reproductive success and survival (e.g., Kitaysky et al., 2003, 2005).

In Gray-faced Petrels, *Pterodroma macroptera gouldi*, there were no sex differences or changes with breeding substage in baseline corticosterone levels, but there was a weak negative relationship of the adrenocortical response to capture stress (Adams et al., 2005). Stress responses were also higher during the incubation phase than other stages. Thus it is necessary to control for stage in breeding when investigating such environmental effects as ENSO. For Nazca Boobies, *Sula granti*, breeding on the Galapagos Islands moonlight may affect distribution of the main prey species that include sardines (Clupeids) and flying fish (Exocetids). Frequency and availability of prey, possibly affected by weather variables such as cloud cover, can in turn affect corticosterone plasma levels (Tarlow et al., 2003).

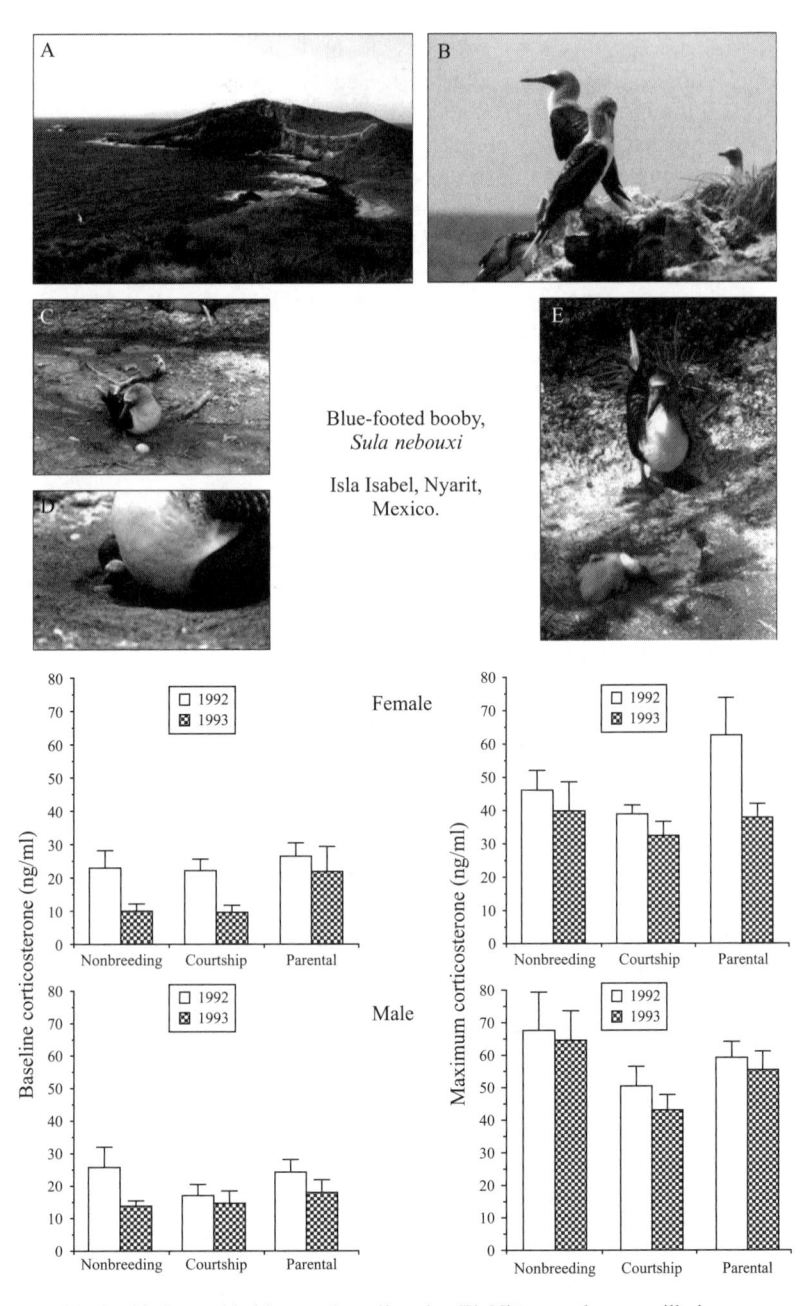

Blue-footed booby,
Sula nebouxi

Isla Isabel, Nyarit,
Mexico.

Fɪɢ. 31. Seabirds worldwide can be affect by El Niño southern oscillation events as abundance of food and weather change dramatically. The blue-footed booby, *Sula nebouxi*, (panel b) breeds extensively on Isla Isabel (panel a) off the coast of Nyarit, Mexico. They lay

A weak ENSO in 2003 resulted in late breeding in Rhinoceros Auklets, *Cerorhinca monocerata*, whereas in 2004 (cooler waters and greater primary production in the north eastern Pacific Ocean), laying dates occurred earlier (Addison et al., 2008). Interestingly, females tend to rear more sons in good years and more daughters in poorer years, but there was no difference in baseline corticosterone (Addison et al., 2008). It is interesting to note that in an urban population of white-crowned sparrows, *Zonotrichia leucophrys pugetensis*, females with higher baseline corticosterone tended to produce more female chicks. Further, treatment of females with corticosterone implants (that raised baseline levels but well within the normal, unstressed, range) also resulted in more female chicks (Bonier et al., 2007). It is possible that weather events may result in skews of sex ratios in some species. In rhinoceros auklets and common murres, there were no differences in chick responses to stress such as reduced food being fed by parents suggesting that parents feed sons and daughters differentially according to environmental conditions such as ENSO (Addison et al., 2008; Cameron-Macmilan et al., 2007). Whether baseline corticosterone levels are truly related to reproductive success (fitness) is still debatable (Bonier et al., 2009; Hau et al., 2010).

In seabirds in general, baseline corticosterone appears to be an excellent indicator of foraging conditions with high corticosterone related to poor conditions (weather and food availability) and low corticosterone to good conditions (e.g., in least auklets, *Aethia pusilla*, and Thick-billed murres, *Uria lomvia*, Benowitz-Fredericks et al., 2008; black-legged kittiwakes, Buck et al., 2007; Kitaysky et al., 2003). Corticosterone is also high in years when breeding common murres chick stage did not match with fish population increases compared with years in which parental phase and maximum fish populations did coincide (Doody et al., 2008).

Experimentally increased foraging effort (by clipping wing feathers to raise $E_e + E_i + E_o$) in little auks, *Alle alle*, resulted in a decline in body mass and increases in baseline corticosterone in both clipped adults and their chicks compared with controls (Harding et al., 2009). However, increasing allostatic load by raising wing loading by adding 45 g weights to Cory's Shearwaters, *Calonectris diomedea*, during incubation increased foraging time at sea and a lower rate of mass gain while at sea but no change in baseline corticosterone compared with controls (Navarro et al.,

---

one or two eggs (panel c), and chicks (panel d) are entirely dependent upon fish brought by the parents. In the ENSO event of 1993, very few blue-footed boobies attempted to breed and the young of those that did died of starvation (panel d). Because adults chose a self-preservation strategy, corticosterone levels were not elevated (lower panel). From Wingfield et al. (1999) courtesy of Elsevier. All photos by J. C. Wingfield.

2008). More research is needed in different ecological contexts to resolve the relationships of baseline and stress-induced corticosterone levels and energy demand (Hau et al., 2010).

In a review of the avian literature, Angelier and Chastel (2009) suggest that the adrenocortical stress response during the parental phase can be modulated (degree of increase) and also the prolactin (a pituitary hormone with multiple actions including parental behavior) stress response, a decrease, may be involved in parental investment. Interaction of these two may be very important in determining the degree of parental effort in relation to environmental perturbations, both acute and chronic (e.g., ENSO events). Moreover, experimental elevation of corticosterone in black-legged kittiwakes resulted in a decrease in prolactin compared to controls (Angelier et al., 2009a). Spontaneous abandonment of the egg or chick in king penguins occurs primarily when their fat reserves fall to a critical level. This spontaneous abandonment is accompanied by increases in baseline corticosterone and a decrease in plasma levels of prolactin (Groscolas et al., 2008). In the Snow Petrel, *P. nivea*, the corticosterone response to stress was negatively correlated with body condition during incubation but not the prolactin response. Further, in contrast to kittiwakes, injection of ACTH (to increase endogenous corticosterone) had no effect on circulating prolactin (Angelier et al., 2009b). For black-legged kittiwakes, birds breeding in poorer condition have higher baseline corticosterone and experimentally increased corticosterone results in increased body condition presumably through foraging (Angelier et al., 2007b; Kitaysky et al., 2003; Lanctot et al., 2003). Breeding black-legged kittiwakes had a higher response of corticosterone and lower prolactin response to acute stress whereas failed breeders showed the opposite (Chastel et al., 2005). Clearly, breeding status and body condition are important and in ENSO years adding to the complexity of environmental factors to consider. More studies are needed on corticosterone and prolactin stress responses to acute perturbations to determine the ecological bases of variation particularly in response to weather.

Baseline corticosterone increased each year during the parental phase of breeding, stabilized, and then declined in older wandering albatrosses, *Diomedea exulans*, (Angelier et al., 2006). Baseline corticosterone levels were high after arriving at the nest from a foraging trip and declined proportional to the success of that foraging trip (Angelier et al., 2007a). In contrast to Adélie penguins, postforaging corticosterone was lower (Angelier et al., 2008; McQueen et al., 1999) suggesting that success of the foraging trip (environmental conditions) and length of the trip allowing replenishment of condition are important factors. Beaulieu et al. (2010) also found no correlation of baseline corticosterone with length of foraging trips associated with extent and rate of melt of sea ice.

Aging effects, that could influence how individuals cope with perturbations, are also not always consistent. In black-browed albatrosses, *Thallasarche melanophris*, although corticosterone levels were highest in first time breeders (and reproductive success lowest), they did not change with age (Angelier et al., 2007c). In common terns, *Sterna hirundo*, however, the adrenocortical response to acute stress did decline with age. This decline appears to be decreased capacity of the adrenal gland to secrete corticosterone because injections of ACTH did not enhance the corticosterone response in older birds (Heidinger et al., 2006, 2008). Whether these differences can be explained by the allostatic load framework (Fig. 7) remains to be determined.

It is also very important to consider the role that blood-binding proteins (e.g., CBG) may have in regulating how much free corticosterone (i.e., not bound to CBG) is available to enter target cells and bind to receptors (Breuner and Orchinik, 2002). Again in black-legged kittiwakes, baseline and maximum corticosterone, and CBG varied from year to year and colony to colony but appeared to be driven by such environmental cues as local food supplies as might be predicted for long-lived seabirds (Shultz and Kitaysky (2008). In the Laysan albatross, corticosterone levels rise during incubation fasts while body condition declines but this may be accompanied by an increase in CBG to protect the reproductive attempt (Sprague, 2009), whereas in tufted puffins, *Fratercula cirrhata*, total and free baseline and maximum corticosterone (after capture stress) were higher prior to egg laying than during incubation. CBG levels were positively correlated with body condition during the chick rearing phase, whereas free corticosterone baselines were negatively correlated (Williams et al., 2008).

III. Conclusions

There is no question that weather has profound influences on behavior and that physiological and endocrine mechanisms have evolved to cope. It is also clear that many other factors, such as territory or home range quality, access to shelter and food, social status, body condition, parasite infection, and injuries all contribute to allostatic load, the daily expenditure required to go about daily and seasonal routines. Add to this the burgeoning allostatic load of human disturbance through exploitation of natural resources, urbanization, pollution, and global climate change, and it is not surprising that many organisms are declining and potential catastrophic loss of biodiversity looms. The concept of allostasis, stability through change, and the phenomena of allostatic load and allostatic overload may provide a framework by which we can understand the cumulative wear and tear that individuals must endure through their life cycles. No one individual experiences the environment in exactly the same way as another and we must understand coping mechanisms at the individual level. Responses to weather are no exception because so many factors may contribute to how an individual may respond to the same climatic event. First, it is important to distinguish between climate, ambient conditions averaged over many years, and current weather to which an individual is exposed. The latter may be very different from the former.

A. Coping Mechanisms for Weather Versus Climate

Climate is defined by average weather conditions over many years. Organisms may time life-history stages, such as breeding, to occur at optimal times for reproductive success. Only when weather events go beyond the climatic norm for a particular time of year are allostatic overload and stress likely. It is at this time that increases in corticosterone would be important resulting in activation of the emergency life-history stage and coping. If such events become more permanent (such as in global climate change), then there will be selection for those individuals that can adjust timing of life-history stages to changing phenology. Many individuals may not be able to do so.

Weather events are short lived (hours to days) after which the normal life-history stage can be resumed quickly, but note that intensity of the weather event is proportional to allostatic load. Coping strategies allow individuals to survive short-lived perturbations in the best condition possible. Climatic events that change timing of life-history stages such as breeding and migration act within the norms of seasonality in relation to phenology without necessarily any corticosteroid related stress effects.

It is becoming clear that elevated circulating levels of corticosterone in response to unpredictable and potentially deleterious environmental events such as inclement weather are a common feature in several taxa studied to date, and in diverse ecological contexts. Further, increased circulating levels of corticosterone in birds responding to these labile perturbation factors appear independent of season and habitat. Opportunistic field observations coupled with experimental evidence for the actions of corticosteroids in many physiological and behavioral changes associated with responses to the unpredictable suggest common mechanisms, perhaps across vertebrates. However, because the number of species studied is limited and the spectrum of habitats and unpredictable events for which samples are available are still rather small, we should be cautious in generalizing too far. Nonetheless, meta-analyses and thoughtful reviews of existing literature on well over 100 species point the way for further investigations (e.g., Bókony et al., 2009; Bonier et al., 2009; Goymann and Wingfield, 2004; Hau et al., 2010). The allostatic overload framework allows hypotheses to be generated for future experimental tests. Data from a variety of vertebrate taxa are also needed, from oceans to mountains, the poles, forests, and deserts to truly understand how responses to weather may have common mechanisms. Changes in hormone levels, such as corticosterone, when in a refuge or when on the move, and then during *recovery* will be critical. Also essential are data related to the physiological and behavioral patterns themselves. Such detailed quantitative (rather than anecdotal) observations are still few. It should also be noted that other hormones play a major role in orchestrating these facultative physiological and behavioral responses characteristic of the emergency life-history stage, although these too remain much less well known with the possible exception of the interrelationship of corticosterone and prolactin in the stress responses of breeding birds (Angelier and Chastel, 2009).

B. DIVERSITY OF MECHANISMS—FUTURE DIRECTIONS

Much remains to be revealed in the hormone–behavior interrelationships and ecological factors associated with coping with weather events. Do different species integrate the physiology and behavior of coping in similar or different ways and are similar control mechanisms in place? Other intriguing questions include: What are the environmental cues triggering changes in CBG, and genomic and membrane receptors in target cells associated with coping? Will global climate change increase environmental unpredictability, making phenotypic flexibility a critical factor in dealing with long-term changes in the environment? Will the highly plastic hormone–behavior interaction system underlying coping in relation to weather enable them to adjust? It is hoped that this chapter will have heuristic value in characterizing the phenomenon of hormone–behavior interactions and the natural history of coping with weather. The possibilities for truly integrative research from molecules to populations are challenging but are now within reach.

Acknowledgments

Much of the research conducted on weather and hormone responses to stress were supported by a series of grants from the National Science Foundation (most recent IOS-0750540), the Russell F. Stark University Professorship from the University of Washington, and an Endowment in Physiology from the University of California, Davis, to J. C. W. Both authors are extremely grateful to well over a hundred former undergraduate and graduate students, and postdoctoral fellows who contributed to the fieldwork in many of the studies cited and endured unpleasant weather to collect relevant samples and record novel behavior. We also thank the family of Professor Sievert Rohwer for permission to sample birds on their land on Whidbey Island.

References

Adams, N.J., Brown, C.R., 1990. Energetics of molt in penguins. In: Davis, L.S., Darby, J.T. (Eds.), Penguin Biology. Academic Press, San Diego, pp. 297–315.

Adams, N.J., Cockrem, J.F., Taylor, G.A., Candy, E.J., Bridges, J., 2005. Corticosterone responses of grey-faced petrels (*Pterodroma macroptera gouldi*) are higher during incubation than other breeding stages. Physiol. Zool. 78, 69–77.

Addison, B., Kitaysky, A.S., Hipfner, J.M., 2008. Sex allocation in a monomorphic seabird with a single-egg clutch: test of the environment hypothesis, mate quality, and female condition hypotheses. Behav. Ecol. Sociobiol. 63, 135–141.

Andreev, A.V., 1991a. Winter adaptation in the willow ptarmigan. Arctic 44, 106–114.

Andreev, A.V., 1991b. Winter habitat segregation in the sexually dimorphic black-billed capercaillie Tetrao urogalloides. Ornis Scand. 22, 287–291.

Andreev, A.V., 1999. Energetics and survival of birds in extreme environments. Ostrich 70, 13–22.

Angelier, F., Chastel, O., 2009. Stress, prolactin and parental investment in birds: a review. Gen. Comp. Endocrinol. 163, 142–148.

Angelier, F., Shaffer, S.A., Weimerskirch, H., Chastel, O., 2006. Effect of age, breeding experience and senescence on corticosterone and prolactin levels in a long-lived seabird: the wandering albatross. Gen. Comp. Endocrinol. 149, 1–9.

Angelier, F., Clément-Chastel, C., Gabrielsen, G.W., Chastel, O., 2007a. Corticosterone and time-activity budget: an experiment with black-legged kittiwakes. Horm. Behav. 52, 482–491.

Angelier, F., Schaffer, S.A., Weimerskirch, H., Trouve, C., Chastel, O., 2007b. Corticosterone and foraging behavior in a pelagic seabird. Physiol. Biochem. Zool. 80, 283–292.

Angelier, F., Weimerskirch, H., Dano, S., Chastel, O., 2007c. Age, experience and reproductive performance in a long-lived bird: a hormonal perspective. Behav. Ecol. Sociobiol. 61, 611–621.

Angelier, F., Bost, C.-A., Giraudeau, M., Bouteloup, G., Dano, S., Chastel, O., 2008. Corticosterone and foraging behavior in a diving seabird: the Adélie penguin, *Pygoscelis adeliae*. Gen. Comp. Endocrinol. 156, 134–144.

Angelier, F., Clément-Chastel, C., Welcker, J., Gabrielseb, G.W., Chastel, O., 2009a. How does corticosterone affect parental behavior and reproductive success? A study of prolactin in black-legged kittiwakes. Funct. Ecol. 23, 784–793.

Angelier, F., Moe, B., Blanc, S., Chastel, O., 2009b. What factors drive prolactin and corticosterone responses to stress in a long lived bird species (snow petrel *Pagodroma nivea*)? Physiol. Biochem. Zool. 82, 590–602.

Astheimer, L.B., Buttemer, W.A., Wingfield, J.C., 1992. Interactions of corticosterone with feeding, activity and metabolism in passerine birds. Ornis Scand. 23, 355–365.

Astheimer, L.B., Buttemer, W.A., Wingfield, J.C., 1994. Gender and seasonal differences in the adrenocortical response to ACTH challenge in an arctic passerine, *Zonotrichia leucophrys gambelii*. Gen. Comp. Endocrinol. 94, 33–43.

Astheimer, L.B., Buttemer, W.A., Wingfield, J.C., 1995. Seasonal and acute changes in adrenocortical responsiveness in an arctic-breeding bird. Horm. Behav. 29, 442–457.

Avery, M.I., Krebs, J.R., 1984. Temperature and foraging success of great tits, *Parus major*, hunting for spiders. Ibis 126, 33–38.

Axelrod, J., Reisine, T.D., 1984. Stress hormones: their interaction and regulation. Science 224, 452–459.

Barclay, R.M.R., Lausen, C.L., Hollis, L., 2001. What's hot and what's not: defining torpor in free-ranging birds and mammals. Can. J. Zool. 79, 1885–1890.

Barré, H., 1984. Metabolic and insulative changes in winter- and summer-acclimatized king penguin chicks. J. Comp. Physiol. 154, 317–324.

Beal, K.G., 1978. Temperature-dependent reduction of individual distance in captive house sparrows. Auk 95, 195–196.

Beaulieu, M., Dervaux, A., Thierry, A.-M., Lazin, D., Le Maho, Y., Ropert-Coudert, Y., et al., 2010. When sea-ice clock is ahead of Adélie penguin's clock. Funct. Ecol. 24, 93–102.

Benowitz-Fredericks, Z.M., Shultz, M.T., Kitaysky, A.S., 2008. Stress hormones suggest opposite trends of food availability for planktivorous and piscivorous seabirds in 2 years. Deep Sea Res. Part II 55, 1868–1876.

Bize, P., Klopfenstein, A., Jeanneret, C., Roulin, A., 2007. Intra-individual variation in body temperature and pectoral muscle size in nestling Alpine swifts *Apus melba* in response to an episode of inclement weather. J. Ornithol. 148, 387–393.

Boix-Hinzen, C., Lovegrove, B.G., 1998. Circadian metabolic and thermoregulatory patterns of red-billed woodhoopoes (*Phoeniculus purpureus*): the influence of huddling. J. Zool. (Lond.) 244, 33–41.

Bókony, V., Lendvai, A.Z., Liker, A., Angelier, F., Wingfield, J.C., Chastel, O., 2009. Stress response and the value of reproduction: are birds prudent parents? Am. Nat. 173, 589–598.

Bonier, F., Martin, P.R., Wingfield, J.C., 2007. Maternal corticosteroids influence primary offspring sex ratio in a free-ranging passerine bird. Behav. Ecol. 18, 1045–1050.

Bonier, F., Martin, P.R., Moore, I.T., Wingfield, J.C., 2009. Do baseline glucocorticoids predict fitness? Trends Ecol. Evol. 24, 634–642.

Braun, C.E., Martin, K., Robb, L.A., 1983. White-tailed ptarmigan (*Lagopus leucurus*). Poole, A., Gill, F. (Eds.), In: The Birds of North America, vol. 68. The Academy of Natural Sciences, Philadelphia Washington, DC; The American Ornithologists' Union.

Brenner, F.J., 1965. Metabolism and survival time of grouped starlings at various temperatures. Wilson Bull. 77, 388–395.

Breuner, C.W., Hahn, T.P., 2003. Integrating stress physiology, environmental change and behavior in free-living sparrows. Gen. Comp. Endocrinol. 43, 115–123.

Breuner, C.W., Orchinik, M., 2001. Seasonal regulation of membrane and intracellular corticosteroid receptors in the house sparrow brain. J. Neuroendocrinol. 13, 412–420.

Breuner, C.W., Orchinik, M., 2002. Plasma binding proteins as mediators of corticosteroid action in vertebrates. J. Endocrinol. 175, 99–112.

Breuner, C.W., Orchinik, M., Hahn, T.P., Meddle, S.L., Moore, I.T., Owen-Ashley, N.T., et al., 2003. Differential mechanisms for plasticity of the stress response across latitudinal gradients. Am. J. Physiol.: Regul. Integr. Comp. Physiol. 285, R594–R600.

Brigham, R.M., Barclay, R.M.R., 1992. Lunar influence on foraging and nesting activity of common poorwills (*Phalaenoptilus nuttallii*). Auk 109, 315–320.

Brigham, R.M., Körtner, G., Maddocks, T.A., Geiser, F., 2000. Seasonal use of torpor in free-ranging Australian owlet-nightjars (*Aegotheles cristatus*). Physiol. Biochem. Zool. 73, 613–620.

Brown, L.H., Britton, P.L., 1980. The Breeding Seasons of East African Birds. East Africa Nat. Hist. Soc, Nairobi, 164 pp.

Brown, C.R., Brown, M.B., Raouf, S.A., Smith, L.C., Wingfield, J.C., 2005a. Effects of endogenous steroid hormone levels on annual survival in cliff swallows. Ecology 86, 1034–1046.

Brown, C.R., Brown, M.B., Raouf, S.A., Smith, L.C., Wingfield, J.C., 2005b. Steroid hormone levels are related to choice of colony size in cliff swallows. Ecology 86, 2904–2915.

Buck, C.L., O'Reilly, K.M., Kildaw, S.D., 2007. Interannual variability of black-legged kittiwake productivity is reflected in baseline plasma corticosterone. Gen. Comp. Endocrinol. 150, 430–436.

Cain, J.R., Lien, R.J., 1985. A model for drought inhibition of bobwhite quail (*Colinus virginianus*) reproductive systems. Comp. Biochem. Physiol. 82A, 925–930.

Calder, W.A., King, J.R., 1974. Thermal and caloric relations of birds. Farner, D.S., King, J.R. (Eds.), In: Avian Biology, vol. 3. Academic Press, New York, pp. 259–413.

Calf, K., Adams, N., Slotow, R., 2002. Dominance and huddling behavior in bronze manikin *Lonchura cucullata* flocks. Ibis 144, 488–493.

Cameron-Macmilan, M.L., Walsh, C.J., Wilhelm, S.L., Storey, A.E., 2007. Males chicks are more costly to rear than females in a monogamous seabird, the common murre. Behav. Ecol. 18, 81–85.

Chaplin, S.B., 1982. The energetic significance of huddling behavior in common bushtits (*Psaltriparus minimus*). Auk 99, 424–430.

Chastel, O., Lacroix, A., Weimerskirch, H., Gabrielsen, G.W., 2005. Modulation of prolactin but not corticosterone responses to stress in relation to parental effort in a long-lived bird. Horm. Behav. 47, 459–466.

Cherel, Y., Le Maho, Y., 1985. Five months of fasting in king penguin chicks: body mass loss and fuel metabolism. Am. J. Physiol. 249, R387–R392.

Cherel, Y., Stahl, J.C., Le Maho, Y., 1987. Ecology and physiology of fasting in king penguin chicks. Auk 104, 254–262.

Cherel, Y., Robin, J.-P., Le Maho, Y., 1988. Physiology and biochemistry of long-term fasting in birds. Can. J. Zool. 66, 159–166.

Cockrem, J.F., Potter, M.A., Candy, E.J., 2006. Corticosterone in relation to body mass in Adelie penguins (*Pygoscelis adeliae*) affected by unusual sea ice conditions at Ross Island, Antarctica. Gen. Comp. Endocrinol. 149, 244–252.

Coppens, C.M., de Boer, S.F., Koolhaas, J.M., 2010. Coping styles and behavioral flexibility: towards underlying mechanisms. Philos. Trans. R. Soc. B 365, 4021–4028.

Corbel, H., Geiger, S., Groscolas, R., 2009. Preparing to fledge: the adrenocortical and metabolic responses to stress in king penguin chicks. Funct. Ecol. 24, 82–92.

Crespi, E.J., Denver, R.J., 2005. Ancient origins of human developmental plasticity. Am. J. Human Biol. 17, 44–54.

Csada, R.D., Brigham, R.M., 1992. Common poorwill, *Phalaenoptilus nuttalli*. Poole, A., Gill, F. (Eds.), In: The Birds of North America, vol. 32. The Academy of Natural Sciences, Philadelphia, Washington, DC; The American Ornithologists' Union.

Davidson, N.C., Evans, P.R., 1982. Mortality of redshanks and oystercatchers from starvation during severe weather. Bird Study 29, 183–188.

Dawson, R.D., Bortolotti, G.R., 2000. Reproductive success of American kestrels: the role of prey abundance and weather. Condor 102, 814–822.

Dawson, W.R., Hudson, J.W., 1970. Birds. Whittow, G.C. (Ed.), In: Comparative Physiology of Thermoregulation, vol. 1. Acad. Press, New York, pp. 233–310.

Dawson, W.R., Carey, C., Van't Hof, T.J., 1992. Metabolic aspects of shivering thermogenesis in passerines during winter. Ornis Scand. 23, 381–387.

Decker, K.L., Conway, C.J., 2009. Effects of an unseasonal storm on red-faced warbler nesting success. Condor 111, 392–395.

Deviche, P., Small, T.W., Sharp, P.J., Tsutsui, K., 2006. Control of luteinizing hormone and testosterone secretion in a flexibly breeding male passerine, the rufous-winged sparrow, *Aimophila carpalis*. Gen. Comp. Endocrinol. 149, 226–235.

DeWoskin, R., 1980. Heat exchange influence on foraging behavior of *Zonotrichia* flocks. Ecology 61, 30–36.

Dhabhar, F.S., 2002. A hassle a day may keep the doctor away: stress and the augmentation of immune function. Integr. Comp. Biol. 42, 556–564.

Dittami, J.P., 1986. Seasonal reproduction, molt and their endocrine correlates in two tropical Ploceidae species. J. Comp. Physiol. B 156, 641–647.

Dittami, J.P., 1987. A comparison of breeding and molt cycles and life histories in two tropical starling species: the blue-eared glossy starling, *Lamprotornis chalybaeus*, and Rüppell's long-tailed glossy starling, *L. purpuropterus*. Ibis 129, 69–85.

Dolby, A.S., Grubb, T.C., 1999. Effects of winter weather on horizontal and vertical use of isolated forest fragments by bark-foraging birds. Condor 101, 408–412.

Doody, L.M., Wilhelm, S.I., McKay, D.W., Walsh, C.J., Storey, A.E., 2008. The effects of variable foraging conditions on common murre (*Uria aalge*) corticosterone concentrations and parental provisioning. Horm. Behav. 53, 140–148.

Drent, R.H., 1972. Adaptive aspects of the physiology of incubation. In: Voous, K.H. (Ed.), Proceedings of the XV International Ornithological Congress. E.J. Brill, Leiden, Netherlands, pp. 255–280.

Drent, P.J., van Oers, K., van Noordwijk, A.J., 2003. Realized heritability of personalities in the great tit (*Parus major*). Proc. R. Soc. B 270, 45–51.

du Plessis, M.A., Williams, J.B., 1994. Communal cavity roosting in green woodhoopoes: consequences for energy expenditure and the seasonal pattern of mortality. Auk 111, 292–299.

du Plessis, M.A., Weathers, W.W., Koenig, W.D., 1994. Energetic benefits of communal roosting by acorn woodpeckers during the non-breeding season. Condor 96, 631–637.

Dunn, E.K., 1973. Changes in fishing ability of terns associated with wind speed and sea surface conditions. Nature 244, 520–521.

Edwards, J.S., 1987. Arthropods of alpine aeolian ecosystems. Annu. Rev. Entomol. 32, 163–179.

Edwards, J.S., Banko, P.C., 1976. Arthropod fallout and nutrient transport: a quantitative study of Alaskan snowpatches. Arct. Alp. Res. 8, 237–245.

Eeva, T., Lehikoinen, E., Rönkä, M., Lummaa, V., Currie, D., 2002. Different responses to cold weather in two pied flycatcher populations. Ecography 25, 705–713.

Elkins, N., 1983. Weather and Bird Behavior. Poyser Press, Calton, UK.

Enfield, D.B., 2001. Evolution and historical perspective of the 1997–1998 El Niño-Southern Oscillation event. Bull. Mar. Sci. 69, 7–25.

Ettinger, A.O., King, J.R., 1980. Time and energy budgets of the willow flycatcher (*Empidonax traillii*) during the breeding season. Auk 97, 533–546.

Evans, P.R., 1969. Winter fat deposition and overnight survival of yellow buntings (*Emberiza citrinella* L.). J. Anim. Ecol. 38, 415–423.

Evans, P.R., 1976. Energy balance and optimal foraging strategies in shorebirds: some implications for their distributions and movements in the non-breeding season. Ardea 64, 117–139.

Flemming, S.P., Smith, P.C., 1990. Environmental influences on osprey foraging in northeastern Nova Scotia. J. Raptor Res. 24, 64–67.

Formozov, A.N., 1946. Snow cover as an integral factor of the environment and its importance in the ecology of mammals and birds. In: New Series, Zoology, vol. 5. Moscow Soc. Natur, pp. 1–152, English translation, Occ. Papers No.1 (1963), Boreal Institute, University of Alberta, Edmonton.

Foster, M.S., 1974. Rain, feeding behavior, and clutch size in tropical birds. Auk 91, 722–726.

Gavrilova, O., Leon, L.R., Marcus-Samuels, B., Mason, M.M., Castle, A.L., Refetoffs, S., et al., 1999. Torpor in mice is induced by both leptin-dependent and -independent mechanisms. Proc. Natl. Acad. Sci. USA 96, 14623–14628.

Geiser, F., 1998. Evolution of daily torpor and hibernation in birds and mammals: importance of body size. Clin. Exp. Pharmacol. Physiol. 25, 736–740.

Geiser, F., 2010. Hibernation, daily torpor and aestivation in mammals and birds: behavioral aspects. In: Breed, M., Moore, J. (Eds.), Encyclopedia of Animal Behavior. Eslevier Press, New York.

Geleon, A., 1981. Modifications du comportement au cours du cycle annuel de l'oie landaise. Can. J. Zool. 63, 2810–2816.

Gessamen, J.A., Worthen, G.L., 1982. The Effects of Weather on Avian Mortality. Utah State University Printing Services, Logan, Ut.

Gibbs, H.R., Grant, P.R., 1987. Ecological consequences of an exceptionally strong El Niño event on Darwin's finches. Ecology 68, 1735–1746.

Gilbert, C., Robertson, G., Le Maho, Y., Naito, Y., Ancel, A., 2006. Huddling behavior in emperor penguins: dynamics of huddling. Physiol. Behav. 88, 479–488.

Gilbert, C., Le Maho, Y., Perret, M., Ancel, A., 2007. Body temperature changes induced by huddling in breeding male emperor penguins. Am. J. Physiol. Regul. Integr. Comp. Physiol. 292, R176–R185.

Gill, F.B., 1995. Ornithology. W.H. Freeman, New York, 766 pp.

Gluck, E.F., Stephens, N., Swoap, S.J., 2006. Peripheral ghrelin deepens torpor bouts in mice through the arcuate nucleus neuropeptide Y signaling pathway. Am. J. Physiol. Regul. Integr. Comp. Physiol. 291, R1303–R1309.

Goymann, W., Wingfield, J.C., 2004. Allostatic load, social status, and stress hormones—the costs of social status matter. Anim. Behav. 67, 591–602.

Grant, P.R., Grant, B.R., 1980. The breeding and feeding characteristics of Darwin's finches in Islas Galapagos. Ecol. Monogr. 50, 381–410.

Groscolas, R., Cherel, Y., 1992. How to molt while fasting in the cold: the metabolic and hormonal adaptations of Emperor and king penguins. Ornis Scand. 23, 328–334.

Groscolas, R., Robin, J.-P., 2001. Long-term fasting and re-feeding in penguins. Comp. Biochem. Physiol. A 128, 645–655.

Groscolas, R., Lacroix, A., Robin, J.-P., 2008. Spontaneous egg or chick abandonment in energy-depleted king penguins: a role for corticosterone and prolactin? Horm. Behav. 53, 51–60.

Grossman, A.F., West, G.W., 1977. Metabolic rate and temperature regulation of winter acclimatized black-capped chickadees, *Parus atricapillus*, of interior Alaska. Ornis Scand. 3, 127–138.

Grubb, T.C., 1973. Absence of "individual distance" in the tree swallow during adverse weather. Auk 90, 432–433.

Grubb, T.C., 1975. Weather-dependent foraging behavior of some birds wintering in a deciduous woodland. Condor 77, 175–182.

Grubb, T.C., 1977. Weather-dependent foraging in ospreys. Auk 94, 146–149.

Grubb, T.C., Greenwald, L., 1982. Sparrows and a brush pile: foraging responses to different combinations of predation risk and energy costs. Anim. Behav. 30, 637–640.

Hahn, T.P., Wingfield, J.C., Deviche, P., Mullen, R., 1995. Spatial and temporal opportunism in Arctic birds. Am. Zool. 35, 259–273.

Hannon, S.J., Eason, P.K., Martin, K., 1998. Willow ptarmigan (*Lagopus lagopus*). Poole, A., Gill, F. (Eds.), In: The Birds of North America, vol. 369. The Academy of Natural Sciences, Philadelphia, Washington, DC; The American Ornithologists' Union.

Harding, A.M.A., Kitaysky, A.S., Hall, M.E., Welsker, J., Karnovsky, N.J., Talbot, S.L., et al., 2009. Flexibility in the parental effort of an arctic-breeding seabird. Funct. Ecol. 23, 348–358.

Hart, B.L., 1988. Biological basis of the behavior of sick animals. Neurosci. Biobehav. Rev. 12, 123–137.

Hau, M., Ricklefs, R.E., Wikelski, M., Lee, K.A., Brawn, J.D., 2010. Corticosterone, testosterone and life history strategies of birds. Proc. R. Soc. Lond. B 277, 3203–3212.

Heidinger, B.J., Nisbet, I.C.T., Ketterson, E.D., 2006. Older parents are less responsive to a stressor in a long-lived seabird: a mechanism for increased reproductive performance with age? Proc. R. Soc. B 273, 2227–2231.

Heidinger, B.J., Nisbet, I.C.T., Ketterson, E.D., 2008. Changes in adrenal capacity contribute to a decline in the stress response with age in a long-lived seabird. Gen. Comp. Endocrinol. 156, 564–568.

Hendricks, P., 2009. Snow bathing by house finches: a review of this behavior by North American birds. Wilson J. Ornithol. 121, 834–838.

Hiebert, S.M., 1993. Seasonal changes in body mass and use of torpor in a migratory hummingbird. Auk 110, 787–797.

Hiebert, S.M., Ramenofsky, M., Salvante, K., Wingfield, J.C., Gass, C.L., 2000a. Non-invasive methods for measuring and manipulating corticosterone in hummingbirds. Gen. Comp. Endocrinol. 120, 235–247.

Hiebert, S.M., Salvante, K.G., Ramenofsky, M., Wingfield, J.C., 2000b. Corticosterone and nocturnal torpor in the rufous hummingbird (*Selasphorus rufus*). Gen. Comp. Endocrinol. 120, 220–234.

Hiebert, S.M., Wingfield, J.C., Ramenofsky, M., Deni, L., 2004. Sex differences in the response of torpor to exogenous corticosterone during the onset of the migratory season in rufous hummingbirds. Barnes, B.M., Carey, H.V. (Eds.), Life in the Cold: Evolution, Mechanisms, Adaptation and Application. In: Twelfth International Hibernation Symposium, Institute of Arctic Biology, University of Alaska Fairbanks, AK, USA, pp. 221–230.

Hiraldo, F., Veiga, J.P., Mañez, M., 1990. Growth of nestling black kites, *Milvus nigrans*: effects of hatching order, weather and season. J. Zool. (Lond.) 222, 197–214.

Holberton, R., Wingfield, J.C., 2003. Modulating the corticosterone stress response: a mechanism for balancing risk and reproductive success in arctic breeding sparrows? Auk 120, 1140–1150.

Holder, K., Montgomerie, R., 1993. Rock ptarmigan (*Lagopus mutus*). Poole, A., Gill, F. (Eds.), In: The Birds of North America, vol. 51. The Academy of Natural Sciences, Philadelphia Washington, DC; The American Ornithologists' Union.

Irving, L., 1972. Arctic Life of Birds and Mammals Including Man. In: Zoophysiol Ecology, vol. 2. Springer Verlag, Berlin, 192 pp.

Jacobs, J.D., 1996. Regulation of Life History Strategies Within Individuals in Predictable and Unpredictable Environments. Ph.D. Thesis: University of Washington.

Jacobs, J.D., Wingfield, J.C., 2000. Endocrine control of lifecycle stages: a constraint on response to the environment? Condor 102, 35–51.

Jenni-Eiermann, S., Glaus, E., Grüebler, M., Schwabl, H., Jenni, L., 2008. Glucocorticoid response to food availability in breeding barn swallows (*Hirundo rustica*). Gen. Comp. Endocrinol. 155, 558–565.

Johnson, H.M., 1954. Winter microclimates of importance to Alaskan small mammals and birds. Ph.D. Thesis, Cornell Univ. New York.

Ketterson, E.D., King, J.R., 1977. Metabolic and behavioral responses to fasting in the white-crowned sparrow (*Zonotrichia leucophrys*). Physiol. Zool. 50, 115–129.

Kissner, K.J., Brigham, R.M., 1993. Evidence for the use of torpor by incubating and brooding common poorwills, *Phalaenoptilus nuttallii*. Ornis Scand. 24, 333–334.

Kitaysky, A.S., Wingfield, J.C., Piatt, J.F., 1999. Dynamics of food availability, body condition and physiological stress response in breeding black-legged kittiwakes. Funct. Ecol. 13, 577–584.

Kitaysky, A.S., Kitaiskaia, E.V., Piatt, J.F., Wingfield, J.C., 2003. Benefits and costs of increased levels of corticosterone in seabird chicks. Horm. Behav. 43, 140–149.

Kitaysky, A.S., Romano, M.D., Piatt, J.F., Wingfield, J.C., Kikuchi, M., 2005. The adrenocortical response of tufted puffin chicks to nutritional deficits. Horm. Behav. 47, 606–619.

Kitaysky, A.S., Piatt, J.F., Wingfield, J.C., 2007. Stress hormones link food availability and population processes in seabirds. Mar. Ecol. Prog. Ser. 352, 245–258.

Kitaysky, A.S., Piatt, J.F., Hatch, S.A., Kitaiskaia, E.V., Benowitz-Fredericks, Z.M., Shultz, M.T., et al., 2010. Food availability and population processes: severity of nutritional stress during reproduction predicts survival of long-lived seabirds. Funct. Ecol. 24, 625–637.

Koolhaas, J.M., Korte, S.M., Bper, S.F., Van Der Vegt, D.J., Van Renen, C.G., Hopster, H., et al., 1999. Coping styles in animals: current status in behavior and stress-physiology. Neurosci. Biobehav. Rev. 23, 925–935.

Koolhaas, J.M., de Boer, S.F., Buwalda, B., van Reenen, K., 2007. Individual variation in coping with stress: a multidimensional approach of ultimate and proximate mechanisms. Brain Behav. Evol. 70, 218–226.

Korhonen, K., 1980. Microclimate in the snow burrows of willow grouse (*Lagopus lagopus*). Ann. Zool. Fenn. 17, 5–9.

Korhonen, K., 1981. Temperature in the nocturnal shelters of the redpoll (*Acanthis flammea* L.) and the Siberian tit (*Parus cinctus* Budd.) in winter. Ann. Zool. Fenn. 18, 165–167.

Korte, S.M., Koolhaas, J.M., Wingfield, J.C., McEwen, B.S., 2005. The Darwinian concept of stress: benefits of allostasis and costs of allostatic load and the trade-offs in health and disease. Neurosci. Biobehav. Rev. 29, 3–38.

Körtner, G., Brigham, R.M., Geiser, F., 2001. Torpor in free-ranging tawny frogmouths (*Podargus strigoides*). Physiol. Biochem. Zool. 74, 789–797.

Lack, D., 1950. Breeding season in the Galapagos. Ibis 92, 268–278.

Lanctot, R.B., Hatch, S.A., Gill, V.A., Eens, M., 2003. Are corticosterone levels a good indicator of food availability and reproductive performance in a kittiwake colony? Horm. Behav. 43, 489–502.

Landys, M., Ramenofsky, M., Wingfield, J.C., 2006. Actions of glucocorticoids at a seasonal baseline as compared to stress-related levels in the regulation of periodic life processes. Gen. Comp. Endocrinol. 148, 132–149.

Laurie, W.A., 1989. Glynn, P. (Ed.), Global Ecological Consequences of the 1982–1983 El Niño-Southern Oscillation. Elsevier Press, New York, pp. 121–141.

Le Maho, Y., 1983. Metabolic adaptations to long term fasting in Antarctic penguins and domestic geese. J. Therm. Biol 8, 91–96.

Le Maho, Y., Delclitte, P., Chatonnet, J., 1976. Thermoregulation in fasting penguins under natural conditions. Am. J. Physiol. 231, 913–922.

Le Maho, Y., Kha, V.V., Koubi, H., Dewasmes, G., Girard, J., Ferre, P., et al., 1981. Body composition, energy expenditure, and plasma metabolites in long-term fasting geese. Am. J. Physiol. 241, E342–E354.

Lewis, D.M., 1982. Cooperative breeding in a population of white-browed sparrow weavers, *Plocepasser mahali*. Ibis 124, 511–522.

Ligon, J.D., 1970. Still more responses of the poor-will to low temperatures. Condor 72, 496–498.

Lobato, E., Merino, S., Moreno, J., Morales, J., Tomás, G., Martínez-de la Puente, J., et al., 2008. Corticosterone metabolites in blue tit and pied flycatcher droppings: effects of brood size, ectoparasites and temperature. Horm. Behav. 53, 295–305.

Lynn, S.E., Breuner, C.W., Wingfield, J.C., 2003. Short-term fasting affects locomotor activity, corticosterone, and corticosterone-binding globulin in a migratory songbird. Horm. Behav. 43, 150–157.

Machmer, M.M., Ydenberg, R.C., 1990. Weather and osprey foraging energetics. Can. J. Zool. 68, 40–43.

Marsh, R.L., 1980. Development of temperature regulation in nestling tree swallows. Condor 82, 461–463.

Marshall Jr., J.T., 1963. Rainy season nesting in Arizona. In: Proceedings of the XIIIth International Ornithological Congress, 620–622.

Martin, L.B.I.I., Rubenstein, D.R., 2008. Stress hormones in tropical birds: patterns and future directions. Ornithol. Neotropical 19 (Suppl.), 207–218.

Martin, K., Wiebe, K.L., 2004. Coping mechanisms of alpine and Arctic breeding birds: extreme weather and limitations to reproductive resilience. Integr. Comp. Biol. 44, 177–185.

McEwen, B., 2000. Allostasis and allostatic load: implications for neuropsychopharmacology. Neuropsychopharmacology 22, 108–124.

McEwen, B.S., 2006. Protective and damaging of stress mediators: central role of the brain. Dialouges Clin. Neurosci. 8, 367–381.

McEwen, B.S., Wingfield, J.C., 2003. The concept of allostasis in biology and biomedicine. Horm. Behav. 43, 2–15.

McEwen, B.S., Wingfield, J.C., 2010. What is in a name? Integrating homeostasis, allostasis and stress. Horm. Behav. 57, 105–111.

McKechnie, A.E., Lovegrove, B.G., 2001. Thermoregulation and the energetic significance of clustering behavior in the white-backed mousebird (Colius colius). Physiol. Biochem. Zool. 74, 238–249.

McKechnie, A.E., Lovegrove, B.G., 2002. Avian facultative hypothermic responses: a review. Condor 104, 705–724.

McKechnie, A.E., Ashdown, R.A.M., Christian, M.B., Brigham, R.M., 2007. Torpor in an African caprimulgid, the freckled nightjar, Caprimulgus tristigma. J. Avian Biol. 38, 261–266.

McQueen, S.M., Davis, L.S., Young, G., 1999. Sex steroid and corticosterone levels of Adélie penguins (Pygoscelis adeliae) during courtship and incubation. Gen. Comp. Endocrinol. 114, 11–18.

Mercer, J.B., Simon, E., 1987. Appropriate and inappropriate hypothalamic cold thermosensitivity in willow ptarmigan. Acta Physiol. Scand. 131, 73–80.

Merola-Zwartjes, M., Ligon, J.D., 2000. Ecological energetics of the Puerto Rican tody: heterothermy, torpor, and intra-island variation. Ecology 81, 990–1003.

Meservey, W.R., Kraus, G.F., 1976. Absence of "individual distance" in three swallow species. Auk 93, 177–178.

Miller, A.H., 1963. Desert adaptations in birds. In: Proceedings of the XIIIth International Ornithological Congress, 666–674.

Mrosovsky, N., Sherry, D.F., 1980. Animal anorexias. Science 207, 837–842.

Munck, A., Guyre, P., Holbrook, N., 1984. Physiological functions of glucocorticosteroids in stress and their relation to pharmacological actions. Endocr. Rev. 5, 25–44.

Navarro, J., González-Solis, J., Viscor, G., Chastel, O., 2008. Ecophysiological response to an experimental increase of wing loading in a pelagic seabird. J. Exp. Mar. Biol. Ecol. 358, 14–19.

Nelson, R.J., 2004. Leptin: the "skinny" on torpor. Am. J. Physiol. Regul. Integr. Comp. Physiol. 287, R6–R7.

Newton, I., 1986. Population regulation in sparrowhawks. J. Anim. Ecol. 55, 463–480.

Newton, I., 1998. Population Limitation in Birds. Academic Press, Boston.

Novikov, G.A., 1972. The use of under-snow refuges among small birds of the sparrow family. Aquilo Ser. Zool. 13, 95–97.

O'Reilly, K.M., Wingfield, J.C., 1995. Spring and autumn migration in Arctic shorebirds: same distance, different strategies. Am. Zool. 35, 222–233.

Øverli, Ø., Sørenson, C., Pulman, K.G.T., Pottinger, T.G., Korzan, W., Summers, C.H., et al., 2007. Evolutionary background for stress-coping styles: relationships between physiological, behavioral, and cognitive traits in non-mammalian vertebrates. Neurosci. Biobehav. Rev. 31, 396–412.

Owen-Ashley, N.T., Turner, M., Hahn, T.P., Wingfield, J.C., 2006. Hormonal, behavioral, and thermoregulatory responses to bacterial lipopolysaccharide in captive and free-living white-crowned sparrows (*Zonotrichia leucophrys gambelii*). Horm. Behav. 49, 15–19.

Pereyra, M.E., Wingfield, J.C., 2003. Changes in plasma corticosterone and adrenocortical responses to stress during the breeding cycle in high altitude flycatchers. Gen. Comp. Endocinol. 130, 222–231.

Perfito, N., Schirato, G., Brown, M., Wingfield, J.C., 2002. Response to acute stress in the harlequin duck (*Histronicus histronicus*) during the breeding season and moult: relationships to gender, condition and life history stage. Can. J. Zool. 80, 1334–1343.

Perfito, N., Bentley, G., Hau, M., 2006. Tonic activation of brain GnRH immunoreactivity despite reduction of peripheral reproductive parameters in opportunistically breeding zebra finches. Brain Behav. Evol. 67, 123–134.

Perfito, N., Zann, R.A., Bentley, G.E., Hau, M., 2007. Opportunism at work: habitat predictability affects reproductive readiness in free-living zebra finches. Funct. Ecol. 21, 291–301.

Perfito, N., Kwong, J.M.Y., Bentley, G.E., Hau, M., 2008. Cue hierarchies and testicular development: is food a more potent stimulus than day length in an opportunistic breeder (*Taenopygia g. guttata*)? Horm. Behav. 53, 567–572.

Perrins, C.M., 1979. British Tits. Collins Co. Ltd., London, 304 pp.

Pielou, E.G., 1994. A Naturalist's Guide to the Arctic. University of Chicago, Chicago 327 pp..

Piersma, T., 1994. Close to the edge: energetic bottlenecks and the evolution of migratory pathways in knots. Ph.D. Thesis, Rijksuniversiteit Groningen, 366 pp. Published by Uitgeverij Het Open Boek, Texel, Netherlands.

Pravosudov, V.V., 2003. Long-term moderate elevation of corticosterone facilitates avian food-caching behavior and enhances memory. Proc. R. Soc. Lond. B 270, 2599–2604.

Pravosudov, V.V., 2005. Corticosterone and memory in birds. In: Dawson, A., Sharp, P.J. (Eds.), Functional Avian Endocrinology. Narosa Press, New Delhi, pp. 271–284.

Pravosudov, V.V., Kitaysky, A.S., Wingfield, J.C., Clayton, N.S., 2001. Long-term unpredictable foraging conditions and physiological stress responses in mountain chickadees (*Poecile gambeli*). Gen. Comp. Endocrinol. 123, 324–331.

Pravosudov, V.V., Kitaysky, A.S., Saldanha, C., Wingfield, J.C., Clayton, N.S., 2002. The effects of photoperiod on adrenocortical stress response in mountain chickadees (*Poecile gambeli*). Gen. Comp. Endocrinol. 126, 242–248.

Pravosudov, V.V., Mendoza, S.P., Clayton, N.S., 2003. The relationship between dominance, corticosterone, memory, and food caching in mountain chickadees (*Poecile gambeli*). Horm. Behav. 44, 93–102.

Pruitt Jr., W.O., 1970. Some ecological aspects of snow. In: Ecology of the Subarctic Regions. United Nations Educational Scientific and Cultural Organization, Paris, pp. 83–99.

Pruitt Jr., W.O., 1978. Boreal Ecology. Edward Arnold Ltd., London, 73 pp.

Pruitt Jr., W.O., 2005. Why and how to study a snowcover. Can. Field Nat. 119, 118–128.

Putaala, A., Hohtola, E., Hissa, R., 1995. The effect of group size on metabolism in huddling grey partridge (*Perdix perdix*). Comp. Biochem. Physiol. 111B, 243–247.

Ramenofsky, M., Gray, J., Johnson, R., 1992. Behavioral and physiological adjustments of birds living in winter flocks. Ornis Scand. 23, 371–380.

Ramenofsky, M., Agatsuma, R., Ramfar, T., 2008a. Environmental conditions affect the behavior of captive migratory white-crowned sparrows. Condor 110, 658–671.

Ramenofsky, M., Moffat, J., Bentley, G.E., 2008b. Corticosterone and migratory behavior of captive white-crowned sparrows. In: Morris, S., Vosloo, A. (Eds.), Molecules to Migration: The Pressures of Life. Medimond Publishing Co., via Maserati 6/2, 40124 Bologna, Italy, pp. 575–582.

Raouf, S.A., Smith, L.C., Brown, M.B., Wingfield, J.C., Brown, C.R., 2006. Glucocorticoid hormone levels increase with group size and parasite load in cliff swallows. Anim. Behav. 71, 39–48.

Redpath, S.M., Arroyo, B.E., Etheridge, B., Leckie, F., Bouwman, K., Thirgood, S.J., 2002. Temperature and hen harrier productivity: from local mechanisms to geographical patterns. Ecography 25, 535–540.

Reinertsen, R.E., 1983. Nocturnal hypothermia and its energetic significance for small birds living in the arctic and subarctic regions. A review. Polar Res. 1, 269–284.

Reinertsen, R.E., Haftorn, S., 1983. Nocturnal hypothermia and metabolism in the willow tit *Parus montanus* at 63°N. J. Comp. Physiol. 151, 109–118.

Reneerkens, J., Morrison, R.I.G., Ramenofsky, M., Piersma, T., Wingfield, J.C., 2002a. Baseline and stress-induced levels of corticosterone during different life cycle stages in a shore bird on the high Arctic breeding grounds. Physiol. Biochem. Zool. 75, 200–208.

Reneerkens, J., Piersma, T., Ramenofsky, M., 2002b. An experimental test of the relationship between temporal variability of feeding opportunities and baseline levels of corticosterone in a shorebird. J. Exp. Zool. 293, 81–88.

Richdale, L.E., 1945. Supplementary notes on the diving petrel. Trans. R. Soc. NZ 75, 42–53.

Ricklefs, R.E., Hainsworth, F.R., 1968. Temperature dependent behavior of the cactus wren. Ecology 49, 227–233.

Ricklefs, R.E., Reed-Hainsworth, F.R., 1969. Temperature regulation in nestling cactus wrens: the nest environment. Condor 71, 32–37.

Robin, J.-P., Boucontet, L., Chilet, P., Groscolas, R., 1998. Behavioral changes in fasting emperor penguins: evidence for a "re-feeding" signal linked to a metabolic shift. Am. J. Physiol. 43, R746–R753.

Rogers, C.M., Ramenofsky, M., Ketterson, E.D., Nolan Jr., V., Wingfield, J.C., 1993. Plasma corticosterone, adrenal mass, winter weather, and season in non-breeding populations of dark-eyed juncos (*Junco hyemalis hyemalis*). Auk 110, 279–285.

Rohwer, S., Wingfield, J.C., 1981. A field study of social dominance; plasma levels of luteinizing hormone and steroid hormones in wintering Harris' sparrows. Z. Tierpsychol. 47, 173–183.

Romero, L.M., 2002. Seasonal changes in plasma glucocorticoid concentrations in free-living vertebrates. Gen. Comp. Endocrinol. 128, 1–24.

Romero, L.M., Wingfield, J.C., 1998. Seasonal changes in adrenal sensitivity alter corticosterone levels in Gambel's white-crowned sparrows (*Zonotrichia leucophrys gambelii*). Comp. Biochem. Physiol. 119C, 31–36.

Romero, L.M., Wingfield, J.C., 1999. Alterations in hypothalamic-pituitary-adrenal function associated with captivity in Gambel's white-crowned sparrows (*Zonotrichia leucophrys gambelii*). Comp. Biochem. Physiol. B 122, 13–20.

Romero, L.M., Ramenofsky, M., Wingfield, J.C., 1997. Season and migration alters the corticosterone response to capture and handling in an arctic migrant, the white-crowned sparrow (*Zonotrichia leucophrys gambelii*). Comp. Biochem. Physiol. 116C, 171–177.

Romero, L.M., Reed, J.M., Wingfield, J.C., 2000. Effects of weather on corticosterone responses in wild free-living passerine birds. Gen. Comp. Endocrinol. 118, 113–122.

Romero, L.M., Dickens, M.J., Cyr, N.E., 2009. The reactive scope model—a new model integrating homeostasis, allostasis and stress. Horm. Behav. 55, 375–389.

Ropelewski, C.F., Halpert, M.S., 1987. Global and regional scale precipitation patterns associated with the El Niño/southern oscillation. Monthly Weather Rev. 115, 1606–1626.

Rotenberry, J.T., Wiens, J.A., 1991. Weather and reproductive variation in shrubsteppe sparrows: a hierarchical analysis. Ecology 72, 1325–1335.

Rubenstein, D.R., 2007. Stress hormones and sociality: integrating social and environmental stressors. Proc. R. Soc. B 274, 967–975.

Saether, B.E., Tufto, J., Engen, S., Jerstad, K., Røstad, O.W., Skåtan, J.E., 2000. Population dynamical consequences of climate change for a small temperate songbird. Science 287, 854–856.

Saldanha, C.J., Schlinger, B.A., Clayton, N.S., 2000. Rapid effects of corticosterone on cache recovery in mountain chickadees (*Parus gambeli*). Horm. Behav. 37, 109–115.

Sapolsky, R.M., 1987. Stress, social status, and reproductive physiology in free-living baboons. In: Crews, D. (Ed.), Psychobiology of Reproductive Behavior, An Evolutionary Perspective. Prentice-Hall, New Jersey, pp. 291–322.

Sapolsky, R.M., 2002. Endocrinology of the stress response. In: Becker, J.B., Breedlove, S.M., Crews, D., McCarthy, M.M. (Eds.), Behavioral Endocrinology. 2nd edition MIT Press, Cambridge MA, London UK, pp. 409–450.

Sapolsky, R.M., Romero, L.M., Munck, A.U., 2000. How do glucocorticosteroids influence stress responses? Integrating permissive, suppressive, stimulatory, and preparative actions. Endocr. Rev. 21, 55–89.

Schulkin, J., 2003. Rethinking Homeostasis. Allostatic regulation in physiology and pathophysiology. MIT Press, Cambridge.

Schwabl, H., Wingfield, J.C., Farner, D.S., 1985. Influence of winter on behavior and endocrine state in European blackbirds (*Turdus merula*). Z. Tierpsychol. 68, 244–252.

Scott, I., Evans, P.R., 1992. The metabolic output of avian (*Sturnus vulgaris, Calidris alpina*) adipose tissue liver and skeletal muscle: implications for BMR/body mass relationships. Comp. Biochem. Physiol. 103A, 329–332.

Sealy, S.G., 1966. Swallow mortality at Moose Mountain. Blue Jay 24, 17–18.

Sergio, F., 2003. From individual behavior to population pattern: weather-dependent foraging and breeding performance in black kites. Anim. Behav. 66, 1109–1117.

Sharbaugh, S.M., 2001. Seasonal acclimatization to extreme climatic conditions by black-capped chickadees (*Poecile atricapilla*) in interior Alaska (64°N). Physiol. Biochem. Zool. 74, 568–575.

Shultz, M.T., Kitaysky, A.S., 2008. Spatial and temporal dynamics of corticosterone and corticosterone—binding globulin are driven by environmental heterogeneity. Gen. Comp. Endocrinol. 155, 717–728.

Sih, A., Bell, A., Johnson, J.C., 2004. Behavioral syndromes: an ecological and evolutionary overview. Trends Ecol. Evol. 19, 372–378.

Silverin, B., Wingfield, J.C., 2010. Wintering strategies. In: Breed, M., Moore, J. (Eds.), Encyclopedia of Animal Behavior. Elsevier press, London.

Silverin, B., Wingfield, J.C., Stokkan, K.-A., Massa, R., Järvinen, A., Anderson, N.Å., et al., 2008. Ambient temperature effects on photo-induced gonadal cycles and hormonal secretion patterns in great tits from three different breeding latitudes. Horm. Behav. 54, 60–68.

Small, T.W., Sharp, P.J., Deviche, P., 2007. Environmental regulation of the reproductive system in a flexibly breeding Sonoran Desert bird, the rufous-winged sparrow, *Aimophila carpalis*. Horm. Behav. 51, 483–495.

Smith, S.M., 1972. Roosting aggregations of bushtits in response to cold temperatures. Condor 74, 478–479.

Smith, G.T., Wingfield, J.C., Veit, R.R., 1994. Adrenocortical response to stress in the common diving-petrel, *Pelecanoides urinatrix*. Physiol. Zool. 67, 526–537.

Sprague, R.S., 2009. Glucocorticoid physiology and behavior during life history transitions in Laysan albatross (*Phoebastria immutabilis*). Ph.D. Thesis, Univ. Montana, Missoula. 89 pp.

Steen, J., 1958. Climatic adaptation in some small northern birds. Ecology 39, 625–629.

Steenhof, K., Kochert, M.N., McDonald, T.L., 1997. Interactive effects of prey and weather on golden eagle reproduction. J. Anim. Ecol. 66, 350–362.

Sterling, P., Eyer, J., 1988. Allostasis: a new paradigm to explain arousal pathology. In: Fisher, S., Reason, J. (Eds.), Handbook of Life Stress, Cognition and Health. John Wiley & Sons, New York, pp. 629–649.

Stokkan, K.-A., 1992. Energetics and adaptations to cold in ptarmigan in winter. Ornis Scand. 23, 366–370.

Stokkan, K.-A., Sharp, P.J., Unander, S., 1986. The annual breeding cycle of the high arctic Svalbard Ptarmigan (*Lagopus mutus hyperboreus*). Gen. Comp. Endocrinol. 61, 446–451.

Storey, K.B., 2001. Turning down the fires of life: metabolic regulation of hibernation and estivation. In: Storey, K.B. (Ed.), Molecular Mechanisms of Metabolic Arrest. BIOS Sci. Publ., Oxford, pp. 1–21.

Strand, C.R., Small, T.W., Deviche, P., 2007. Plasticity of the rufous-winged sparrow, *Aimophila carpalis*, song control regions during the monsoon-associated summer breeding period. Horm. Behav. 52, 401–408.

Streich, W.J., Litzbarski, H., Ludwig, B., Ludwig, S., 2006. What triggers facultative winter migration of great bustards (*Otis tarda*) in Central Europe? Eur. J. Wildl. Res. 52, 48–53.

Sulkava, S., 1969. On small birds spending the night in the snow. Aquilo Series Zool 7, 33–37.

Swenson, J.E., Olssen, B., 1991. Hazel grouse night roost site preferences when snow-roosting is not possible in winter. Ornis Scand. 22, 284–286.

Tarlow, E.M., Hau, M., Anderson, D.J., Wikelski, M., 2003. Diel changes in plasma melatonin and corticosterone concentrations in tropical Nazca boobies (*Sula granti*) in relation to moon phase and age. Gen. Comp. Endocrinol. 133, 297–304.

Tieleman, B.I., Williams, J.B., Buschur, M.E., 2002. Physiological adjustments to arid and mesic environments in larks (Alaudidae). Physiol. Zool. 75, 305–313.

Tielemann, B.I., 2002. Avian adaptation along an aridity gradient. Ph.D. Thesis, University of Groningen, The Netherlands, 366 pp.

Travis, J.M.J., 2003. Climate change and habitat destruction: a deadly anthropogenic cocktail. Proc. R. Soc. Lond. B 270, 467–473.

Trenberth, K.E., 1997. The definition of El Niño. Bull. Am. Meteorol. Soc. 78, 2771–2777.

Van Hierden, Y.M., Korte, S.M., Ruesink, E.W., van Reenen, C.G., Engel, B., Korte-Bouws, A.H., et al., 2002. Adrenocortical reactivity and central serotonin and dopamine turnover in young chicks from a high and low feather-pecking line of laying hens. Physiol. Behav. 75, 653–659.

Veit, R., Hunt Jr., G.L., 1991. Broad scale density and aggregation of pelagic birds from a circumnavigational survey of the Antarctic Ocean. Auk 108, 790–800.

Vickery, W.L., Millar, J.S., 1984. The energetics of huddling by endotherms. Oikos 43, 88–93.

Vleck, C.M., 1993. Hormones, reproduction, and behavior in birds of the Sonoran Desert. In: Sharp, P.J. (Ed.), Avian Endocrinology. Journal of Endocrinology Ltd., Bristol, pp. 73–86.

Vleck, C.M., Priedkalns, J., 1985. Reproduction in zebra finches: hormone levels and effect of dehydration. Condor 87, 37–46.

Vleck, C.M., Vleck, D., 2002. Physiological and reproductive consequences in Adélie Penguins. Integr. Comp. Biol. 42, 76–83.

Walls, S.S., Kenward, R.E., Holloway, G.J., 2005. Weather to disperse? Evidence that climatic conditions influence vertebrate dispersal. J. Anim. Ecol. 74, 190–197.

Walsberg, G.E., 1990. Communal roosting in a very small bird: consequences for the thermal and respiratory gas environments. Condor 92, 795–798.

Wang, P.C., Wolowyk, M.W., 1988. Torpor in mammals and birds. Can. J. Zool. 66, 133–137.

Warham, J., 1996. The behavior, population biology and physiology of the petrels. Academic Press, New York, London, 613 pp.

Weatherhead, P.J., Sealy, S.G., Barclay, R.M.R., 1985. Risks of clustering in thermally-stressed swallows. Condor 87, 443–444.

Welty, J.C., Baptista, L., 1988. The Life of Birds. W.B. Saunders, New York, 581 pp.

White, F.N., Bartholomew, G.A., Howell, T.R., 1975. The thermal significance of the nest of the sociable weaver *Philetairus socius*: winter observations. Ibis 117, 171–179.

Wikelski, M., Trillmich, F., 1997. Body size and sexual size dimorphism in marine iguanas fluctuate as a result of opposing natural and sexual selection: an island comparison. Evolution 51, 922–936.

Williams, T.D., 2008. Individual variation in endocrine systems: moving beyond the tyranny of the "Golden Mean" Philos. Trans. R. Soc. Lond. B. Biol. Sci. 363, 1687–1698.

Williams, J.B., Tieleman, B.I., 2001. Physiological ecology and behavior of desert birds. In: Nolan, V., Thompson, C.F. (Eds.), Current Ornithology, vol. 16. Plenum Press, New York, pp. 299–353.

Williams, C.T., Kitaysky, A.S., Kettle, A.B., Buck, C.L., 2008. Corticosterone levels of tufted puffins vary with breeding stage, body condition index and reproductive performance. Gen. Comp. Endocrinol. 158, 29–35.

Wilson, E.O., 1975. Sociobiology. Belknapp Press, Cambridge, MA.

Wilson, S., Norris, D.R., Wilson, A.G., Arcese, P., 2007. Breeding experience and population density affect the ability of a songbird to respond to future climate variation. Proc. R. Soc. B 274, 2539–2545.

Wingfield, J.C., 1980. Fine temporal adjustment of reproductive functions. In: Epple, A., Stetson, M.H. (Eds.), Avian Endocrinology. Academic Press, New York, pp. 367–389.

Wingfield, J.C., 1983. Environmental and endocrine control of reproduction: an ecological approach. In: Mikami, S.-I., Wada, M. (Eds.), Avian Endocrinology: Environmental and Ecological Aspects. Japanese Scientific Societies Press, Tokyo, pp. 205–288. Springer-Verlag, Berlin.

Wingfield, J.C., 1984. Influences of weather on reproduction. J. Exp. Zool. 232, 589–594.

Wingfield, J.C., 1985a. Influences of weather on reproductive function in male song sparrows, *Melospiza melodia*. J. Zool. (Lond.) 205, 525–544.

Wingfield, J.C., 1985b. Influences of weather on reproductive function in female song sparrows, *Melospiza melodia*. J. Zool. (Lond.) 205, 545–558.

Wingfield, J.C., 1988. Changes in reproductive function of free-living birds in direct response to environmental perturbations. In: Stetson, M.H. (Ed.), Processing of Environmental Information in Vertebrates. Springer-Verlag, Berlin, pp. 121–148.

Wingfield, J.C., 1994. Modulation of the adrenocortical response to stress in birds. In: Davey, K.G., Peter, R.E., Tobe, S.S. (Eds.), Perspectives in Comparative Endocrinology. National Research Council Canada, Ottawa, pp. 520–528.

Wingfield, J.C., 2003. Control of behavioral strategies for capricious environments. Anim. Behav. 66, 807–816.

Wingfield, J.C., 2004. Allostatic load and life cycles: implications for neuroendocrine mechanisms. In: Schulkin, J. (Ed.), Allostasis, Homeostasis and the Costs of Physiological Adaptation. Cambridge University Press, Cambridge, pp. 302–342.

Wingfield, J.C., 2006. Communicative behaviors, hormone-behavior interactions, and reproduction in vertebrates. In: Neill, J.D. (Ed.), Physiology of Reproduction. Academic Press, New York, pp. 1995–2040.

Wingfield, J.C., 2008. Organization of vertebrate annual cycles: implications for control mechanisms. Philos. Trans. R. Soc. B 363, 425–441.

Wingfield, J.C., Farner, D.S., 1978. The endocrinology of a naturally breeding population of the white-crowned sparrow (Zonotrichia leucophrys pugetensis). Physiol. Zool. 51, 188–205.

Wingfield, J.C., Jacobs, J.D., 1999. The interplay of innate and experiential factors regulating the life history cycle of birds. In: Adams, N., Slotow, R. (Eds.), Proceedings of the 22nd International Ornithological Congress. BirdLife South Africa, Johannesburg, pp. 2417–2443.

Wingfield, J.C., Kenagy, G.J., 1991. Natural regulation of reproductive cycles. Schreibman, M., Jones, R.E. (Eds.), In: Vertebrate Endocrinology: Fundamentals and Biomedical Implications, vol. 4. Academic Press, New York, pp. 181–241, Part B.

Wingfield, J.C., Kitaysky, A.S., 2002. Endocrine responses to unpredictable environmental events: stress or anti-stress hormones? Integr. Comp. Biol. 42, 600–610.

Wingfield, J.C., Ramenofsky, M., 1997. Corticosterone and facultative dispersal in response to unpredictable events. Ardea 85, 155–166.

Wingfield, J.C., Ramenofsky, M., 1999. Hormones and the behavioral ecology of stress. In: Balm, P.H.M. (Ed.), Stress Physiology in Animals. Sheffield Academic Press, Sheffield, UK, pp. 1–51.

Wingfield, J.C., Romero, L.M., 2001. Adrenocortical responses to stress and their modulation in free-living vertebrates. In: McEwen, B.S. (Ed.), Handbook of Physiology, Section 7: The Endocrine System, Volume 4: Coping With The Environment: Neural and Endocrine Mechanisms. Oxford University Press, Oxford, pp. 211–236.

Wingfield, J.C., Moore, M.C., Farner, D.S., 1983. Endocrine responses to inclement weather in naturally breeding populations of white-crowned sparrows. Auk 100, 56–62.

Wingfield, J.C., Hegner, R.E., Lewis, D., 1991. Circulating levels of luteinizing hormone and steroid hormones in relation to social status in the cooperatively breeding white-browed sparrow weaver, Plocepasser mahali. J. Zool. (Lond.) 225, 43–58.

Wingfield, J.C., Vleck, C.M., Moore, M.C., 1992. Seasonal changes in the adrenocortical response to stress in birds of the Sonoran Desert. J. Exp. Zool. 264, 419–428.

Wingfield, J.C., Kubokawa, K., Ishida, K., Ishii, S., Wada, M., 1995a. The adrenocortical response to stress in male bush warblers, Cettia diphone: a comparison of breeding populations in Honshu and Hokkaido, Japan. Zool. Sci. 12, 615–621.

Wingfield, J.C., O'Reilly, K.M., Astheimer, L.B., 1995b. Ecological bases of the modulation of adrenocortical responses to stress in Arctic birds. Am. Zool. 35, 285–294.

Wingfield, J.C., Hahn, T.P., Wada, M., Schoech, S., 1997. Effects of day length and temperature on gonadal development, body mass and fat depots in white-crowned sparrows, Zonotrichia leucophrys pugetensis. Gen. Comp. Endocrinol. 107, 44–62.

Wingfield, J.C., Breuner, C., Jacobs, J., Lynn, S., Maney, D., Ramenofsky, M., et al., 1998. Ecological bases of hormone-behavior interactions: the "emergency life history stage" Am. Zool. 38, 191–206.

Wingfield, J.C., Ramos-Fernandez, G., Nuñez-de la Mora, A., Drummond, H., 1999. The effects of an "El Niño" Southern Oscillation event on reproduction in male and female blue-footed boobies, Sula nebouxii. Gen. Comp. Endocrinol. 114, 163–172.

Wingfield, J.C., Hahn, T.P., Maney, D.L., Schoech, S.J., Wada, M., Morton, M.L., 2003. Effects of temperature on photoperiodically-induced reproductive development, circulating plasma luteinizing hormone and thyroid hormones, body mass, fat deposition and molt in mountain white-crowned sparrows, *Zonotrichia leucophrys oriantha*. Gen. Comp. Endocrinol. 131, 143–158.

Wingfield, J.C., Owen-Ashley, N.T., Benowitz-Fredericks, Z.M., Lynn, S.E., Hahn, T.P., Wada, H., et al., 2004. Arctic spring: the arrival biology of migrant birds. Acta Zool. Sin. 50, 948–960.

Wingfield, J.C., Hau, M., Boersma, P.D., Romero, L.M., Hillgarth, N., Ramenofsky, M., et al., submitted. Effects of El Niño and La Niña southern oscillation events on the adrenocortical responses to stress in birds of the Galapagos Islands.

Wingfield, J.C., Wada, H., Helm, J., Sullivan, K., Meddle, S.L., submitted. The presence of water influences reproductive function in a semi-aquatic sparrow, the song sparrow (*Melospiza melodia morphna*). Gen. Comp. Endocrinol.

Wolf, B.O., 2000. Global warming and avian occupancy of hot deserts: a physiological and behavioral perspective. Rev. Chil. Hist. Nat. 73, 1–13.

Wolf, B.O., Walsberg, G.E., 1996. Thermal effects of radiation and wind on a small bird and implications for microsite selection. Ecology 77, 2228–2236.

Wolf, B.O., Wooden, K.M., Walsberg, G.E., 1996. The use of thermal refugia by two small desert birds. Condor 98, 424–428.

Zann, R.A., Morton, S.R., Jones, K.R., Burley, N.T., 1995. The timing of breeding in zebra finches in relation to rainfall in Central Australia. Emu 95, 208–222.

Conflict, Cooperation, and Cognition in the Common Raven

BERND HEINRICH

DEPARTMENT OF BIOLOGY, UNIVERSITY OF VERMONT,
BURLINGTON, VERMONT

I. INTRODUCTION

The common raven, *Corvus corax*, is an enigmatic corvid. It is not only a foraging generalist but also a carcass specialist. It is a close commensal with carnivores (Mech, 1970) that can potentially kill it. It is a solitary breeder yet commonly aggregates with up to thousands of others. It is one of the shyest of birds in some parts of its range and mingles closely with people in others. It forms social relationships with others of its kind that both aid it in getting food and that provide strong competition as well. The raven is also one of the best-known wild birds native to most of the Northern Hemisphere (Boarman and Heinrich, 1999), with some 1400 papers published on it. It is both hated as a killer and loved as a creator of life in legends. No other wild bird has had such a lengthy and extensive close association with humans and generated as much interest and attention in folklore of peoples in Europe, Asia, and North America. In the Norse legends, the chief god Odin had two ravens Hugin (thought) and Munin (memory), who rode on his shoulders and sallied forth daily into the world to bring him the news. Because they saw and remembered everything, Odin used them to counsel the other gods. His two wolves were at his side in a hunting partnership with the ravens. Ravens are even now known for their close associations with wolves wherever they occur, yet until recently their behavior had been a mystery masked by prejudice and assumptions. I examine here how the ravens' unique mix of behavioral characteristics evolved to allow it to become the ecologically and geographically most widely distributed bird on the planet.

Ravens are perhaps best known as northern carcass specialists who, with their long and narrow wings, are superb long-distance flyers capable not only of being vulture but also raptor analogues (Bruggers, 1988). They hunt birds,

189

0065-3454/11 $35.00
DOI: 10.1016/B978-0-12-380896-7.00004-6

small mammals, and other small prey and sometimes kill young ungulates. They not only stay together year-round as mated territorial pairs but also gather in large crowds at ephemeral, rich, clumped food resources. Much of the natural history of this bird (Boarman and Heinrich, 1999) has been common knowledge for at least a century. Although the raven has been acknowledged as clever and intelligent, there were no studies of its psychological attributes until Koehler (1943) published a study suggesting that his 10-year-old pet raven Jakob could count to seven.

Koehler had trained Jakob to open a box with up to six spots on it. To obtain a reward from the box, it had to open the correct one, which was identified by a specific number of spots. The spots varied from one trial to the next in their size, shape, and arrangement. (The identification of numbers was extended by Pepperberg (1998) in her African gray parrot, Alex, who learned to squawk in English and used words to identify the number of blocks, up to six, in front of him). Konrad Lorenz followed up the raven cognition experiment with his 1949 popular book on animal behavior, *King Solomon's Ring*, in which he described how he presented his own head to his pet raven, Roah, who preened it meticulously (Lorenz, 1949). Roah never poked Lorenz and gently preened him around the eyes. Lorenz concluded that ravens have evolved a strong instinctive restraint in the use of their bill in dealing with associates because it could inflict potential harm. In contrast, he suggested that doves with their weak bill had no need to evolve such restraint and therefore do not display it. Additional or alternate explanations were at that time not considered in the realm of science, presumably for fear of anthropomorphizing of which Lorenz was already being accused, despite Darwin's insight of continuity between species. Griffin (1976) reawakened the issue of continuity of mental experience, which was difficult to prove, although as Klopfer (2005) points out, recent methods of accessing direct brain activity "will carry the day" and resolve these issues.

Lorenz's observations suggested rich avenues for future research on bird behavior in relation to as yet unknown cognitive skills. Much new has come to light. Fifteen years later, in 1964, Eberhard Gwinner, Gustav Kramer's, and Lorenz's PhD student at the University of Tuebingen, completed his dissertation study of communication and signaling in the social behavior of ravens. This first systematic long-term study of ravens' interactions with each other provided behavioral insights and became a benchmark for later work in understanding raven cognition, although its relation to adaptation in the birds' ecological setting was left vague.

Adaptive behavior involves a complex of trade-offs and combinations cobbled together from various mechanisms or phenomena roughly categorized as "instincts," trial-and-error learning, culture, "intelligence," and "theory-of-mind" phenomena, even though there are no strict boundaries between them. The first includes the strictly and accurately programmed behavior that is suitable to a narrow set of circumstances. The second involves learning broadens possibilities by permitting programming to meet new contingencies. Culture allows for learning what has not been experienced directly by the individual, and thirdly "intelligence" yields unprogrammed, potentially unreliable behavior that nonetheless permits appropriate responses to shifting scenarios. The end result of any one specific behavior displayed by a vertebrate animal, however, is likely a mix of a number of components that vary from one species, and one situation, to another. Ravens are perhaps an iconic example of a bird from which we can expect adaptations to both fixed and fluid features, and from whom we have an opportunity to make a synthesis of how the various response types can be brought into play and examined in the context of its evolutionary history in its adaptive niche.

As a member of the Corvidae in the genus *Corvus*, the raven may be expected to reveal innate behavior as seen in the comparative behavior of other corvids. Some of the presumably basic or innate corvid characteristics include a generalist diet of animal protein, fruits, and grains; bill-foot coordination in food handling; "caw"-like vocalizations; monogamous pair-bond relationships; open stick nest frames; female incubation; biparental care; and gregariousness.

The raven, however, has evolved in a unique feeding niche. As a carcass specialist, its social contacts regularly include predators. In northern climates, where a carcass could potentially last months rather than days as in southern climates, the raven may regularly and for long periods of time encounter not only carnivores but also other individuals of its own kind. It might be expected to have evolved innate caution and to be able to anticipate the responses of others in order to coexist with them and get food from them.

Many aspects of animal social structure and foraging can also be understood in terms of the dispersion of resources. For example, rich clumped resources are both defensible and worth defending. In what follows, I attempt to put communicative and cognitive functions of ravens into the framework of the whole behavior of this species, highlighting the importance of conflict and cooperation, as centered on and revealed primarily through, their feeding ecology.

II. Feeding Crowds

One of the most well-known behaviors of ravens is their aggregation into crowds at large food bonanzas (Coombes, 1948; Hauri, 1956; Mylne, 1961). My own involvement with ravens for research was sparked by what appeared to me to be enigmatic: a group of them at the remains of a moose (*Alces*) carcass in dense forest. It did not seem likely that more than a dozen birds would have independently found this carcass. Ravens were rare in that mountainous forested area of western Maine, and the crowd could have been assembled from a large area. The birds were noisy enough to attract me from more than a kilometer away, yet it would have been easy for the discoverer to keep it a secret, simply by staying quiet. Why did ravens, who were supposedly "intelligent," fail to remain silent when they discovered a prized food bonanza so that they could keep the food for themselves?

The birds were making what seemed like an odd call at the moose. These "yell" vocalization (Fig. 1) are relatively high-pitched calls compared to the more familiar guttural raven "quorks." Spectrograms of the yell reveal several harmonics, around 1.8, 2.5, and 3.5 kHz (Heinrich, 1988c). The calls were given singly or in irregular sequences in contrast to many other raven calls that are repeated at regular sequences. When yells were recorded and later played back in the field with a loudspeaker at about

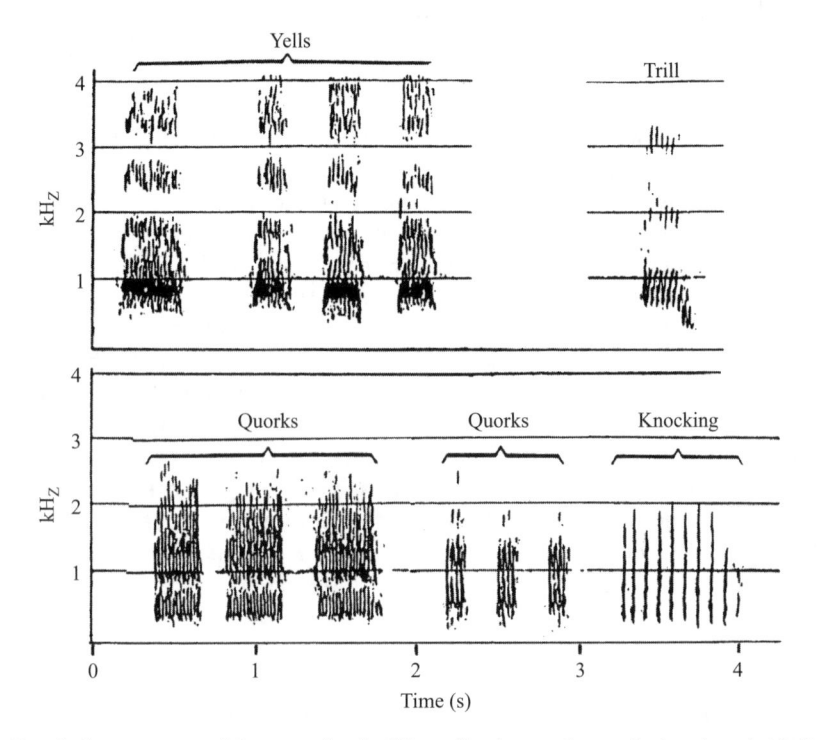

FIG. 1. Spectrograms of the attracting "yell" vocalizations and several others heard at baits. Reprinted from Heinrich (1988c).

65 db at 75 m, they attracted 1–5 ravens within 1 min in 18 of 22 trials (Heinrich, 1988c). The birds approached despite the fact that no others had done so in the 15 min preceding playbacks. Although the yell attracted other ravens, no ravens appeared at playbacks administered at random places in the forest out of earshot (several kilometers) of the existing feeding aggregation, casting doubt on the idea that yelling could account for the crowds of ravens at the bait. In sum, results of these experiments generated more questions than answers. Were the crowds the result of recruitment to food? Alternatively, were they a by-product of attraction of carnivores to open carcasses, stray discovery by a passing crowd, or some other phenomenon?

A. COMPARATIVE BEHAVIOR

To investigate whether food was discovered by individuals or crowds, I distributed piles of open meat and animal carcasses in the woods, and observed them continuously from concealed hides to monitor birds that flew over or came near. I compared these observations of ravens with those of other species, such as blue jays, crows, nuthatches, woodpeckers, chickadees, who also fed on meat. All the other species were routinely seen on almost any day, whereas ravens only rarely. However, although blue jays (*Cyanocitta cristata*) and several black-capped chickadees (*Poecile atricapillus*) travel in flocks of up to about a dozen, none ever assembled in any way that would suggest recruitment. American crows (*Corvus brachyrhynchos*) were the least common of the birds in the heavily wooded study area and they were potentially the most relevant in a comparative analysis, and I therefore distributed both meat and piles of cracked corn in a highly visible manner (on a golf course near a communal crow roost in Burlington, Vermont) where crows were guaranteed to find the food. During the four winters of the comparative study, nothing that could be construed as conspicuous vocalizations or recruitment occurred in any of the other species even though these other birds were orders of magnitude more common than ravens (Heinrich, 1988c; Heinrich, unpublished data). The raven aggregations therefore involved a potentially unique social mechanism.

B. RECRUITMENT?

To determine if raven crowds can be recruited by individual discoverers of a food bonanza, it had to be established to what extent crowds may exist in the ambient environment in the vicinity of baits. In the 4 years of study (1984–1988), I monitored the number of ravens seen flying together in areas other than the vicinity where baits were distributed (Heinrich, 1988c,d). Of 87 incidents of ravens seen flying at large, 69% were single and 25% in pairs. Only two sighting of groups of five and six individuals were made. Similarly, in 25 independent incidents of bait discovery, 72% (18) were by apparently single and 28% (7) were by pairs. However, during approach to baits, ravens routinely came in groups (Fig. 2). These data indicated that the bait where crowds later assembled are seldom if ever discovered by crowds and that information transfer from individuals or pairs to others occurred at a distance from the food source. The origin of these birds was traced to distant nocturnal roosts.

Long-range recruitment from communal nocturnal roosts was inferred by visually monitoring carcasses from the tops of tall trees. In the small relatively ephemeral communal raven roosts, such as those in the forests of Maine, a large portion of the whole roost may depart relatively synchronously in one or two directions in the morning but then return independently as singletons, pairs, and small groups in the evening. The largest group of birds (up to 52 birds at once) arrived at baits in the half hour before dawn (Heinrich, 1994c). These groups of birds flew in a direct line to the bait, were noisy and could often be heard when they were still over a

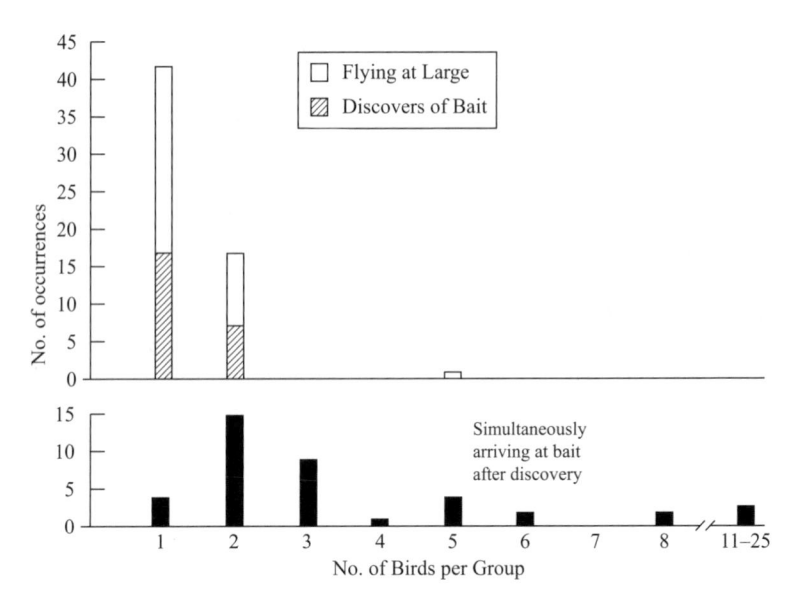

FIG. 2. Ravens' distribution in the field versus discovering and arriving at baits after discovery. Birds flying at large and discovering baits were the same, singles and pairs, while groups arrived only after the bait had been discovered. Reprinted with permission from Heinrich (1988d).

kilometer away. After the second day of feeding at the carcass, the birds presumably left the roost less synchronously and arrived later. They were strung out in much smaller groups and arrived over a longer time span (Fig. 3). The groups of ravens of various sizes came repeatedly on successive days from the same directions at some baits (Heinrich, 1988c; Marzluff et al., 1996). But groups also arrived simultaneously from different directions on successive days. Most of the roosts from where these groups originated were temporary, lasting only a few days, but some, such as one at a dump, a permanent food source, lasted throughout the year. Social soaring of a crowd of birds was associated with roosts and bait locations (Heinrich, 1988c; Marzluff et al., 1996).

The hypothesis that information transfer occurred at communal nocturnal roosts (Ward and Zahavi, 1973) was examined experimentally in the field (Marzluff et al., 1996) using naïve ravens who had no knowledge of current carcass locations. Wild nonterritorial "floater" birds (Heinrich, 1988c,d) were captured and held in a large (17,000 m^3) aviary complex for

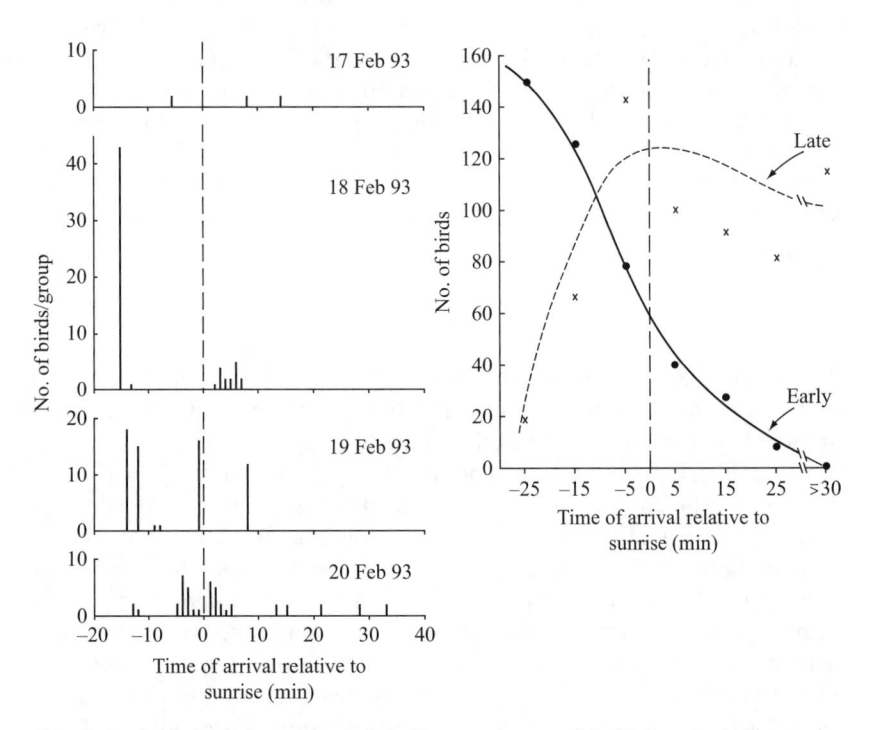

FIG. 3. In the first 2–3 days after a bait is discovered, most of the birds arrive in large groups 15–25 min before sunrise. After 3 or more days, they arrive in small groups over a long time span. Reprinted with permission from Heinrich (1994c).

at least 2 months to erase their knowledge of currently available carcasses in the field. Such naïve birds, equipped with a radio transmitter, were carried in a pet carrier into the crown of a tree near a roost and released there at dusk (Marzluff et al., 1996). The hungry released birds almost immediately joined the roost. On the next morning, in 9 out of 10 trials, the naïve bird followed its new roost-mates to the food bonanza where the birds of that roost were currently feeding. In a control test, birds released in the evening the same distance from the food bonanza, but not into a roost, failed to show up at local baits.

In an additional experiment, hungry birds were released from a pet carrier (pulling the door open from hiding by a long string) in front of a pile of meat. These hungry birds fed there after being released. Would they, now being knowledgeable of a food bonanza, bring recruits the next morning? Results were mixed and difficult to interpret, as it could not be assumed that the released bird would be able to locate a roost that night because its knowledge of current roost locations had been erased as well. Nor could one know, if a bird did find a roost, if the birds at that particular roost were ready to feed somewhere else (most roost birds regularly visited the same feeding place until it was exhausted). Despite these complicating factors, in two of 20 tests the next dawn after the "discoverer" had found the food bonanza, it led a group directly to the bait. Although the hypothesis that communal roosts serve as "information centers" as proposed by Ward and Zahavi was supported by six lines of empirical evidence (Marzluff et al., 1996), the mechanism of long-range recruitment from a distant roost was, and still remains, unanswered.

C. Assembly and Recruitment Mechanism

As shown experimentally, the vocalizations acted to assemble nearby ravens, but they did not account for the crowds at baits. This can be explained in part by their developmental origin. The yells are derived from the begging vocalizations of the young in the nest (Heinrich and Marzluff, 1991), and they are the same as those made by the female while incubating, presumably when she is indicating hunger to her mate and thus "asking" to be fed. They could, however, also be construed to be part of an adaptive mechanism for recruitment in forming or maintaining the crowds because (1) in ravens, they are retained in the young, whereas in most other birds, they are lost soon after fledging and (2) although the yells proximally indicate hunger under conditions of expectation to be fed, such as when food is near, they are functionally referential because individuals call more when there is better food. Thus, recipients obtain information about the presence of food and also its desirability (Bugnyar et al., 2001).

The referential aspects of yelling are perhaps reinforced shortly after the birds fledge when they are still fed by the parents. When one of a group of hungry young sees a parent arrive with food, it begs to be fed. The others are then alerted by these yells that food is coming. Similarly, later in the winter when the birds are near food but do not have access to it, they yell and nearby birds gather until a quorum is reached and they descend to feed. If the birds fear the food or are prevented from accessing it, the calls continue, but after feeding starts, the calls subside or stop. Semantically, therefore, the short-range recruitment call does not mean the birds want to share food. Instead, the calls mean they want to get access to that food.

In an experimental study of a group of captive subadult ravens, yelling was induced by hunger but strongly influenced by status (Heinrich and Marzluff, 1991). The dominant juveniles do most of the yelling and they suppress calling by subordinates. When successive dominants were removed, replacements immediately took their place to yell (Fig. 4). The mated pairs always outrank the juveniles, but unlike the dominant subadults, they rarely yell despite their high social rank. In fact, the adults inhibit the juveniles from making them. Baits thus serve as arenas to establish and demonstrate status, and status in ravens may ultimately function in sexual selection (Gwinner, 1964).

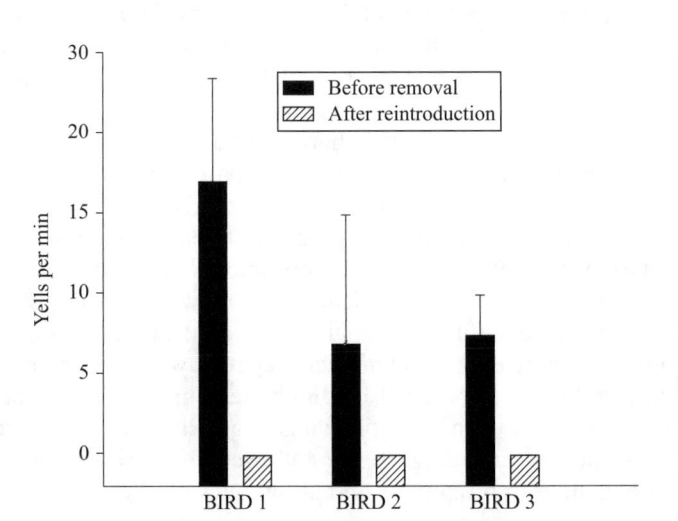

Fig. 4. Dominance rank affects the production of yells. Hungry birds yell frequently. Calling by subordinates is typically suppressed, but when the dominants are gone, others take their place to yell. When the former dominants are reintroduced, their yelling is reduced due to the presence of new dominant individuals. Shown here is yell frequency by three alpha males in a group held in an aviary before and after reintroduction to the group. Reprinted from Heinrich and Marzluff (1991).

In contrast to the yell given by dominants at food, the subordinate ravens also give a similar-sounding "begging" or appeasement call when they are attacked during dominance contests at food. These calls (Bugnyar et al., 2001) are also a local cue indicating the presence of food, and they also act an attractant (Heinrich et al., 1993).

Over 400 ravens were feeding (but not all at once) at one super bonanza (two-skinned adult cows) even though on average only one bird was observed per 300 km of travel on roads through forest in that study area (Heinrich, 1988a,b,c,d). Neither the short-range recruitment yell nor the appeasement vocalizations can alone account for raven crowds at baits (Heinrich et al., 1993). As already suggested, only long-range recruitment from communal roosts could account for the dozens of ravens that sometimes arrive almost at once.

Thus far, it has been impossible to monitor the behavior of the discoverer of a bait when it returns to a roost and how it acts there to recruit roost-mates to the bait at some subsequent time. The birds roost high on cliffs or in dense conifers, and they leave in the morning when it is still dark. No obviously conspicuous vocalizations are evident as the birds leave. However, the recruiter must provide some signal, whether intentional or not, so that roost-mates follow it rather some other bird who is ignorant of a food location. The roost probably contains many birds who do not know the whereabouts of food, and they would not be expected to leave the roost before knowledgeable birds but instead follow those who leave early. Possibly recruitment works in the same manner as we do in a strange city. In this situation, we do not know where to find a restaurant at dawn. We know, however, that residents of a nearby apartment building will all be heading toward one to eat breakfast, and we could find a restaurant simply by following someone who appears to be confident in leaving. One could label such following behavior either "recruitment" or "information parasitism." It is parasitism if those who lead (are followed) pay a cost, and it is recruitment if they benefit. If a signal is given that induces following (say, calling and/or leaving early) and impacts negatively on the signaler, then it would predictably be minimized or eliminated through evolution. If the effect of the signal is to induce following to a valued food resource, then there is an inferred advantage to be followed. As I will suggest below, recruiters benefit both proximally and ultimately.

D.   THE EVOLUTION OF RECRUITMENT

Over a half dozen proximate and ultimate hypotheses of why vagrant subadult ravens recruit each other to winter carcasses were considered (Heinrich, 1988d, 1989), and the most plausible were tested by combinations of field observations and experiments. First, it seemed possible that individual ravens, unable to penetrate the hides of a carcass, might call to recruit predators to open them. Other ravens would then come incidentally by parasitizing the yeller's recruitment efforts. This hypothesis was rejected because ravens did not yell nor recruit at unopened carcasses, nor were recruitment calls given by pairs. The idea that the aggregations were kin groups seemed unlikely and was rejected because ravens clutches usually consist of four to five young, and all the marked young from local nests dispersed in the fall. Further, DNA fingerprinting confirmed that feeding groups do not represent genetic clans (Parker et al., 1994).

The temporary alliances between birds at roosts likely have the advantage of "many eyes" in finding carcasses. Fifty or more birds who have each traversed hundreds of kilometers of forest have collectively more information than any one bird, and if all birds share information of large carcasses that they themselves can not possibly consume, then all can feed on a regular basis, at little cost to each. But such a "rational" solution is not likely invoked by choice since each bird acts for its own benefit. It might, however, be the product of evolution if it is connected to an immediate advantage and a proximally selfish motive.

Ungulate carcasses are rare but large, and the benefit of sharing reciprocally could be great, yet cost little. However, such sharing is not likely based on such logic since it is prone to invasion by cheaters. The possibility that the birds share reciprocally with others also seemed unlikely, because unlike house sparrows whose chirps attract flock mates (Elgar, 1986), ravens do not stay in flocks. If there was an *evolved* strategy, it had to be based on selfishness. I was even more intrigued when I noted at times vicious fighting at carcasses to which birds had presumably recruited each other. Of the various hypotheses considered (Heinrich, 1988c), the one that ultimately received the most empirical support related to dominance contests at the bait, where gangs of juveniles or subadults overpower the defenses of the much stronger territorial mated adults (Heinrich, 1989; Heinrich et al., 1993).

To test this hypothesis, it was necessary to identify individuals and to age them. In previous studies of ravens, juveniles had been determined mainly on the basis of their pink mouth linings. In contrast, adults possess black linings, while 2–3-year-old subadults display mottled mouth linings; plumage is a second less commonly used criterion to age ravens (Heinrich, 1994a, b,c). Most birds (81 of 91) from four feeding crowds that we captured were assigned as juveniles or subadults. These birds were highly mobile and considered to be "floaters." They ranged over at least 1800 km^2 while foraging, with some of the 463 marked birds having been seen even beyond New England, in New York, and into Canada in Quebec, New Brunswick, and Nova Scotia. In one set of experiments (Heinrich, 1988c), groups of ravens in western Maine appeared at most of 135 baits (totaling about 8 tons of meat). In the presence of the vagrants at baits, the individually marked adults assumed the dominant postures (Gwinner, 1964) and were aggressive to the juveniles and subadults, suggesting that recruitment by the juveniles could be a mechanism for them to gain access to the meat (Heinrich, 1988c). The juvenile floaters appeared to form *ad hoc* alliances or "gangs" that overpowered the resident territorial pair or pairs at rich food bonanzas. The floaters also destroyed the adults' nests (Heinrich, unpublished data).

The gang hypothesis was confirmed in the field and in simulated conditions in a large aviary with different compartments to separate vagrants and a territorial pair who nested there. Six to nine of the nonbreeding floaters were required to gain access to a pile of meat defended by a mated resident pair (Marzluff and Heinrich, 1991). These gangs, however, do not always consist entirely of juveniles because mouth color is not always a reliable indicator of age as was at first thought.

Ravens usually do not breed until they are at least 3 years old and may still not have a mate and territory at 8 years of age (Gruenkorn, pers. comm.). Feather color is a poor age indicator (Heinrich, 1994b) and mouth color is only a partial indicator of age (Kerttu, 1973). Young birds raised in aviaries also changed mouth color as a function of status (Heinrich and Marzluff, 1992). The highest ranking birds in a group of 17 had black mouth linings 8 months after fledging. These birds formed pair bonds. By 22 months postfledging, there were still unpaired, pink-mouthed birds. Paired birds always had black mouth linings. The mouth color change of the subordinate and/or unpaired birds is a slow process, and the "gangs of juveniles," although largely younger birds, were therefore mostly low-status vagrants.

Is there an advantage for low-status birds to recruit others to a food bonanza if, in the resulting dominance hierarchies, they end up as subordinates? I addressed this question by examining weight changes of 22 ravens over a series of feeding bouts (Heinrich, 1994a). In this study, the dominance hierarchy of the birds was established through observation of 517 dominance interactions over 2 months. The birds displayed their status while feeding at carcasses by yelling, their aggressive actions and feather posture, and their feeding positions (Fig. 5). The subordinant individual was defined as the one backing away from others and assuming a submissive posture by lowering its head and fluffing out its head feathers. The highest ranking individuals were 64 times more likely than subordinates to perch on top of the carcass during feeding. Their head feathers were flattened and their feathers around the legs flared prominently to the

FIG. 5. Ravens form social relationships between different individuals. Relationships involve interactions that include aggression, tolerance, and affiliation. These interactions occur while individuals perch, allopreen, and maintain contact with each other over varying lengths of time. In this photograph of birds that have mutual bonds, the feather displays are subtle. But in the presence of strangers, full-blown displays erupt frequently, with dominant subadult ravens perching on top of a carcass while feeding with a crowd of other ravens (see Fig. 1 in Heinrich 1994a).

sides. The "top-birds," however, did not pick on the lowest-status birds. To the contrary, dominance interactions occurred primarily between adjacently ranked individuals. For example, the four most dominant birds scored 92 wins over the next four highest ranking birds, 25 over the next four individuals, 14 over next four ravens, and finally only 3 wins over the remaining birds at the bottom of the hierarchy. Interactions with the latter occur infrequently as they stay largely out of reach of the dominant birds.

After feeding on the carcasses of cut-open raccoons (*Procyon*) for the same duration, high ranking ravens gained 100 g on average, while middle and low ranking birds gained 115 g. In contrast, pronounced differences in weight gain between birds of different status emerged when birds were given restricted access to meat. When ravens were presented with a frozen carcass with only one hole to access the meat, high ranking birds gained about the same weight as before, middle ranking individuals gained 20 g less, and the lowest ranking animals only half as much as the dominant birds (Heinrich, 1994a). These results suggest that the subordinates gain even under restrictive conditions among strong competition, and in fact, may gain even more than the dominants at an open carcass (Fig. 6).

Birds joining large groups experienced fewer attacks than those who joined smaller groups (Fig. 7). This effect probably resulted because aggression by the defending pair of territorial birds is diluted per individual as group size increases (Marzluff and Heinrich, 1991). It thus appears that

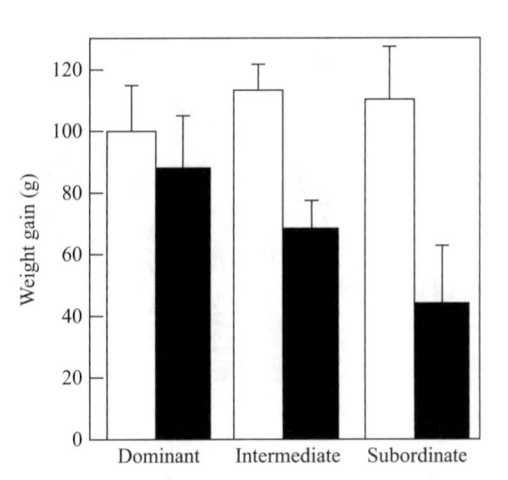

FIG. 6. The dominant birds of a feeding crowd do not ordinarily gain more weight per unit time than the subordinates at a carcass unless access is restricted to a small feeding hole. In this figure, weight gain at a cut-open unfrozen raccoon (open bars) is compared to that at a frozen calf carcass with one feeding hole (closed bars). Reprinted with permission from Heinrich (1994a).

birds who recruit others suffer few costs. Recruited individuals do constitute additional feeding competitors, but this effect is compensated; recruited ravens obtain greater access to food and experience decreased aggression by the defenders. An added benefit of large feeding flocks is that they offer an opportunity for status signaling (Fig. 8), which facilitates mate choice by ravens (Gwinner, 1964). The number of birds recruited both at carcasses and at fresh wolf kills (Stahler et al., 2002) often increases linearly and not exponentially, suggesting that information transfer is directed toward specific individuals or small groups of them, with information gradually spreading to ever-more individuals and/or groups of them.

Recent work in the sheep-farming country of Wales at one of the largest relatively permanent raven roosts in the world provides further evidence for the raven roost information center hypothesis and the "gang" hypothesis to overpower superior competitors (Dall and Wright, 2009). Sheep carcasses with small plastic pellets embedded in the meat were set out, with different colored pellets in different carcasses. The ravens feeding at these carcasses ingested the beads and expelled them in their regurgitated pellets at their nocturnal roosts. Where a particular-colored pellet fell indicated where a raven feeding from a particular carcass in the day had roosted at night. In the large roosts, pellet colors were clumped, indicating that the ravens feeding on any one carcass roosted in clusters that were

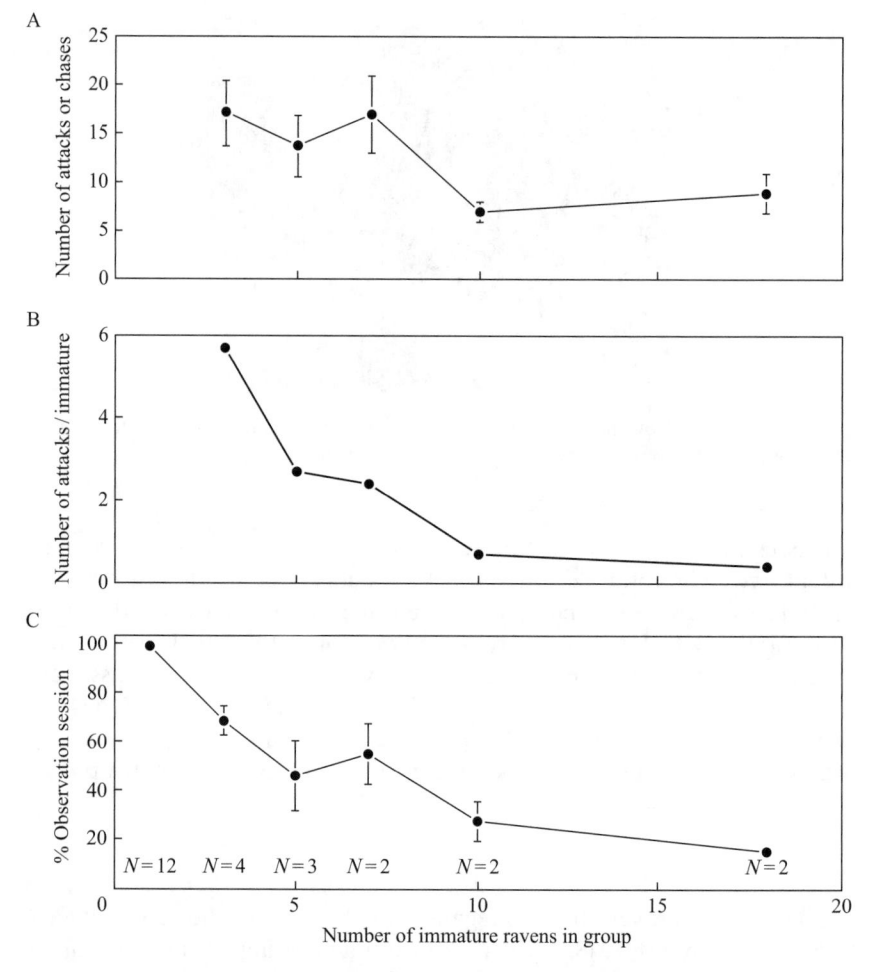

FIG. 7. As the number of immature ravens at a food bonanza increases, the birds feed more continuously, are flushed fewer times off the bait, and as shown here, the number of attacks by the territory holders decreases (A) and those on the individuals plummets (B). Reprinted with permission from Marzluff and Heinrich (1991).

somewhat separated from the main roost aggregation (Wright et al., 2003). These results, involving roosts of some 2000 birds, suggest that the roost was divided into different subpopulations that each exploited separate food bonanzas. Dall and Wright (2009) suggest that the subgroups of birds from their giant roosts stay together and forage in the roost vicinity and can then almost immediately overpower superior competition. Distant

Fig. 8. Photograph of a pair of adult territorial ravens (male right, female left) displaying at a feeding crowd of juvenile vagrant birds at a carcass in winter.

carcasses that were defended by territorial pairs were discovered by individual birds who returned to the roost and had to recruit their gangs from there to then chase off the pair and then feed. The Wales sheep country with a reliably high food density permits long-lived roosts. In contrast, in the Maine forest there are very few and very widely scattered carcasses and the roosts are very short-lived (usually several days; Fig. 9). They are composed of *ad hoc* crowds (Heinrich et al., 1994) and are apparently not together long enough to form bonds for long-term gang membership.

E.   RAVEN ASSOCIATIONS

The crowds of ravens that aggregate at food have often been described as "flocks" (Coombes, 1948; Mylne, 1961), but a flock implies membership to a group where individuals stay together. This is seldom ascertained. At our study site in western Maine, there were generally 10—50 ravens feeding at any one time at the carcasses in winter, although 463 had been captured and marked at the site. The same individuals never congregated at different baits. A similar number of birds were often at any one bait at any time throughout most of the day and on subsequent days, but different birds arrived and left throughout the day. One individually marked bird might come and feed for perhaps half an hour in the morning and then leave, and return a day or two later, or not at all. Another might stay a few hours in the morning; a third might do so in the afternoon. But although the birds did not stay together, possible long-term association was not precluded.

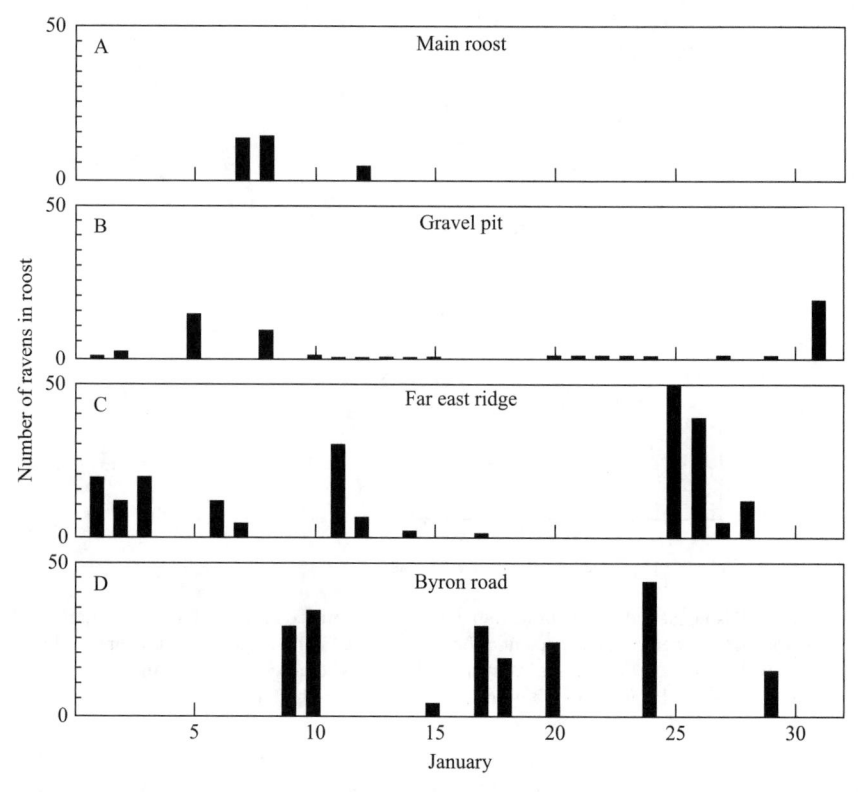

Fɪɢ. 9. Roost occupancy in four different pine groves in the core of the western Maine study area. Roosts tended to form within about a kilometer of a feeding site, and local shifts in roost location and numbers of birds in them were frequent. Reprinted with permission from Marzluff et al. (1996).

Group cohesion and dispersal were examined by capturing 10 individuals from one Maine feeding "flock" and monitoring them over 70 consecutive days and nights (Fig. 10). The birds were equipped with radio transmitters and their locations checked in the daytime and again at night. The survey was conducted from back-country roads over an approximately 5000 km^2 area, centering on the place where they were captured at a carcass. The results gave no indication of a flock structure; all these birds roosted and dispersed independently of one another. They took up residency from one to several weeks in ranges from about 190 to 3100 km^2. Two of the birds stayed for only 2 days, whereas another was located almost every day and night for the entire 70 days (Heinrich et al., 1994). Had the birds associated together, then if one was found, the others should have been with it. These

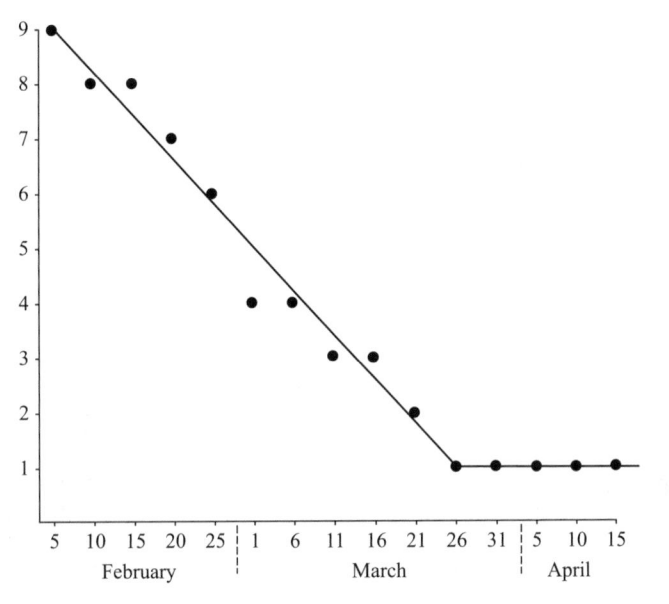

FIG. 10. Dispersal and association among 10 ravens captured at one bait on 5 February 1993 What year? Birds were radio-tagged and then monitored for 70 consecutive days and nights in an approximately 5000 km² Maine study area. The birds steadily dispersed, and by 26 March only one remained. Reprinted with permission from Heinrich et al. (1994).

data indicate that, at any one bait or carcass, the crowds of birds in this forested area do not constitute flocks. Nevertheless, associations that could be considered flocks do form under some conditions.

When new individuals or two groups that had been held separately were brought together in the aviary, all the aggressive interactions, including chases, fights, jabs, feather displays, and vocalizations occurred at the start and diminished within 2 h. Dominance hierarchies were established, aggression decreased, and associations formed. In one case, a group of four birds that had been kept together for several weeks killed a newcomer introduced into their enclosure, after they had not allowed it to feed at their frozen calf carcass, and it then fed by raiding their caches. These observations of "artificial" groups suggest that flocks could potentially form under ecological conditions where ravens encounter one another frequently (such as in an area where food is abundant and they disperse less). In the aviary, the formation of "friendships" among nonbreeders ranged from various levels of tolerance at food to apparent pair formation with considerable allo-preening. Mated pairs in the wild sometimes alternately preen each other in sessions lasting a half hour. In the pairs formed in the aviary, a released bird would not leave the area until its partner was also released (Heinrich, unpublished data). Hormone profiles are correlated with behavioral patterns; levels of the stress hormone, corticosterone, are elevated both in the young crowded in the nest and in non-breeding flock members (Stoewe et al., 2008) relative to territorial paired birds even when they interact with the crowd birds at food bonanzas (Lelva et al., 2010).

Social coordination is difficult to document in the field, but anecdotes suggest that it may occur. I once saw several hundred ravens all flying in a long strung-out queue in the same direction near midday in northern Germany. Recently on 12 September 2010, a loosely aggregated group of 20 ravens flew about 500 m above my house in Vermont at 07:30 h, heading northwest. Flights similar to these were noted on other rare occasions over the years, but no systematic records of times and flight directions are available. The group flights could be recruitment flights from roosts to food carcasses, although that seems unlikely for many since group flights to food occur at dawn or earlier. At least in one large (approximately 1500 ravens) roost in California the birds arrived *de novo* on 8 November and then all left on 15 December. During the 36 nights that the ravens were observed at that roost they arrived from "all directions" singly or in group of up to 40 birds; they left before light in the morning. On the evening before leaving for good, they stayed vocal until midnight. In contrast, they typically were silent by 2000 h on most other nights. As usual they left before dawn, but none came back that evening (Cotterman and Heinrich, 1993). Taken together, these observations raise several unanswered questions about raven communication, roost dynamics and possible long-range movements to seasonal food supplies. Apparently birds that pair up reduce their stress levels because they have, in the presence of feeding crowds, lower levels of corticosterone (stress-indicating) hormones than birds in crowds (Selva et al., 2011). Similarly, nestlings prior to fledging also have higher corticosterone hormone levels than after they fledge and are no longer crowded together (Stoewe et al., 2008).

Roosting behavior, associations, and movements are related to food supply. In Maine and Vermont, winter roosts rarely exceed 80 individuals and roost locations and occupancy are erratic when the birds feed on deer carcasses, and more rarely, on moose. In contrast, roosts were larger and more "permanent" when there were (previously) still open landfills. In Idaho and Oregon where the birds forage on grain left from industrial agriculture, hundreds to 2000 ravens roost annually on power lines at predictable locations; the occupancy of these nocturnal roosts increases and decreases seasonally (Engel et al., 1992; Stiel, 1981). In Welsh sheep country, where there is a steady year-long supply of meat, ravens have similarly large-sized and long-lived communal roosts.

III. Food Hoarding

Caching behavior is variously adaptive and an ecologically relevant solution that has evolved in many birds to deal with a fluctuating food supply (De Kort et al., 2007; Grodzinski and Clayton, 2010). By recruiting others to a food bonanza, ravens benefit by gaining access to defended food, increasing their opportunity to display status, and diluting the risks. But after access to the food has been achieved, the birds immediately begin to haul off one load of food after another and hide them in multiple, widely dispersed caches. During cache-making, the bird shoves the food into a crevice (usually on the ground) and then picks up nearby debris and covers it. In snow, the birds usually lay the meat down and then use their bills in sideway flips to excavate a small cavity. They then pick up the meat, lay it into the hole and then again use the bill to shovel snow in. During cache recovery, birds use their bills to shovel away snow, perhaps digging down 10 or more centimeters if it had snowed in the meantime. Many aspects of cache-making depend strongly on the presence of others.

Given the birds' apparent haste and eagerness to carry off meat rather than staying to feed, two aspects of this caching behavior seemed puzzling. First, birds that had been recruited to crowds (but not in mated pairs working alone) made their caches far from the food source and the crowd; the birds did not just cache the meat nearby, they flew out of sight. Second, after a crowd had removed all the meat from a carcass the ravens were not seen in the area as would be expected if they stayed to recover their caches. It seemed likely that the vagrant crowds, as the radio-tagging study had also suggested, either dispersed too widely to recover their caches, unless they had a very long-term memory and came back much later.

Memory for cache locations was examined in a large ($17,000 \text{ m}^3$) outdoor aviary complex with trees, boulders, and natural ground cover as in neighboring natural habitat. Birds were allowed into a main compartment and permitted to cache meat in snow, and then afterward held in side aviaries for varying lengths of time for up to 2 weeks before being again let into the main aviary to retrieve their caches (Heinrich and Pepper, 1998). Introduction of fake caches served as controls. No control caches were ever recovered, proving that cache recoveries depended on memory of site rather than on scent. After several days, the birds easily recovered their caches, but after 2 weeks their apparent site memory seemed to fade and they failed to check (dig) their old cache locations. Possibly meat would either spoil or be relatively quickly retrieved by mammals such as shrews and other carnivores so that it does not pay a nonterritorial bird to return and dig where it has cached food. The durability of frozen meat and/or memory in relation to longevity of food type (Clayton and Dickinson, 1998) is not known. It would be instructive to investigate in jays and ravens, especially comparing winter versus summer caches for the same perishable food (Fig. 11).

When more than one raven had been in the experimental aviary at the same time to cache, they recovered their own as well as some of the other's when they were let in days later to recover caches. These observations explained much of the birds' caching behavior. Depending on circumstances, the birds either hurried or delayed caching (Fig. 12). When there was a large pile of food and competitors present, the ravens hurried to make one cache after another, but still took care to distance themselves from the others to cache. When there was no more food left and/or they had only one piece in their bill and the other ravens had none (and were no longer distracted by their own caching), the birds took time to hide their food. Before they cached, they took care to distance themselves from the other bird(s) and/or to cache behind obstructions such as large rocks or trees (Heinrich and Pepper, 1998). These behaviors in the aviary, where the birds could escape the notice of each other only with difficulty (relative to being free in the field), probably explains why birds in the wild flew far from the bait in order to cache. They also highlight the fact that sharing food at the

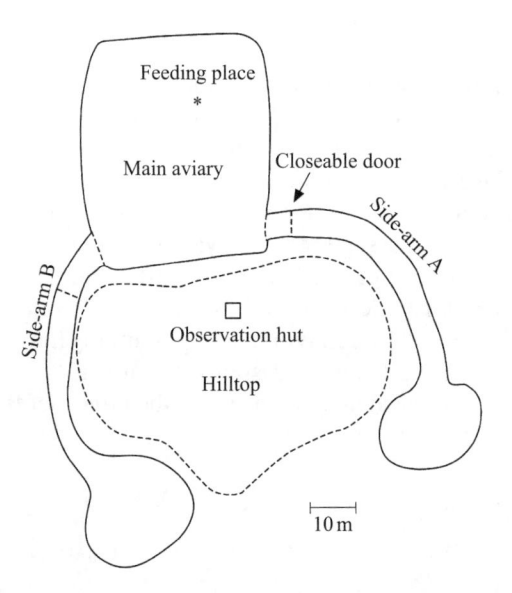

FIG. 11. The aviary complex used for controlled experiments of caching behavior. Note the main compartment where the food for the caching was provided and the sidearms where birds could cache at a distance and in privacy from the main crowd gathered at the food. Reprinted with permission from Heinrich and Pepper (1998).

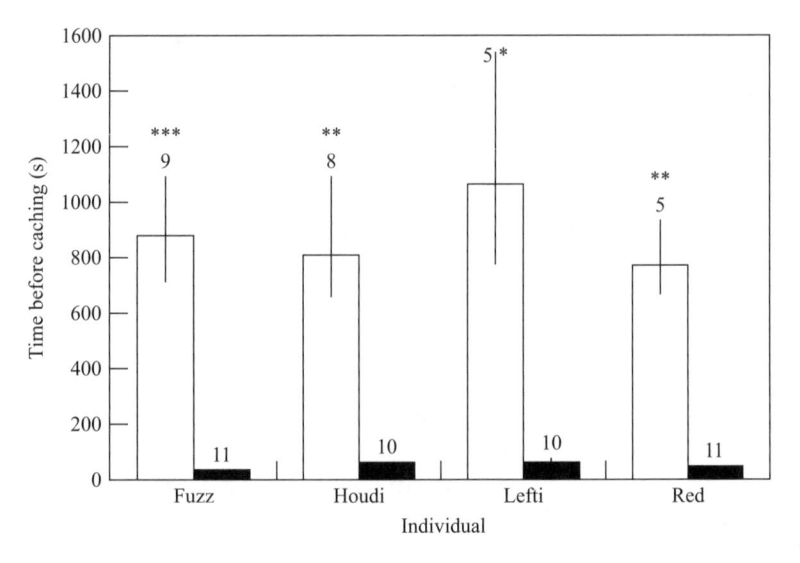

Fɪɢ. 12. When the birds are in a crowd and provided with a pile of 15 pieces of food, they hurry and cache immediately until all the food is gone (black bars). When given only one piece and when only one piece remains that they own, then they greatly delay caching (open bars). Reprinted with permission from Heinrich and Pepper (1998).

carcass is a strategy to gain access to it and not to share it. The difference between the behavior of ravens in crowds and that of mated pairs is, however, dramatic in this respect. Mated pairs, if alone, often cached near the carcass and were not observed to raid each other's caches.

Although the apparent cache memory duration (or willingness to attempt cache recovery after a passage of time) was restricted to less than a month, the bird's actions often suggested apparent understanding of the intentions of others as potential raiders, as well as the ability to thwart those intentions. Up to this point their behavior could potentially have been accounted for by innate reflexes and learned responses. But what are they? Additionally, do the birds have a capacity to visualize the effects of their actions, and to thus plan ahead?

IV. Instinct, Learning, and Insight

What might a raven's behavior look like without the shaping influence of the outside world? Except perhaps for the gaping behavior of the just-hatched young, it is difficult to know because the animals live from birth in a world of many stimuli. To determine innate responses, the best we can probably do is to withhold specific stimuli and later test responses to them under conditions of suitable motivation. This requires the use of hand-reared birds, because it is only in these animals that access to some stimuli can be controlled.

A. Neophobia

Although neophobia in birds is associated with narrow ecological specificity (Greenberg, 1990a,b), in ravens, who are generalist feeders, it is considered an exaggerated trait (Gwinner, 1964). Why do the birds conspicuously exhibit apparent fear of food carcasses? In the forests of Maine, for example, ravens did not approach an opened calf carcass with prominently exposed meat until at least 2 days after discovering it (Heinrich, 1988c, 1989). When they did finally approach it, they did so cautiously, and only after a long series of backward jumps (jumping jacks) and finally a peck, followed by a period of waiting and then another approach and peck and wait. These behaviors were usually delayed until several birds had gathered. They then advanced and retreated together. Is their apparent fear a learned response from prior negative conditioning, cultural learning from the example of others, or is it largely innate? To investigate the contributing factors, five sibling groups of ravens were reared as chicks out of the nest and kept at separate locations so that they could not have learned to either fear or be attracted to calf, deer, or other animal carcasses, nor be influenced by watching others' responses who had learned before. They were reared on small pieces of meat, dog, chow, and chicken starter and later presented with novel test items after they had been kept a day without food.

Results from the naïve hand-reared birds (Heinrich et al., 1996) were unequivocal; all young who were long out of the nest (up to 9 months after fledging), and who also had no prior experience with carcasses nor seen others react to them, exhibited apparently exaggerated fear of animal carcasses and other large potential food items that ravens in the wild normally encounter and depend on for their food (Fig. 13). A dead raccoon or similarly sized mammal, for example, drove all the naïve young birds to roost in the top-most perches of their aviary, and they would not come back down to feed for at least 24 h even though the carcass had been opened to expose the meat (Heinrich et al., 1996). Smaller carcasses, such as those of mice or large moths, also induced initial avoidance and caution, but for short durations. Size, as such, as well as shape and texture mattered. Some naïve young ravens immediately approached and ate smooth caterpillars, but fuzzy ones elicited the jumping jack response and were contacted

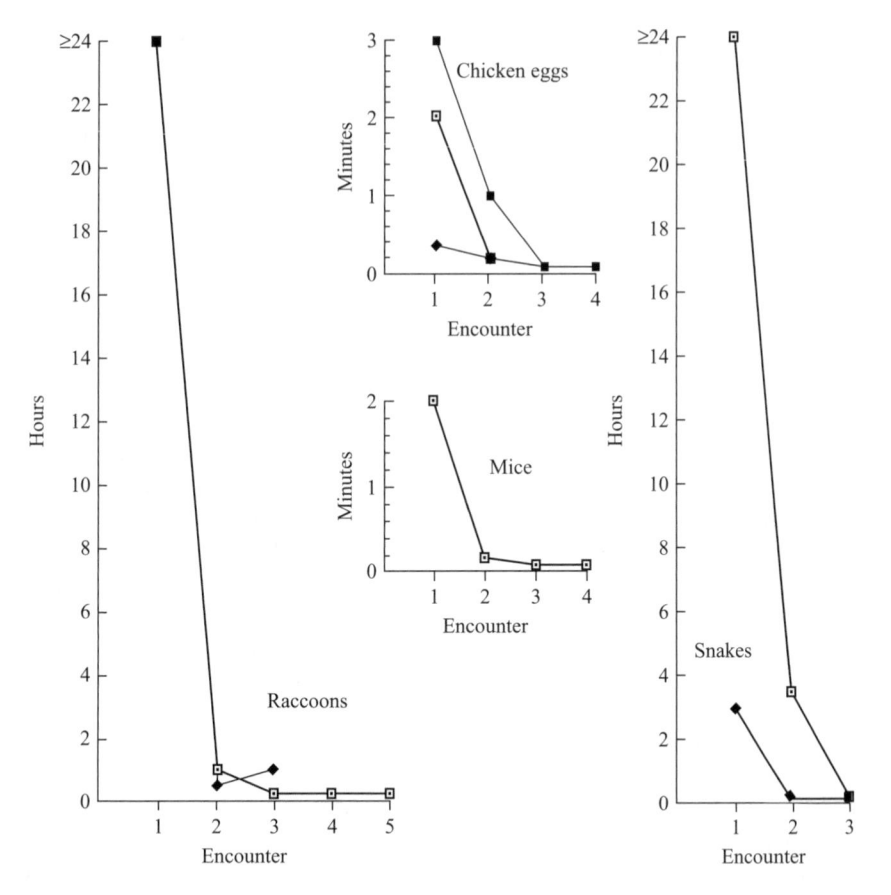

Fig. 13. Highly preferred food, such as meat visible in a cut-open carcass of a large animal such as a raccoon, may not be contacted by juvenile ravens until more than a day after discovered, although small carcasses such as mice and other food such as eggs may be taken in minutes. Reprinted with permission from Heinrich et al. (1996).

gradually (Heinrich, 1988a, 1989). A pile of cereal elicited avoidance, but as soon as the food-pile was dispersed and divided into smaller portions the birds immediately fed from it (Heinrich, 1989). Their neophobia is, however, not general. Naïve young ravens approached any smooth round objects within seconds regardless of its size and color, whereas long thin objects were ignored. It appears, therefore, that ravens have an innate attention to, but also fear of, large things that resemble an animal. On the other hand, objects with shapes that resemble eggs or fruit, regardless of size or color, attract them. That is, they have an innate filter that helps to identify likely food items. But, as I will show, it does not end there. It sets the stage for learning.

B. NEOPHILIA

Neophilia in ravens is most apparent to small items (probably because they are not feared), although attraction is not likely restricted to them because they are small. During the summer ravens feed on small items that vary greatly in shape, texture, and color. In addition to eggs and fruit, they include insects, seeds, and all sorts of other invertebrate animals that come in a large range of shapes, textures, and colors. Are they innately attracted to any of them?

The problem in determining precisely what kind of items naïve birds are attracted to initially (instinctively) is difficult to determine due to the effects of learning. Ravens already a week or more before fledging have already routinely pecked and manipulated their nest material and anything else within reach, and as soon as they leave the nest, this tendency to approach, touch, and manipulate all objects in their path increases. It potentially represents an innate mechanism of a generalist feeder to encounter non-dangerous potential food items that are of general type, and hence not easily programmed specifically prior to learning.

I tested whether or not neophilia is an exploratory behavior for eventual food identification in four tame ravens in a natural forest environment. In these experiments, I walked with them for 38 half-hour "exploring sessions" starting on the day they left the nest (Heinrich, 1995a,b). During the first 10 sessions, the birds made 980 contacts of 95 kinds of objects. In the subsequent 28 sessions, 44 new items were added, and the birds' reactions to them compared to the previously encountered background items (Fig. 14). The birds were led daily over the same ground where the inedible items from the previous sessions were left. They highly preferred the novel (from 42 to 24,000 times) above previously encountered items. Although previously novel inedible items were soon ignored, the novel if edible items, in contrast, became highly preferred if reintroduced in subsequent sessions.

The birds' neophilia, in conjunction to their habituation and learning and group size which affects it (Stoewe et al., 2006), should allow them to exploit the available food within various ecological settings. This idea was tested by subjecting these forest birds to a range of items from the Atlantic seashore (Heinrich, 1995a,b). As predicted, within one trial, the novel edible items were identified and used, and the inedible one soon ignored. It has been proposed that the well-known characteristic of hand-reared ravens to take shiny objects, such as coins and jewelry, may be attempts to take what they have forcibly been denied (Goodwin, 1986). This study, however, suggests that it is proximally related to novelty and ultimately to food-finding. Although the neophilia and neophobia are innate

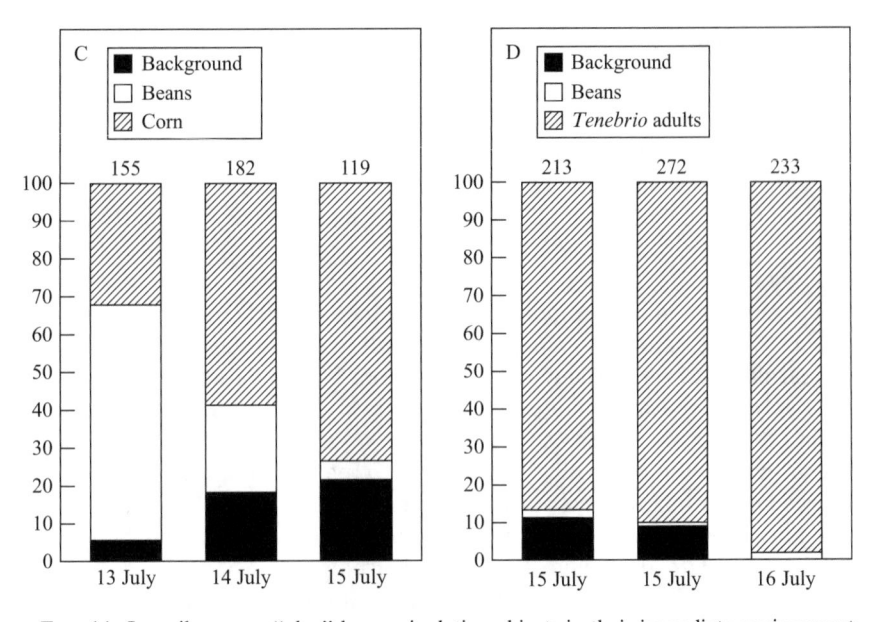

Fig. 14. Juvenile ravens "play" by manipulating objects in their immediate environment and show a preference for new items they had not encountered before. Shown here are object choices during six consecutive half-hour periods in the percentage of choices of dried (inedible) beans, yellow maize kernels (edible), and background (natural ground in forest) where after the third trial (on 15 July) tenebrio adults were introduced. Reprinted with permission from Heinrich (1995b).

characteristics, they are the substrate for learning that will later specify what to search for, ignore, or fear and avoid as food. Functionally, it helps the birds to "cast a wide net" and to find potential food whatever it may turn out to be and regardless of where they grow up.

The birds' neophilia is not restricted to small objects. As the birds became older, they feared large objects less and thus their attraction to them, which was previously masked by fear, became apparent. They showed a special attraction to large live animals, although that attraction was tempered with much caution. Animals to which they were attracted included live dogs, cats, chickens, and geese. When encountered for the first time, the live animals were approached cautiously in much the same way as carcasses were approached, first from behind and then springing back repeatedly until making contact with the tail end. In smaller animals, such as live chickens, the ravens' probes led to aggression and may have resulted in killing the chicken and subsequent feeding. But in the larger potentially dangerous animals such as dogs, such play behavior led to eventual mutual tolerance. In these cases, food could result not from eating the animal as such, but as I will later indicate, it may have ultimate evolutionary significance by using what it provides instead.

C. LEARNING AND KNOWING

A change in response to produce an ultimately more rewarding behavior through experience does not necessarily mean conscious understanding of cause and effect. Ravens' behavior, however, often appeared to involve more than trial-and-error learning. Sometimes they acted as if they could predict what another individual might do before it acted. Such ability should be especially valuable in a highly unpredictable social environment involving a life-style of close association with conspecific and heterospecific competitors aggregated at piles of meat.

Ravens the world over associate closely with carnivores, such as wolves, bears, cats, raptors, and humans. Any and all could provide food on the one hand and kill them in the process on the other. Each has different behavioral characteristics, as a species and as individuals. As I will indicate, the key to getting food in these situations probably involves the combination of curiosity, play, and learning, and perhaps ultimately also understanding.

The balance of the conflicting and mutually reinforcing tendencies change with age and learning experience and bring new behaviors into play. On their first encounters, my tame ravens intently watched a new cat, dog, domestic fowl, or sometimes strange person before approaching them from the rear, edging up, and pecking them while simultaneously jumping back. The birds made increasingly bolder probes and learned the limits of the animals' responses, and thus became able to gauge the limits of safety (Heinrich, 1999a). But at the same time that a raven is getting to know the other individual, the latter is learning as well. Changes in behavior of the other individual may be as important, if not more so, for the raven. Eventually, as the raven learns what it can get away with (literally and figuratively) and the novelty wears off, a potential predator, such as a wolf, might ignore the raven. In the process, the raven has a secured a new feeding niche as it is able feed beside the other at its kills.

Learning behavior on an innate substrate may also involve another social task, namely food caching. Food caching is a typical corvid characteristic instinct. However, the behavior involves many components, some of which are probably modified by learning. The first antecedents to the differentiated caching and retrieval responses appear shortly after fledging when the birds manipulate objects, pecking, billing, and carrying them, mock fighting over them in tug-of-wars with siblings, and with mock caching. After carrying an object, a bird may drop it and pick up another, and/or tuck the original object into a crevice or under grass before leaving it. The young shows interest in what interests others, and such dropped or apparently cached objects are often preferentially taken by siblings since the family travels together. The "cachers" learn how others respond to their caching attempts. This play-caching and subsequent retrieval of seemingly "worthless" non-food objects may represent half of all objects cached (Bugnyar et al., 2007a), and it would be a cheap way to learn what "works" and what does not in the mutual cache-making and retrieval game. This game becomes useful later when it is practiced with food because it increases the skills in food hiding and in pilfering (Bugnyar et al., 2007b, Bugnyar and Kotrschal, 2002, 2004). The young birds' improvement in their cache-making and cache-retrieval develops along with their object permanence, that is, representation of objects that are temporarily out of sight (Piaget, 1954).

I conclude that ravens learn by building on innate tendencies that ultimately promote experience. Experience is facilitated by the tendency of "play" that both facilitates the identification of and ultimately access to food. (Heinrich and Smolker, 1998). This neophilia, although tempered by neophobia of large-sized objects, might not fully preclude the birds from approaching the potentially new and dangerous large animals that they are sure to encounter at close range at carcasses. However, in this case they take advantage of the previous learning experience gained by others (i.e., culture).

D. CULTURE

Unlike many other passerine birds, who become independent of their parents either immediately or several days after fledging, ravens associate with their parents for 2–3 months after fledging. This prolonged association with their parents, and later for perhaps several years with other juveniles at carcasses and roosts, combined with alertness provides opportunity to learn from the lifetime experience of others. The recently fledged birds follow one or both of their parents, and during their "apprenticeship" with them, the fledglings learn what from the past has proven to be worthy of fear or food. In an aviary, for example, recently fledged naïve ravens who are without their parents are almost bizarrely frightened of any animal carcass provided to them (Heinrich, 1999a,b,c). However, wild ravens of the same age, who have followed their (experienced) parents to carcasses, approach them without hesitation (Heinrich, 1999a,b,c). Conversely, wild ravens instantly leave a feeding spot if one bird among them leaves in fright, such as after seeing a person (Heinrich, 1989). The ravens' close reference and attention to each other is also reflected in their ability to follow the gaze of others, even humans, with whom they are associated (Bugnyar et al., 2004; Schloegl et al., 2007).

Individual identification may be particularly relevant and important for culturally transmitted knowledge because it concerns "insider knowledge" that may be difficult to acquire but can be easy to transmit. In my aviary, ravens routinely recognized humans as individuals (Heinrich, 1999a,b,c). Alternatively, I could identify few of them as individuals. Whenever I walked into the aviary the wild-caught birds came to me to be fed, but when a stranger approached, they flew out of sight. Individual recognition may be a general ability of many birds; gull researchers need to conceal their identity in order to visit the same colony repeatedly to band birds (Spear, 1988). The ability to recognize and remember individual humans has been recently experimentally examined in American crows (Marzluff et al., 2010). Urban wild crows, *C. brachyrhynchos*, in Seattle, Washington, quickly recognized a dangerous person (one who trapped, banded, and released them) and continue to scold them for at least several years. The ravens' attention to individual humans is presumably an extension of a more general pattern to recognize enemies individually and to develop and maintain social relations in their own species. In ravens and jackdaws, it is used to identify and favor kin and associates (Scheid et al., 2007; Schwab et al., 2008). Those birds, who can identify enemies, mob them, and associates then identify them as well.

While raven's fear of humans is widespread and has presumably spread and perhaps been maintained by cultural transmission, acceptance could potentially also be similarly attained. In the Bay Area of California, at least some ravens follow one person regularly. Dadre Traughber (pers. comm.) has now had a "relation" with a pair of ravens and their offspring and associates in Marin County, California, for 7 years. On 6 September 2010, when Traughber visited with "her" ravens for the 244th time, she wrote in one of her notes that she had gone to see her three new "kids" weekly since the beginning of July when they were still with their parents. Now they often meet her when she arrives in her car, and they sometimes follow her the entire 3–4 h of her hike. She only occasionally now drops them a peanut, although she fed them more generously at the beginning of their relationship in 2003. Similarly, Guenther Bloch (pers. comm.), while studying wolves in Banff National Park in Canada, reports ravens meeting up with a mammal at a rendezvous point, the animal's home site. When the animal leaves, the ravens follow it. It is always the same raven pair that follows but sometimes others join in. The inference of these cases is that ravens are adaptable, and they presumably would have followed northern human Pleistocene hunters as well since they would have reliably left meat at their encampments.

In the northeastern United States, ravens seldom come near humans in the wild. It is difficult to imagine how the cycle of fear of humans can be broken. I assume it would require a sparse population with isolated individuals so that fear cannot be spread socially. (It is unlikely that trust will spread as easily as fear, because while learning trust in one area or situation could earn a meal or be neutral, it could be deadly in another place). Presently in New England, ravens have not been hunted or killed at poison baits for perhaps a half century, but the fear of man remains. I know of only one exception of these otherwise fearful local birds learning trust; after daily continuous (forced) contact with my wild-captured ravens in an aviary, they became tame enough, after several months of daily contact, to feed in groups with me in the aviary standing within 3 m of them. Once released back into the wild, however, they again contact wild fearful ravens, and that fear would presumably take precedence over trust.

Ravens are well known to associate with wolves (Mech, 1966, 1970). At the Canadian Wolf Research Center at Shubernacadie, Nova Scotia, where I observed ravens and wolves at close range for 4 days, the ravens almost invariably fed along with wolves, who also fed as a group. Food (dog chow, skinned beef, and cut-open deer) was invariably left untouched by the ravens until the wolves started to feed on it (Heinrich, 1999a). In 1996, I examined nine wolf-killed elk carcasses in north Yellowstone National Park. All were being fed on by 6–30 ravens at any one time. Several kilometers outside the park boundary where elk were hunted, I examined 34 elk gut piles (with entrails, spleens, lungs, and diaphragm) and none of these were attended by ravens (Heinrich, 1999a). In a follow-up study in the same area (Stahler et al., 2002), ravens required about 35 min to discover experimental carcasses, but discovery time of wolf-killed carcasses was zero; several ravens were already present at the kill and they fed almost immediately. Raven numbers at the food site then increased quickly (Fig. 15). In Banff National Park in Canada, ravens make contact and play with wolf pups as soon as they leave the den, and when the pack leaves on a hunt, the ravens follow, or vice versa (Gunther and Karin Bloch, pers. comm.).

Wolves were reintroduced to Yellowstone National Park in 1995–1996 after a 70-year absence. Five years after their introduction, ravens were already preferentially associating with wolves (*Canis lupus*) in a kleptoparasitic foraging strategy (Stahler et al., 2002). They did not follow elk (*Cervus elaphus*), the wolves's primary prey. Amazingly, the ravens also did not follow coyotes (*Canis latrans*), which to us look like smaller wolves. Given that, ravens may follow humans as well as wolves but do not associate with coyotes or elk (Stahler et al., 2002). Nevertheless, despite the birds' quick acceptance of and close association with wolves, it is highly unlikely that ravens associate with wolves is solely instinctive since following behavior involves sometimes acute discrimination, and associations are based on

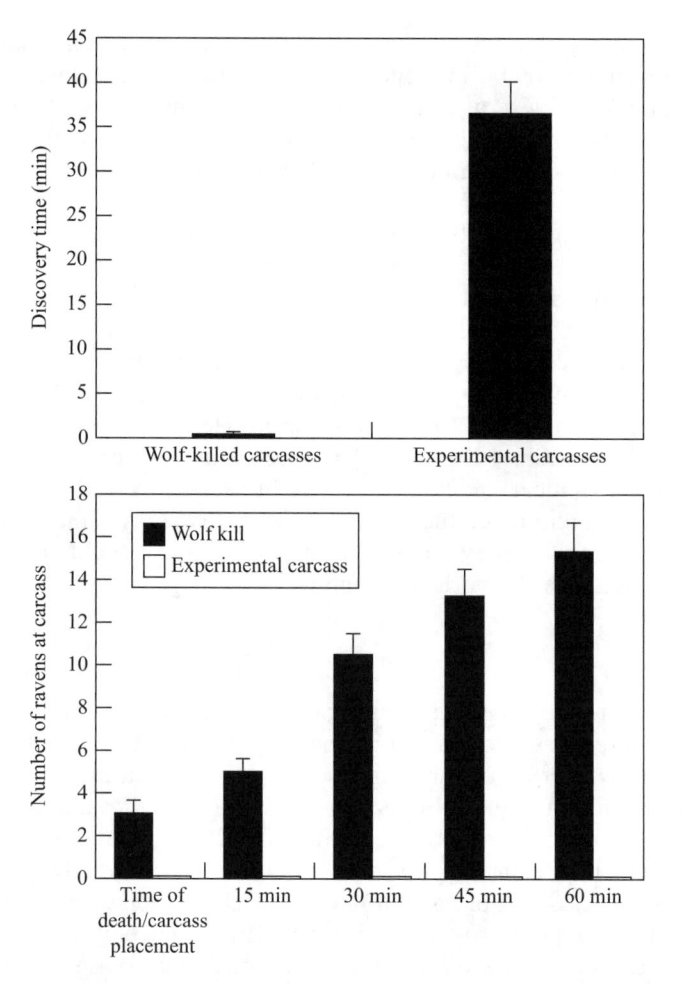

FIG. 15. In Yellowstone National Park, ravens were present at wolf-killed elk carcasses, whereas experimental carcasses were not discovered until at least a half hour (top). Subsequently, the numbers of ravens at the wolf-killed carcass increased, while no ravens appeared at the experimental carcasses even though they had been discovered. Reprinted with permission from Stahler et al. (2002).

learning cues which include attraction to wolf howls in Nova Scotia (Harrington, 1978) and to gunshots (but not other human-created loud noises), during the elk hunting season in Wyoming (White, 2005).

In Yellowstone, as in Banff, ravens also start their association with wolf pups at the den (Stahler, personal communication) where they interact with them, scavenge on their scat, and pick up scraps of their food. After the pups leave the den and the wolves travel in a pack, the ravens continue to stay in touch with them. In Yellowstone, ravens are present when a pack attacks an elk, and several land and feed with them moments after the elk is down. At this point in time, ravens are regular commensals with wolves, as has been observed by literally all people who have studied wolves (Mech, 1966,1970).

It has been suggested that ravens associated with northern aboriginal human hunters regardless of kind, and symbiotic relationships may have developed through a combination of learning based on instinctual tendencies and from the example of others, but also by direct mutual experience with the specific carnivores. As any pet owner of dogs and cats knows well, otherwise fierce predators come to ignore or even to be attached to those animals they get to know. A possible scenario (Heinrich, 1999a,b,c) is that a raven gave food calls (the "yells") in frustration at a carcass because it could not access meat (Heinrich and Marzluff, 1991). A wolf hearing them came by, which reinforced the raven to call near live prey, which in turn led the raven to seek live prey. Thus, a culture of symbiosis could develop with wolves as well as with aboriginal hunters.

E. INSIGHT

Knowing or understanding (seeing causal connections) permits rapid and appropriate responses to novel situations. Appropriate behavior to any one situation can also result from lengthy trial-and-error learning, which need not include insight (quick understanding) or going through some steps mentally before or without performing them. Examples of what looks like, but may not be, insight are common in ravens. As already mentioned, ravens at a carcass tear or hack off meat to cache. When working in mated pairs in the winter on frozen meat, each bird could only chip off small pieces. It can store a few pieces in its gular pouch and continue to hack off more, but soon the bird can no longer hack meat when also holding a beak-full at the same time. Ravens then lay their loosened meat down until a large pile is made, and then cram it into their wide-open beak before departing with it. Birds in crowds never set food aside, presumably because they potentially know that it would "instantly" be stolen by the others. When confronted with large hunks of suet that were too heavy to carry off, ravens in pairs solved a different potential means-end problem that, to my knowledge, has not been seen in other birds. Rather than hacking off the fat in bits and pieces like all other birds (crows, blue jays, woodpeckers, nuthatches, chickadees) on the same suet did, they hammered out a deep groove to cut off thick manageable pieces that could be carried off (Comstock, 2007; Heinrich, 1999a,b,c). The hacking out of small bits of suet to make the groove to get the big piece of fat later was not just incidental to getting a proximate reward since small pieces of fat hacked off in the process were left in the apparent haste to get the big piece.

The preceding examples could be the result of learning. There is no way of knowing because the individuals were wild ravens whose previous experience was unknown. Similarly, the use of rocks as tools to throw at nest robbers can also be attributed to causes other than insight (Heinrich, 1988b). However, neither the suet cutting nor the stone dropping on intruders was seen in any other birds who make use of the same food (woodpeckers, nuthatches, chickadees, blue jays, and crows) or the same nest sites (birds of prey) and who could presumably all learn by trial and error but apparently do not. Is one the result of insight and the other not? Unfortunately, despite the suggestive comparative differences, there is no way of knowing. Can tool use address these possibilities?

The making and use of tools often requires the ability to perform a sequence of actions to bring about an effect and has typically been used to infer understanding or insight (e.g., Griffin, 1984; Piaget, 1954; Povinelli, 2000; Thorpe, 1956). Among birds, New Caledonia crows *Corvus moneduloides* (Chappell and Kacelnik, 2002, 2004; Hunt, 1996; Weir et al., 2002) and woodpecker finches (Tebbich and Bshary, 2004) routinely manufacture and use tools, but show mixed results in means–ends understanding of tools. Although impressive, these behaviors by birds and those resulting in the most impressive constructions by social hymenoptera (von Frisch, 1974) are performed by animals with minute brains. They require no or only minimal learning and insight does not have to be invoked to account for them.

Proof of involvement of understanding requires experimental examination of tasks for which the animal could not have been specifically programmed by either evolution or by learning. One of the commonly used tests for understanding has involved strings attached to food to assess if the animal performs the appropriate steps to access the food (Harlow and Settlage, 1934). This method had been used for a variety of birds including finches, tits, and budgerigars. The problem with the tests was that although insight could have occurred, the role of learning could not be ruled out (Ducker and Rensch, 1977; Heinrich, 1995a,b; Taylor et al., 2010; Thorpe, 1956; Vince, 1961).

The proof of mental phenomena is probably never possible using observations of behavior alone. It requires instead the elimination of alternatives, which is difficult to achieve because most behavior contains various elements. The question is whether the task is "solved" mostly by chance, trial-and-error learning or instinct (Hauser et al., 2002). To examine whether ravens have the capacity for insight, experiments were performed using hand-reared birds that had no experience with pulling up food that was suspended by string and who during their evolutionary history would not have had opportunity or need to secure food by that method.

As expected, ravens naïve to food attached to a long (70 cm) string exhibited a variety of responses (Heinrich, 1995a,b). One common initial response (of young birds) was to examine the food from a perch and then either ignore it or fly at it to grasp it with the bill and then dangle from it. Others appeared to try to sever the string where it was attached to the perch. But other (especially older) birds tried something different during their first and then all later trials. They perched above the string attachment, reached down below the perch, grasped a length of string with their bill, pulled the loop of string up above the perch, laid it down upon the perch, then stepped on that loop of string and applied enough pressure on it so it would not slip, then let go of the string, reached down below the perch again, all the while maintaining pressure on the previously pulled-up string. They then lifted the second loop of string and repeated the sequence 6–10 times until the meat was obtained, at which point they stayed in place until they had removed the meat from the string, and then left. A second similar technique used by others was pulling up successive loops but then stepping *sideways* along the perch until the string was taut and only then stepping on the string before reaching down again. The birds also repeated this sequence until the entire length of the string had been stretched across the horizontal perch and the meat was obtained.

The preceding results (Heinrich, 1995a,b) appeared to demonstrate that some individuals possessed knowledge of cause-and-effect of their actions. That is, they appeared to "know" that the food was attached to the string and that by pulling the string up, they would reach the food. But if so, then an additional prediction is that they should be reluctant to try to fly off with the meat on the string that they had just pulled up onto their perch. Alternatively, they *should be* willing to fly off with meat that they found on the perch but that they had *not* pulled up. Indeed, three of the five ravens (in the first study) that had pulled up meat on string were very reluctant to leave. They fed on the meat as soon as they got it up to their perch, but always stayed in the place where they were perched. They did not leave their perch spontaneously, and could not easily be shooed away by my deliberate attempts to do so (Heinrich, unpublished data). If, on the other hand, I agitated them enough to fly away, they almost invariably *dropped* the meat (172 times out of 184 trials). The ravens' behavior differed when meat with the same (loose) string attached to it was laid (by me) onto the perch. In these cases, the birds picked the meat up and "always" flew off with it without hesitation (157 times out of 157 trials). Since they eagerly flew off with meat attached to string that they had *not* pulled up, it was apparently the knowledge of the anticipated event of having the meat yanked out of their bill after pulling it up that prevented them from flying off. In other words, they apparently anticipated a result that they had not experienced.

Additional experiments suggest that ravens have "rational expectations" that are predicated on understanding the connection between cause and effect. We expect, for example, that objects will fall. To find out if ravens have the same expectation, and simultaneously "see" in their minds what is out of sight, I allowed six tame birds to get acclimated for 2 weeks to an opaque 120-cm long PVC tube on the ground in their aviary. I occasionally inserted food, including live frogs so that they had experience looking in and supposedly through the tube. During subsequent experimental trials, when they were no longer frightened of the tube, I set it up vertically at a slight angle with one end stuck into the soil so that any food that dropped down could not be visible from the ground. A perch at the open end was also positioned so that, although a bird could see into the top, it could not see down to the bottom. When I dropped food into the tube all six birds responded within 10 s. Four of six flew first to the top to look in, and the other two flew first directly to the bottom to attempt to excavate food there. On their second trial, three of the four that had looked first into the top checked instead first at the bottom (Heinrich, unpublished data).

What happens when an animal with "rational" expectations is confronted with the irrational? To investigate this question, I performed a test where a phenomenon that is routinely encountered and ignored is experienced but in an unusual context. Psychologists "ask" preverbal children if they notice unusual events by monitoring increases in their attention. I did the same with ravens (who show alarm by sleeking their feathers, standing erect, and then flying off). Ravens routinely see branches wiggle when they land on them and when there is wind. I attached thin monofilament line to twigs and waited until birds rested on a windless day. When I pulled on the monofilament line, they showed instant fright the moment a branch moved in apparent spontaneous fashion. That is, they reacted as we might to an unusual event, one that to them had no apparent cause and that to us in an analogous experiment would have seemed "spooky."

After having spontaneously pulled up food on string, the birds could be assumed to have been trained according to the rule, "pull up on string that is directly above the meat," because that is what they did in the test and may subsequently assume. They may, after that, no longer check to make sure that the string they pull on is indeed actually connected to the meat below them; they investigate what they knew; I suspended two 70-cm long strings side by side. Only one held meat, while the other was attached to a stone of equal weight. Two strings were presented in three ways: (a) normally with the weight pulled straight down by gravity; (b) crossed so that by pulling on the string above the meat the bird would pull up the stone; and (c) the stone was held by the same kind of string as during the prior tests, but the meat was now attached to a new string of novel color (red), versus white, the color of the string which they had previously been "trained" to associate with the food reward (Heinrich, 1995a,b).

The results of these tests were telling. Having been "trained" to pull up a certain *kind* of string of a certain color and texture that dangled directly above the food, some birds pulled instead on the novel string that connected to the food on their very first trials. If they initially contacted the "wrong" string, they then immediately corrected themselves and moved over to pull up the other string, the one with meat.

A recent experiment showed that New Caledonia crows can use a 40-cm long string to reach food (Taylor et al., 2010). The authors, however, concluded that the birds did *not* require insight to solve the task, but instead their behavior represented "operant conditioning mediated by a perceptual-motor feedback cycle." Ravens display the same behavior, even after making mistakes. Their string-pulling is based on their ability to coordinate their feet with their eyes and is influenced by feedback and learning which enhances speed and smoothness. For example, using 70-cm long string, the birds took on average 4–46 s to obtain the meat. By the fifteenth trial, birds acquired food three to four times faster than they did during the first five trials (Heinrich, unpublished data). Some birds did not hold the string tightly enough so that the string slipped. This increased the number of steps the bird had to perform before obtaining the meat. But this need not have anything to do with insight. Feedback is always a necessary part of the behavior.

By pulling on a string, a bird might see the meat come closer, and the sensation of seeing it at a distance of 65 cm from them, rather at 70 cm, could at least theoretically be perceived as a reward. One test of such presumptive reward involved an experiment where the birds had to perform the illogical task of pulling *down* on a string above them (Fig. 16). This caused another string below them to come *up* by the same increments that the other was pulled down (Heinrich and Bugnyar, 2005). Not surprisingly (if the birds had some insight into the situation but not enough), all six *naive* ravens failed to solve the preceding nonintuitive test. Most birds did not pull the string at all in this pull-down task. The two birds that did yank on the string failed to show the sequence of pulling and stepping on loops; they could see the food but that did not improve their performance. Only those birds who had previous experience in pulling up meat in the straight pull-up task persisted in the pull-down task. They then learned to pull on strings that were reversed in orientation and required pulling down to get the meat

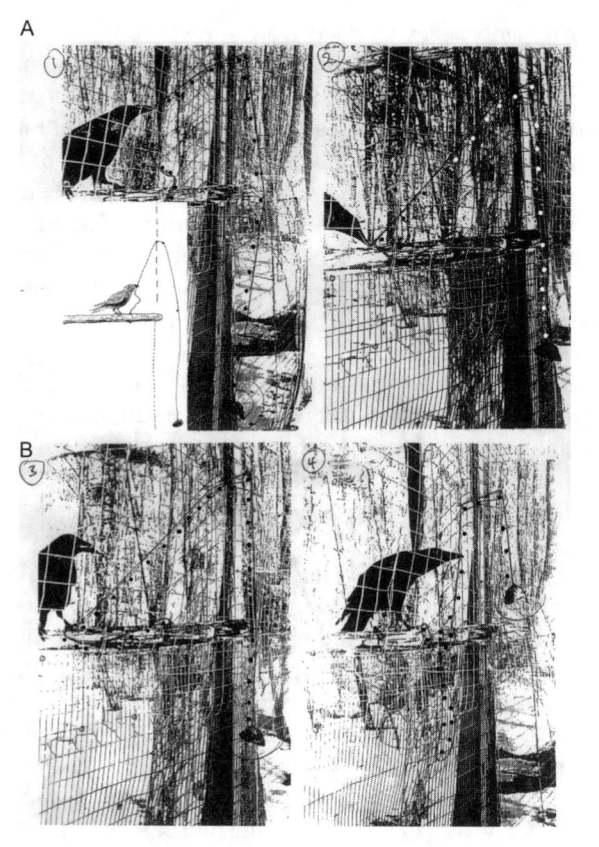

FIG. 16. Setup for (A) vertical pull-up task versus (The white and dark dots are here added onto the photograph to help guide the viewer to see the string; they were not available to the bird.) (B) pull-down task for set of experiments on a group of ravens tested for solving an "illogical" solution. Reprinted with permission from Heinrich and Bugnyar (2005).

to come up. These results proved two things. First, ravens who are successful string-pullers did not pull on string *simply* because it was in the vicinity of food even though food was attached to string. Second, after they were successful at string pull-ups their rewarded behavior was reinforced; after they had experienced the logical behavior of pulling up meat that was dangled below, they also *learned*, but the learning was that of being predisposed to an awareness of the food and string connection and thus an increased motivation to pull strings. Such trained birds could be retrained to learn to pull the string down to get the meat to come up. In contrast, the logical leap to accomplish this task was apparently too great for naïve birds.

In addition to inferences gleaned from the speed of acquisition of correctly performing complex multistep behavior, insight could also be potentially inferred using physiological data. For example, in rats obtaining food by a new and more effective rule was associated with a simultaneous abrupt shift in neural activity in the prefrontal cortex area of their brains (Durstewitz and Seamans, 2010). The association between the sudden acquisition of the skill in parallel with a sudden new neural activity in a specific brain area strongly suggests a causal relationship and hence could potentially become a diagnostic tool for gauging whether insight learning (or other cognitive functions, as for example, self-awareness; Epstein et al., 1981), has occurred.

Tool use in conjunction with body movements would appear to involve willful manipulation of at least parts of oneself. Does this imply self-awareness, and can it be shown by mirror experiments?

F. SELF-AWARENESS AND SOCIAL KNOWLEDGE

Ravens establish a dominance hierarchy at food and typically show their dominance by feather postures (Gwinner, 1964) as well as by the positions they take on the carcass while feeding. The most dominant birds attack or feign attacks at their near-status rivals (Heinrich, 1994a). If they recognize themselves in a mirror, then they should not attack their reflection. However, if they recognize only the dominance posture as such, then they should attack or feign attack at their images in a mirror. The question is still open, but I raise it because of some anecdotal observations. I once put a large mirror in front of a group of ravens feeding at a carcass, but saw no change in behavior and thus dropped the project. However, I have received three reports of "ravens" (often not differentiated from "crows") beating themselves bloody on window panes of remote cabins in the woods, apparently treating their reflections as rivals like most other birds do. Whether or not they recognize themselves is not clear, but ravens and other crows can recognize each other as individuals. Do they also have knowledge about what others might know?

We performed an experimental study of caching and cache-raiding to answer this question (Bugnyar and Heinrich, 2005, 2006). Cachers were allowed to cache in private. However, a window into another compartment permitted a putative cache-raider to view the cacher. When the bird (the "knower"), who had visual access to the cacher, was allowed to enter the compartment with the cache, the cacher attacked the putative cache-raider (knower) when the latter went near the hidden food (Fig. 17). When another bird (the "guesser"), who had also been in the other compartment but whose view into the caching area had been blocked by a curtain, entered the compartment, the cacher allowed it to approach its caches. In both of these cases, the ravens acted as though they knew what the other birds knew or did not know about cache locations. An alternate interpretation is that the knowledgeable putative cache-raider behaved differently when it neared the cache and by its behavior divulged that it knew the cache location. However, in both situations, cache owners "knew" something about what others knew. In the first situation, it knew that the cache-raider knew the cache location because the cache-making had been *observed by it*. In the other case, the cache owner knew what the other knew *from its behavior*.

We found no evidence that ravens in their cache-raiding cued on behavior that might reveal they were near a cache. Observers of caches did not differ from nonobservers when they were tested together with the cachers; like the nonobservers, the observers went indiscriminately to the "wrong" places thus potentially concealing their knowledge of cache locations. However, in private these observers went more quickly, and directly, to the others' caches.

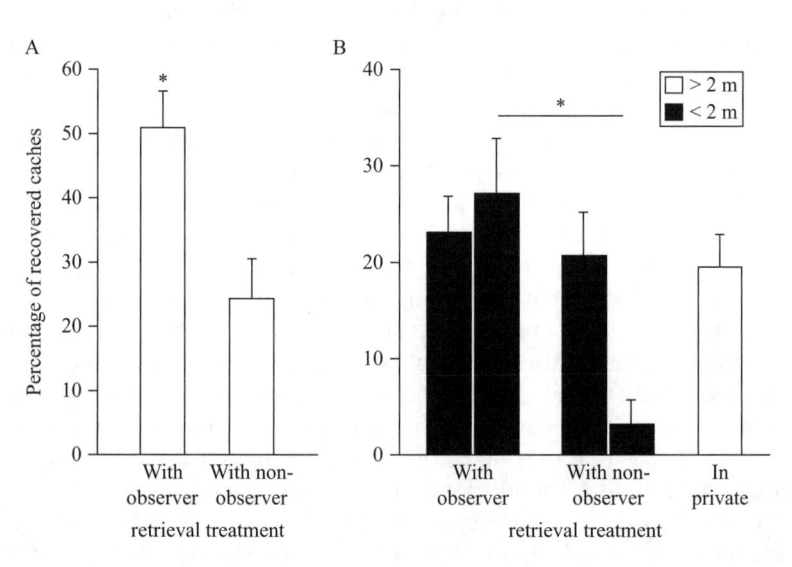

FIG. 17. Cache-makers attempted to recover their caches when they were in danger of being raided by a competitor. They were (left panel) twice as likely to recover their cache in the presence of an observer than a nonobserver of the cache-making (left panel). The likelihood of retrieving the cached food by the cache-maker was markedly lower when a nonobserver approached its cache than when a putative observer came near it. Reprinted with permission from Bugnyar and Heinrich (2005).

Knowledge of putative cache-raiders has recently been corroborated in other experiments. In these, a human experimenter hid food, while the visual field of raven bystanders was manipulated (Bugnyar, 2011). Three competitor ravens had been visually present at two, one, or none of the caching events and thus had full, partial, or no knowledge of cache locations. Predictably, they should therefore prioritize retrieving *those* caches their competitor had seen being made. As expected, the pilfering ravens were quicker to raid caches made by fully informed competitors, that is, those that had been present during the caching event by the human. Birds in this way seemed to be "mind reading" and not reacting to possible behavioral cues given by the cache defender. How far removed is knowing what another knows relative to what he "feels"?

G. EMPATHY AND TOLERANCE

A recent study suggests the possibility of empathy in ravens (Fraser and Bugnyar, 2010a)—the ability to infer feelings in others, which would then permit action to intervene on their behalf. Ravens have been shown to do both. A group of 13 young ravens reared together in an aviary were monitored to quantify their many fights (during which loud rasping calls are typical) and the opposite of fights, their sitting closely next to each other during which mutual preening (and low soft comfort sounds are typical). The latter acts were defined as "consolation" behavior if they were carried out by a third party, that is, a bystander not involved in the original aggression. The researchers watched birds for 10 min after each of 152 conflicts and recorded all affiliative and aggressive acts during that time. These were compared with control observations of the victim of the aggression the next day at the same time, also for 10 min. The surprising result of this study was that within the 2 min after an aggressive encounter (of 152 recorded) the victims were 2.5 more likely to be approached by a *bystander* for consolation than during the control period. The bystanders most likely to affiliate with the victim were its prior associates with whom it had a bond or relationship. The bystanders' affiliative response to those who had been attacked suggests that they acted out of proximate empathy for the others' feelings, potentially to bond friendship in future partnerships.

Ravens are often highly aggressive, but they are often also loyal and tolerant of associates. Empathy is an important psychological state that may proximally inform and guide behavior and thus be an ultimately adaptive social behavior. It may involve an individual's boundaries relative to others, as Konrad Lorenz in his book *King Solomon's Ring* (1949) indicated in his example of the raven and the dove. As previously mentioned, his pet raven

Roah showed great restraint when it preened Lorenz near the eyes. Lorenz inferred from this that social animals that possess dangerous weapons, such as ravens with the big powerful bill or wolves with their sharp teeth, have along with their weapons also evolved an ability to restrain their use around their associates or kin. Lorenz did not invoke empathy, but he drew inferences about the birds' evolved behavior involving aggression, weapons, and restraint. However, as the previously mentioned experiments show, tolerance from empathy is not excluded as a possible proximate mechanism for the raven's behavior. In light of this work, it can now be suggested that Roah knew the effects that might result by poking his friend in the eye without actually poking him in the eye. I do know that ravens are not always inhibited to poke the eyes of others, since Scott Lindsey, a helper of mine received a bloody peck wound under his right eyebrow when he tried to hold a recently captured wild raven at slightly less than arm's length. Empathy could have been involved in exercising the inhibition with Lorenz, as well as in the aggression on Scott Lindsey, since the same ability to calculate the effect of the action on others could be used not only to prevent harm, but also to inflict it. (But even if either is true, the role of instinct is not precluded).

Observers of ravens in the wild have reported seeing ravens attacking others, with one or several ganging up on one. The victim may sustain wounds, usually on the wing tips, but usually escapes. Almost nothing is known about what motivates these attacks that are not at food as we have no knowledge of the antecedents to the behavior. Quick retaliations by threats to raiding of caches is routine (Bugnyar and Heinrich, 2006), but in the wild the raider can almost always escape and need not face potential attackers. In captive birds, there is more to be learned. In one group of ravens that had also been together for several weeks in an aviary, a frozen calf provided them adequate food. In this case, the calf was chopped open on all sides regularly so that the meat was always accessible and the birds could cache what they could not immediately consume. An additional bird was innocently added to the same *ad hoc* group, and this bird was repeatedly chased from the carcass that the four normally fed from together. The newcomer then stayed away from the carcass but instead tried to feed itself solely by raiding the other's caches. Presumably as a result, it was one day found hacked to death by the others. This was the only "murder" observed in the two decades-long study. This anecdote suggests that attacks are "punishment" for transgressions. Did the birds attack, knowing they would inflict harm, or were they reacting solely to stimulus? It also raises the issue of "morals," group norms that are expected and enforced. Is this a uniquely human phenomenon?

In contrast to the treatment of victims of attacks, ravens also sidle up to and preen each other in ways that in primates are signs of friendship. In mated raven pairs, one member routinely stacks meat next to itself when the two are working together, and they do not take food from one another. Instead, the male brings his mate food while she incubates and broods the small young. In short, the birds observe rules of behavior. If we observed them in ourselves, we might say they were behaving according to expected norms that are based on empathy and that could promote tolerance and cooperation.

Tolerance in ravens needs to be based on trust, and that cannot be counted on. But it does occur. I observed vigorous chases that lasted for over an hour when a group of six ravens arrived near a calf bait in Vermont, and at the end of that time the vagrants left without feeding. Finally (February 1998) a group of 15 did get at the meat and the adults eventually became tolerant. The feeding site was surrounded by four active raven nests within 2–10 km, and at least three pairs also utilized the same bait over several days of feeding as the adults' aggression subsided. The bait (which was next to a blind near my house) may have been feared by them. They always waited until the vagrants had started to feed and then flew down immediately behind them (Heinrich, 1999a,b,c). The newcomers and possibly the neighboring pairs helped them dilute the perceived risk of feeding there, or perhaps after a large crowd assembled, it became counter-productive to be aggressive and chase individuals away because they would have been immediately replaced by others.

Similarly, my tame ravens, Goliath and his mate Whitefeather, engaged in an aerial battle (on 6 January 1997) with one or two other ravens for 23 min over a calf carcass I had provided them in Maine. The pair then fed alone on the carcass. However, on the next day, a crowd of six juveniles fed there instead. They were not the pair's young from the previous year as they had been banded. The pair later joined the group, and although both of the pair put on dominance displays, they did not give chase. The next day the vagrants and the pair fed there again, but there was never any recruitment of a crowd (Heinrich, 1999a,b,c). Not enough details are available to decipher the meaning of this incident. It would seem, for example, to be less selfish if territorial raven pairs were tolerant of a few hungry stray vagrant birds and allow them to feed along-side themselves. If they did so, then these weaker birds would have no reason to recruit and if they then did not recruit, then the powerful adults' sharing would result in them possessing most of the carcass for themselves (rather than the roost crowd getting it instead). The adult's tolerance and sharing would then be construed as selfish behavior, but if this were the case, it required putting themselves into the mind of the others.

These anecdotes suggest that social relationships of ravens are not absolute. Mirroring those of chimpanzees (De Waal, 1996), they vary in value, and depend on compatibility and stability (Fraser and Bugnyar, 2010b). As expected, kin relations have high value and depend on sex (female— female relationships are less compatible and more insecure).

We cannot ask a raven how it feels about another, but we can "read" their love versus hate, and we now know ravens can read other's intentions. *A priori*, one would predict that feelings are irrelevant and that only effects matter. However, some of the ravens' behavior is apparently associated with a knowledge of the feelings of others. Feelings generate acts, and it is therefore useful for ravens to empathize to anticipate feelings, so that they desist from acts that will result in reprisal, and to induce acts that will create allies.

V. Summary and Discussion

Corvids, including the raven, are generalists who hunt small, generally invertebrate prey. The raven, *C. corax*, however, is adapted to utilize prey that is even larger that it can kill. It has evolved to utilize the prey provided by other, more powerful, hunters. Yet although a generalist feeder, it may be predisposed to access a variety of food and thus also live in several situations or habitats. In this way, the raven is at the far end of the generalist spectrum. It is able to feed and reproduce over the widest geographical and ecological range of any bird on earth. It stays year-round and breeds in the high arctic, northern tundra, and northern taiga forests. It lives on oceanic coastlines and islands, on the Himalayan mountain peaks and (formerly) on the American prairies, and now also in some cities. Wherever wolves roam in packs, ravens are there as close commensals (and possible symbionts) with them. Their close association with humans in areas they are not persecuted is likely a change from their former, and still widespread, association with wolves.

One of the most conspicuous aspects of this solitary-nesting bird is its appearance in crowds at carcasses. The crowds are composed primarily of nonbreeding subadults assembled by recruitment from nocturnal roosts. These roosts may be small and temporary in areas of rapidly shifting resources, such as small widely dispersed carcasses, or they can be year-round at temporally reliable resources. The entire roost, if small, or subgroups of it, if large, act as "gangs" that overpower territorial adults otherwise defending access to a carcass. Aside from the primary long-range recruitment of generally nonkin groups from roosts, the ravens are also attracted to bait by aural and visual signals associated with it, as well as by the food call, developed from a retention of their juvenile begging calls that are given by dominant, hungry juveniles directly at the bait.

After a food bonanza is found, the birds concentrate their efforts to haul off successive loads of meat during scatter hoarding for their own consumption later. The caches are generally far removed from the original food source. They are a valuable resource even when coming from a large carcass because winter carcasses are often frozen solid and it takes much work to chip off a load of meat. Ravens observe others making caches and may later raid those caches. Cache-makers therefore take great care to avoid being seen by others making a cache, or if they are (experimentally) confined in the presence of others, they greatly delay making caches, or quickly retrieve just-made caches and make false caches. They defend caches if raiding conspecifics approach.

The raven's anticipation of the intentions of others suggests "theory-of-mind" abilities. Such capacity may be especially useful in their association with dangerous carnivores with whom they associate. Various experiments indicate (by inference through exclusion; Schloegl et al., 2009) that innate programming, learning, and chance are not the prime causative factors and that ravens are capable of cause-and-effect reasoning. Cultural learning from parents and associates is involved in their adaptation, and empathy and tolerance are discussed as a possible part of their behavioral and social repertoire.

Mutual habituation of ravens to the predators they depend on for food, and conversely to others who may prey on them, is achieved from a combination of neophobia and neophilia of large furry objects. The first leads ravens to distance themselves to food, but combined with neophilia and learning facilitated through play, leads to "tests" of the reactions of the live versus dead animals. Neophilia, without any apparent neophobia, is also shown to round smooth objects. This combination of traits facilitates ravens to find, and then quickly learn, the most appropriate food in any of a great range of seasons and ecological settings.

It is impossible to say whether the flexibility of behavior is responsible for the ravens' expansion over this large range, or if its flexibility came instead from the access to and necessity of encountering this diversity of environments. It seems likely, however, that one feeds the other in a mutually reinforcing feedback loop; the more flexible the behavior the more new situations and habitats could be exploited, which in turn selected for more flexible behavior. However, since flexibility always means less-than-perfect responses locally, this leads to the question of why the birds would then not succumb to local adaptation and "freeze" their behavior into adapted patterns that would decrease the need for costly trial-and-error learning? I suspect that part of the answer is that even if the raven were to be adapted with perfect innate responses to deal effectively with a local environment, it would still have to deal with inherent unpredictability and risk in the form of conspecific and heterospecific competitors.

In the tropics such as the African plains, animal carcasses are almost exclusively provided by carnivores, and what they do not eat is almost completely inundated by maggots in 2 or 3 days. Ravens like fresh meat. For an ephemeral, but valuable, resource that in open country is located quickly, a mass frenzy of mammals and vultures clean it up in about a day or less. In short, the southern plains engender a brief but intense scramble competition where what is not eaten within a day or two is left only for the insects. There is little chance and need for individual recognition of other carnivores or members of the same species. In the northern forests, in contrast, a carcass in winter might last weeks and potentially also months. At such long-lasting resources, ravens meet dangerous carnivores on whom they depend. Such resources are also places for long-term repeated meetings of the same individuals of their own kind. Frequent encounters and simultaneous access of many individuals for long periods of time would favor individuals who show restraint, who achieve social dominance and/or whose access is not only dependent on the responses of the others of their own kind but also those of other species and individuals. That is, they face a formidably socially challenging task. If they can handle it with their social knowledge, they may then also be predisposed to face other environmentally challenging situations as they occur. As a consequence, the world is open to them, wherever large food bonanzas can be found.

Acknowledgments

I am grateful to the many researchers who have been fascinated by this enigmatic and complex bird, the raven, and I especially thank John Marzluff and Thomas Bugnyar for their dedication and recent work with whom and which I have had the pleasure and honor to be associated with in our mutual endeavor to try to understand the life and the mind of this bird and to bring it into the light of science.

References

Boarman, W.I., Heinrich, B., 1999. Common raven (*Corvus corax*). In: Poole, A., Gill, F. (Eds.), The Birds of North America, No. 476. The Birds of North America, Inc., Philadelphia, PA, pp. 1–32.

Bruggers, J.D., 1988. The Behavior and Ecology of the Common Raven in Northeastern Minnesota. PhD thesis, University of Minnesota, Minneapolis.

Bugnyar, T., 2011. Knower–guesser differentiation in ravens: others' viewpoints matter. Proc. R. Soc. B 278, 634–640.

Bugnyar, T., Heinrich, B., 2005. Food-storing ravens, *Corvus corax*, differentiate between knowledgeable and ignorant competitors. Proc. R. Soc. B 272, 1641–1646.

Bugnyar, T., Heinrich, B., 2006. Pilfering ravens, *Corvus corax*, adjust their behaviour to social context and identity of competitors. Anim. Cogn. 9, 369–376.

Bugnyar, T., Kotrschal, K., 2002. Observational learning and the raiding of food caches in ravens, *Corvus corax*: is it "tactical deception" Anim. Behav. 64, 185–195.

Bugnyar, T., Kotrschal, K., 2004. Leading a conspecific away from food in ravens, *Corvus corax*? Anim. Cogn. 7, 69–76.

Bugnyar, T., Kijne, T.M., Kotreschal, K., 2001. Food calling in ravens: are yells referential signals? Anim. Behav. 61, 949–958.

Bugnyar, T., Stoewe, M., Heinrich, B., 2004. Ravens, *Corvus corax*, follow gaze direction of humans around obstacles. Proc. R. Soc. Lond. B 271, 1331–1336.

Bugnyar, T., Stoewe, M., Heinrich, B., 2007a. The ontogeny of caching behaviour in ravens, *Corvus corax*. Anim. Behav. 74, 757–767.

Bugnyar, T., Schwab, C., Schloegl, C., Kotrschal, K., Heinrich, B., 2007b. Ravens judge competitors through experience with play caching. Curr. Biol. 17, 1804–1808.

Chappell, J., Kacelnik, A., 2002. Tool selectivity in a non-mammal, the New Calidonia crow (*Corvus monelduloides*). Anim. Cogn. 5, 71–78.

Chappell, J., Kacelnik, A., 2004. Selection of tool diameter by New Caledonia crows (*Corvus monelduloides*). Anim. Cogn. 7, 121–127.

Clayton, N.S., Dickinson, A., 1998. Episodic-like memory during cache recovery by scrub jays. Nature 395, 272–278.

Comstock, C., 2007. Suet carving to maximize foraging efficiency by common ravens. Wilson J. Ornithol. 119, 95–99.

Coombes, R.A.H., 1948. The flocking of the raven. Br. Birds 41, 290–294.

Cotterman, V., Heinrich, B., 1993. A large temporary raven roost. The Auk 110, 395.

Dall, S.R.X., Wright, J., 2009. Rich pickings near large communal roost favor 'gang' foraging by juvenile common ravens, *Corvus corax*. PLoS ONE 4 (2), e4530.

De Kort, S.R., Tebbich, S., Dally, J.M., Emery, N.J., Clayton, N.S., 2007. The comparative cognition of caching. In: Zentall, T.R., Wasserman, E. (Eds.), Comparative Cognition. Oxford University Press, New York.

De Waal, F.B.M., 1996. Good Natured: The Origin of Right and Wrong in Human and Other Animals. Harvard University Press, Cambridge and London.

Ducker, G., Rensch, B., 1977. The solution of patterned string problems by birds. Behaviour 62, 164–173.

Durstewitz, D., Seamans, J., 2010. Abrupt transitions between prefrontal neural ensemble states accompany behavioral transitions during rule learning. Neuron 66, 438–448.

Elgar, M.A., 1986. House sparrows establish foraging flocks by giving chirrup calls if the resource is divisible. Anim. Behav. 34, 169–174.

Engel, K.A., Young, L.S., Steenhof, K., Roppe, J.A., Kochert, M.W., 1992. Communal roosting of common ravens in southwestern Idaho. Wilson Bull. 104, 105–121.

Epstein, R., Lanza, R.P., Skinner, B.F., 1981. "Self-awareness": the pigeon. Science 212 (4495), 695–696.

Fraser, O.N., Bugnyar, T., 2010a. Do ravens show consolation? Responses to distress in others. PLoS ONE 5 (5), doi:10.1371/journal.pone.0010605.

Fraser, O.N., Bugnyar, T., 2010b. The quality of social relationships in ravens. Anim. Behav. 79, 927–933.

Goodwin, D., 1986. Crows of the World, second ed. University of Washington Press, Seattle.

Greenberg, R., 1990a. Ecological plasticity, neophobia, and resource use in birds. Stud. Avian Biol. 13, 431–437.

Greenberg, R., 1990b. Feeding neophobia and ecological plasticity: a test of the hypothesis with captive sparrows. Anim. Behav. 39, 375–379.

Griffin, D.R., 1976. The Question of Animal Awareness: Evolutionary Continuity of Mental Experience. Rockefeller University Press, New York.

Griffin, D., 1984. Animal Thinking. Harvard University Press, Cambridge, MA.

Grodzinski, U., Clayton, N.S., 2010. Problems faced by food-caching corvids and the evolution of cognitive solutions. Phil. Trans. R. Soc. B 365, 977–987.

Gwinner, E., 1964. Untersuchungen ueber das Ausdrucks- und Sozialverhalten des Kolkraben (*Corvus corax* corax L.). Z. Tierpsychol. 21, 657–748.

Harlow, H.F., Settlage, P.H., 1934. Comparative behavior of primates. VII. Capacity to solve patterned string tests. J. Comp. Psychol. 18, 423–435.

Harrington, F.H., 1978. Ravens attracted to wolf howling. Condor 80, 236–237.

Hauri, R., 1956. Beitrage zur Biologie des Kolkraben (*Corvus corax*). Ornithol. Beob. 53, 28–53.

Hauser, M.D., Peterson, H., Seelig, D., 2002. Ontogeny of tool use in cottontop tamarins, *Saguinus oedipus*: innate recognition of functional relevant features. Anim. Behav. 64, 299–311.

Heinrich, B., 1988a. Why do ravens fear their food? Condor 90, 950–952.

Heinrich, B., 1988b. Raven tool use? Condor 90, 270–271.

Heinrich, B., 1988c. Winter foraging at carcasses by three sympatric corvids, with emphasis on recruitment by the raven *Corvus corax*. Behav. Ecol. Sociobiol. 23, 141–156.

Heinrich, B., 1988d. Food sharing in the raven, *Corvus corax*. In: Slobodchikoff, C.N. (Ed.), The Ecology of Social Behavior. Academic Press, New York, pp. 285–311.

Heinrich, B., 1989. Ravens in Winter. Summit Books of Simon & Schuster, New York, NY, 379 pp.

Heinrich, B., 1994a. Dominance and weight-changes in the common raven, *Corvus corax*. Anim. Behav. 48, 1463–1465.

Heinrich, B., 1994b. When is the common raven black? Wilson Bull. 106 (3), 571–572.

Heinrich, B., 1994c. Does the early bird get (and show) the meat? The Auk 111, 764–769.

Heinrich, B., 1995a. An experimental investigation of insight in common ravens, *Corvus corax*. The Auk 112, 994–1003.

Heinrich, B., 1995b. Neophilia and exploration in juvenile common ravens *Corvus corax*. Anim. Behav. 50, 695–704.

Heinrich, B., 1999a. Mind of the Raven: Investigations and Adventures with Wolf-Birds. Cliff Street Books/HarperCollins, New York.

Heinrich, B., 1999b. Sociobiology of ravens: conflict and cooperation. Sitzungberichte Ges. Naturforschender Freunde Berlin 37, 13–22.

Heinrich, B., 1999c. Planning to facilitate caching: possible suet cutting by a common raven. Wilson Bull. 111, 276–278.

Heinrich, B., Bugnyar, T., 2005. Testing problem solving in ravens: string-pulling to reach food. Ethology 111, 962–976.

Heinrich, B., Marzluff, J.M., 1991. Do common ravens yell because they want to attract others? Behav. Ecol. Sociobiol. 28, 13–21.

Heinrich, B., Marzluff, J.M., 1992. Age and mouth color in common ravens, *Corvus corax*. The Condor 94, 549–550.

Heinrich, B., Pepper, J., 1998. Influence of competitions on caching behavior in the common raven, *Corvus corax*. Anim. Behav. 56, 1083–1090.

Heinrich, B., Smolker, R., 1998. Play in common ravens (*Corvus corax*). In: Bekoff, M., Byers, J.A. (Eds.), Animal Play: Evolutionary, Comparative and Ecological Perspectives. Cambridge University Press, Cambridge, UK.

Heinrich, B., Marzluff, J.M., Marzluff, C.S., 1993. Ravens are attracted to the appeasement calls of discoverers when they are attacked at defended food. The Auk 110, 247–254.

Heinrich, B., Kaye, D., Knight, T., Schaumburg, K., 1994. Dispersal and association among a "flock" of common ravens, *Corvus corax*. The Condor 96, 545–551.

Heinrich, B., Marzluff, J.M., Adams, W., 1996. Fear and food recognition in naive common ravens. The Auk 112 (2), 499–503.

Hunt, G.R., 1996. Manufacture and use of hook-tools by New Caledonia crows. Nature 397, 149–151.

Kerttu, M.E., 1973. Aging Techniques for the Common Raven Corvus corax principalis Ridgeway. MS Thesis. Michigan Tech Univ. Houghton, p. 55.

Klopfer, P., 2005. Animal cognition and the new anthropomorphism. Int. J. Comp. Psychol. 18, 202–206.

Koehler, O., 1943. Zahl-Versuche an einem Kolkraben und Vergleichende Versuche an Menschen. Z. Tierpsychol. 5, 575–712.

Lorenz, K., 1949. King Solomon's Ring.

Marzluff, J.M., Heinrich, B., 1991. Foraging by common ravens in the presence and absence of territory holders: an experimental analysis of social foraging. Anim. Behav. 42, 755–770.

Marzluff, J.M., Heinrich, B., Marzluff, C.S., 1996. Raven roosts are mobile information centers. Anim. Behav. 51, 89–103.

Marzluff, J.M., Walls, J., Cornell, H.M., Withey, J.C., Craig, D.P., 2010. Lasting recognition of threatening people by wild American crows. Anim. Behav. 79, 699–707.

Mech, L.D., 1966. The Wolves of Isle Royale. US National Park Service, US Government Printing Office, Washington, DC.

Mech, L.D., 1970. The Wolf. The Natural History Press, Garden City, New York.

Mylne, C.K., 1961. Large flocks of ravens at food. Br. Birds 54, 206–207.

Parker, P.G., Waite, F.A., Heinrich, B., Marzluff, J.M., 1994. Do common ravens share food bonanzas with kin? DNA fingerprinting evidence. Anim. Behav. 48, 1085–1093.

Pepperberg, I., 1998. Talking with Alex: logic and speech in parrots. Sci. Am. 9 (4), 60–65.

Piaget, J., 1954. The Construction of Reality in the Child. Norton, New York.

Povinelli, D.J., 2000. Causality, tool use, and folk physics: a comparative approach. In: Povinelli, D.J. (Ed.), Folk Physics for Apes. Oxford University Press, New York.

Scheid, C., Range, F., Bugnyar, T., 2007. When, what, and whom to watch? Quantifying attention in ravens (Corvus corax) and jackdaws (Corvus mendula). J. Comp. Psychol. 121, 380–386.

Schloegl, C., Kotrschal, K., Bugnyar, T., 2007. Gaze following in common ravens (Corvus corax): ontogeny and habituation. Anim. Behav. 74, 769–778.

Schloegl, C., Dierks, A., Gayton, G.K., Huber, L., Kotrschal, K., Bugnyar, T., 2009. What you see is what you get? Inferences by exclusion in ravens (Corvus corax) and keas (Nestor notabilis). PLoS ONE 4, e6368.

Schwab, C., Bugnyar, T., Schloegl, C., Kotrschal, K., 2008. Enhanced social learning between siblings in common ravens, Corvus corax. Anim. Behav. 75, 501–508.

Selva, N., Cortes-Avizanda, A., Lemus, J.A., Blanco, G., Mueller, T., Heinrich, B., et al., 2011. Stress associated with group living in a long-lived bird. Biol. Lett. doi:10.1098/rsbl.2010.1204.

Spear, L., 1988. The Halloween mask episode. Nat. Hist. 6/88, 4–8.

Stahler, D.R., Heinrich, B., Smith, W.D., 2002. The raven's behavioral association with wolves. Anim. Behav. 64, 283–290.

Stiel, R.B., 1981. Observations of a large roost of common ravens. The Condor 83, 78.

Stoewe, M., Bugnyar, T., Heinrich, B., Kotrschal, K., 2006. Effect of group size on approach to novel objects in ravens (Corvus corax). Ethology 112, 1079–1088.

Stoewe, M., Bugnyar, T., Schloegl, C., Heinrich, B., Kotrschal, K., Moestl, E., 2008. Corticosterone excretion patterns and different affiliative behavior over development in ravens (Corvus corax). Horm. Behav. 53, 208–216.

Taylor, A.H., Medina, F.S., Holzheier, J.C., Hearne, L.J., Hunt, G.R., Gray, R.D., 2010. An investigation into the cognition behind spontaneous string pulling in New Caledonia crows. PlosOne 5, e9345, doi:10.1371/journal.pone.0009345.

Tebbich, S., Bshary, R., 2004. Finch physics: cognitive abilities related to tool-use in the woodpecker finch *Cactospiza pallida*. Anim. Behav. 67, 689–697.

Thorpe, W.H., 1956. Learning and Instinct in Animals. Methuen and Co., London.

Vince, M.A., 1961. String-pulling: in birds. III. The successful responses in greenfinches and canaries. Behaviour 17, 103–129.

von Frisch, K., 1974. Animal Architecture. Harcourt Brae Jovanovich, New York.

Ward, P., Zahavi, A., 1973. The importance of certain assemblages of birds as "information centers" for food finding. Ibis 115, 517–534.

Weir, A.S., Chappell, J., Kacelnik, A., 2002. Shaping of hooks in New Caledonia crows. Science 297, 981.

White, C., 2005. Hunters ring dinner bell for ravens: experimental evidence of a unique hunting strategy. Ecology 86, 1057–1060.

Wright, J., Stone, R.E., Brown, N., 2003. Communal roosts as structured information centres in the raven, *Corvus corax*. J. Anim. Ecol. 72, 1003–1014.

Communication Networks and Spatial Ecology in Nightingales

Marc Naguib,* Hansjoerg P. Kunc,[†] Philipp Sprau,*
Tobias Roth,[‡,§] and Valentin Amrhein[‡,§]

*DEPARTMENT OF ANIMAL ECOLOGY, NETHERLANDS INSTITUTE OF ECOLOGY
(NIOO-KNAW), WAGENINGEN, THE NETHERLANDS
[†]SCHOOL OF BIOLOGICAL SCIENCES, QUEEN'S UNIVERSITY BELFAST,
BELFAST, UNITED KINGDOM
[‡]RESEARCH STATION PETITE CAMARGUE ALSACIENNE, RUE DE LA
PISCICULTURE, SAINT-LOUIS, FRANCE
[§]ZOOLOGICAL INSTITUTE, UNIVERSITY OF BASEL, BASEL, SWITZERLAND

I. Introduction

In most animals, communication plays a central role in a variety of contexts, often having direct consequences for reproduction and survival. Among the diversity of signals used in communication, sexually selected elaborate displays have received specific attention in research on causes and consequences of complex behavioral traits (Danchin et al., 2008). Sexually selected signals usually provide information on the quality, condition, and motivation of the signaler and have important fitness consequences when being used in resource defense and acquisition and in mate attraction. Moreover, sexually selected signals often are long-range advertisement signals connecting distant individuals with each other, making such signals an important feature to be considered in social networks. Among the different advertisement signals, bird song as research model has provided important insights into the evolution of behavioral mechanisms and functions (Beecher and Brenowitz, 2005; Catchpole and Slater, 2008; Gil and Gahr, 2002; Searcy and Nowicki, 2005). In most songbirds that breed in the temperate zones, only males sing to defend a territory against other males and to attract or stimulate females (Catchpole and Slater, 2008); but female song in several species has been reported as well (Price, 2009; Riebel et al., 2005).

0065-3454/11 $35.00
DOI: 10.1016/B978-0-12-380896-7.00005-8

A. SINGING AND RECEIVER SEX

One persistent question in sexual selection and in animal communication has been which kind of information is signaled when using structurally complex displays like bird song. Like most sexual displays, bird song is a multicomponent signal. Depending on the complexity of the signal, studies showed that the different song components can be under particular selection, such as repertoire size (Catchpole, 1980; Hasselquist et al., 1996; McGregor and Krebs, 1982; Rivera-Gutierrez et al., 2010), production quality of particular song components (Ballentine, 2009; Ballentine et al., 2004; Botero et al., 2009; Forstmeier et al., 2002), or use of songs that include specific song components (Vallet and Kreutzer, 1995; Vallet et al., 1998). In species with vocal repertoires, evidence from several studies suggests that repertoire size is intersexually selected, with males having a larger repertoire being more attractive to females and more successful in reproduction. Classic studies by Catchpole (1980) on sedge warblers, *Acrocephalus schoenobaenus*, by McGregor and colleagues on great tits, *Parus major* (McGregor and Krebs, 1982; McGregor et al., 1981), and by Hasselquist and colleagues (1996) on great reed warblers, *Acrocephalus arundinaceus*, are good examples of female preferences for males with a larger song repertoire, even though repertoire size presumably is also under other selection pressures (Byers and Kroodsma, 2009).

Because females and males may be interested in different characteristics of a singer, and different motivational and qualitative differences may be coded in different singing traits, the sexes may select for different structural traits. Females may be more interested in traits that signal parasite resistance or immune competence (Buchanan et al., 1999; Dreiss et al., 2008; Saino et al., 1997), in traits that reflect the genetic or developmental background (Holveck and Riebel, 2010; Nowicki et al., 1998a; Riebel et al., 2009; Searcy et al., 2010), or in traits that are linked to future parental care (Buchanan and Catchpole, 2000; Halupka and Borowiec, 2006). Males, in contrast, may be more interested in traits signaling resource holding potential and motivation to defend a resource (Naguib and Mennill, 2010; Searcy and Beecher, 2009). Traits like song rate may provide information on the personality of the singer (Naguib et al., 2010) or on the immediate condition of a singer, or of the territory, such as food availability (Berg et al., 2005; Clarkson, 2007; Strain and Mumme, 1988). Performance-related characteristics such as trills that depend on neuromuscular coordination (Westneat et al., 1993) are suggested to be affected specifically by developmental conditions (Hoese et al., 2000; Podos, 1996; Podos et al., 2009). Therefore, performance-related characteristics may be more relevant for females (Ballentine et al., 2004; Byers et al., 2010; Caro et al., 2010), as they can indicate male developmental background (Buchanan et al., 2003; Nowicki et al., 1998a; Searcy et al., 2010; but see Gil et al., 2006) or health (Dreiss et al., 2008), and thus predict qualitative aspects of the mate and possibly of its future offspring. Recent studies showed that such performance-related song traits are also used by males to assess the signaler (Cramer and Price, 2007; de Kort et al., 2009; DuBois et al., 2011; Schmidt et al., 2008; Sprau et al., 2010b). Thus, bird song as a multicomponent signal can reflect the different aspects of quality in different traits, which may also differ among species. Moreover, within the same signal, the relevant traits of a signal may depend on the sex of the receiver.

B. THE TERRITORIAL FUNCTION OF BIRD SONG

Many male songbirds respond aggressively to conspecific male intruders into their territories, but in some species, males may be more tolerant to intrusions as long as their reproduction or territory tenure is not at risk. Thus, silent intrusions without singing by the intruder may be tolerated to some extent. However, intruders that start singing within an already occupied territory typically elicit aggressive responses involving singing and approach by the territory holder. Playback experiments commonly simulate such intrusions by a singing rival to measure vocal and spatial responses of the territory holder (Catchpole and Slater, 2008; Gil and Gahr, 2002). Indeed, most of our knowledge on the territorial function of bird song is based on playback experiments, simulating an intruder into the territory or a rival singing nearby (Catchpole and Slater, 2008). A few studies tested directly the keep-out function of song using speaker-replacement experiments in which the resident male was temporally removed from a territory and replaced by a loudspeaker playing conspecific song or control sounds (Krebs et al., 1978; Nowicki et al., 1998b). A few other studies further investigated functions of singing over longer distances across territory boundaries (Simpson, 1985; Sprau et al., 2010a). All these studies support the idea that song serves as a keep-out signal to other males, and playback experiments have been powerful in determining which song traits and singing strategies yield strong responses by territorial males and their neighbors. The intensity of response toward simulated intruders usually is interpreted as reflecting the aggressiveness of the intruder as it is perceived by the resident male. Determining which signaling traits constitute an intensive and aggressive response is not always unambiguous, and there has been some debate on which criteria have to be met for a trait to be identified as an aggressive signal (Laidre and Vehrencamp, 2008; Naguib and Mennill, 2010; Searcy and Beecher, 2009; Searcy et al., 2006). Most commonly, changes in singing style such as more irregular singing, an increase in use of certain song traits, and physical approaches are interpreted as reflecting arousal. Traits that predict an escalation toward an actual physical attack have been argued to be of particular value in assigning an aggressive signal value (Searcy and Beecher, 2009). As signaling interactions commonly are used to avoid physical attacks, most commonly researchers rely on changes in vocal and spatial behavior to assess the function of a signal (Naguib and Mennill, 2010). Experiments using dummy birds which also add visual cues to the acoustic signal may prove to be a useful addition for some species (Balsby and Dabelsteen, 2002; Searcy et al., 2006), even though the use of dummies also has some limitations (Laidre and Vehrencamp, 2008) and is restricted to study short-range signaling. Thus, researchers usually rely on contextual changes in singing or on physical approach as measures of arousal and as an operational measure of aggressive response.

Studies have shown that male responses to playback depend on several factors including structural traits and the timing of playback songs relative to those of the subject (Todt and Naguib, 2000), the level of song degradation (Brumm and Naguib, 2009; Naguib and Wiley, 2001), changes in song amplitude (Naguib, 1997), or song familiarity (Falls et al., 1982). Moreover, responses may vary with time of day (Shy and Morton, 1986) or may depend on the habitat heterogeneity (Naguib and Todt, 1998). In addition, the nature of the territorial response also depends on the condition, rank, or quality of the territory owners themselves (Kunc et al., 2006; Mennill and Ratcliffe, 2004; Mennill et al., 2002; Schmidt et al., 2006; Sprau et al., 2010b), including elementary behavioral characteristics such as exploratory behavior that is commonly used as a proxy for personality (Amy et al., 2010), and previous experience with intruders (Amrhein and Erne, 2006; Godard, 1993; Hall et al., 2006; Schmidt et al., 2007). Moreover, recent studies simulating a more dynamically moving intruder revealed that spatial behavior of intruders effect responsiveness of residents (Amrhein and Lerch, 2010; Poesel and Dabelsteen, 2005).

C. BIRD SONG AS MEDIATOR IN SOCIAL NETWORKS

Bird song is a long-range signal, and a singing individual as well as its singing interactions with conspecifics usually can be heard by other individuals at various distances (Brumm and Naguib, 2009; Wiley and Richards, 1982). Thus, song can be seen as mediator connecting individuals over distances that are beyond actual close-range encounters. Such connectivity through long-range signals is important in understanding the network structure of a territorial neighborhood, where physical encounters are much more infrequent than in group living species. The signals connecting individuals are sources of information to be used in decision making in current and future territorial or mating contexts. Despite the territoriality, an individual's spatial behavior is not confined to its territory, as birds make silent excursions beyond the own territorial boundaries (Chandler et al., 1997; Hanski and Haila, 1988; Naguib et al., 2001, 2004; Pitcher and Stutchbury, 2000). Such excursions and singing by residents may partly have coevolved; territorial birds may sing to repel intruders, and intruders may use the song of residents to gather information that they may then use in future decision making, for example, for extrapair copulations, future encounters, or in decisions on settlement or mating in the following breeding season. Thus, to fully understand the function of song in a territorial neighborhood, the singing and territorial behavior of the resident individuals need to be considered along with the spatial and movement behavior of the territorial residents or nonterritorial floaters. Yet, as it is practically difficult to follow small songbirds over prolonged periods of time, there is still little information available on their spatial behavior and how it is linked to song. A few radio-tracking studies, including our own studies, have shown that the spatial behavior of nonterritorial prospecting individuals is linked to song, as we will discuss in Sections III.B and III.C. An additional consequence of singing in a social network is that vocal interactions between two individuals can be heard by others. These nonparticipating listening individuals (the audience; eavesdroppers) then can use asymmetries in vocal interaction to assess relative differences among the singers. Such eavesdropping has been shown to be an important source of information in communication networks (McGregor and Dabelsteen, 1996; Peake, 2005; Todt and Naguib, 2000), as discussed in Section III.C.

D. THE NIGHTINGALE

Male nightingales, *Luscinia megarhynchos*, have a high singing activity both at night and during the day (Amrhein et al., 2002; Thomas, 2002b), raising questions on functional differences in singing at different times of day. Nightingales are long-distant migrants and males start nocturnal song upon arrival from their wintering grounds on their breeding territories and usually cease nocturnal song once being paired (Amrhein et al., 2002). Females usually arrive about a week to 10 days after the males (Amrhein et al., 2007) so that data on singing behavior collected before pairing can be used to predict the future pairing success. In our study population, a large proportion of up to 50% of males remain unpaired throughout the season (Amrhein and Zwygart, 2004; Amrhein et al., 2004b, 2007), allowing us to compare song traits before pairing of males that become paired and males that remain unpaired (bachelors). Moreover, during nocturnal song, males engage in hourly long vocal interactions raising specific questions on the function of nocturnal song and on nocturnal male–male vocal interactions. Nocturnal song also has the practical advantage that functional aspects of vocal signals can be studied in the absence of visual cues or changes in spatial configurations. Moreover, in nightingales, territory boundaries are mostly defined by habitat characteristics such as bordering open fields, rivers, or grassland (Amrhein et al., 2002; Grüll, 1981; Wilson et al., 2005), so that loudspeakers can be placed at defined distances within or outside territorial boundaries. Nightingales also use a few preferred song posts during nocturnal song, and they spend about 90% of the time within their song territory (Naguib et al., 2001) so that the identity of the male can be determined by its singing location with high reliability. As in other songbirds, playback simulating territorial intrusions during the day elicit strong territorial responses including physical approach and singing (Sections II.C.4 and III.C). However, responses at night commonly are almost exclusively vocal and over longer distances with only rare occasions of approach (Section II.B).

By reviewing literature on the function of male song in nightingales, we integrate different aspects of communication and of the territorial system, and place our findings into a broader context of animal communication. Nightingales are an excellent model species to study song acquisition, song development, and the organization of large song repertoires (Hultsch and Todt, 2004; Kipper and Kiefer, 2010; Todt and Hultsch, 1996), as well as to study functional aspects of singing in the wild, which is the focus of this chapter. By bringing together different aspects of the singing behavior that has been studied both descriptively and experimentally along with more ecologically focused studies on settlement and spatial behavior, we provide a comprehensive overview of the complexity of the territorial system of a songbird. In Section II, we focus on descriptive studies on male singing activity in relation to pairing status and season (Section II.A) and on nocturnal vocal interactions (Section II.B). In Section III, we discuss playback experiments conducted during the day, which mainly were conducted within a communication network framework (Section III.C), and discuss translocation experiments with radio-tagged individuals in which we studied spatial behavior of prospecting males and females with respect to resident males' singing activity. In Section IV we integrate the main findings.

II. SINGING AND TERRITORIAL BEHAVIOR IN NIGHTINGALES

The dual function of bird song, i.e.. territory defense and mate attraction, raises a number of specific issues on how the two functions of bird song are integrated into one signal (Ratcliffe and Otter, 1996). In addition to differences in the song traits to which males and females may attend to, as discussed above, another question is, whether females searching a mate and males listening to a rival's song both attend to song at the same time, as discussed in the following section.

A.   VARIATION IN SINGING ACTIVITY WITH TIME OF DAY, SEASON, AND PAIRING STATUS

One conspicuous aspect of bird song is that it varies on different time scales. Male singing activity varies over the year, with a peak of singing during the breeding season. Singing also varies within the breeding season, often with a peak in singing during earlier stages of the season. Moreover, singing varies with time of day and the actual timing of single songs varies with respect to the timing of songs of other males. Thus, one question is whether or not these various levels of temporal variation in singing have functional correlates that may explain the evolution of such time patterning.

Part of the temporal variation of singing behavior may have evolved as a result of different selection pressures by male and female receivers. Females usually make decisions on mating at specific periods in the season, when choosing a social mate or when making decisions on extrapair copulations. Males are most vigorous in territory defense also during this period, but the territorial function of song usually persists beyond the period of female reproductive decision making. In several species, males sing differently during the period of mate attraction compared to when singing to other males in a territorial context. For example, before attracting a mate, males in some species sing more complex songs and show higher singing activity than after mate attraction (Catchpole and Slater, 2008), suggesting that in such cases the primary function of male song is to initially establish a territory and to attract a female.

In Section II.A.1, we will consider variation of nocturnal and diurnal song in nightingales with respect to the time of season and the pairing status of males. The focus of this section is on descriptive data from nightingales allowing to make inferences on the possible function of singing at different times of day with respect to receiver sex. The timing of single songs within nocturnal vocal interactions will be discussed in Section II.B.1 where it is linked to other aspects of singing and territorial behavior. Responses to diurnal playback are considered within Sections II.C.4 and III.C.

1.   Variation in Nocturnal Singing Activity

The most apparent characteristic of the temporal variation of singing in nightingales is the extensive nocturnal song in addition to diurnal song (Amrhein et al., 2002; Hultsch and Todt, 1982; Thomas, 2002b). Nightingales have a diurnal singing routine like most other songbirds, so that nocturnal song is an extension of the diurnal singing routine rather than merely a temporal shift away from times when most other songbirds sing. As nocturnally singing males lose more weight over night than males which do not sing, nocturnal song may carry substantial physiological costs (Thomas, 2002a). Even though nocturnal song is more widespread across birds than often thought (Amrhein et al., 2002), the predictability and regularity of nocturnal song in nightingales along with its sibling species, the thrush nightingale (*Luscinia luscinia*; Griessmann and Naguib 2002), is outstanding, as males then sing at high song rates over several hours without changing song posts. The existence of diurnal as well as of nocturnal song raises the question of whether the function of song differs between times of the day. The observation that the number of nocturnally singing males decreases with the ongoing breeding season has led to the idea that males sing at night to attract nocturnally migrating females (Glutz von Blotzheim, 1988; Hultsch, 1993). In surveys on the occurrence of nocturnal song and on the pairing status of territorial males, we indeed found that males usually cease singing at night after a female has settled in their territory (Amrhein et al., 2002, 2004a, 2007). These findings suggest that nocturnal song plays an important role in female attraction. Findings that females prospect an area by sampling several singing males at night (Roth et al., 2009), as discussed in Section III.B, support this conclusion.

Interestingly, paired males often resume nocturnal song for some nights at a later stage, mainly during female egg-laying (Amrhein et al., 2002; Kunc et al., 2007). These findings suggest that while nocturnal song appears to be import in attracting a female for social pair formation, the function is not restricted to that (see also Section II.B). The nocturnal song of a paired male during its mate's egg-laying period is likely to have a different function given that social pair formation with several females is an extreme exception in nightingales (Glutz von Blotzheim, 1988). Nocturnal song during the egg-laying period may have several other functions (Amrhein et al., 2002), such as to stimulate his mate to invest more into egg production (Gil et al., 2004), to mimic a bachelor and thus to reduce the probability of intrusions by males seeking extrapair copulations, or to attract females seeking extrapair copulations. Despite this correlative evidence suggesting that nocturnal song is under main selection by females, experimental studies show that nocturnal song also is of intrasexual relevance, as discussed in Section II.B.1.

2. Variation in Dawn Singing Activity

In contrast to nocturnal song, singing activity at dawn does not vary significantly with pairing status or with the stages of the breeding cycle (Amrhein et al., 2004a). Also, dawn song rate does not correlate with subsequent pairing status and with the breeding stages, contrasting some studies in other species (Kunc et al., 2005a). Currently, we cannot exclude that the specific characteristics of singing at dawn differ over the season or among males differing in pairing success. Yet, the mere presence of dawn song over the season suggests that its function is important to defend the territory against rival males and for regulating social relationships among territorial neighbors. A high singing activity at dawn is widespread among songbirds (Staicer et al., 1996) and has been linked to female fertility (Cuthill and Macdonald, 1990; Mace, 1987; Welling et al., 1997), nest defense, parental care and survival (Welling et al., 1997), territory defense (Poesel et al., 2004), male rank (Otter et al., 1997), previous territorial intrusions (Amrhein and Lerch, 2010; Erne and Amrhein, 2008), population density (Sexton et al., 2007), or to ecological factors like environmental pollution (Gorissen et al., 2005). The link between dawn song and female fertility, as reported in some studies (also see Suter et al., 2009), suggests a specific intersexual function of dawn song. Yet, even in species with a peak of dawn singing around female fertility, dawn singing often extends beyond the fertile period of the mate (Amrhein et al., 2008; Saggese et al., 2011), and it can involve a complex signaling network among many individuals (Fitzsimmons et al., 2008a,b; Foote et al., 2008, 2010). Dawn song thus may well be of general importance for males and females to assess singers, even if it may have evolved initially due to stronger selection pressure from one sex.

Thus, the temporally different singing behavior of paired and unpaired males at night and the lack of differences at dawn along with apparent sex-specific differences in the time of day at which nightingales explore the area (Amrhein et al., 2004b; Roth et al., 2009; see Section III.B) suggest that intra- and intersexual selection has led to the temporal segregation of singing and prospecting.

B. Vocal Interactions

When males sing, they often also vocally interact with each other. Such vocal interactions are characterized by temporal and/or structural relations of the songs of the singers to each other (Todt and Naguib, 2000). Males occasionally reply with the same song type to each other (song type matching) or specifically select songs with certain structural characteristics when counter singing with each other. Moreover, song birds (Brumm, 2006; Ficken et al., 1974, 1985) as well as chorusing insects and frogs (Grafe, 1996; Greenfield, 1994; Schwartz, 1987) generally avoid acoustic masking so that call or song alternating is widespread. However, males frequently also start a song before the other male has finished, thus overlapping the song of

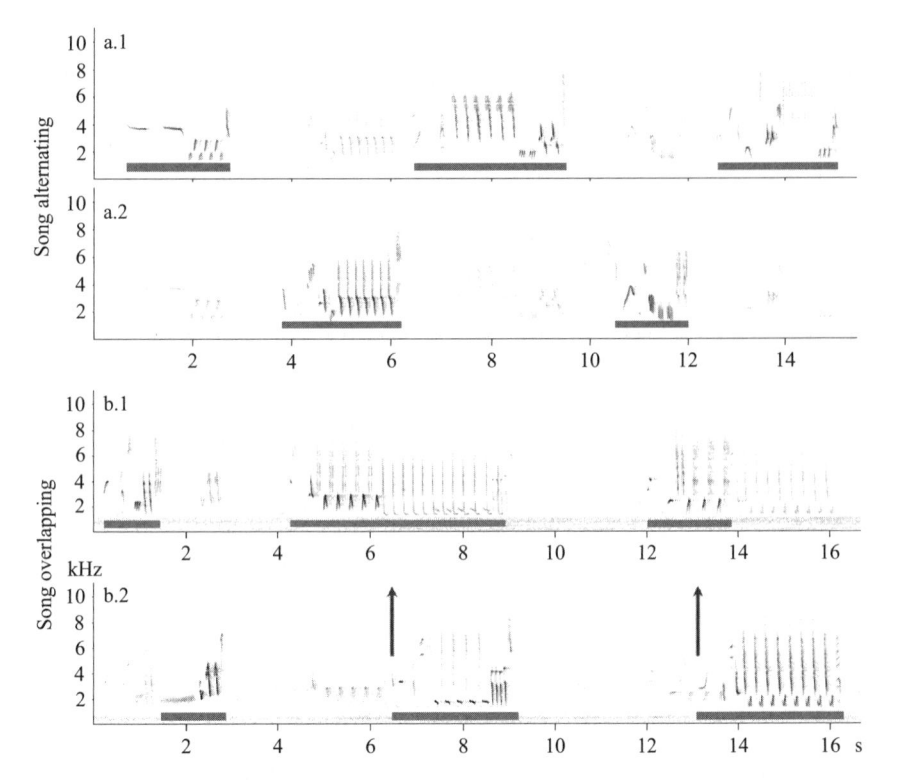

FIG. 1. Sound spectrograms from two vocal interactions in male nightingales, exemplifying song alternating (a.1 and a.2) and song overlapping (b.1 and b.2). Overlapping events are marked with arrows and the duration of a song is highlighted by gray bars below each song. Songs from interacting individuals are faintly visible also in the spectrogram of songs from its counterpart.

the counterpart (Fig. 1). Possibly resulting from such general mechanisms to avoid signal overlap, persistent song overlapping by playback simulating close rivals in songbirds often elicits changes in singing and aggressive responses such as approach to the loudspeaker (Naguib and Mennill, 2010). Song overlapping has been shown in many species to act as a signal and indeed can be used more universally than song type matching, which requires a song repertoire as well as songs that are shared among singers. Vocal interactions in nightingales are most apparent during long nocturnal singing bouts, but males also vocally interact with each other during the day. In the following sections, we will first address experiments in which we tested vocal response of male nightingales to song overlapping during nocturnal song (Section II.B.1) and then (Section II.B.2) the relation between nocturnal singing interactions between unpaired males and their future pairing success. As most of the playbacks that we conducted during the day were conducted in a communication network framework or tested the territorial response to specific song traits, we consider these diurnal responses in Sections II.C.4 and III.C.

1. Song Overlapping at Night

During nocturnal song, nightingales often interact vocally with each other mainly by alternating songs and by occasional song type matching or overlapping (Todt and Naguib, 2000). Even though the primary function of nocturnal song appears to be attracting females, as discussed in Section II.A.1, descriptive and experimental data suggest that nocturnal song is relevant also in male–male interactions. Playback studies on night-ingale nocturnal song have shown that males respond in specific ways depending on the timing of an opponent's song, such as when their songs are overlapped by playback or when playback songs alternate with them (Hultsch and Todt, 1982; Naguib, 1999; Naguib and Kipper, 2006; Schmidt et al., 2006; Sprau et al., 2010b; Fig. 1). The most frequent response to song overlapping during nocturnal song in nightingales is a more irregular sing-ing pattern (Naguib and Kipper, 2006; Naguib et al., 1999; Schmidt et al., 2006), suggesting that males try to avoid being overlapped and perceive song overlapping as a disturbing and presumably aggressive signal (Naguib and Mennill, 2010; Todt and Naguib, 2000). Most commonly, interacting nightingales alternate their songs during nocturnal singing interactions, with 20–30% of songs overlapping the songs of a rival during long distance interactions between neighboring males (Naguib and Kipper, 2006). Night-ingales also have been shown to increasingly interrupt their nocturnal singing the more their songs are being overlapped during nocturnal play-back (Naguib and Kipper, 2006). Interestingly, after playback, males continued to sing with the more interruptions the more songs were over-lapped by playback, indicating that responses to song overlapping are not just reactions to avoid jamming but lead to more persistent arousal. This also suggests that song overlapping can be used as a graded signal by adjusting the number of songs of a rival that are overlapped (Naguib and Kipper, 2006). Yet, to date studies have treated song overlapping as a strategy with binary options for choice, that is, song alternating or song overlapping. Thus, there is still little understanding on how the signal value of song timing varies on a more gradual level, and whether or not the function of song overlapping is also affected by the latency with which a male starts a song after the rival started its song and thus by the proportion of a song that is being overlapped.

While playback experiments at night provide insights into which song traits males use and respond to vocally, the territorial consequences of such singing strategies are not as apparent as during the day, when patterns of singing can have immediate consequences leading to physical retreat or approach. The value of the information obtained during nocturnal listening or interacting thus can be expected to be important also in decision making during the day. As proposed by the social dynamic hypothesis discussed in the context of dawn singing (Staicer et al., 1996), males may exchange information during nocturnal interactions that is relevant for their general social relations. This could include learning individual characteristics of the song of particular male rivals (Kiefer et al., 2010) or assessing motivational characteristics that may affect also territorial behavior during the day. If so, one would predict that during the day males would respond more aggressively to a male which they already had experienced as singing aggressively at night. To test this idea, Schmidt et al. (2007) presented males with either an alternating or overlapping playback at night, played from outside their territory. When simulating an intrusion the next morning using a standard noninteractive playback, males showed a stronger territorial response when they had been exposed to an overlapping rather than to an alternating playback the night before (Schmidt et al., 2007). These findings show that male vocal interactions at night have consequences for territorial behavior during the day and that song overlapping at night leads to more aroused singing during the night as well as to more aggressive territorial responses during the day. Such long-term effects are also supported by playback studies on banded wrens, *Thryothorus pleurostictus*, and on winter wrens, *Troglodytes troglodytes*, which revealed changes in singing and territorial behavior 1–5 days after an intruder was simulated (Amrhein and Erne, 2006; Amrhein and Lerch, 2010; Erne and Amrhein, 2008; Illes et al., 2006).

2. Correlates of Future Pairing Status

The vocal interactions between males provide information on differences in motivation or quality of the male, or they may be linked to differences in territory quality. Such information is also relevant for females, which thus may impose a selection pressure on male–male nocturnal interactions. Females may attend specifically to these interactions and be influenced in their mating decisions depending on relative differences in the performance of males in their vocal interactions (Wiley and Poston, 1996). A network of nocturnally singing males thus even may be considered as a sort of hidden lek in which territorial males display relative to each other (Cockburn et al., 2009; Wagner, 1998) during the time of female prospecting (Roth et al., 2009). Studies on diurnal song in other species support this idea, as laboratory studies on canaries, *Serinus canaria*, showed that female song preference is affected by the way songs are used in a vocal interactions between males (Amy et al., 2008; Leboucher and Pallot, 2004). Also field studies on great tits (Otter et al., 1999) and black-capped chickadees, *Poecile atricapilla*, (Mennill et al., 2002) showed that females attend to male–male vocal interactions and subsequently use the obtained information in their mating decisions.

In nightingales, several nocturnal playback experiments showed that males that are unpaired at the time of playback but later become paired respond differently to playback than males that remain unpaired throughout the breeding season. Males that remain bachelors overlap fewer playback songs (Kunc et al., 2006), interrupt their singing more when their songs are overlapped (Schmidt et al., 2006), and more frequently add high-frequency whistles to their songs than males that will become paired (Sprau et al., 2010b). Moreover, during the period when females of paired males lay eggs, their mates respond with a lower song rate and lower extent of song overlapping to nocturnal playback compared to bachelors' responses during the same time of the season, indicating that males become less aroused when challenged by nocturnal song after pairing (Kunc et al., 2007). In contrast, males that remain unpaired throughout the breeding season do not strongly vary in their response to an opponent across the season. Thus, males apparently vary the level of aggression in vocal interactions according to their pairing status and to the stage of the breeding season (Kunc et al., 2007). Yet, it remains to be shown whether the relation between singing and successful pairing results from females preferring males that interact more aggressively or whether males interacting more aggressively also differ in other traits affecting female choice.

C. STRUCTURAL SONG TRAITS AND THEIR SPECIFIC FUNCTIONS

In the following subsections, we will highlight some structural characteristics of nightingale song and consider the currently available data from nightingales on the possible function of different structural traits.

1. Song Repertoires

Nightingales are renowned for their singing versatility and their large vocal song repertoire consisting of 150–200 different song types (Kipper et al., 2006). Further, each song is composed of a complex series of repeated and unrepeated elements (Todt, 1970). The repertoire and its organization are acquired through vocal learning during early life (Hultsch, 1992; Hultsch and Todt, 1989, 1992, 1996a). Yet, males can also be inventive when developing their repertoire (Hughes et al., 2002) and modulate their repertoire later in life, with the main changes occurring from the first to the second breeding season (Kiefer et al., 2006, 2009), leading to more repertoire similarities among males in their second breeding season (Kiefer et al., 2010). In line with such repertoire modulation, male nightingales actually may sing songs learned early in life only when hearing that particular song. Otherwise they retain certain songs as "silent song types" that are not produced during noninteractive singing (Geberzahn and Hultsch, 2003; Geberzahn et al., 2002).

While the song repertoire has been intensively studied to address questions on rules of song acquisition and of storing and retrieving large amounts of serial information, less is known on the factors that have led to the evolution of the large repertoires in the first place. To date, a few studies have shown that the song repertoire of male nightingales provides information that could be relevant in female choice. Kipper et al. (2006) showed that males arriving earlier in the season have larger song repertoires and a larger body mass, suggesting that repertoire size encodes information on male quality. Moreover, 1-year old males have smaller repertoires than older males (Kiefer et al., 2006) and age can be one of the important factors reflecting quality. Given that the vocal repertoire is delivered in singing bouts lasting over several hours at night, which is the time of female mate prospecting, it seems reasonable to assume that females indeed attend to structural singing traits in nocturnal song, even though they probably will not actually count the number of song types to determine repertoire size. Neighboring males also share a substantial proportion of their song repertoire of up to 60% (Kipper et al., 2004) and commonly alternate songs with each other during nocturnal singing with occasional song type matching and overlapping songs of the rival (Todt and Naguib, 2000). The fact that male nightingales acquire both the songs shared by many males as well as songs that are not shared with others may enable them to match the songs of rivals as well as to avoid being matched by rivals (Sprau and Mundry, 2010). Such social effects may thus also have played a role in the evolution of large repertoires (Byers and Kroodsma, 2009).

2. Whistle Songs

Among the diversity of nightingale songs, one song category sticks out syntactically and auditorily, which are the so-called whistle songs (Hultsch and Todt, 1996b; Kunc et al., 2005b). Unlike most other nightingale songs that start with a series of nonrepeated structurally different notes, whistle songs begin with a series of repeated notes with a narrow frequency bandwidth leading to a whistle-like structure. Each male has a repertoire of different whistle songs differing in frequency, duration, and modulation of the whistles (Kunc et al., 2005b; Naguib et al., 2002). Whistle songs are used at all times of the day but are most common during nocturnal song where up to 20% of the songs can be whistle songs (Kunc et al., 2005b; Naguib et al., 2002). Early in the breeding season, whistle songs sung at dawn make up less than 14% of songs (Kunc et al., 2005a). In contrast to soft initial whistles (see Section II. C.3), the conspicuous whistles at the onset of whistle songs appear to be designed for long-range transmission and as alerting component (Richards, 1981), and whistle songs have a considerably longer transmission distance than more broadband frequency song components (Naguib et al., 2008). The increased use of whistle songs at night, their decreased use during male–male close-range interactions (Kunc et al., 2006), and their long transmission range combined with nocturnal migratory and mate searching behavior of females suggests that they have a specific function in alerting and attracting females. Nevertheless, males also are responsive to whistle songs at night as they occasionally match the same song category and thereby often even use whistles that also match the frequency of the whistles of rival males (Naguib, 2005). Such frequency matching occurs more often and with more precision with increasing distance (Naguib et al., 2002) and thus can be seen as a less aggressive long distance signal to attract attention. Such whistle frequency matching over long distances possibly serves to draw attention of females to the song of the matching male and away from competitors. This long distance matching adds a new aspect to the general view on the function of signal matching as it contrasts the more common findings that vocal matching is associated with aggressive close-range contexts (Searcy and Beecher, 2009; Todt and Naguib, 2000).

3. Songs Preceded by High-Frequency Whistles

In addition to the distinct song category of whistle songs, nightingales occasionally also use softer high-frequency whistles as the first elements preceding any song. Such an initial whistle is of higher frequency compared to the whistle in whistle songs, it is of lower amplitude, and usually it is not repeated (Fig. 2). The more frequent use of initial whistles in territorial disputes and short-range vocal interactions suggests that they function primarily as short-range signals in aggressive contexts (Sprau et al., 2010a,b). These findings suggest that initial whistles are functionally similar to soft song that has been described in other songbird species as agonistic signal in intrasexual interactions (Anderson et al., 2007; Dabelsteen et al., 1998; Hof and Hazlett, 2010; Searcy and Nowicki, 2006). Soft song with its low amplitude is considered to signal high arousal to an opponent, while reducing the probability that eavesdroppers receive the signal content (McGregor and Dabelsteen, 1996). Initial whistles could expand on this function, as the low amplitude may signal high arousal only to close rivals while hiding this arousal from more distant individuals that are exposed to the regular songs (Sprau et al., 2010a).

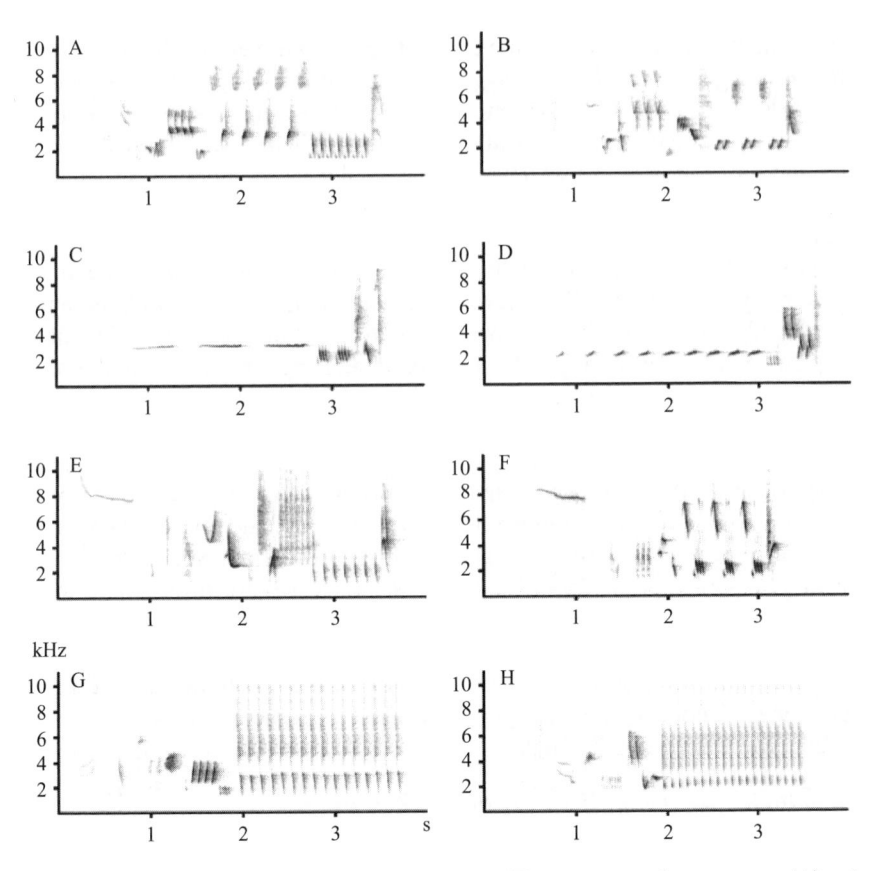

Fig. 2. Sound spectrograms nightingale songs with different structural components. (A) and (B) represent ordinary nightingale songs; (C) and (D) represent whistle songs, characterized by the series of whistles in the first part of the song; (E) and (F) represent songs preceded by initial whistles which are higher in frequency and lower in volume than the whistle in whistle songs. They also are usually not repeated within a song but often precede subsequent ordinary songs; (G) and (H) represent songs containing rapid broadband trills.

4. Songs with Rapid Broadband Trills

Another song category that appears to have a specific signal value consists of songs that contain rapid broadband trills. Trills occur in many songbird species and often are used in aggressive contexts (Cramer and Price, 2007; DuBois et al., 2009; Illes et al., 2006), but they have also been shown to be used by females to assess males (Ballentine et al., 2004; Caro et al., 2010; Vallet and Kreutzer, 1995). Because the production of trills is physically constrained (Hoese et al., 2000; Podos, 1996), they can contain specific information on the quality of the singing male that can be used by females (Ballentine, 2009; Ballentine et al., 2004; Caro et al., 2010; Draganoiu et al., 2002) as well as by males (Illes et al., 2006; Schmidt et al., 2008). Rapid trills degrade quickly over distance (Naguib, 2003; Naguib et al., 2008) so that the signal content is probably most easily received in close-range interactions even though in nightingales rapid broadband trills are still perceived as an aggressive signal at far distances (Sprau et al., 2010a). We also found that males increase the percentage of songs containing rapid broadband trills in response to nocturnal playback (Kunc et al., 2006; Schmidt et al., 2006; Sprau et al., 2010b) and sing more songs with rapid broadband trills to near than to far nocturnal playback (Sprau et al., 2010a). Further, in a playback experiment during the day using two loudspeakers, we showed that territorial males approach and respond more to the loudspeaker playing songs with rapid broadband trills than to the loudspeaker playing songs without trills (Schmidt et al., 2008). Males approached faster and stayed longer and sang more near the loudspeaker broadcasting songs with these trills, compared to the loudspeaker playing songs without such trills. These findings suggest that rapid broadband trills have an aggressive signal value, confirming the interpretation from studies on rapid broadband trills during nocturnal songs (Kunc et al., 2006; Sprau et al., 2010a,b).

Rapid broadband trills thus seem to have a similar signal value as song overlapping (also see Section II.B.1). Unlike song overlapping, though, trills can be sung independently of whether or not a rival is singing and thus are suitable signals also in noninteractive singing bouts. In a study testing whether trills can enhance the agonistic function of song overlapping, we found a moderate enhancing effect of trills on song overlapping (Sprau et al., 2010b).

III. SPATIAL ECOLOGY AND COMMUNICATION NETWORKS

A. SONG AND TERRITORIAL SETTLEMENT

Territorial songbirds are model organisms to address a number of issues in behavioral ecology that are related to division of space and defense of resources. At the onset of each breeding season, space has to be divided up among individuals, as many resident species are not strictly territorial outside the breeding season (Stamps, 1994; Stamps and Krishnan, 1997, 2001), and because migratory birds have to establish territories upon arrival on the breeding ground. The factors affecting the decisions where to settle are often difficult to disentangle. Presumably, a complex set of factors is involved in the decision process including individual-specific traits such as the experience with a particular site, individual age, time of arrival, as well as environmental factors such as territory location, quality, and spatial arrangement of the males that are already present (Hoover, 2003; Naguib, 2005; Reed et al., 1999).

In a survey of settlement patterns in nightingales, we found that males that arrive earlier are more likely to become paired than later arriving males. Early arriving males on average also were older than late arriving males, but this difference was not significant (Amrhein et al., 2007). Nevertheless, these data fit well with findings by Kipper et al. (2006) that males arriving earlier have larger song repertoires, and that song repertoire also increases with age, at least from the first to the second breeding season (Kiefer et al., 2006; Kipper and Kiefer, 2010). Even though it is not possible with our current data to disentangle the role of male characteristics and territorial characteristics with respect to female choice, the data suggest that it is beneficial for males to arrive a few days before the majority of females arrive. Such an earlier male arrival generally might have evolved as a consequence of male–male competition for the best territories (Kokko et al., 2006). It may also make them more attractive, as longer residency could have positive effects on current physical condition after a long migration. Longer residency and familiarity with the site and the neighborhood may also affect other behavioral traits that females may attend to, such as attention and response to stimuli, or exploratory and foraging behavior.

Male songbirds often are highly philopatric, with males returning to the same territory they had occupied the previous year (Greenwood, 1980), and this is also common in our nightingale population. Using long-term territory-occupancy data, Roth and Amrhein (2010) proposed a new model to estimate local survival, which is the probability that a male survives from one breeding season to the next and settles in the same territory as in the previous breeding season. They then compared local survival with apparent survival obtained from a traditional analysis of the capture–recapture data from the same population, determining the probability an individual survives from one breeding season to the next and settles in the same study area (as opposed to the same territory in local survival). As local survival in nightingales is virtually the same as apparent survival, it appears that most of the surviving males settle not only in the same study area, but also in the same territory as in the previous breeding season. For the moderate proportion of males that switch territories, males may often select new territories at some larger distance from the previous territory and thus also outside our study site (Roth and Amrhein, 2010).

The spatial configuration of territories is the result of the decision of each individual where to settle and may explain part of the variation in breeding success among males (Formica et al., 2004). It is also likely that the spatial configuration of the territories have direct implications on vocal communication and likewise that vocal communication may affect the spatial configuration (Naguib, 2005; Waser and Wiley, 1980). For instance, it is known for several bird species that distance to the closest neighbor or the number of neighbors may affect singing (Cockburn et al., 2009; Liu, 2004). A survey of the settlement pattern in male nightingales confirmed that the distance to the closest neighbor decreases and the number of neighbors increases during the course of the breeding season (Naguib et al., 2008). One thus may argue that a seasonal change in the spatial configuration of territories could explain at least part of the seasonal variation in singing of nightingales (Amrhein et al., 2004a; Kunc et al., 2005a) as well as the seasonal changes in vocal interactions (Kunc et al., 2006, 2007). Although still understudied, the interplay of the spatial configuration of territories and of song received increasing attention over the past years. Current research indicates that vocal communication in many species is best viewed as a communication network with stationary as well as moving senders and receivers.

B. Spatial Behavior Within and Beyond Territory Boundaries

While a territory is the most obvious central component of a territorial individual's spatial ecology, behavior does not stop at a territorial boundary. For example, singing interactions usually involve communication across territory boundaries among two or more territorial males. Moreover, many territorial systems also incorporate nonterritorial individuals, so-called floaters (Bruinzeel and van de Pol, 2003; Campioni et al., 2010; Kempenaers et al., 2001). Male floaters usually do not sing (Amrhein et al., 2004b), but they may impose selection pressures on territorial males that are difficult to assess, given the often hidden behavior of floating individuals (Smith, 1978). Due to the general difficulty of observing individual songbirds over a prolonged time while they are exploring space, most information on spatial behavior beyond territorial boundaries results from radio-tracking studies (Chandler et al., 1994, 1997; Hanski, 1992; Maciejok et al., 1995; Naef-Daenzer, 1994; Pitcher and Stutchbury, 2000; Rätti and Siikamki, 1993; Stutchbury, 1998). These studies have well documented that males as well as females can leave their territory and explore the neighborhood, showing that understanding territorial systems requires a more holistic view incorporating a larger area.

In a series of studies, we investigated the spatial behavior of both male and female nightingales, combining radio-tracking and translocation studies with descriptive and experimental work on singing behavior of territorial males. Our aim was to determine whether and to what extent spatial relations exist among individuals within a larger neighborhood and how these are linked to or mediated by the singing behavior of residents. By radio-tracking males throughout the breeding season, we found that most of the time, males indeed remain on their territory, defined as the area they use for singing (Naguib et al., 2001). Interestingly, males that sang at higher rates also made more forays while receiving fewer forays from neighbors. Yet, we found the opposite pattern when following males whose neighbor was challenged by a simulated territorial intrusion using playback (Naguib et al., 2004). In this case, males were more likely to intrude into a neighbor's territory when that neighbor sang more in response to a simulated intruder. These findings show that song has both repelling and attracting functions to other males, depending on the context in which it is used.

On a larger scale, male song also appears to have an attracting function to rival males exploring a neighborhood. We occasionally observed that during extraterritorial forays, radio-tagged males move straight close to the song posts of their singing neighbors. We made similar observations in a radio-tracking study where males were translocated from a remote site to our site. Translocated males almost exclusively prospected the neighborhood at dawn, which also is the time of day with the highest probability to encounter a resident male singing (Amrhein et al., 2004b). During these dawn excursions, translocated males visited several resident males (Fig. 3), often sitting close to the singing resident, suggesting that they were attracted by the song of the residents (Amrhein et al., 2004b). Interestingly, translocated males spent more time in territories of paired males than in those of unpaired males, suggesting that the short period of prospecting at dawn is sufficient to assess the pairing status of a resident. We do not know whether this information is provided by a possibly different singing style at dawn of paired and unpaired males or by the female itself. Information on pairing status otherwise is more readily available at night, when paired males usually do not sing (Amrhein et al., 2002, 2004a). Yet, due to an apparent lack of nocturnal movements by males, they are unlikely to use nocturnal song to assess pairing status of males within a larger neighborhood.

In contrast to territory-prospecting males, prospecting unpaired females moved over large distances specifically at night and moved less at dawn or other times of the day (Roth et al., 2009). These findings support the idea that females use nocturnal song to assess pairing status and quality of males. Yet, it remains unclear whether nocturnal singing is a cause for, or an effect of, nocturnally prospecting by females, and how nocturnal song evolved in the first place (Roth et al., 2009). Both, the translocated females at night and the translocated males at dawn, covered distances during one prospecting foray of up to 6 km. Such extended movements of potential receivers reveal that singing males indirectly compete with other singing males that are further away than the hearing distance. As a consequence, coevolution

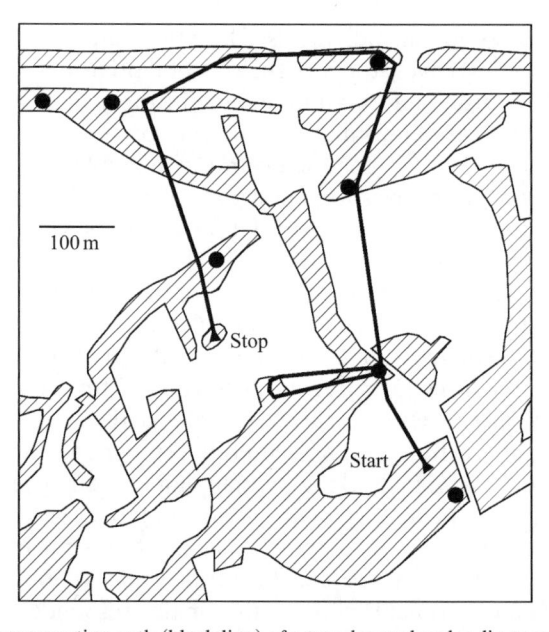

FIG. 3. Dawn prospecting path (black line) of a translocated and radio-tagged male nightingale (based on data in Amrhein et al., 2004b). Hatched areas indicate reed, bushes, or woods separated by fields and meadows. Black dots indicate singing territorial males.

between vocal and spatial behavior warrants an integrated view of vocal signaling on the one hand and of use of space on the other hand. Studies on spatial behavior of information-seeking individuals have a great potential to improve our understanding of vocal communication, as the movements of receivers within and among territories may influence and connect individual males singing in their territories, resulting in social networks (Croft et al., 2007, 2009). Such an integrated view is emphasized by studying vocal communication within a network of signalers and receivers, as discussed in the following section.

C. STRATEGIES IN COMMUNICATION NETWORKS: SIGNALING AND
    INFORMATION GATHERING

One aspect of territorial systems that has been emphasized in recent years is that animals using long-range signals can be heard simultaneously by several receivers. Animals are well known to be able to obtain information about relative differences between individuals by observing their interactions (Danchin et al., 2004; Whitfield, 2002). Signaling interactions with asymmetries in the way signalers use their signals provide information on relative differences among individuals. This information may be important for nonparticipating eavesdroppers such as potential mates or rivals that may benefit from using information obtained from signaling asymmetries. To emphasize this way of information gathering, McGregor and Dabelsteen (1996) introduced the term communication networks highlighting the potential for individuals to eavesdrop on signaling interactions between others and to extract information from the relation of their signals to each other. Signalers even may interact in certain ways to signal specifically to eavesdroppers rather than to their direct interacting counterpart (Zahavi, 1979). The idea of communication networks stimulated research activities focusing on more than two individuals being involved in a communication event in a range of organisms (McGregor, 2005). In nightingales, we used two-loudspeaker setups to test whether territorial males extract information from signaling interactions and respond differently depending on the relation between the two signals. Song overlapping and other temporal asymmetries in singing appeared as a particularly suitable example, as the two loudspeakers could be set to only differ in the temporal relations of the songs but not to differ in any absolute trait, such as song rate or song complexity. The experiments showed that males responded more aggressively to a loudspeaker playing song that overlapped the songs of another loudspeaker placed 20 m away (Naguib and Todt, 1997). These findings indicate that males can indeed extract information from signaling interactions between other males, and that song overlapping is interpreted as aggressive signal also by eavesdroppers and not only by the individuals directly involved in the interaction. Moreover, a subsequent experiment in which songs from two loudspeakers alternated with each other in asymmetric ways revealed that asymmetries in vocal interactions are relevant for eavesdroppers also in the absence of song overlapping (Naguib et al., 1999). The experiment demonstrates the existence of vocal leader–follower relations, with males responding stronger to vocal leaders when songs were alternating asymmetrically without any vocal overlap (Naguib et al., 1999). Also Mennill and colleagues found a stronger response by male black-capped chickadees to the overlapping speaker (Mennill and Ratcliffe, 2004), and they further showed that females are more likely to engage in extrapair copulations when they heard their mate losing a vocal interaction as imposed by interactive playback (Mennill et al., 2002). Studies on great tits also found that females respond differently depending on whether or not their mate is overlapped by playback (Otter et al., 1999), but this did not lead to changes in extrapair paternity (Otter et al., 2001). Peake and colleagues showed that great tit males use information obtained by eavesdropping differently depending on whether they are themselves challenged by a winner or a loser of the interaction they could listen to (Peake et al.,

2001; Peake et al., 2002). The presumably most common context for eavesdropping on others' interactions involves an interaction of a territorial male with a singing stranger or a neighbor. Interactions of a territorial male with a stranger can be valuable to eavesdropping neighboring males, because they could use the response by their known neighbor as yard stick to assess the stranger. In order to test this idea, we conducted playback experiments with males but focused on the spatial behavior of their neighbors, which we recorded using radio telemetry (Naguib et al., 2004). This experiment revealed that nightingales indeed attend to their neighbors' interactions and respond depending on how their neighbor responds. Males intruded into the neighboring territory earlier when the challenged neighbor responded stronger. Yet, they did not intrude when the rival was simulated to have left the territory shortly after the intrusion (Naguib et al., 2004). Such eavesdropping on neighbor interactions and responses that depend on the neighbors behavior toward an unfamiliar rival may be adaptive as any new individual settling in the neighborhood may cause an at least temporal instability of an established system. Some studies indeed showed that birds benefit by being surrounded by familiar neighbors (Beletsky and Orians, 1989). Other laboratory studies showed that eavesdropping females respond differently to overlapped and overlapping songs (Amy and Leboucher, 2009; Garcia-Fernandez et al., 2010; Leboucher and Pallot, 2004). These studies show that signaling interactions provide important information for decision making, in addition to information derived from a single male singing. Recently, Amy et al. (2010) even showed that great tits respond to playback in their neighboring territory depending on personality traits of that neighbor. These findings indicate that individual information about the neighbor affects their own decision making in response to threats in the neighborhood. Such eavesdropping, extraterritorial forays, or in resident birds also previous encounters in winter flocking suggest that territorial systems should be seen as a larger social network with social relations extending in time and space beyond a mere presence and defense of territorial boundaries.

Taken together, the studies outline three lines of evidence that a songbird communication system such as in nightingales is best viewed as a large-scale communication network. First, singing is likely to depend on the spatial configuration of the territories. Second, because prospecting individuals are exposed to the singing of several males over a large spatial range, singing males may compete for access to females or territories with many other males, some of them even outside their own hearing distance. And third, songbirds obtain information by listening to the contests of other individuals, thus emphasizing the network character of communication systems involving multiple senders and receivers.

IV. Summary and Conclusion

Here we synthesize studies on vocal communication and spatial behavior in nightingales with research on other songbirds and emphasize the functions of advertisement signals in territorial systems and their role linking individuals in a social network. Nightingales with their hour-long singing bouts at night and their substantial singing activity at day have been a rewarding model to provide answers for a number of functional issues in vocal communication. Studying vocal behavior at night has yielded insights into the functions of vocal signals in the absence of changes in spatial location and the risk of immediate physical escalation. Playback experiments during the day have complemented nocturnal playbacks and revealed the importance of vocal interactions for eavesdropping territorial males and their neighbors. The combination of descriptive and experimental studies on song with a communication network approach and translocation experiments to test prospecting behavior of males and females have provided insights into a more ecological perspective of communication, enhancing the understanding of general principles of temporal and structural variation in advertisement signaling across species. The integration of singing and spatial behavior emphasizes the importance of network characteristics in the evolution of communication systems, with selection pressures imposed by territorial neighbors and nonterritorial individuals that intrude into occupied territories or eavesdrop from the distance on singing and singing interactions. More research on singing and spatial behavior will be important to broaden our view on such complex communication systems. Also playback studies may continue to develop a more dynamic approach, simulating intruding strangers as well as intruding neighbors that show natural spatial behavior by moving within the territory of a resident. Automated devises for song recordings and tracking movements and the use of populations with well-characterized individuals may become an essential component for future studies. Such studies will be able to generate novel insights into animal communication by integrating signaling and spatial behavior, as we have highlighted in this chapter.

Acknowledgments

We thank Rouven Schmidt and all assistants and students who contributed to the research that has been going on for more than 10 years and without whose dedicated work at all times of the day we would not have been able to maintain the project. We further thank the Basler Stiftung für biologische Forschung, the Basler Stiftung für experimentelle Zoologie, the Foundation Emilia Guggenheim-Schnurr, the Freie Universität Berlin, the Freiwillige Akademische Gesellschaft Basel, the German Research Foundation (grants Na335/4, Na335/5,

Na335/8), the Netherlands Institute of Ecology (NIOO-KNAW), the Ornithologische Gesellschaft Basel, the Swiss National Science Foundation, the Treubel-Fonds, and the University Bielefeld for funding. We are also grateful to the Swiss Association Pro Petite Camargue Alsacienne for funding, maintaining the research station, and enabling us to work with the study population of nightingales. We are grateful to Joseph Waas and an anonymous reviewer for constructive and helpful comments on the chapter.

References

Amrhein, V., Erne, N., 2006. Dawn singing reflects past territorial challenges in the winter wren. Anim. Behav. 71, 1075–1080.

Amrhein, V., Lerch, S., 2010. Differential effects of moving versus stationary territorial intruders on territory defence in a songbird. J. Anim. Ecol. 79, 82–87.

Amrhein, V., Zwygart, D., 2004. Bestand und Verpaarungsstatus von Nachtigallen *Luscinia megarhynchos* im elsässischen Rheintal bei Basel. Ornithol. Beobachter 101, 19–24.

Amrhein, V., Korner, P., Naguib, M., 2002. Nocturnal and diurnal singing activity in the nightingale: correlations with mating status and breeding cycle. Anim. Behav. 64, 939–944.

Amrhein, V., Kunc, H.P., Naguib, M., 2004a. Seasonal patterns of singing activity vary with time of day in the nightingale. Auk 121, 110–117.

Amrhein, V., Kunc, H.P., Naguib, M., 2004b. Non-territorial nightingales prospect territories during the dawn chorus. Proc. R. Soc. B 271, S167–S169.

Amrhein, V., Kunc, H.P., Schmidt, R., Naguib, M., 2007. Temporal patterns of territory settlement and detectability in mated and unmated nightingales *Luscinia megarhynchos*. Ibis 149, 237–244.

Amrhein, V., Johannessen, L.E., Kristiansen, L., Slagsvold, T., 2008. Reproductive strategy and singing activity: blue tit and great tit compared. Behav. Ecol. Sociobiol. 62, 1633–1641.

Amy, M., Leboucher, G., 2009. Effects of eavesdropping on subsequent signalling behaviours in male canaries. Ethology 115, 239–246.

Amy, M., Monbureau, M., Durand, C., Gomez, D., Thery, M., Leboucher, G., 2008. Female canary mate preferences: differential use of information from two types of male–male interaction. Anim. Behav. 76, 971–982.

Amy, M., Sprau, P., de Goede, P., Naguib, M., 2010. Effects of personality on territory defence in communication networks: a playback experiment with radio-tagged great tits. Proc. R. Soc. B 277, 3685–3692.

Anderson, C.A., Nowicki, S., Searcy, W.A., 2007. Soft song in song sparrows: response of males and females to an enigmatic signal. Behav. Ecol. Sociobiol. 61, 1267–1274.

Ballentine, B., 2009. The ability to perform physically challenging songs predicts age and size in male swamp sparrows, *Melospiza georgiana*. Anim. Behav. 77, 973–978.

Ballentine, B., Hyman, J., Nowicki, S., 2004. Vocal performance influences female response to male bird song: an experimental test. Behav. Ecol. 15, 163–168.

Balsby, T.J.S., Dabelsteen, T., 2002. Female behaviour affects male courtship in whitethroats, *Sylvia communis*: an interactive experiment using visual and acoustic cues. Anim. Behav. 63, 251–257.

Beecher, M.D., Brenowitz, E.A., 2005. Functional aspects of song learning in songbirds. Trends Ecol. Evol. 409.

Beletsky, L.D., Orians, G.H., 1989. Familiar neighbors enhance breeding success in birds. Proc. Natl. Acad. Sci. USA 86, 7933–7936.

Berg, M.L., Beintema, N.H., Welbergen, J.A., Komdeur, J., 2005. Singing as a handicap: the effects of food availability and weather on song output in the Australian reed warbler *Acrocephalus australis*. J. Avian Biol. 36, 102–109.

Botero, C.A., Rossman, R.J., Caro, L.M., Stenzler, L.M., Lovette, I.J., de Kort, S.R., et al., 2009. Syllable type consistency is related to age, social status and reproductive success in the tropical mockingbird. Anim. Behav. 77, 701–706.

Bruinzeel, L.W., van de Pol, M., 2003. Site attachment of floaters predicts success in territory acquisition. Behav. Ecol. 15, 290–296.

Brumm, H., 2006. Signalling through acoustic windows: nightingales avoid interspecific competition by short-term adjustment of song timing. J. Comp. Physiol. A 192, 1279–1285.

Brumm, H., Naguib, M., 2009. Environmental acoustics and the evolution of bird song. Adv. Study. Behav. 40, 1–33.

Buchanan, K.L., Catchpole, C.K., 2000. Song as an indicator of male parental effort in the sedge warbler. Proc. R. Soc. B 267, 321–326.

Buchanan, K.L., Catchpole, C.K., Lewis, J.W., Lodge, A., 1999. Song as an indicator of parasitism in the sedge warbler. Anim. Behav. 57, 307–314.

Buchanan, K.L., Spencer, K.A., Goldsmith, A.R., Catchpole, C.K., 2003. Song as an honest signal of past developmental stress in the European starling (*Sturnus vulgaris*). Proc. R. Soc. B 270, 1149–1156.

Byers, E.B., Kroodsma, D.E., 2009. Female mate choice and songbird song repertoirs. Anim. Behav. 77, 13–22.

Byers, J., Hebets, E., Podos, J., 2010. Female mate choice based upon male motor performance. Anim. Behav. 79, 771–778.

Campioni, L., Delgado, M.D.M., Penteriani, V., 2010. Social status influences microhabitat selection: breeder and floater eagle owls *Bubo bubo* use different post sites. Ibis 152, 569–579.

Caro, S.P., Sewall, K.B., Salvante, K.G., Sockman, K.W., 2010. Female Lincoln's sparrows modulate their behavior in response to variation in male song quality. Behav. Ecol. 21, 562–569.

Catchpole, C.K., 1980. Sexual selection and the evolution of complex songs among European warblers of the genus *Acrocephalus*. Behaviour 74, 149–166.

Catchpole, C.K., Slater, P.J.B., 2008. Bird Song: Biological Themes and Variation. Cambridge University Press, New York.

Chandler, C.R., Ketterson, E.D., Nolan, V., Ziegenfus, C., 1994. Effects of testosterone on spatial activity in free-ranging male dark-eyed juncos, *Junco hyemalis*. Anim. Behav. 47, 1445–1455.

Chandler, C.R., Ketterson, E.D., Nolan, V., 1997. Effects of testosterone on use of space by male dark-eyed juncos when their mates are fertile. Anim. Behav. 54, 543–549.

Clarkson, C.E., 2007. Food supplementation, territory establishment, and song in the Prothonotary Warbler. Wils. J. Ornithol. 119, 342–349.

Cockburn, A., Dalziell, A.H., Blackmore, C.J., Double, M.C., Kokko, H., Osmond, H.L., et al., 2009. Superb fairy-wren males aggregate into hidden leks to solicit extragroup fertilizations before dawn. Behav. Ecol. 20, 501–510.

Cramer, E.R.A., Price, J.J., 2007. Red-winged blackbirds *Agelaius phoeniceus* respond differently to song types with different performance levels. J. Avian Biol. 38, 122–127.

Croft, D.P., James, R., Krause, J., 2007. Exploring Animal Social Networks. Princeton University Press, Princeton.

Croft, D.P., Krause, J., Darden, S.K., Ramnarine, I.W., Faria, J.J., James, R., 2009. Behavioural trait assortment in a social network: patterns and implications. Behav. Ecol. Sociobiol. 63, 1495–1503.

Cuthill, I.C., Macdonald, W.A., 1990. Experimental manipulation of the dawn and dusk chorus in the blackbird *Turdus merula*. Behav. Ecol. Sociobiol. 26, 209–216.

Dabelsteen, T., McGregor, P., Lampe, H.M., Langmore, N., Holland, J., 1998. Quiet song in song birds: an overlooked phenomenon. Bioacoustics 9, 89–105.

Danchin, E., Giraldeau, L.A., Valone, T.J., Wagner, R.H., 2004. Public information: from nosy neighbors to cultural evolution. Science 305, 487–491.

Danchin, É., Giraldeau, L.-A., Cézilly, F., 2008. Behavioural Ecology. Oxford University Press, New York.

de Kort, S.R., Eldermire, E.R.B., Valderrama, S., Botero, C.A., Vehrencamp, S.L., 2009. Trill consistency is an age-related assessment signal in banded wrens. Proc. R. Soc. B 276, 2315–2321.

Draganoiu, T.I., Nagle, L., Kreutzer, M., 2002. Directional female preference for an exaggerated male trait in canary (*Serinus canaria*) song. Proc. R. Soc. B 269, 2525–2531.

Dreiss, A.N., Navarro, C., de Lope, F., Møller, A.P., 2008. Effects of an immune challenge on multiple components of song display in barn swallows *Hirundo rustica*: implications for sexual selection. Ethology 114, 955–964.

DuBois, A.L., Nowicki, S., Searcy, W.A., 2009. Swamp sparrows modulate vocal performance in an aggressive context. Biol. Lett. 5, 163–165.

DuBois, A., Nowicki, S., Searcy, W., 2011. Discrimination of vocal performance by male swamp sparrows. 65, 717–726.

Erne, N., Amrhein, V., 2008. Long-term influence of simulated territorial intrusions on dawn and dusk singing in the winter wren: spring versus autumn. J. Ornithol. 149, 479–486.

Falls, J.B., Krebs, J.R., McGregor, P.K., 1982. Song matching in the great tit (*Parus major*)—the effect of similarity and familiarity. Anim. Behav. 30, 997–1009.

Ficken, R.W., Ficken, M.S., Hailman, J.P., 1974. Temporal pattern shifts to avoid acoustic interference in singing birds. Science 183, 762–763.

Ficken, R.W., Popp, J.W., Matthiae, P.E., 1985. Avoidance of acoustic interference by ovenbirds. Wilson Bull. 97, 569–571.

Fitzsimmons, L.P., Foote, J.R., Ratcliffe, L.M., Mennill, D.J., 2008a. Eavesdropping and communication networks revealed through playback and an acoustic location system. Behav. Ecol. 19, 824–829.

Fitzsimmons, L.P., Foote, J.R., Ratcliffe, L.M., Mennill, D.J., 2008b. Frequency matching, overlapping and movement behaviour in diurnal countersinging interactions of black-capped chickadees. Anim. Behav. 75, 1913–1920.

Foote, J.R., Fitzsimmons, L.P., Mennill, D.J., Ratcliffe, L.M., 2008. Male chickadees match neighbors interactively at dawn: support for the social dynamics hypothesis. Behav. Ecol. 19, 1192–1199.

Foote, J.R., Fithsimmons, L.P., Mennill, D.J., Ratcliffe, L.M., 2010. Black-capped chickadee dawn choruses are interactive communication networks. Behaviour 147, 1219–1248.

Formica, V.A., Gonser, R.A., Ramsay, S., Tuttle, E.M., 2004. Spatial dynamics of alternative reproductive strategies: the role of neighbors. Ecology 85, 1125–1136.

Forstmeier, W., Kempenaers, B., Meyer, A., Leisler, B., 2002. A novel song parameter correlates with extra-pair paternity and reflects male longevity. Proc. R. Soc. B 269, 1479–1485.

Garcia-Fernandez, V., Amy, M., Lacroix, A., Malacarne, G., Leboucher, G., 2010. Eavesdropping on male singing interactions leads to differential allocation in eggs. Ethology 116, 662–670.

Geberzahn, N., Hultsch, H., 2003. Long-time storage of song types in birds: evidence from interactive playbacks. Proc. R. Soc. B 270, 1085–1090.

Geberzahn, N., Hultsch, H., Todt, D., 2002. Latent song type memories are accessible through auditory stimulation in a hand-reared songbird. Anim. Behav. 64, 783–790.

Gil, D., Gahr, M., 2002. The honesty of bird song: multiple constraints for multiple traits. Trends Ecol. Evol. 17, 133–141.

Gil, D., Leboucher, G., Lacroix, A., Cue, R., Kreutzer, M., 2004. Female canaries produce eggs with greater amounts of testosterone when exposed to preferred male song. Horm. Behav. 45, 64–70.

Gil, D., Naguib, M., Riebel, K., Rutstein, A., Gahr, M., 2006. Early condition, song learning and the volume of brain song nuclei in the zebra finch (*Taeniopygia guttata*). J. Neurobiol. 66, 1602–1612.

Glutz von Blotzheim, U.N., 1988. Nachtigall. In: Glutz von Blotzheim, U.N. (Ed.), Handbuch der Vögel Mitteleuropas, Band 11/I. Aula Verlag, Wiesbaden, pp. 137–194.

Godard, R., 1993. Tit-for-tat among neighboring hooded warblers. Behav. Ecol. Sociobiol. 33, 45–50.

Gorissen, L., Snoeijs, T., Van Duyse, E., Eens, M., 2005. Heavy metal pollution affects dawn singing behaviour in a small passerine bird. Oecologia 145, 504–509.

Griessmann, B., Naguib, M., 2002. Song sharing in neighboring and non neighboring thrush nightingales (*Luscinia luscinia*) and its implications for communication. Ethology 108, 377–387.

Grafe, T.U., 1996. The function of call alternation in the Arican reed frog (*Hyperolius marmoratus*): precise call timing prevents auditory masking. Behav. Ecol. Sociobiol. 38, 149–158.

Greenfield, M.D., 1994. Synchronous and alternating choruses in insects and anurans: common mechanisms and diverse functions. Am. Zool. 34, 605–615.

Greenwood, P.J., 1980. Mating systems, philopatry and dispersal in birds and mammals. Anim. Behav. 28, 1140–1162.

Grüll, A., 1981. Untersuchungen über das Revier der Nachtigall (*Luscinia megarhynchos*). J. Ornithol. 122, 259–285.

Hall, M.L., Illes, A., Vehrencamp, S.L., 2006. Overlapping signals in banded wrens: long-term effects of prior experience on males and females. Behav. Ecol. 17, 260–269.

Halupka, K., Borowiec, M., 2006. Male whitethroats, *Sylvia communis*, advertise their future contribution to parental care. Behaviour 143, 1–14.

Hanski, I.K., 1992. Territorial behaviour and mixed reproductive strategy in the chaffinch. Ornis Scand. 23, 475–482.

Hanski, I.K., Haila, Y., 1988. Singing territories and home ranges of breeding chaffinches: visual observation vs. radiotracking. Ornis Fenn. 65, 97–103.

Hasselquist, D., Bensch, S., vonSchantz, T., 1996. Correlation between male song repertoire, extra-pair paternity and offspring survival in the great reed warbler. Nature 381, 229–232.

Hoese, W.J., Podos, J., Boetticher, N.C., Nowicki, S., 2000. Vocal tract function in birdsong production: experimental manipulation of beak movements. J. Exp. Biol. 203, 1845–1855.

Hof, D., Hazlett, N., 2010. Low-amplitude song predicts attack in a North American wood warbler. Anim. Behav. 80, 821–828.

Holveck, M.J., Riebel, K., 2010. Low-quality females prefer low-quality males when choosing a mate. Proc. R. Soc. B 277, 153–160.

Hoover, J.P., 2003. Decision rules for site fidelity in a migratory bird, the prothonotary warbler. Ecology 84, 416–430.

Hughes, M., Hultsch, H., Todt, D., 2002. Imitation and invention in song learning in nightingales (*Luscinia megarhynchos* B., Turdidae). Ethology 108, 97–113.

Hultsch, H., 1992. Time window and unit capacity—dual constraints on the acquisition of serial information in songbirds. J. Comp. Physiol. A 170, 275–280.

Hultsch, H., 1993. Psychobiological and ecological aspects of song learning and memorization. Etología 3, 309–323.

Hultsch, H., Todt, D., 1982. Temporal performance roles during vocal interactions in nightingales (*Luscinia megarhynchos*). Behav. Ecol. Sociobiol. 11, 253–260.

Hultsch, H., Todt, D., 1989. Memorization and reproduction of songs in nightingales (*Luscinia megarhynchos*): evidence for package formation. J. Comp. Physiol. A 165, 197–203.

Hultsch, H., Todt, D., 1992. The serial order effect in the song acquisition of birds—relevance of exposure frequency to song models. Anim. Behav. 44, 590–592.

Hultsch, H., Todt, D., 1996a. Discontinuous and incremental processes in the song learning of birds: evidence for a primer effect. J. Comp. Physiol. A 179, 291–299.

Hultsch, H., Todt, D., 1996b. Rules of parameter variation in homotype series of birdsong can indicate "sollwert" significance. Behav. Proc. 38, 175–182.

Hultsch, H., Todt, D., 2004. Learning to sing. In: Slabbekoorn, H., Marler, P. (Eds.), Nature's Music: The Science of Birdsong. Elsevier, San Diego.

Illes, A.E., Hall, M.L., Vehrencamp, S.L., 2006. Vocal performance influences male receiver response in the banded wren. Proc. R. Soc. B 27, 1907–1912.

Kempenaers, B., Everding, S., Bishop, C., Boag, P., Robertson, R.J., 2001. Extra-pair paternity and the reproductive role of male floaters in the tree swallow (*Tachycineta bicolor*). Behav. Ecol. Sociobiol. 49, 251–259.

Kiefer, S., Spiess, A., Kipper, S., Mundry, R., Sommer, C., Hultsch, H., et al., 2006. First-year common nightingales (*Luscinia megarhynchos*) have smaller song-type repertoire sizes than older males. Ethology 112, 1217–1224.

Kiefer, S., Sommer, C., Scharff, C., Kipper, S., Mundry, R., 2009. Tuning towards tomorrow? Common nightingales *Luscinia megarhynchos* change and increase their song repertoires from the first to the second breeding season. J. Avian Biol. 40, 231–236.

Kiefer, S., Sommer, C., Scharff, C., Kipper, S., 2010. Singing the popular songs? Nightingales share more song types with their breeding population in their second season than in their first. Ethology 116, 619–626.

Kipper, S., Kiefer, S., 2010. Age related changes in birds' singing styles: on fresh tunes and fading voices? Adv. Study Behav. 41, 77–118.

Kipper, S., Mundry, R., Hultsch, H., Todt, D., 2004. Long-term persistence of song performance rules in nightingales (*Luscinia megarhynchos*): a longitudinal field study on repertoire size and composition. Behaviour 141, 371–390.

Kipper, S., Mundry, R., Sommer, C., Hultsch, H., Todt, D., 2006. Song repertoire size is correlated with body measures and arrival date in common nightingales, *Luscinia megarhynchos*. Anim. Behav. 71, 211–217.

Kokko, H., Gunnarsson, T.G., Morrell, L.J., Gill, J.A., 2006. Why do female migratory birds arrive later than males? J. Anim. Ecol. 75, 1293–1303.

Krebs, J.R., Ashcroft, R., Webber, M., 1978. Song repertoires and territory defense in the great tit *Parus major* L. Nature 271, 539–542.

Kunc, H.P., Amrhein, V., Naguib, M., 2005a. Seasonal variation of dawn song and its relation to mating success in the nightingale (*Luscinia megarhynchos*). Anim. Behav. 70, 1265–1271.

Kunc, H.P., Amrhein, V., Naguib, M., 2005b. Acoustic features of song categories of the nightingale (*Luscinia megarhynchos*) and its implications for communication. Behaviour 142, 1083–1097.

Kunc, H.P., Amrhein, V., Naguib, M., 2006. Vocal interactions in nightingales (*Luscinia megarhynchos*): more aggressive males have higher pairing success. Anim. Behav. 72, 25–30.

Kunc, H.P., Amrhein, V., Naguib, M., 2007. Vocal interactions in common nightingales (*Luscinia megarhynchos*): males take it easy after pairing. Behav. Ecol. Sociobiol. 61, 557–563.

Laidre, M.E., Vehrencamp, S.L., 2008. Is bird song a reliable signal of aggressive intent? Behav. Ecol. Sociobiol. 62, 1207–1211.

Leboucher, G., Pallot, K., 2004. Is he all he says? Intersexual eavesdropping in the domestic canary, *Serinus canaria*. Anim. Behav. 68, 957–963.

Liu, W.C., 2004. The effect of neighbours and females on dawn and daytime singing behaviours by male chipping sparrows. Anim. Behav. 68, 39–44.

Mace, R., 1987. The dawn chorus in the great tit *Parus major* is directly related to female fertility. Nature 330, 745–746.

Maciejok, J., Saur, B., Bergmann, H.H., 1995. Was tun Buchfinken (*Fringilla coelebs*) zur Brutzeit außerhalb ihrer Reviere. J. Ornithol. 136, 37–45.

McGregor, P.K., 2005. Communication Networks. Cambridge University Press, Cambridge.

McGregor, P.K., Dabelsteen, T., 1996. Communication networks. In: Kroodsma, D.E., Miller, E.H. (Eds.), Ecology and Evolution of Acoustic Communication in Birds. University Press, Cornell, pp. 409–425.

McGregor, P.K., Krebs, J.R., 1982. Mating and song types in the great tit. Nature 297, 60–61.

McGregor, P.K., Krebs, J.R., Perrins, C.M., 1981. Song repertoires and lifetime reproductive success in the great tit (*Parus major*). Am. Nat. 118, 149–159.

Mennill, D.J., Ratcliffe, L.M., 2004. Do male black-capped chickadees eavesdrop on song contests? A multi-speaker playback experiment. Behaviour 141, 125–139.

Mennill, D.J., Ratcliffe, L.M., Boag, P.T., 2002. Female eavesdropping on male song contests in songbirds. Science 296, 873.

Naef-Daenzer, B., 1994. Radiotracking of great and blue tits: new tools to assess territoriality, home-range and ressource distribution. Ardea 82, 335–347.

Naguib, M., 1997. Use of song amplitude for ranging in Carolina wrens, *Thryothorus ludovicianus*. Ethology 103, 723–731.

Naguib, M., 1999. Effects of song overlapping and alternating on nocturnally singing nightingales. Anim. Behav. 58, 1061–1067.

Naguib, M., 2003. Reverberation of rapid and slow trills: implications for signal adaptations to long range communication. J. Acoust. Soc. Am. 133, 1749–1756.

Naguib, M., 2005. Singing interactions in song birds: implications for social relations, territoriality and territorial settlement. In: McGregor, P.K. (Ed.), Communication Networks. Cambridge University Press, Cambridge, pp. 300–319.

Naguib, M., Kipper, S., 2006. Effects of different levels of song overlapping on singing behaviour in male territorial nightingales (*Luscinia megarhynchos*). Behav. Ecol. Sociobiol. 59, 419–426.

Naguib, M., Mennill, D., 2010. The signal value of bird song: empirical evidence suggests song overlapping is a signal. Anim. Behav. 80, e11–e15.

Naguib, M., Todt, D., 1997. Effects of dyadic vocal interactions on other conspecific receivers in nightingales. Anim. Behav. 54, 1535–1543.

Naguib, M., Todt, D., 1998. Recognition of neighbors' song in a species with large and complex song repertoires: the thrush nightingale. J. Avian Biol. 29, 155–160.

Naguib, M., Wiley, R.H., 2001. Estimating the distance to a source of sound: mechanisms and adaptations for long-range communication. Anim. Behav. 62, 825–837.

Naguib, M., Fichtel, C., Todt, D., 1999. Nightingales respond more strongly to vocal leaders in simulated dyadic interactions. Proc. R. Soc. B 265, 537–542.

Naguib, M., Altenkamp, R., Grießmann, B., 2001. Nightingales in space: song and extra-territorial forays of radio tagged song birds. J. Ornithol. 142, 306–312.

Naguib, M., Mundry, R., Hultsch, H., Todt, D., 2002. Responses to playback of whistle songs and normal songs in male nightingales: effects of song category, whistle pitch, and distance. Behav. Ecol. Sociobiol. 52, 216–223.

Naguib, M., Amrhein, V., Kunc, H.P., 2004. Effects of territorial intrusions on eavesdropping neighbors: communication networks in nightingales. Behav. Ecol. 6, 1011–1015.

Naguib, M., Schmidt, R., Sprau, P., Roth, T., Floercke, C., Amrhein, V., 2008. The ecology of vocal signaling: male spacing and communication distance of different song traits in nightingales. Behav. Ecol. 19, 1034–1040.

Naguib, M., Kazek, A., Schaper, S.V., van Oers, K., Visser, M.E., 2010. Singing activity reveals personality traits in great tits. Ethology 116, 1–7.

Nowicki, S., Peters, S., Podos, J., 1998a. Song learning, early nutrition and sexual selection in songbirds. Am. Zool. 38, 179–190.

Nowicki, S., Searcy, W.A., Hughes, M., 1998b. The territory defense function of song in song sparrows: a test with the speaker occupation design. Behaviour 135, 615–628.

Otter, K., Chruszcz, B., Ratcliffe, L., 1997. Honest advertisement and song output during the dawn chorus of black-capped chickadees. Behav. Ecol. 8, 167–173.

Otter, K., McGregor, P.K., Terry, A.M.R., Burford, F.R.L., Peake, T.M., Dabelsteen, T., 1999. Do female great tits (Parus major) assess males by eavesdropping? A field study using interactive song playback. Proc. R. Soc. B 266, 1305–1309.

Otter, K.A., Stewart, I.R.K., McGregor, P.K., Terry, A.M.R., Dabelsteen, T., Burke, T., 2001. Extra-pair paternity among great tits Parus major following manipulation of male signals. J. Avian Biol. 32, 338–344.

Peake, T.M., 2005. Communication Networks. In: McGregor, P.K. (Ed.), Communication Networks. Cambridge University Press, Cambridge.

Peake, T.M., Terry, A.M.R., McGregor, P.K., Dabelsteen, T., 2001. Male great tits eavesdrop on simulated male-to-male vocal interactions. Proc. R. Soc. B 268, 1183–1187.

Peake, T.M., Terry, A.M.R., McGregor, P.K., Dabelsteen, T., 2002. Do great tits assess rivals by combining direct experience with information gathered by eavesdropping? Proc. R. Soc. B 269, 925–1929.

Pitcher, T.E., Stutchbury, B.J.M., 2000. Extraterritorial forays and male parental care in hooded warblers. Anim. Behav. 59, 1261–1269.

Podos, J., 1996. Motor constraints on vocal development in a songbird. Anim. Behav. 51, 1061–1070.

Podos, J., Lahti, D.C., Moseley, D.L., 2009. Vocal performance and sensorimotor learning in songbirds. Adv. Study Behav. 40, 159–195.

Poesel, A., Dabelsteen, T., 2005. Territorial responses of male blue tits to simulated dynamic intrusions: effects of song overlap and intruder location. Anim. Behav. 70, 1419–1427.

Poesel, A., Dabelsteen, T., Pedersen, S.B., 2004. Dawn song of male blue tits as a predictor of competitiveness in midmorning singing interactions. Acta. Ethol. 6, 65–71.

Price, J.J., 2009. Evolution and life-history correlates of female song in the new world blackbirds. Behav. Evol. 20, 967–977.

Ratcliffe, L., Otter, K., 1996. Sex differences in song recognition. In: Kroodsma, D.E., Miller, D.E. (Eds.), Ecology and Evolution of Acoustic Communication in Birds. Cornell University Press, Ithaca, pp. 339–355.

Rätti, O., Siikamki, P., 1993. Female attraction behavior of radio tagged polyterritorial pied flycatcher males. Behaviour 127, 279–288.

Reed, J., Boulinier, R., Danchin, E., Oring, L., 1999. Informed dispersal: prospecting by birds for breeding sites. Curr. Ornithol. 15, 189–259.

Richards, D.G., 1981. Alerting and message components in songs of rufous-sided towhees. Behaviour 76, 223–249.

Riebel, K., Hall, M.L., Langmore, N.E., 2005. Female songbirds still struggling to be heard. Trends Ecol. Evol. 20, 419–420.

Riebel, K., Naguib, M., Gil, D., 2009. Experimental manipulation of the rearing environment influences adult female zebra finch song preferences. Anim. Behav. 78, 1397–1404.

Rivera-Gutierrez, H.F., Pinxten, R., Eens, M., 2010. Multiple signals for multiple messages: great tit, *Parus major*, song signals age and survival. Anim. Behav. 80, 451–459.

Roth, T., Amrhein, V., 2010. Estimating individual survival using territory occupancy data on unmarked animals. J. Appl. Ecol. 47, 386–392.

Roth, T., Sprau, P., Schmidt, R., Naguib, M., Amrhein, V., 2009. Sex-specific timing of mate searching and territory prospecting in the nightingale: nocturnal life of females. Proc. R. Soc. B 276, 2045–2050.

Saggese, K., Korner-Nievergelt, F., Slagsvold, T., Amrhein, V., 2011. Wild bird feeding delays start of dawn singing in the great tit. Anim. Behav. 81, 361–365.

Saino, N., Galeotti, P., Sacchi, R., Møller, A.P., 1997. Song and immunological condition in male barn swallows (*Hirundo rustica*). Behav. Ecol. 8, 364–371.

Schmidt, R., Kunc, H.P., Amrhein, V., Naguib, M., 2006. Responses to interactive playback predict future mating status in nightingales. Anim. Behav. 72, 1355–1362.

Schmidt, R., Kunc, H.P., Amrhein, V., Naguib, M., 2007. The day after: effects of vocal interactions on territory defence in nightingales. J. Anim. Ecol. 76, 168–173.

Schmidt, R., Kunc, H.P., Amrhein, V., Naguib, M., 2008. Aggressive responses to broadband trills are related to subsequent pairing success in nightingales. Behav. Ecol. 19, 635–641.

Schwartz, J.J., 1987. The function of call alternation in anuran amphibians: a test of three hypotheses. Evolution 41, 461–471.

Searcy, W.A., Beecher, M.D., 2009. Song as an aggressive signal in songbirds. Anim. Behav. 78, 1281–1292.

Searcy, W.A., Nowicki, S., 2005. The Evolution of Animal Communication. Reliability and Deception in Signaling Systems. Princeton University Press, Princeton, USA.

Searcy, W.A., Nowicki, S., 2006. Signal interception and the use of soft song in aggressive interactions. Ethology 112, 865–872.

Searcy, W.A., Anderson, R.C., Nowicki, S., 2006. Bird song as a signal of aggressive intent. Behav. Ecol. Sociobiol. 60, 234–241.

Searcy, W.A., Peters, S., Kipper, S., Nowicki, S., 2010. Female response to song reflects male developmental history in swamp sparrows. Behav. Ecol. Sociobiol. 64, 1343–1349.

Sexton, K., Murphy, M.T., Redmond, L.J., Dolan, A.C., 2007. Dawn song of eastern kingbirds: intrapopulation variability and sociobiological correlates. Behaviour 144, 1273–1295.

Shy, E., Morton, E.S., 1986. The role of distance, familiarity, and time of day in Carolina wrens responses to conspecific songs. Behav. Ecol. Sociobiol. 19, 393–400.

Simpson, B.S., 1985. Effects of the location in territory and distance from neighbors on the use of song repertoires by Carolina wrens. Anim. Behav. 33, 793–804.

Smith, S.M., 1978. Underworld in a territorial sparrow—adaptive strategy for floaters. Am. Nat. 112, 571–582.

Sprau, P., Mundry, R., 2010. Song type sharing in common nightingales, *Luscinia mega-rhynchos*, and its implications for cultural evolution. Anim. Behav. 80, 427–434.

Sprau, P., Roth, T., Schmidt, R., Amrhein, V., Naguib, M., 2010a. Communication across territory boundaries: distance-dependent responses in nightingales. Behav. Ecol. 21, 1011–1017.

Sprau, P., Schmidt, R., Roth, T., Amrhein, V., Naguib, M., 2010b. Effects of rapid broadband trills on responses to song overlapping in nightingales. Ethology 115, 300–308.

Staicer, C.A., Spector, D.A., Horn, A.G., 1996. The dawn chorus and other diel patterns in acoustic signaling. In: Kroodsma, D.E., Miller, E.H. (Eds.), Ecology and Evolution of Acoustic Communication in Birds. Cornell University Press, London.

Stamps, J., 1994. Territorial behavior: testing the assumptions. Adv. Study Behav. 23, 173–232.

Stamps, J.A., Krishnan, V.V., 1997. Functions of fights in territory establishment. Am. Nat. 150, 393–405.

Stamps, J.A., Krishnan, V.V., 2001. How territorial animals compete for divisible space: a learning-based model with unequal competitors. Am. Nat. 157, 154–169.

Strain, J.G., Mumme, R.L., 1988. Effects of food supplementation, song playback, and temperature on vocal territorial behavior of Carolina wrens. Auk 105, 11–16.

Stutchbury, B.J.M., 1998. Extra-pair mating effort of male hooded warblers, Wilsonia citrina. Anim. Behav. 55, 553–561.

Suter, S.M., Ermacora, D., Rieille, N., Meyer, D.R., 2009. A distinct reed bunting dawn song and its relation to extrapair paternity. Anim. Behav. 77, 473–480.

Thomas, R.J., 2002a. The costs of singing in nightingales. Anim. Behav. 63, 959–966.

Thomas, R.J., 2002b. Seasonal changes in the nocturnal singing routines of common nightingales Luscinia megarhynchos. Ibis 144, E105–E112.

Todt, D., 1970. Zur Ordnung im Gesang der Nachtigall (Luscinia megarhynchos). Verh. Dtsch. Zool. Ges 1970, 249–252.

Todt, D., Hultsch, H., 1996. Acquisition and performance of song repertoires: ways of coping with diversity and versatility. In: Kroodsma, D.E., Miller, E.H. (Eds.), Ecology and Evolution of Acoustic Communication in Birds. Cornell University Press, Ithaca, London, pp. 79–96.

Todt, D., Naguib, M., 2000. Vocal interactions in birds: the use of song as a model in communication. Adv. Study Behav. 29, 247–296.

Vallet, E., Kreutzer, M., 1995. Female canaries are sexually responsive to special song phrases. Anim. Behav. 49, 1603–1610.

Vallet, E., Beme, I., Kreutzer, M., 1998. Two-note syllables in canary songs elicit high levels of sexual display. Anim. Behav. 55, 291–297.

Wagner, R.H., 1998. Hidden leks: sexual selection and the clustering of avian territories. Ornithol. Monogr. 49, 123–145.

Waser, P.M., Wiley, R.H., 1980. Mechanisms and evolution of spacing in animals. In: Marler, P., Vandenbergh, J.G. (Eds.), Handbook of Behavioral Neurobiology: Social Behavior and Communication. Plenum Publishing Cooperation, New York, pp. 159–233.

Welling, P.P., Rytkönen, S.O., Koivula, K.T., Orell, M.I., 1997. Song rate correlates with paternal care and survival in willow tits: advertisement of male quality? Behaviour 134, 891–904.

Westneat, M.W., Long, J.H., Hoese, W., Nowicki, S., 1993. Kinematics of birdsong—functional correlation of cranial movements and acoustic features in sparrows. J. Exp. Biol. 182, 147–171.

Whitfield, J., 2002. Nosy neighbors. Nature 419, 242–243.

Wiley, R.H., Poston, J., 1996. Indirect mate choice, competition for mates, and coevolution of the sexes. Evolution 50, 1371–1379.

Wiley, R.H., Richards, D.G., 1982. Adaptations for acoustic communication in birds: sound transmission and signal detection. In: Kroodsma, D.E., Miller, E.H. (Eds.), Acoustic Communication in Birds, Vol. 2. Academic Press, New York, pp. 131–181.

Wilson, A.M., Fuller, R.J., Day, C., Smith, G., 2005. Nightingales Luscinia megarhynchos in scrub habitats in the southern fens of East Anglia, England: associations with soil type and vegetation structure. Ibis 147, 498–511.

Zahavi, A., 1979. Why shouting? Am. Nat. 113, 155–156.

Direct Benefits and the Evolution of Female Mating Preferences: Conceptual Problems, Potential Solutions, and a Field Cricket

WILLIAM E. WAGNER JR.

SCHOOL OF BIOLOGICAL SCIENCES, UNIVERSITY OF NEBRASKA, LINCOLN, NEBRASKA, USA

I. INTRODUCTION

A. THE EVOLUTION OF FEMALE MATING PREFERENCES

Females often preferentially mate with males with particular traits, such as larger morphological traits, bigger and brighter color patterns, more vigorous visual displays, and faster, longer, and louder calls (Andersson, 1994; Ryan and Keddy-Hector, 1992). These mating decisions can have important fitness consequences for females; males with preferred traits can provide material resources that increase female or offspring fitness (direct benefits; Heywood, 1989; Hoelzer, 1989; Price et al., 1993), alleles that increase offspring viability (good genes; Fisher, 1930; Grafen, 1990; Pomiankowski, 1988; Zahavi, 1975), or alleles that affect the attractiveness of male offspring (sexy sons; Fisher, 1930; Kirkpatrick, 1982; Lande, 1981). In addition, females may express preferences because alleles that are beneficial in another context incidentally bias female responses to male traits in a mating context (Basolo, 1990, 1995; Christy, 1995; Endler and Basolo, 1998; Kirkpatrick, 1987a; Ryan, 1990).

There has been substantial debate over the past three decades about the viability and importance of the good genes, sexy sons, and receiver bias mechanisms (e.g., Jones and Ratterman, 2009; Kirkpatrick and Ryan, 1991; Kokko et al., 2003). In contrast, there has been very little debate about the viability and importance of the direct benefits mechanism. It is generally regarded as a straightforward, relatively uncomplicated hypothesis, broadly important but conceptually uninteresting. Indeed, most experimental and theoretical work on mate choice over the past two decades has focused on

273

0065-3454/11 $35.00
DOI: 10.1016/B978-0-12-380896-7.00006-X

the good genes mechanism, and in many reviews of the state of the field, the direct benefits hypothesis has received little more than a passing acknowledgment (for a recent example, which is by no means unique, see Jones and Ratterman, 2009). Kotiaho and Puurtinen (2007) criticized this distorted focus, noting that there has been excessive enthusiasm for a mechanism that has not been adequately tested and which, at best, has only small effects on female fitness (e.g., Kirkpatrick and Barton, 1997; Møller and Alatalo, 1999). Because the good genes hypothesis has been overemphasized, the direct benefits hypothesis is conceptually underdeveloped, some of the complexities of the hypothesis have been unexplored, and some of the problems with the hypothesis are not widely appreciated.

My goals for this chapter are to highlight a few of the problems with the direct benefits hypothesis that might not be widely known, and to discuss some potential solutions to these problems. I begin with an overview of the hypothesis and a discussion of some of the challenges in testing whether females directly benefit from their mating preferences. I will discuss some conceptual problems with the hypothesis and some potential solutions to these problems. I conclude by illustrating some of these issues using the work that my colleagues and I have done with a field cricket. I make five major points: (1) a strong test of the hypothesis is more difficult than most authors (myself included) may have suggested; (2) we do not understand why males provide some types of direct benefits; (3) the handicap mechanism, which is the major hypothesis for why male signals provide reliable information about benefit quality, is insufficient for direct benefits; (4) environmental effects on signal reliability may be widespread; and (5) because of environmental effects on signal reliability, female choice based on male signals of direct benefit quality may require the evolution of complex assessment strategies.

B. THE BROAD REACH OF DIRECT BENEFITS

There are two general pathways through which females can directly benefit from expressing preferences. First, females may have higher fitness if they respond to some types of signals, independently of the costs and benefits of mating with particular males (reviewed by Reynolds and Gross, 1990). For example, females might incur lower search costs if they preferentially respond to more localizable signal types. Similarly, females might incur lower costs of associating with males if they preferentially respond to signal types that are less likely to attract predators. Second, females may have higher fitness if they mate with particular types of males. For example, some males may provide greater material contributions to females or offspring, or some males may impose lower costs on females (reviewed by Andersson, 1994; Halliday, 1978; Reynolds and Gross, 1990; Searcy, 1982; Thornhill and Alcock, 1983). The material contributions that male animals provide to females take a bewildering variety of forms. Some common types of male-provided benefits are: nutrients, such as prey items, body parts, and secretions (Gwynne, 1988; Sakaluk, 1984; Thornhill, 1976); access to resources on a territory, including refuges, oviposition or nesting sites, and food (Howard, 1978; Pleszynska, 1978; Searcy, 1979); more sperm, more viable sperm, or better fertilization ability (Drnevich et al., 2001; Matthews et al., 1997; Robertson, 1990); a variety of products transferred in seminal fluid, including nutritive and defensive compounds (Boggs and Gilbert, 1979; Dussourd et al., 1989; Iyengar and Eisner, 1999; Markow, 1988); male protection, including protection from harassment by other males and from predators (Borgia, 1981; González et al., 1999); and male care of offspring, including care that frees females to engage in other activities and care that increases offspring fitness (Downhower and Brown, 1980; Hill, 1991; Knapp and Kovach, 1991; Pampoulie et al., 2004). These male contributions can thus increase female fitness because of their effects on female survivorship and reproduction, or because of their effects on offspring survivorship and reproduction. While the former might more accurately be referred to as direct, nongenetic benefits, and the latter as indirect, nongenetic benefits (e.g., Grether, 2010), their effects on preference evolution should be similar. Females may also benefit from mating with some types of males, not because these males provide greater benefits *per se*, but because they impose lower costs on females. For example, females might risk damage from mating with males of all types, but the risk or magnitude of the damage may be lower for some types of males.

In contrast to genetic benefits, which tend to have only small effects on female fitness (e.g., Hadfield et al., 2006; Kirkpatrick and Barton, 1997; Møller and Alatalo, 1999; Qvarnström et al., 2006), these direct benefits, when present, can have large effects (e.g., Møller and Jennions, 2001). There are two reasons that genetic benefits tend to have relatively weak effects on female fitness. First, if genetic variation for fitness is limited, the benefit to females of mating with higher fitness males will be small (e.g., Qvarnström et al., 2006). Second, if the genetic correlation between male signal expression and male fitness is relatively small, females may often mate with low fitness males when they choose mates based on the signal. In contrast, direct benefits tend to have larger effects on female fitness because it does not matter whether variation in benefit quality results from genetic or environmental effects (i.e., the total variance for direct benefit quality, rather than the genetic variance, will determine the extent to which females can benefit from their mate choices). However, as with genetic benefits, imperfect correlations between male signals and direct benefit quality could reduce the ability of females to select high-benefit males, depending upon what females assess during mate choice. If females choose mates based on a direct assessment of benefit quality, trait-benefit correlations are irrelevant. If, however, females indirectly assess benefit quality based on correlated male signals, the ability of females to select high-benefit males will be reduced if the phenotypic correlation between the trait and benefit quality is low (see also Section II.A).

The broad reach of the direct benefits hypothesis is commonly misunderstood or misrepresented. For example, in work on animals in which males provide no resources to females, such as lekking birds, it is relatively common for direct benefits to be dismissed because females "only receive sperm" from their mates. An absence of evidence, however, is not evidence of an absence; there are literally dozens of types of direct benefits that would be undetectable based on casual observation, including signal-related search and association costs, and mate-related predation, parasitism, injury, sperm quantity, sperm quality, and seminal fluid benefits. Indeed, there is no animal with internal fertilization, and very few with external fertilization, for which the direct benefits hypothesis can be rejected without explicitly testing for direct benefits. This has long been known (e.g., Reynolds and Gross, 1990) but is often ignored. In addition, in studies that measure offspring fitness components rather than female fitness components, direct benefits are sometimes dismissed based on the mistaken assumption that direct benefits only affect female fecundity, fertility, or longevity. There is no offspring fitness component that is inherently invulnerable to the effects of direct benefits.

C. Testing the Direct Benefits Hypothesis: Some Complications

Studies of direct benefits sometimes begin by testing the fitness consequences for females of repeated and/or multiple mating (e.g., Wagner et al., 2001a). For example, some females might be mated once to a given male, some females might be mated repeatedly to given male, and some females might be mated once to each of a number of different males. Female life span, female lifetime fecundity, offspring size, and/or offspring survivorship might then be measured. The logic of this approach is that if females receive material contributions from males, then females that mate repeatedly and/or multiply should have higher fitness or produce offspring of higher fitness. While such studies can provide information about the fitness consequences of repeated and multiple mating, they may provide misinformation about the benefits of female mating preferences. First, a positive effect of mating rate on female fitness does not necessarily support the direct benefits hypothesis. Females might benefit from repeated and multiple mating, but preferred males might not provide greater benefits than less preferred males. Second, neither the absence of an effect of mating rate on female fitness, nor a negative effect of mating rate on female fitness, necessarily rejects the direct benefits hypothesis. For example, while higher mating rates might reduce female fitness, females may nonetheless have higher fitness when they mate with preferred males. To test whether females directly benefit from their mating preferences, it is instead necessary to test the fitness consequences of variation in female mating preferences.

The good genes and sexy sons hypotheses are notoriously difficult to test because they require showing that females with stronger preferences produce offspring of higher fitness as a result of alleles that females receive from males with preferred traits (Kokko et al., 2003). This is difficult in many animals, particularly under ecologically relevant conditions, because of difficulties with tracking offspring and measuring offspring reproductive success. Although rarely acknowledged, the direct benefits hypothesis is equally difficult to test; it also predicts that females with stronger preferences have higher fitness, either because of nongenetic benefits that females receive from males with preferred traits or because of nongenetic benefits that offspring receive. The latter component of this prediction requires just as much effort to test as do the predictions of the good genes and sexy sons hypotheses. Moreover, for all three hypotheses, it is necessary to disentangle paternal genetic and nongenetic effects on offspring fitness to separate the effects of direct and genetic benefits. Finally, even if females benefit from mating with preferred males because of nongenetic male effects on female or offspring fitness, manipulative experiments will usually be necessary to determine why females benefit (i.e., the benefit mechanism).

An additional complication for testing the direct benefits, good genes, and sexy sons hypotheses is that the predictions about the fitness consequences of female preferences are limited to nonequilibrium conditions. At equilibrium, the fitness benefits of female preferences should be balanced by the costs of expressing preferences and by trade-offs between preferences and other traits (e.g., Kirkpatrick, 1987b). Whether the preferences of most populations are at or near their optima, however, is unknown.

Because of the difficulty of measuring female and offspring fitness under natural conditions, or because the necessity of these measures has not been appreciated, past studies of direct benefits have mostly taken an atomistic approach in which the investigators have tested for specific benefit mechanisms using observational studies in the field and/or controlled experiments in the field or laboratory. For example, a number of studies have tested whether females that mate with preferred males produce more surviving offspring because preferred males provide more parental care (reviewed by Andersson, 1994). These types of studies can tell us whether a specific benefit mechanism increases a given female fitness component, or set of fitness components, in a given environment. While we might then use the results to make inferences about the direct benefits of female mating preferences, the validity of such inferences is nearly always unknown. A given fitness component, for example, may be positively correlated, uncorrelated, or even negatively correlated with overall fitness (e.g., because the purported male contributions increase one component of female fitness but reduce other components of fitness; e.g., Fedorka and Mousseau, 2004). In addition, a given benefit mechanism may increase a given female fitness component in only a subset of environments (e.g., Tolle and Wagner, 2011). Finally, the direct benefits hypothesis includes an eclectic set of mechanisms, and different mechanisms can require very different types of experiments to test. Rejection of a given benefit mechanism cannot be used to reject the hypothesis itself (see Section I.B).

Regardless of whether a study measures the fitness consequences of female preferences or measures the effect of a given benefit mechanism on components of female fitness, it is necessary to ensure that variation among females is not confounded with variation among males. First, females with stronger preferences may differ in a variety of ways from females with weaker preferences (Jennions and Petrie, 1997), and the fitness consequences of these differences can be confused with the fitness consequences of preferences. Second, females in a number of animals are known to produce more offspring, or invest more in each offspring they produce, when they mate with more attractive males (reviewed by Møller and Thornhill, 1998). It may thus appear that preferred males provide direct benefits even if they provide nothing. This problem can be avoided by experimentally randomizing the association between trait attractiveness and direct benefit quality. Numerous studies, for example, have experimentally manipulated the morphological structures, color patterns, or acoustic signals that a given male expresses (e.g., Basolo, 1990; Møller and de Lope, 1994; Wagner et al., 2007) and some have experimentally manipulated the direct benefits that specific males provide (e.g., Sakaluk et al., 2006; Wright and Cuthill, 1989).

Strong support for the direct benefits hypothesis requires a demonstration that (a) preferences increase female or offspring fitness; (b) the effect of preference on fitness is due to either signal-related effects on female fitness or nongenetic material effects on female or offspring fitness (see Section I.B for this distinction), not due to genetic or female effects; and (c) a specific benefit mechanism, or set of benefit mechanisms, can explain the fitness consequences of preferences. Requirement (c) is important because it allows identification of reasons that selection acts on female preferences. While these criteria might seem draconian, this does not mean that we cannot make progress by addressing more limited questions. Rather, the inferences we can make from such studies will necessarily be weak. Strong tests of all hypotheses for preference evolution, including the direct benefits hypothesis, are simply difficult to conduct.

II. THE DIRECT BENEFITS HYPOTHESIS: CONCEPTUAL ISSUES

A. FEMALE CHOICE BASED ON DIRECT BENEFITS

If males vary in the direct benefits that they provide to females, or in the costs that they cause females to incur, and if females can directly or indirectly assess the benefits and/or costs of mating with males (i.e., direct benefit quality), then females preferences based on benefit quality should be favored. Whether preferences actually evolve will depend on a variety of factors, including the costs of being choosy and trade-offs between preferences and other traits. The more difficult issues are why males should provide direct benefits to females, and when male signals are correlated with benefit quality, why male signals provide reliable information. To illustrate the problems, it is potentially useful to divide direct benefits into three classes based on: (a) whether females can directly assess benefit quality prior to mating and (b) whether males use signals to attract females.

The simplest type of female choice occurs when males offer resources to females in the absence of signaling (Fig. 1A). For example, males might search for females and offer them food items (e.g., Thornhill, 1976). When this is the case, females can directly inspect the direct benefit prior to mating. If there are costs of mating, such as a risk of predation or a risk of parasite transmission, or if females only mate once per reproductive bout, selection may favor selective mating with those males that offer the highest-quality food items. Female choice, in turn, should tend to favor the evolution of higher-quality direct benefits (e.g., greater male investment in finding high-quality food items). It is this class of direct benefit that makes the evolution of female choice for direct benefits seem simple and straightforward.

A slightly more complex type of female choice occurs when males produce signals to attract females at a distance and then offer resources to females once they approach (Fig. 1B). The key issue is whether females can directly assess the benefit prior to mating. If they can directly assess the benefit, they should; male signals may not provide reliable information about benefit quality, and or may be less reliable than direct assessment. For example, in a territorial animal, males might signal to attract females and allow females

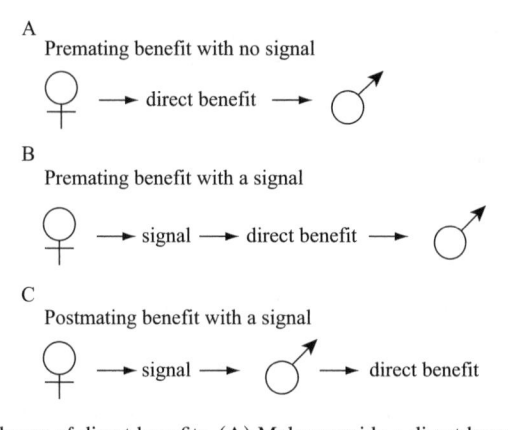

FIG. 1. Three classes of direct benefits. (A) Males provide a direct benefit prior to mating but do not signal to attract females. (B) Males signal to attract females and provide a direct benefit prior to mating. (C) Males signal to attract females and provide a direct benefit after mating. When females can directly assess the quality of the benefit prior to mating, females should choose mates based on benefit quality. When females cannot directly assess the quality of the benefit prior to mating, they instead need to rely on male signals, which may or may not provide reliable information about benefit quality.

to utilize resources on the territory following mating. Male signals may or may not be correlated with territory quality, but females can potentially assess the territory prior to mating (e.g., Howard, 1978). As should be the case when males do not signal, selection should favor female assessment of benefit quality and selective mating with males that offer the highest-quality benefits, which in turn should tend to favor the evolution of higher-quality direct benefits. While females might use male signals for a preliminary assessment of benefit quality, direct benefit quality will evolve primarily as a result of direct female assessment of the benefit. This class of direct benefit is simple and straightforward if the signal provides no information about benefit quality. It is more complicated, however, if the signal is correlated with benefit quality; such a relationship cannot be explained by the prevailing hypothesis for evolution of reliable signaling (see Section II.C).

In my discussion of the first two classes of direct benefits, I have assumed that females either receive the benefit before mating, or if they do not receive the benefit until after mating, that males cannot later choose to withhold the benefit (e.g., that males will not exclude females from accessing resources on their territories once mating has occurred). If females can directly assess benefit quality prior to mating, but males can withhold the benefit once mating has occurred, then these classes of direct benefits may be more similar to the third class (next).

The most complex type of female choice occurs when males produce signals to attract females at a distance, females indirectly assess benefit quality prior to mating based on the signal, and females cannot directly assess the benefit, and do not receive the benefit, until after mating has occurred (Fig. 1C). These types of benefits are sometimes referred to as postmating or postcopulatory direct benefits. For example, males might produce signals correlated with the quality of the nutrients or defensive compounds they will transfer in their seminal fluid, or with the quality of paternal care they will provide to offspring (e.g., Hill, 1991; Wagner and Harper, 2003). The reason that this class of direct benefit is a problem is because males can potentially produce deceptive signals and get away it because females will not be able to tell that they have been cheated until after they have accepted a male's sperm. And if males can get away with deception, why should they pay the cost of providing direct benefits to females? These problems, are not adequately solved by prevailing hypotheses for the evolution of direct benefits and the evolution of signal reliability.

B. THE EVOLUTION OF POSTMATING DIRECT BENEFITS

A number of hypotheses could potentially explain why males provide postmating direct benefits: female choice for higher-quality benefits, natural selection for male investment in females or offspring, female retaliation against low-benefit males, and male signaling of genetic quality via direct benefits. Except for the signaling of genetic quality hypothesis, these hypotheses may be of limited utility (see Wagner and Basolo, 2008). For example, female choice should only favor the evolution of direct benefits if females can directly assess benefit quality prior to mating; if females can only indirectly assess benefit quality based on a correlated male signal, and if males do not benefit in another context from providing higher-quality benefits, selection should break the correlation between the signal and benefit because males will have higher fitness if they provide less than females prefer. Selection for male investment in females or offspring requires female monogamy or limited multiple mating; the greater the extent of female multiple mating, the lower the fitness return for males of providing direct benefits (Vahed, 1998). And female retaliation requires that a low cost to females of punishing low-benefit males and repeated mating interactions between between pairs of males and females (Maynard Smith and Harper, 2003). In addition, the signal of genetic benefits hypothesis, while potentially of broad applicability, may require that genetic benefits have a greater effect on female fitness than does the direct benefit that serves as a signal. Otherwise, selection on female behavior should primarily be a consequence of variation in the direct benefit, and when this is the case, males can potentially profit from cheating on the benefit because females should not exercise cryptic choice based on direct benefits (e.g., female patterns of sperm use should only be based on the future costs and benefits of using a male's sperm, not based on whether a male recently cheated on a direct benefit; Dawkins and Carlisle, 1976; Simmons and Parker, 1989).

An alternative, the incidental sanctions hypothesis, proposes that males provide postmating direct benefits, and perhaps some types of premating direct benefits, because conditional female reproductive tactics incidentally sanction (penalize) low-benefit males (Wagner and Basolo, 2008). This hypothesis has two components. First, the quality of the direct benefit that a male has provided may affect the costs and benefits of a female's current and future reproductive decisions. For example, females that have received low-quality direct benefits from a male may: (1) forego additional matings with the male because the expected benefits of repeated mating are low and there are costs of being near and mating with males; (2) mate sooner with a new male to compensate for the previous low-quality benefit (3) invest less in current egg production because they have fewer resources to allocate to various traits; or (4) invest less in current parental care because the payoffs of investing are lower relative to the benefits of conserving resources for future reproduction. Three types of conditional reproductive responses are illustrated in Fig. 2 (for others, see Wagner and Basolo, 2008). Second, many of these conditional reproductive tactics will tend to incidentally penalize low-benefit males. For example, as a result of the benefit-dependent changes in female reproductive behavior described above, low-benefit males should transfer less sperm, experience more intense sperm competition, have fewer offspring with a given female, and/or have fewer surviving offspring with a given female. Stated colloquially, if a male does not play nice, a female may need to pursue alternative reproductive options, often to the detriment of the male that has not played nice. Incidental sanctions can have the same effect as female retaliation, but in contrast to retaliation, females need not benefit from the negative effects of their behavior on males.

The incidental sanctions hypothesis draws from a number of sources. For example, in some insects, males provide nuptial gifts at the time of mating, and females may remove spermatophores sooner (e.g., Sakaluk, 1984; Wedell, 1991, 1994), show a lower latency to mate with a new male (e.g., Thornhill, 1983), or invest less in offspring (e.g., Wedell, 1996) when a male has provided a low-quality nuptial gift. Similarly, female birds may "divorce" their mates (Lindén, 1991) or show greater extra-pair mating (Freeman-Gallant, 1997) if a male has provided low-quality paternal care in a previous reproductive bout. Wagner and Harper (2003) pointed out

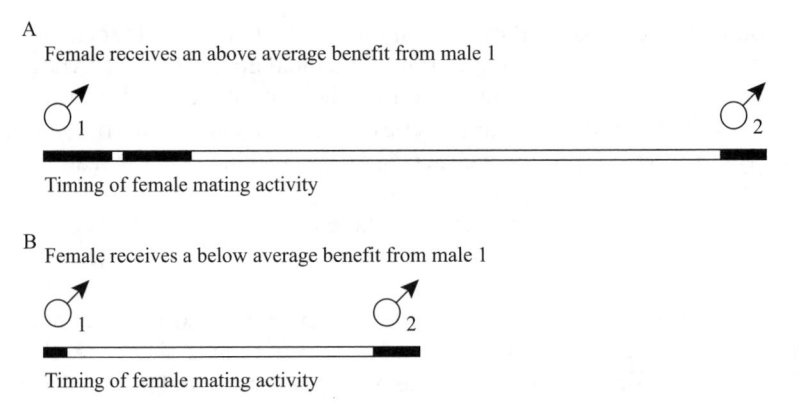

FIG. 2. Potential differences in the mating behavior of females that receive (A) an above average direct benefit from their first mate and (B) a below average direct benefit from their first mate. The bar along the x-axis of each figure represents female mating time: mating (closed bar) and not mating (open bar). The duration of mating is represented by the length of the closed bar (short, intermediate, or long). A single closed bar beneath a female–male pair indicates a single mating with that male, while two closed bars indicate two matings with that male. The numbers associated with males indicate that the males are different individuals. Any mating with a new male is assumed to be with a male that provides average mating benefits, and females are assumed to mate once with such males and to show intermediate mating durations. Females that receive higher-quality benefits from a given male may mate longer, mate repeatedly, and show a longer latency to mate with a new male. Males that provide higher-quality benefits may thus have greater success in sperm competition because they transfer more sperm and experience less intense sperm competition.

that conditional repeated and multiple mating by females could incidentally favor the evolution of higher-quality benefits, and Kvarnemo (2006) pointed out that conditional multiple mating by females could favor the evolution of greater paternal care. In addition, the idea that traits have incidental effects has an extensive history in evolutionary biology. For example, it has long been known that traits that evolve in one context can have pleiotropic consequences in other contexts (Dobzhansky and Holz, 1943; Williams, 1957; Wright, 1968). Building on the pleiotropic effects idea, Williams (1966) pointed out that traits often have incidental consequences not only for the individuals bearing the traits but also for other individuals. A number of authors subsequently applied this idea to the evolution of mating preferences, suggesting that females may respond more strongly to some male traits as an incidental byproduct of sensory or cognitive mechanisms that have evolved in a different context (Basolo, 1990; Christy, 1995; Endler and Basolo, 1998; Kirkpatrick, 1987a; Ryan, 1990). In another application, Tinghitella and Zuk (2009) suggested that plasticity in female reproductive behavior that evolves in one context could incidentally facilitate the evolution of novel male traits. The incidental sanctions hypothesis has the same conceptual foundation as these other ideas: females show plasticity in their reproductive tactics based on current or past benefit quality, and these reproductive tactics, as a byproduct, have negative consequences for males that provide low-quality benefits.

I am not aware of any models that have explored the conditions under which the incidental sanctions hypothesis can and cannot work. There are at least two general issues: the costs and benefits to females of adjusting their reproductive behavior based on benefit quality and the costs and benefits to males of investing in the direct benefit. On the female side, one obvious requirement is simultaneous or sequential polyandry. That is, females must at least sometimes mate with multiple males in a given reproductive bout or with different males in different reproductive bouts (Kvarnemo, 2006; Wagner and Basolo, 2008). If females show lifetime monogamy, any reproductive tactic that penalizes a female's mate will also reduce the fitness of a female (Wagner and Basolo, 2008). In addition, some of the conditional reproductive tactics that would penalize low-benefit males entail costs as well as benefits (e.g., there may be costs of searching for and mating with a new male, and costs of investing less in current offspring). The benefits may or may not outweigh these costs, depending upon social and environmental conditions. On the male side, whether it pays to provide high-quality benefits should depend, in part, on the relative cost imposed by female behavior and the benefit of investing resources in other traits, including traits that allow males to attract more females (e.g., Kokko, 1998; Section I. C). In addition, males can potentially reduce the extent of female multiple mating through two mechanisms: by providing high-quality direct benefits (Wagner and Basolo, 2008) or by manipulating female reproduction (Arnqvist and Rowe, 2005). Whether female behavior favors the evolution of direct benefits or sexually antagonistic traits may depend, in part, on the cost and efficacy of each mechanism for males.

C. The Evolution of Reliable Signaling

Most studies of mating signals either implicitly or explicitly assume that the handicap mechanism ensures signal reliability. The handicap hypothesis is based on the idea that males providing higher-quality benefits to females, such as males of higher genetic quality, pay relatively lower fitness costs of producing expensive, attractive signals (Grafen, 1990; Nur and Hasson, 1984; Zahavi, 1975). For example, while a male of high fitness may experience a small reduction in survivorship if it invests in a costly, attractive signal, a male of low fitness may experience a large reduction in survivorship (i.e., there may be differential fitness costs of signaling). When this is true, the optimal level of signal attractiveness will be higher for high-benefit males.

The handicap hypothesis solves a specific type of signaling problem: deceptive signaling by low-benefit males. This is the primary problem for signals of genetic quality. For signals of direct benefit quality, there are two signaling problems: (1) the production of attractive signals by males that cannot provide high-quality benefits and (2) cheating on the benefit by males that can afford to produce attractive signals (because males cannot cheat on genetic benefits, this is not an issue for signals of genetic quality). While the handicap mechanism can limit the former, it cannot limit the latter and is thus insufficient for reliable signaling of direct benefits (Bussière, 2002; Bussière et al., 2005; Wagner and Basolo, 2008). Consider, for example, a male that can afford to both produce attractive signals and provide high-quality direct benefits to females. Regardless of whether the benefit is provided before or after mating, a high fitness cost of signaling does nothing to prevent this male from withholding the benefit. In fact, a high cost of signaling might promote cheating if the male can use the resources it saves to support the production of more attractive signals (e.g., Kokko, 1998). Reliable signaling of direct benefits thus requires an alternative or additional mechanism that rewards attractive males that also provide high-quality benefits.

A number of alternatives to the handicap hypothesis have been proposed (reviewed by Maynard Smith and Harper, 2003; Searcy and Nowicki, 2005). One of the predominant alternatives is the differential benefits hypothesis (Johnstone, 1997). In the context of direct benefits, this hypothesis proposes that individuals that provide higher-quality benefits receive a greater fitness return from their investment in an attractive signal. Differential benefits have rarely been invoked to explain reliable signaling of direct or genetic benefits (but see Getty, 1998; Searcy and Nowicki, 2005). One reason for this may be the absence of an established mechanism that would produce differential benefits of signaling. However, there are at least two mechanisms that can potentially produce differential benefits of signaling: female rejection of males that provide low-quality premating benefits and female reproductive tactics that incidentally penalize males that provide low-quality postmating benefits (Wagner and Basolo, 2008).

Consider first the case of male signaling in a species in which females can directly assess the benefit prior to mating. A male that provides a low-quality benefit might invest in an expensive, attractive signal, but he will receive a relatively low payoff from his investment; while his signal might attract females, his mating success will be low because females will detect that he provides a low-quality benefit and choose not to mate. In contrast, a male that provides a high-quality benefit, and who invests in the same expensive, attractive signal, will receive a relatively high payoff from his investment; his signal will attract females, and his mating success will be high because females will detect that he provides a high-quality benefit. Female choice based on a direct assessment of benefit quality thus has the potential to produce differential benefits of signaling (e.g., to affect the number of matings per unit of investment in the signal).

Consider next the case of male signaling in a species in which females cannot directly assess benefit quality prior to mating. A male that provides a low-quality benefit might invest in an expensive, attractive signal, but if female behavior incidentally penalizes low-benefit males, he will receive a relatively low payoff from his investment; while his signal might attract females, and while he might mate with those females he attracts, his reproductive success with each female will be low because of female reproductive behavior. In contrast, a male that provides a high-quality benefit and who invests in the same expensive, attractive signal, will receive a relatively high payoff from his investment; his signal will attract females, he will mate with those females he attracts, and his reproductive success with each female will be high because of female reproductive behavior. Incidental sanctions that result from conditional female reproductive tactics thus also have the potential to produce differential benefits of signaling (e.g., the potential to affect the number of offspring sired per unit of investment in the signal).

The primary prediction of the handicap hypothesis is that males that vary in genetic or direct benefits have equivalent mating success when they express preferred signals, but that high-benefit males have higher fitness because they incur lower fitness costs from producing the signal. This is a difficult prediction to test in many animals because it requires experiments in which males that differ in genetic or direct benefit quality are forced to develop and/or express attractive signals, and in which male fitness components are measured under ecologically relevant conditions. In addition, it requires that the manipulations have no effects on fitness other than those that result from developing or expressing the trait (e.g., while diet manipulations often affect the expression of preferred traits, they are also likely to affect the expression of other fitness-related traits). Few studies have attempted this type of experiment (Kotiaho, 2001). The closest is a study by Møller and de Lope (1994), who tested whether there are differential costs of signal expression for a signal of genetic quality. To do so, they asked whether males that naturally vary in signal expression differ in the fitness costs they pay when experimentally forced to express a preferred signal. This study, however, provides only a weak test of the differential costs hypothesis. A stronger test of the hypothesis would ask whether males that vary in benefit quality (i.e., in genetic fitness or in direct benefit quality) differ in the fitness costs they pay when experimentally forced to express a preferred signal. This distinction is important because factors unrelated to benefit quality might have the greatest effect on the costs males pay to express preferred signals. For example, environmental factors that affect signal expression, rather than genetic fitness, may primarily determine the fitness costs that males pay when experimentally forced to express a preferred signal.

The primary prediction of the differential benefits hypothesis is that males that vary in direct benefit quality incur equivalent fitness costs when they express preferred signals, but that high-benefit males have higher reproductive success. As with the differential costs hypothesis, this hypothesis requires experiments in which males that differ in benefit quality are forced to develop and/or express attractive signals and in which the fitness consequences are measured under ecologically relevant conditions. While there is some evidence that female behavior can penalize low-benefit males (some of which is summarized in Wagner and Basolo, 2008), I know of no studies that have explicitly tested whether high-benefit males forced to express attractive signals have higher reproductive success than low-benefit males forced to express the same signals.

There have been few attempts to explicitly model the conditions under which conditional female reproductive tactics might favor the evolution of reliable signaling. Given that there may be a trade-off between benefit quality and signal attractiveness (Burley, 1986), males could potentially reduce their investment in benefit quality in favor of investing in more attractive signals. While this might reduce their reproductive success with each female they attract, they might have higher lifetime reproductive success because they attract more females (Kokko, 1998). A variety of other factors, however, will affect whether it pays for males to cheat on benefits. For example, the shape of the relationship between benefit quality and male reproductive success per female will affect the costs of cheating; if there are increasing marginal gains of investing in benefit quality (i.e., a positive accelerating relationship), males may receive a higher fitness return from investing in the benefit, even though they could attract more females if they cheated on the benefit. That is, an increase in the number of offspring per mating may more than compensate for a decrease in the number of matings.

D. Environmental Effects on Signal Reliability

Almost regardless of why males provide direct benefits, and why male signals at least sometimes provide reliable information about direct benefit quality, spatial and temporal variation in environmental conditions will complicate female assessment based on male signals. The reason for this is that many traits are affected by genotype–environment interactions

(GEIs), including signal attractiveness and, potentially, direct benefit quality. It is becoming increasingly clear, for example, that there are strong GEI effects on male signals (David et al., 2000; Jia et al., 2000; Mills et al., 2007; Rodriguez et al., 2008; Tolle and Wagner, 2011) and that there is often substantial crossover among the reaction norms of different genotypes (Jia et al., 2000; Mills et al., 2007; Rodriguez et al., 2008; Tolle and Wagner, 2011). As a result, the relative attractiveness of the signals produced by a given male, or given male genotype, can be highly environment specific; while a male might produce relatively attractive signals under one set of environmental conditions, the same male commonly produces relatively unattractive signals under other sets of environmental conditions.

GEI effects on male signals create serious complications for the evolution of female choice based on genetic benefits (Greenfield and Rodriguez, 2004; Higginson and Reader, 2009; Hunt et al., 2004; Kokko and Heubel, 2008). Assume, for example, that there are GEI effects on male fitness, such that a given genotype is of relatively high fitness in one environment and of relatively low fitness in another environment. Also assume that, within any given environment, differential costs of signaling ensure that only males of high fitness produce highly attractive signals. While females could use the signal to select mates that are of high fitness in the current environment, they may or may not produce high fitness offspring as a result of these mate choices. If environmental conditions vary temporally or spatially, a female's offspring may have relatively low fitness genotypes, even though the sire was of high fitness at the time of mating.

It is possible that GEI effects on male signals create fewer complications for the evolution of female choice based on direct benefits. Unlike female choice based on genetic benefits, all that may matter for female choice based on direct benefits is that male signals reflect current benefit quality or near-future benefit quality. Thus, even if there are GEI effects on male signals, females might consistently receive high-quality direct benefits as a result of their mate choices, as long as the genotypes that produce the most attractive signals in a given environment also provide the highest-quality direct benefits in that environment. In other words, females could consistently receive high-quality direct benefits if there are congruent GEI effects on signal attractiveness and direct benefit quality (Fig. 3). This might occur, for example, if male fitness is environment dependent, and only those genotypes of high fitness in a given environment can afford to both produce attractive signals and provide high-quality direct benefits. It might also occur if different male genotypes specialize on providing high-quality benefits in different environments, and, within each environment, female behavior incidentally penalizes low-benefit males, producing differential benefits of signaling within each environment.

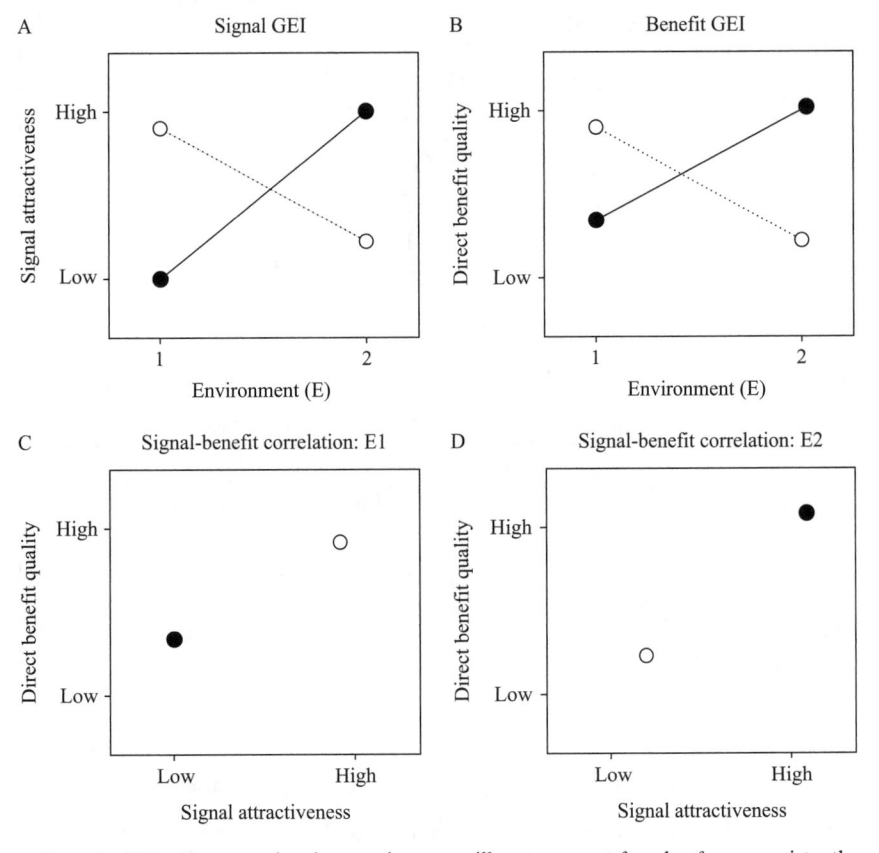

FIG. 3. GEI effects on signal attractiveness will not prevent females from consistently receiving high quality direct benefits if there are congruent GEI effects on direct benefit quality. (A) GEI effect on signal attractiveness: males of genotype 1 (○) produce attractive signals in environment 1 but unattractive signals in environment 2, whereas males of genotype 2 (●) produce unattractive signals in environment 1 but attractive signals in environment 2. (B) GEI effect on direct benefit quality: males of genotype 1 (○) provide high-quality direct benefits in environment 1 but provide low-quality direct benefits in environment 2, whereas males of genotype 2 (●) provide low-quality direct benefits in environment 1 but provide high-quality direct benefits in environment 2. Because there are congruent GEI effects on signal attractiveness and direct benefit quality, the genotype that produces attractive signals in environment 1 (C) and environment 2 (D) is also the genotype that provides high-quality direct benefits in that environment. Adapted from Tolle and Wagner (2011).

I am aware of only one study that has tested for congruent GEI effects on male signals and direct benefits (Tolle and Wagner, 2011; Section III.F). If there are noncongruent GEI effects, the result may be variation among environments in signal reliability; for example, signal attractiveness may be

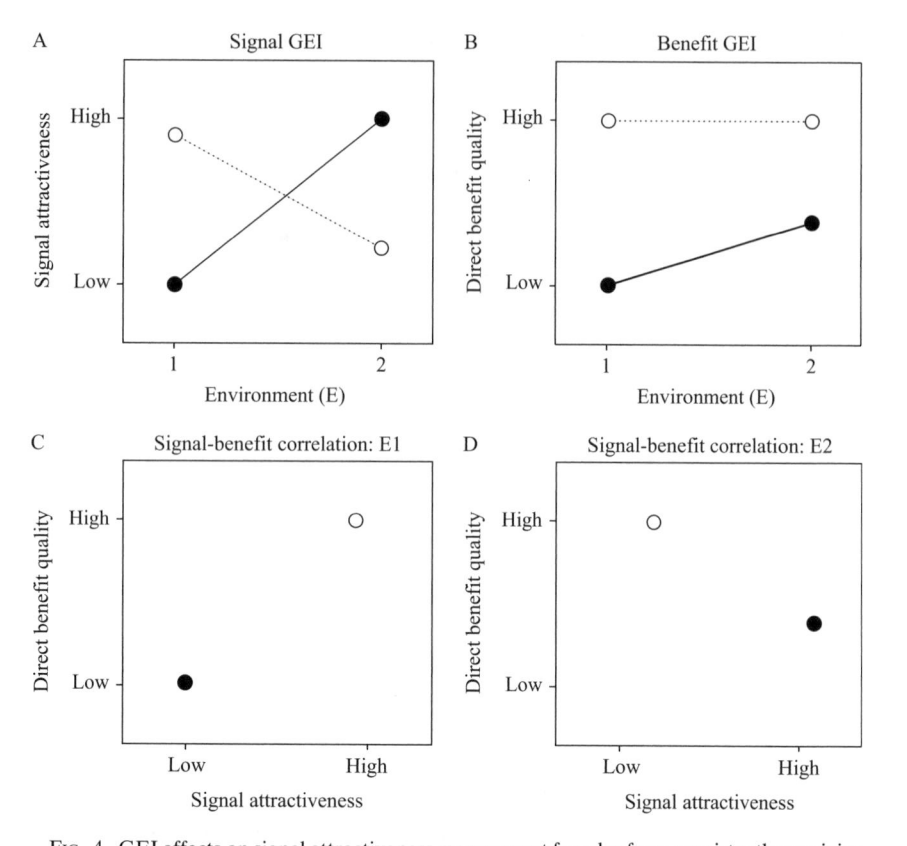

Fig. 4. GEI effects on signal attractiveness may prevent females from consistently receiving high quality direct benefits if there are not congruent GEI effects on direct benefit quality. (A) GEI effect on signal attractiveness: males of genotype 1 (○) produce attractive signals in environment 1 but unattractive signals in environment 2, whereas males of genotype 2 (●) produce unattractive signals in environment 1 but attractive signals in environment 2. (B) No GEI effect on direct benefit quality: males of genotype 1 (○) provide high-quality direct benefits in environment 1 and environment 2, whereas males of genotype 2 (●) provide low-quality direct benefits in environment 1 and environment 2. Because there are noncongruent GEI effects on signal attractiveness and direct benefit quality, the genotype that produces attractive signals in environment 1 provides high-quality direct benefits (C), but the genotype that produces attractive signals in environment 2 provides low-quality direct benefits (D). Adapted from Tolle and Wagner (2011).

positively correlated with direct benefit quality in some environments, but weakly correlated, uncorrelated, or negatively correlated in others (Fig. 4). Given the prevalence of GEI effects on male signals, and given that the reaction norms for signal attractiveness and benefit quality may not be congruent, variation in signal reliability may be common. Some caution, however, is necessary when interpreting studies of GEI effects and studies of environmental effects on signal reliability. It is important to know whether the environmental manipulations used in a study are representative of the environmental conditions encountered by the animal studied. For example, the manipulated environments may span only a portion of natural range of environmental conditions or extend far beyond the natural range of environmental conditions. It is also important to know how frequently the animal encounters the alternative environments. If some environmental conditions are more common than others, it is the more common environmental conditions that will have the predominant effect on the evolution of female mating preferences. Finally, environments vary along many axes, and we known almost nothing about how genotypes respond to multifactorial environmental variation (e.g., whether GEI effects are additive, synergistic, or antagonistic).

Whether variation in signal reliability is a problem for female choice depends upon how signal reliability varies. If there is a positive correlation between signal attractiveness and benefit quality in most environments, females will, on average, benefit from their preferences. If, however, signal attractiveness and benefit quality are positively correlated in some environments and negatively correlated in others, and both environments are relatively common, females will not be able to consistently receive high-quality direct benefits from their signal preferences unless they show plasticity in their mating preferences. While it might seem unlikely that the sign of the relationship between signal attractiveness and benefit quality would vary among environments, this can occur when there are crossing genotypic reaction norms for the signal but only genotypic effects on the benefit (Fig. 4).

The causes of GEI effects are potentially complex, and we know very little about why male genotypes commonly produce relatively attractive signals in some environments but relatively unattractive signals in others. Even the causal relationship between GEI effects and signal reliability is largely unexplored. For example, it is not clear whether selection acts on signal reliability, with consequences for signal and benefit reaction norms, or whether selection acts on signal and benefit reaction norms, with consequences for signal reliability.

E. FEMALE ASSESSMENT STRATEGIES IN VARIABLE ENVIRONMENTS

Females might be able to consistently select high-benefit males, even when the sign of the relationship between signal attractiveness and benefit quality varies among environments, if they show plasticity in their mating preferences. The type of plasticity that would maximize female fitness, however, will depend, in part, on the temporal and spatial scale of environmental variation.

If signal reliability is affected by environmental factors that vary temporally (e.g., factors that vary among seasons or among years) and/or over
large spatial scales (e.g., among populations or subpopulations), such that
most individuals that are reproductively active at a given time in a given
area have experienced similar environmental conditions, females could
consistently receive high-quality benefits if they adjust their preferences
based on their own environmental experience. For example, if males that
produce more extreme trait values provide higher-quality benefits in environment A, while males that produce less extreme trait values provide
higher-quality benefits in environment B, females could assess their own
environment and prefer more extreme trait values in the former and less
extreme trait values in the latter. Depending upon when environmental
factors affect signal attractiveness and benefit quality, females could show
developmental plasticity, behavioral plasticity, or both. Plasticity in female
mating preferences is common (Cotton et al., 2006; Gong and Gibson, 1996;
Hedrick and Dill, 1992; Johnson and Basolo, 2003; Pfennig, 2007;
Qvarnström et al., 2000; Rodriguez and Greenfield, 2003), but it is not
known whether females adjust their preferences to environmental factors
that affect signal reliability.

In contrast, if signal reliability is affected by environmental factors that
vary over short periods of time or over small spatial scales, such that
individuals that are reproductively active at a given time in a given area
have experienced very different environmental conditions, females cannot
simply adjust their preferences based on their own environmental experience. Instead, because a given trait value can indicate high or low-quality
benefits, depending upon what environment a given male has experienced
(see Fig. 4), females would need to assess the environmental history of a
male to determine whether a given trait value indicates that the male will
provide high- or low-quality benefits. This might initially seem implausible,
but females could potentially solve this problem by assessing a second male
trait and by adjusting their preferences for the benefit-related trait on their
assessment of this second trait (Fig. 5). For example, assume that trait X is
positively correlated with benefit quality for males that experience environment 1 but negatively correlated with benefit quality for males that experience environment 2. Also assume that there is a second male trait that is
consistently affected by environment conditions, such that males experiencing environment 1 have trait Y_1, while males experiencing environment
2 have trait value Y_2. Females could use trait Y to determine a male's
environmental history and then selectively mate with Y_1 males with high
values of trait X and/or Y_2 males with low values of trait X.

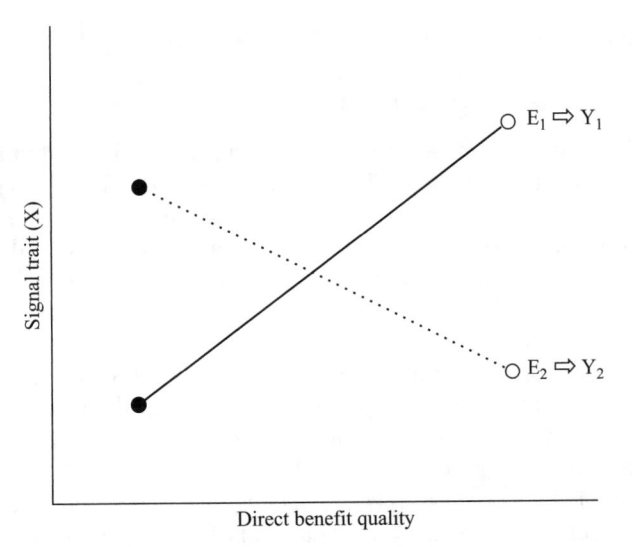

Fɪɢ. 5. A possible solution to variation among environments in signal reliability (see Fig. 4). Within Environment 1 (solid line), males of genotype 1 (○) produce high values of a signal (trait X) and provide high-quality benefits, whereas males of genotype 2 (●) produce low values of the signal and provide low-quality benefits. In contrast, within environment 2 (dashed line), males of genotype 1 (○) produce low values of a signal and provide high-quality benefits, whereas males of genotype 2 (●) produce high values of the signal and provide low-quality benefits. Females could consistently select high-benefit males if (a) a second male trait (trait Y) is consistently affected by environmental conditions, such that males that have experienced E_1 express Y_1 while males that have experienced E_2 express Y_2 and (b) if females selectively mate with Y_1 males with high values of signal and/or Y_2 males with low values of signal.

While females commonly adjust their preferences to environmental conditions, and commonly assess multiple male traits (Bro-Jørgensen, 2009; Hebets and Papaj, 2005), it is not known whether they adjust their preferences for benefit-related traits based on their assessment of environment-specific traits. However, an experimental test of this hypothesis should be relatively straightforward. For example, female responses could be tested to males, models, or signals that vary in both the benefit-related trait and the environment-specific trait. Female responses should be affected by the interaction between the two traits, and they should consistently respond most strongly to the trait combinations that are indicative of the highest-quality direct benefits. Further, females that experience different environmental conditions should show similar patterns of preference plasticity if they cannot use their own environmental experience to assess the environmental conditions experienced by males.

III. EVOLUTION OF POSTMATING DIRECT BENEFITS IN A FIELD CRICKET

A. OVERVIEW AND SOME NATURAL HISTORY

My colleagues and I have conducted a series of studies on female choice for postmating direct benefits in the variable field cricket, *Gryllus lineaticeps*. I describe some of this work in this section, focusing on some of the questions outlined above. Other studies have more thoroughly explored specific benefit mechanisms and their effects on female fitness (e.g., Eisner and Meinwald, 1995; Gwynne, 2001). The field cricket work discussed here, however, has some unique components related to the role of incidental sanctions and variation among environments in signal reliability. As part of my description of this work, I try to identify some of the many gaps in our understanding of why males provide direct benefits and produce signals indicative of benefit quality.

The variable field cricket, *Gryllus lineaticeps*, is a common field cricket of coastal and central California that is particularly abundant in dry grasslands (Weissman et al., 1980). Most breeding activity occurs during the summer, and as is typical for field crickets (Alexander, 1961), males produce a calling song to attract females. The calling song consists of a series of short, rapidly repeated chirps, and males vary in a variety of song characters, including the rate at which they produce chirps and in the duration of their chirps. Males usually sing just outside the entrances of burrows (holes dug by other animals or cracks in the soil), with their heads pointed toward the burrow entrance, which may allow them to quickly escape from potential predators. They defend the space around their burrows from other males using aggressive songs and physical attacks. Unlike some other species of field crickets (e.g., Cade 1979, 1980; Zuk et al., 2006), there is little evidence that males commonly adopt satellite mating tactics (see also Leonard and Hedrick, 2009). For example, it is not obvious that silent males are more common around singing males than in areas away from singing males, or that these males attempt to intercept females.

Gryllus lineaticeps is polymorphic for both wing length and flight muscle size, and as a result, some individuals are capable of flight while other are not (Mitra et al., unpublished). Flightless females walk toward males, while flight-capable females can either walk or fly. The costs and benefits of walking and flying toward males is unknown, but it is known that maintaining large flight muscles is energetically costly for field crickets (Mole and Zera, 1993; Zera et al., 1994, 1997), that flight itself carries high energetic costs (Dudley, 2000), and that females with large flight muscles have lower fecundity, at least partially as a result of these costs (Zera and Cisper, 2001; Zera et al., 1997). In addition, there are at least two predation costs of flight:

flying field crickets are vulnerable to predation by bats (Popov and Shuvalov, 1977), and in *G. lineaticeps*, females that fly to males risk predation by black widow spiders (*Latrodectus hesperus*) when they land near males (Wagner, unpublished observations). There are also likely to be costs of approaching males on the ground, including predation by both spiders (e.g., black widows, tarantulas, and wolf spiders) and small mammals (e.g., shrews and skunks).

Females approach males based on the type of calling song that a male produces (Section III.B). Once a female approaches, the male switches to a mix of calling song and courtship song (these song types are qualitatively distinct). Components of the courtship song, such as the rate of high-intensity clicks, can affect female mating responses (Wagner and Reiser, 2000). Male field crickets may also produce tactile and contact chemical signals (Balakrishnan and Pollack, 1997; Murakami and Itoh, 2003; Ryan and Sakaluk, 2009; Tregenza and Wedell, 1997), but it is not known whether these affect female mating responses in *G. lineaticeps*. If a male is acceptable, and perhaps even before the female has made a decision to mate, the pair moves down into the male's burrow. In contrast to some other field crickets (e.g., Rodríguez-Muñoz et al., 2010), mating in *G. lineaticeps* usually occurs within the burrow. Because any disturbance causes males and females to move down the burrow and sometimes exit via another hole, male mating success is difficult to assess in the field. It is not clear whether male calling areas or burrows contain resources utilized by females. It is possible, for example, that females oviposit in the soil within male burrows.

B. FEMALE PREFERENCES AND MATING BEHAVIOR

A variety of studies have shown that females respond more often and more strongly to male calling songs with higher chirp rates and longer chirp durations. For example, female song preferences have been assessed using a variety of approaches, including single speaker tests that measured female association times (Wagner and Basolo, 2007a; Wagner et al., 2001b), two speaker tests that measured female choices (Wagner, 1996; Wagner and Reiser, 2000), and three speaker tests that measured female association times and choices (Beckers and Wagner, 2011; Bulfer et al., unpublished). In all of these studies, females tended to prefer songs with higher chirp rates and, in at least some studies, tended to prefer songs with longer chirp durations. The strength and form of the preference, however, can vary depending upon how preferences are measured. For example, in single speaker association tests, in which females were presented with only a single song type, there was both a linear and a quadratic component to female preferences; female responses increased with chirp rate, but dropped substantially when the chirp rate was very high (Fig. 6A). In contrast, in two speaker choice tests, females usually preferred the higher of two chirp rates (Fig. 6B). Finally, in three speaker choice and association tests, females showed a threshold response, responding more strongly to high than to low chirp rates, but they did not discriminate between chirp rates that were above the threshold and did not discriminate between chirp rates that were below the threshold (Fig. 6C). These differences suggest that the expression of female mating preferences may depend upon how females encounter males (sequentially or simultaneously, and when simultaneously, in what local densities). However, because the different types of tests were conducted in different years, and used females from different populations, the support for this inference is weak. Female preferences are, however, affected by social experience; females show weaker responses to a low chirp rate song when they have recently heard a high chirp rate song (Wagner et al., 2001b), but these experience effects disappear within 24 h (Beckers and Wagner, 2011). Similar experience effects have been reported for another field cricket (Bailey and Zuk, 2008, 2009).

Of the two traits, chirp rate appears to have a greater effect on female responses than does chirp duration. Wagner and Basolo (2007a) created 25 song types that contained all possible combinations of five chirp rates and five chirp durations (ranging from very low to very high for each song character), and they measured the responses of females to each of the song types. Only chirp rate affected female responses in these tests. The lack of an effect of chirp duration is surprising, given that females from the same population prefer longer chirps in two speaker choice tests (Wagner, 1996). One possible explanation is that the expression of female preferences depends upon how females encounter males (e.g., sequentially or simultaneously). Females may also express preferences based on other calling song traits, but these preferences have not been tested in G. lineaticeps.

Female animals will often mate repeatedly with a given male and mate with multiple males (Hunter et al., 1993). In G. lineaticeps, little is known about female mating patterns in the field. In the lab, however, female G. lineaticeps show extensive repeated mating; females will regularly mate more than once with a given male, and some will mate at least six times over a six-hour period (Wagner et al., 2001a). They also show extensive multiple mating (Wagner et al., 2001a). Approximately 50% of females will mate with a new male the next day, and nearly all will mate with a new male within 7 days (Wagner et al., unpublished). High rates of repeated and

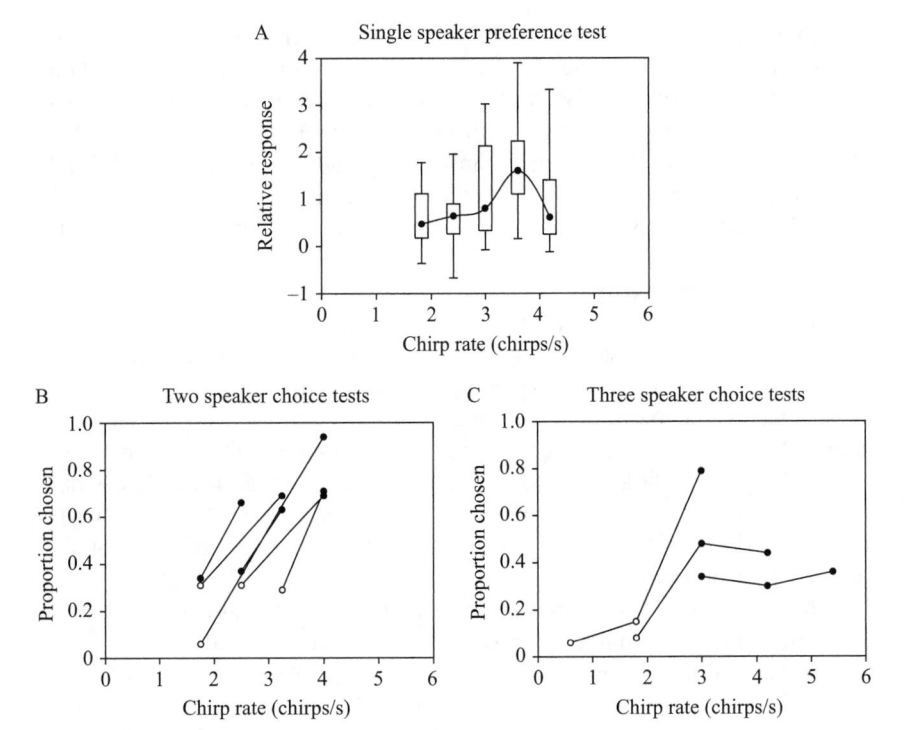

FIG. 6. Female chirp rate preferences in *G. lineaticeps*. (A) Single-speaker response test: females expressed a directional preference for higher chirp rates, but this preference had a strong stabilizing component, with females responding most strongly to moderately high chirp rates than to very high chirp rates. Data are presented as a box plot showing variation in relative female response with variation in chirp rate. Dots within boxes indicate median female responses, upper and lower edges of the boxes indicate 75th and 25th percentiles, respectively, and upper and lower whiskers indicate the maximum and minimum responses, respectively. The curve shows a cubic spline fit to the median response for each chirp rate. Adapted from Wagner and Basolo (2007a). (B) Two speaker choice tests: females more often approach a speaker broadcasting a high chirp rate than a speaker broadcasting a low chirp rate. Each pair of connected dots represents the results of one choice test (total = 6 tests). A significant difference in the number of choices is represented by connected closed and open dots (○–●). A nonsignificant difference in the number of choices is represented by connected closed dots (●–●). Adapted from Wagner and Reiser (2000). (C) Three speaker choice tests: females more often approach a speaker broadcasting an intermediate or high chirp rate than a speaker broadcasting a low chirp rate, but they do not differ in their responses to low chirp rates or in their responses to intermediate and high chirp rates. Each trio of connected dots represents the results of one choice test (total = 3 tests). Within a trio, a significant pairwise difference in the number of choices is represented by connected closed and open dots (○–●). A nonsignificant pairwise difference in the number of choices is represented by connected closed dots (●–●) or connected open dots (○–○). Adapted from Beckers and Wagner (2011).

multiple mating are unlikely to be an artifact of the laboratory environment; observational studies in seminatural enclosures and in the field, as well as paternity studies, indicate that female field crickets regularly mate both repeatedly and multiply (Alexander and Otte, 1967; Rodríguez-Muñoz et al., 2010; Simmons, 1988; Tregenza and Wedell, 1998; Zuk and Simmons, 1997). However, natural rates of repeated and multiple mating may be higher or lower than the laboratory estimates suggest.

Males transfer sperm to females via an external spermatophore. This spermatophore consists of a small ampulla containing sperm and accessory gland secretions (i.e., seminal fluid), but it lacks the nutritious spermatophylax found in some other types of orthopteran insects, such as katydids (Gwynne, 2001). Nonetheless, females often remove and consume the spermatophore some time after it has been attached. There is some evidence that female field crickets may receive a very small fecundity benefit from consuming more spermatophores (Simmons, 1988). It is not known, however, whether there is variation among males in the nutritional quality of their spermatophores.

Female field crickets store sperm in a spermatheca, and when females mate with multiple males, there are often no distinct patterns of sperm precedence (Backus and Cade, 1986; Sakaluk, 1986; Sakaluk and Cade, 1980; Simmons, 1987, 2001). Rather, multiply mated females commonly produce offspring of mixed paternity (but see Simmons et al., 2003). Because the sperm of multiple males can potentially fertilize a female's eggs, the intensity of sperm competition should be high. In addition, because females lay a small number of eggs each day rather than a few large batches of eggs at periodic intervals, a male cannot fertilize an entire batch of eggs by being the only male to mate with a female prior to the initiation of egg laying.

C. Selection on Male Singing Behavior

The results of the female preference studies suggest that sexual selection may favor the evolution of higher chirp rates and, potentially, longer chirp durations. However, because of the difficulty of assessing male mating success in the field, the nature and strength of sexual selection on male song characters have yet to be determined. It is possible, for example, that females do not express preferences in the field because of the difficulty of discriminating between song types in a complex acoustic environment (e.g., Beckers and Wagner, 2011). It is also possible that there are trade-offs among song characters that reduce the net effect of sexual selection on each trait. For example, there is a negative phenotypic correlation between chirp rate and chirp duration. While chirp rate appears to have the greatest effect on female responses (Wagner and Basolo, 2007a), the short chirp durations that are produced by males with high chirp rates may reduce their mating advantage. While field-based measures of male mating success are difficult, it would be possible to use more indirect approaches to assess whether sexual selection occurs on male song characters, such as comparisons of male singing behavior among populations that vary in their preferences.

Producing an attractive calling song is costly for males. For example, Hoback and Wagner (1997) found that the energetic costs of singing in *G. lineaticeps* increased with chirp rate. There was not, however, a significant effect of chirp duration on the energetic costs of singing, although there was a positive trend. Given how male field crickets produce longer chirps, it seems unlikely that males could produce these song types at no cost; longer chirps contain more pulses, and each additional pulse requires an additional cycle of opening and closing of the forewings, each of which requires energy. Males may, however, have adaptations that minimize the cost of producing additional pulses. Insects are known, for example, to have an elastic protein called resilin that reduces the energetic cost of flight (Haas et al., 2000). It is possible that we were not able to detect any energetic cost of producing longer chirps because our sample size was too small to detect a relatively small energetic cost of adding additional pulses to a given chirp.

In addition to the energetic costs of producing higher chirp rates, there are predation costs of producing attractive song types. *G. lineaticeps* is attacked by a parasitoid fly, *Ormia ochracea*. This fly is present across much of the southern United States, from Florida to California, and it attacks different field cricket species in different areas (Cade, 1975; Wagner, 1996; Walker, 1986; Walker and Wineriter, 1991). It has also been introduced to Hawaii, where it attacks an introduced Australasian field cricket (Zuk et al., 1993). Female flies locate males by homing in on male song (Cade, 1975), and they deposit larvae on and around males (Adamo et al., 1995; Cade, 1975). The larvae enter a male and feed, killing the host within 10–12 days (Adamo et al., 1995; Cade, 1975; Walker and Wineriter, 1991; Zuk et al., 1993). Broadcasts of experimental *G. lineaticeps* songs in the field have shown that higher chirp rates and longer chirp durations are more likely to attract flies (Martin and Wagner 2010; Wagner 1996; Wagner and Basolo 2007b), suggesting that males producing preferred song types have a higher risk of fly predation (Fig. 7). Similar results have been found in another species attacked by *O. ochracea* (Gray and Cade, 1999). Of the two traits, chirp rate has a greater effect on fly

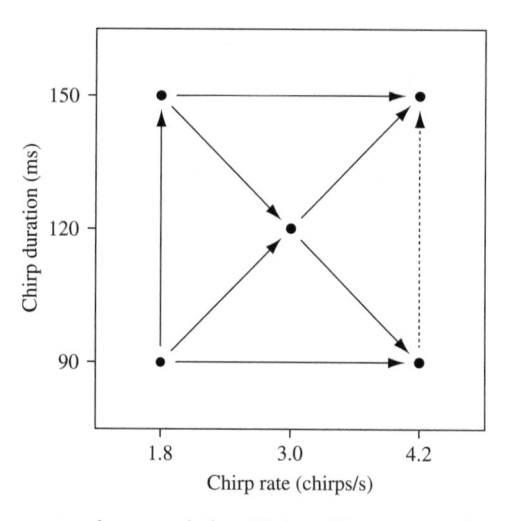

F<small>IG.</small> 7. Parasitism costs of song variation. Higher chirp rates and longer chirp durations increase the risk of attracting parasitoid flies (*Ormia ochracea*). Solid lines connect song types that significantly differed in the number of flies attracted, and their arrows point to the song type that attracted more flies. Dashed lines connect song types that did not significantly differ in the number of flies attracted, and their arrows point to the song type that tended to attract more flies. Adapted from Wagner and Basolo (2007b).

attraction than does chirp duration (Wagner and Basolo, 2007b). It is not known, however, whether male *G. lineaticeps* with preferred song types have higher parasitism rates, or whether fly predation has affected the evolution of male singing behavior, although both appear to be true for another species attacked by *O. ochracea* (Zuk et al., 1995, 2006).

The strength of natural selection due to fly predation is likely to show spatial, seasonal, and diel variation. For example, some *G. lineaticeps* populations are attacked by *O. ochracea* while others are not (Wagner and Beckers, unpublished). In addition, the flies actively orient to male song only during a portion of the cricket's breeding season (Wagner personal observation; see also Velez and Brockmann, 2006). Finally, most flies orient to male song from sunset to a few hours following sunset (Cade et al., 1996). Naturally selection due to fly predation is thus likely to be spatially heterogeneous and, when it occurs, episodic. It is not yet known whether these episodic bouts of selection have affected the evolution of male singing behavior, although this hypothesis can be tested using comparisons of male singing behavior among populations that vary in fly abundance (e.g., Zuk et al., 1993).

D. Selection on Female Mating Preferences

Previous work suggested that females receive fecundity and longevity benefits from repeated and multiple mating (Wagner et al., 2001a). Females in that study were prevented from consuming spermatophores, suggesting that the benefits resulted from products males transfer in their seminal fluid. To test whether males with preferred song types provide more beneficial seminal fluid products to females, we conducted a subsequent mating experiment in which females were mated twice to randomly selected males that varied in chirp rate and chirp duration (Wagner and Harper, 2003). In these matings, females were again experimentally precluded from eating spermatophores, so all that females received from males was sperm, seminal fluid, and perhaps sexually transmitted parasites. In addition, we manipulated the adult diets of the females; some were maintained on a high-nutrition diet as adults, while others were maintained on a low-nutrition diet. For the high-nutrition females, there were no detectable benefits or costs of mating with males with preferred song types. In contrast, for the low-nutrition females, there was a positive relationship between male chirp rate and both female lifetime fecundity and female lifetime fertility, as well as a positive relationship between male chirp duration and female longevity (Fig. 8). These results suggest that males with preferred song types transfer seminal fluid products to females during mating that increase some female fitness components under some environmental conditions. Because we did not experimentally control male singing behavior during the mating interactions, it is possible that the correlation of male chirp rate with female fecundity and fertility was a consequence of females investing more in reproduction when paired with high chirp rate males. A subsequent study, however, found a similar result when males were muted and an average song type was broadcast during the mating interactions (Tolle and Wagner, 2011).

There is indirect evidence that direct benefits may be costly for males to provide (Wagner, 2005). Males placed on a lower-quality diet take longer to produce a new spermatophore, which suggests that spermatophores may be costly to produce. In addition, males that produce higher chirp rates take longer to produce a new spermatophore, which suggests that the cost may be higher for males that provide higher-quality benefits.

We do not yet know what seminal fluid components increase female fecundity and longevity; trace nutrients and chemical compounds that are costly for females to synthesize are among the possibilities. These may or may not be the same seminal fluid products that result in female benefits of repeated and multiple mating. For example, seminal fluid products that increase the fecundity of multiply mated females might be uncorrelated with a male's song phenotype, whereas other seminal fluid products that, on

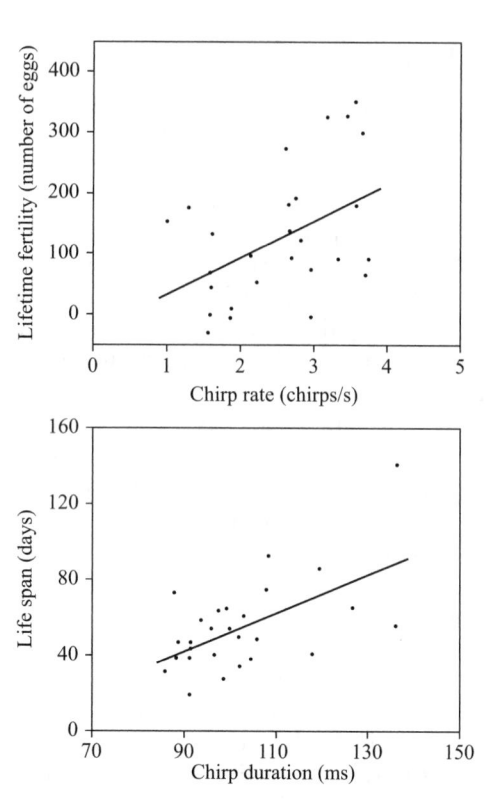

Fɪɢ. 8. Direct benefits of female song preferences. Low-nutrition females mated to males with higher chirp rates had higher lifetime fertilities (upper panel), and low-nutrition females mated to males with longer chirp durations had longer life spans (lower panel). Adapted from Wagner and Harper (2003).

average, reduce female fecundity might be correlated with a male's song phenotype (e.g., males with preferred songs might transfer less costly products).

Because chirp rate and chirp duration are negatively phenotypically correlated in males, females may often have to trade off the fecundity benefits correlated with chirp rate and the longevity benefits correlated with chirp duration. If so, the greater importance of chirp rate in female mate choice suggests that females may sacrifice the longevity benefits in favor of the fecundity benefits (Wagner and Basolo, 2007a).

Expressing preferences for songs with high chirp rates and long chirp durations appears to be costly for females. Female field crickets are occasionally parasitized by *O. ochracea* (Adamo et al., 1995; Walker and

Wineriter, 1991), and in *G. lineaticeps*, up to 6% of the females in a population may be parasitized at a given time (Martin and Wagner, 2010). Because the song types that female prefer are more likely to attract parasitoid flies (Section III.C), females may have a greater risk of parasitism when near preferred males. This risk may arise from a higher probability of a fly arriving when a female is near a male with a preferred song type, or from a higher probability that there are fly larvae on the ground around a male with a preferred song type (larvae can live for up to 8 h after they are deposited; Beckers et al., unpublished). Martin and Wagner (2010) used a field enclosure experiment to examine the cost of being near preferred males. Females were placed in cages with muted males, and the cages were placed above speakers broadcasting either high or low chirp rates. Females in the high chirp rate cages were 1.8 times more likely to be parasitized than females in the low chirp rate cages (Fig. 9). The cost of parasitism is potentially quite severe, particularly for young females, which can lose a substantial proportion of their lifetime reproductive success if they are parasitized (Martin and Wagner, unpublished). It is not yet known whether these costs are high enough to have affected the evolution of female mating preferences. In addition, nothing is known about female search costs, although the general expectation is that females with stronger preferences will incur higher search costs because only a small proportion of the male population will have acceptable traits (reviewed by Andersson, 1994; Jennions and Petrie, 1997).

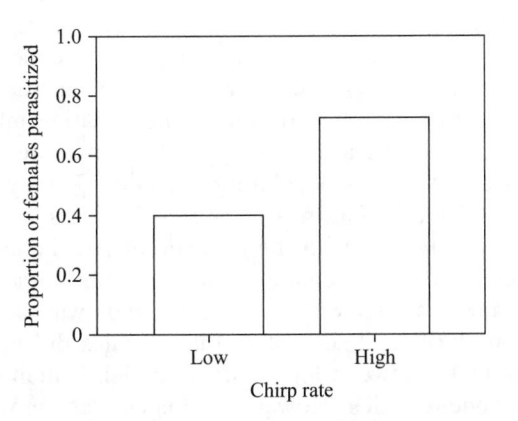

FIG. 9. Parasitism costs of female song preferences. Females had a higher risk of parasitism from parasitoid flies (*Ormia ochracea*) when held in cages with males and high chirp rate song than when held in cages with males and low chirp rate song. Adapted from Martin and Wagner (2010).

E. The Evolution of Direct Benefits

Because females cannot directly assess the fecundity benefits that males provide before they mate with a male, female choice cannot explain why males provide these direct benefits. One might argue that if chirp rate and benefit quality are genetically correlated, female choice based on chirp rate will indirectly favor the evolution of greater fecundity benefits. However, a genetic correlation between signal attractiveness and direct benefit quality should only persist if selection in another context favors the correlation (Wagner and Basolo, 2008). In addition, because females regularly mate with multiple males, it seems unlikely that selection would favor male investment in females or offspring (e.g., Vahed, 1998), although this has not been directly tested in any field cricket. We have, however, tested whether females express conditional reproductive tactics that might incidentally penalize low-benefit males.

First, we tested the hypothesis that females show benefit-dependent repeated mating (Wagner et al., 2007). The strongest test of this hypothesis would be to randomly assign males to high- and low-benefit treatment groups, force the former to provide high-quality benefits and the latter to provide low-quality benefits (without affecting other components of a male's phenotype), and then test whether females are more likely to repeatedly mate with males in the high-benefit group. This would randomize the association between benefit quality and other male traits, and thus ensure that any differences in female repeated mating were due to difference in benefit quality *per se*. Because we could not directly manipulate the direct benefit, we used an alternative approach. First, we measured a male's chirp rate and used chirp rate as an index of direct benefit quality. While this index is crude, males with higher chirp rates provide, on average, higher-quality fecundity benefits under the experimental conditions we used (Section III.D). Second, we muted males by sealing together their forewings with beeswax and, during their mating interactions with females, broadcast an average song type. This prevented male singing behavior from affecting female mating behavior. Finally, we randomly paired males and females and measured each female's latency to initially mate and latency to remate with the assigned male. The latter trials were stopped if a female did not remate within 180 min of the initial mating. The initial latency of a female to mate with a male was uncorrelated with a male's natural chirp rate, suggesting that females did not use nonsong traits to discriminate between high chirp rate/high-benefit males and low chirp rate/low-benefit males. However, females were more likely to remate with high chirp rate/high-benefit males (Fig. 10). This result suggests that females assess benefit quality following an initial mating and selectively remate with high-benefit males. An alternative explanation is that

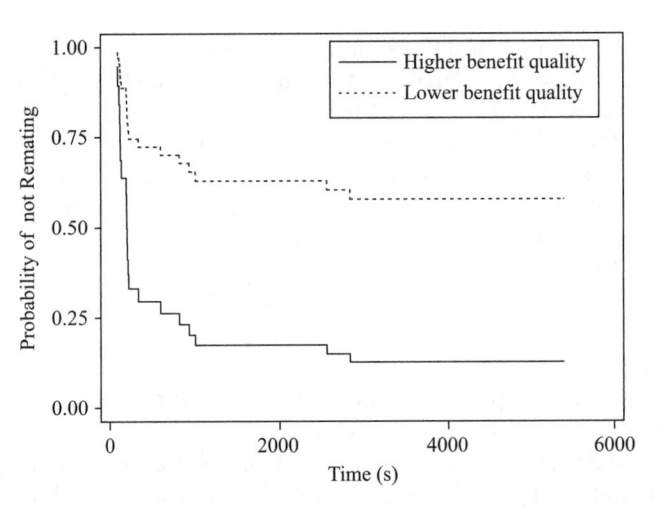

FIG. 10. Conditional female repeated mating. Females were more likely to repeatedly mate with higher chirp rate/higher-benefit males. The figure shows how the probability of not repeatedly mating changed over time (log-normal hazard functions) for females paired with higher-benefit males (natural chirp rate = 3 chirps/s) and lower-benefit males (natural chirp rate = 2 chirps/s). Adapted from Wagner et al. (2007).

females adjust their mating behavior based on nonacoustic traits that are correlated with benefit quality. This is inconsistent with the results of the first mating trials, in which females showed no evidence of having assessed traits correlated with benefit quality. It is possible, however, that females do not assess nonacoustic traits when virgins, but do following an initial mating. To test this possibility, we conducted a control experiment in which we replaced the first male with a new muted male after the initial mating. Females were not more likely to mate with high chirp rate/high-benefit males in the second mating. There is thus no evidence that females assess benefit quality using nonacoustic traits (see also Tolle and Wagner, 2011).

Second, we tested the hypothesis that females show benefit-dependent multiple mating (Wagner et al., unpublished). We used an approach similar to that we used to test for benefit-dependent repeated mating. First, we measured a male's chirp rate and used chirp rate as an index of direct benefit quality. Second, we placed a female with a muted male of known chirp rate, broadcast an average chirp rate, and allowed the female to mate once. Third, every day after the initial mating, we gave the female an opportunity to mate with a new muted male in the presence of an average chirp rate. Approximately 50% of the females mated with a new male the next day, and all females mated with a new male within 7 days. There was no relationship, however, between the chirp rate/benefit quality of the first male and the number of days until a female mated with a new male. This result suggests that females do not change how quickly they mate with a new male based on the quality of the benefit provided by a previous mate. It is possible that this lack of an effect was due to our experimental design; because we placed females in containers with males, females did not have to pay any search costs to locate a new mate, and as they were already near males, they may have perceived that there was little additional risk of fly parasitism from mating with the males they were already near. We thus repeated the experiment, but every day after the initial mating, we tested whether females would approach an average song type broadcast from a speaker at the far end of a large arena. There was no relationship between the initial male's chirp rate/benefit quality and the number of days until a female responded to the song broadcast.

These studies suggest that, because females show conditional repeated mating, high-benefit males will mate more frequently with each female they attract. High-benefit males should thus transfer more sperm to each female, and because females mate with multiple males, this should give them an advantage in sperm competition. However, because females do not show conditional multiple mating, the intensity of sperm competition should differ little for low- and high-benefit males. The net result should be that high-benefit males fertilize a higher proportion of a female's eggs. Conditional female re-mating may thus favor the evolution of higher quality direct benefits and establish the conditions that produce differential benefits of signaling. It is possible, however, that low-benefit males invest in alternative sperm competition traits that compensate for their disadvantage in sperm number. Experiments testing the relationship between direct benefit quality and male reproductive success are thus necessary. The incidental sanctions hypothesis could also be tested in a laboratory evolution study in which all females are mated to multiple males, the number of mates is controlled, but females in some replicates are free to repeatedly mate with each male, whereas females in other replicates are never allowed to repeatedly mate with males.

F. VARIATION IN SIGNAL RELIABILITY

While the handicap mechanism is neither sufficient nor necessary for reliable signaling of direct benefits (Wagner and Basolo, 2008), differential costs of signaling may act in conjunction with other mechanisms to ensure that male signals provide reliable information. The primary prediction of the handicap hypothesis is difficult to test because it requires an experiment that measures the nonreproductive fitness of low- and high-benefit males that have been forced to express attractive signals (Section II.C). There are, however, three weaker predictions that are easier to test. (1) If direct benefit quality is affected by male fitness, and if high fitness genotypes can better afford the costs of producing attractive signals, then benefit quality and signal attractiveness should positively covary among genotypes. (2) If direct benefit quality is affected by a male's environment, and if males that experience better environments can better afford the costs of producing attractive signals, then benefit quality and signal attractiveness should positively covary among environments. Or (3) if direct benefit quality is affected by male fitness, if fitness is environment dependent (i.e., genotypes of high fitness in one environment have relatively low fitness in another environment), and if high fitness genotypes within a given environment can better afford the costs of producing attractive signals, then there should be congruent GEI effects on benefit quality and signal attractiveness (Section II.D).

We tested these weaker predictions in *G. lineaticeps* (Tolle and Wagner, 2011). Males from 24 full-sibling families were split between a low- and high-nutrition juvenile environment, and the males from each juvenile environment were then split between low- and high-nutrition adult environments. Within each environment, males were provided with *ad libitum* food that differed in nutritional value. After 8 days in one of the adult nutritional environments, we measured a male's chirp rate, muted him, mated him to a female in the presence of an average song type, and then measured the number of eggs the female laid. Benefit quality was estimated based on female fecundity. All females experienced the low-nutrition juvenile and adult conditions because previous results suggested that high-nutrition females benefit little from what males provide (Wagner and Harper, 2003).

The juvenile environment did not affect either chirp rate or direct benefit quality. Chirp rate was, however, affected by the interaction of male family and adult environment: males from some families produced higher chirp rates in the high-nutrition environment, while males from other families produced higher chirp rates in the low-nutrition environment (Fig. 11). In contrast, only male family affected benefit quality. As a result, chirp rate and benefit quality did not covary among genotypes, did not covary among environments, and did not have correlated genotypic reaction norms (Fig. 12). None of the predictions of the handicap hypotheses were thus met.

Even worse for the handicap hypothesis, there was variation between the nutritional environments in the relationship between chirp rate and benefit quality: male chirp rate was positively correlated with benefit quality in the low-nutrition environment but negatively correlated with benefit quality in the high-nutrition environment. The handicap hypothesis never predicts that low-benefit males will produce the most attractive signals.

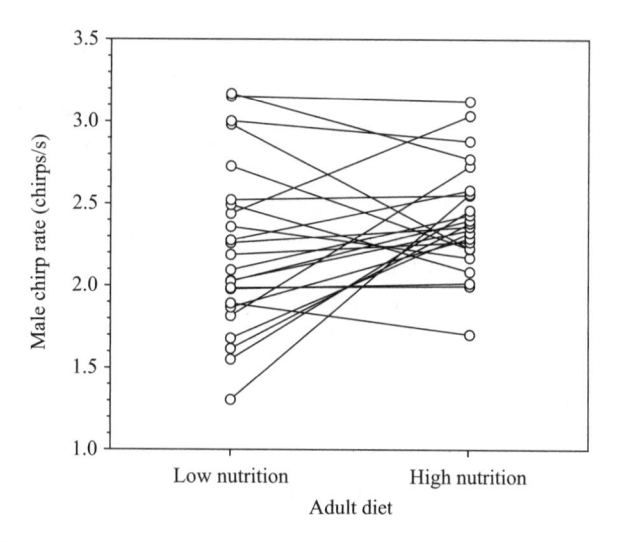

F_{IG}. 11. GEI effect on male chirp rate. There was significant variation among full-sibling families in the effect of adult nutritional environment on male chirp rate: some families produced higher chirp rates in the high-nutrition environment while others produced lower chirp rates in the high-nutrition environment. Symbols (○) show the mean family chirp rates in each environment, and lines connect the means of each family. Adapted from Tolle and Wagner (2011).

Combining the results of our various studies (Fig. 13), whether a female directly benefits from mating with a high chirp rate male appears to depend upon both the female's nutritional history and the male's nutritional history: a female benefits if both she and the male have experienced a low-nutrition environment; a female incurs costs if she has experienced a low-nutrition environment while the male has experienced a high-nutrition environment; and a female neither benefits nor incur costs if she has experienced a high-nutrition environment and the male has experienced a low-nutrition environment. One important caveat to these conclusions is that we do not know how frequently individuals encounter different nutritional environments. It is possible, for example, that most males and females experience nutrient-poor environments, and thus that females usually benefit from mating with high chirp rate males. Detailed information on the nutritional ecology of G. lineaticeps is necessary to make inferences about the extent to which signal reliability varies.

While our results are inconsistent with the predictions of the handicap hypothesis, it is not clear whether they are any more consistent with the predictions of the differential benefits hypothesis. Assume, for example, that the males and females breeding at a given time have experienced

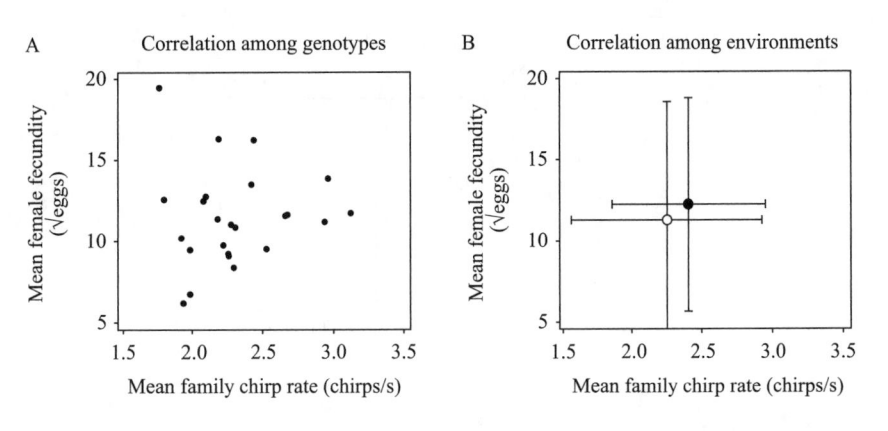

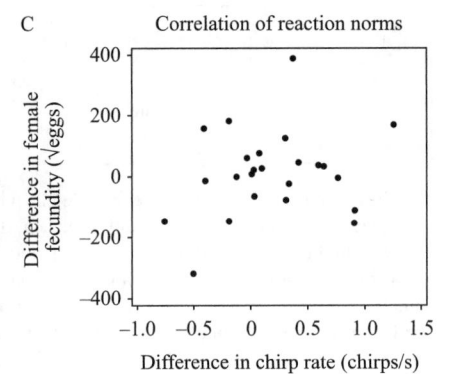

FIG. 12. Covariation among genotypes and among environments, and the correlation of trait plasticity. (A) Correlation of male chirp rate and benefit quality (female fecundity) among full-sibling families ($r_{24} = 0.05$, $P = 0.815$). (B) Male chirp rate and benefit quality in low-nutrition (○) and high-nutrition (●) environments (means ± SD). (C) Correlation of the chirp rate and benefit quality reaction norms ($r_{24} = 0.22$, $P = 0.310$). The figure shows the difference in the mean chirp rate of each full-sibling family (high-nutrition environment–low-nutrition environment) versus the difference in mean benefit quality for each family (high-nutrition environment–low-nutrition environment). Unpublished figures based on data in Tolle and Wagner (2011).

similar nutritional conditions. In a low-nutrition environment, females are more likely to repeatedly mate with high-benefit males (Wagner et al., 2007), and as a result, males that provide high-quality benefits may receive a higher fitness return from their investment in a high chirp rate. Consistent with this hypothesis, there is a positive relationship between male chirp rate and benefit quality in a low-nutrition environment. Whether there is also a positive relationship between chirp rate and benefit quality in a

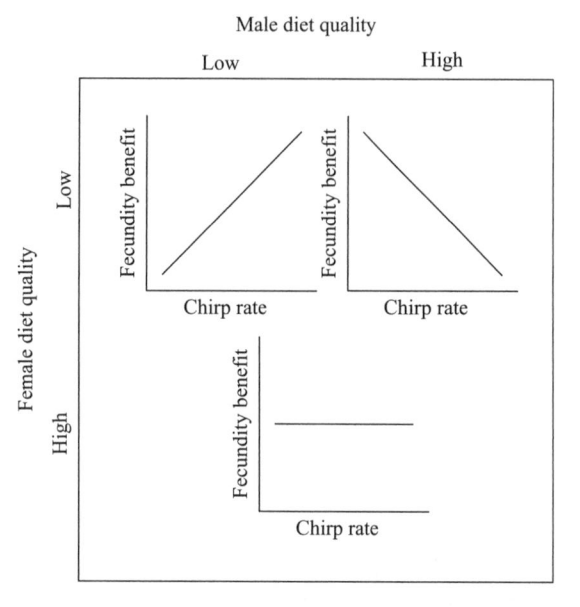

Fig. 13. Summary of results on the relationship between male chirp rate and direct benefit quality. When females have experienced a high-nutrition environment, there are no positive or negative effects of mating with higher chirp rate males (Wagner and Harper, 2003). When females have experienced a low-nutrition environment and males have experienced a low-nutrition environment, females benefit from mating with higher chirp rate males (Tolle and Wagner, 2011; Wagner and Harper, 2003). Finally, when females have experienced a low-nutrition environment and males have experienced a high-nutrition environment, females incur costs from mating with higher chirp rate males (Tolle and Wagner, 2011).

high-nutrition environment should depend upon whether females are also more likely to repeatedly mate with high-benefit males in this environment. Because male-provided direct benefits seem to have little effect on female fecundity when females have experienced a high-nutrition environment (Wagner and Harper, 2003), we might expect benefit quality to have little effect on female repeated mating in high-nutrition environments. If true, female behavior will not produce differential benefits of signaling, and as a result, there will be no incentive for high chirp rate males to provide high-quality benefits. An absence of a relationship between chirp rate and benefit quality in a high-nutrition environment might thus be consistent with an absence of differential benefits. The negative relationship that we found, however, would only be consistent with the differential benefits hypothesis if females, in this environment, were more likely to repeatedly mate with low-benefit males. We do not know whether variation in the nutritional environment affects female repeated mating, but we have no reason to predict that females will be more likely to repeatedly mate with low-benefit males in high-nutrition environments. We are thus left with a puzzling result that may or may not be explainable by either hypothesis for signal reliability.

Regardless of the reason, variation among environments in the relationship between chirp rate and benefit quality may create a problem for the evolution of female mating preferences: unless females can independently assess the environmental histories of males, signal preferences may often result in low-benefit matings. This will be particularly true if individuals breeding at the same time in the same area have experienced different environmental conditions. Field crickets, for example, are omnivores, and they eat everything from low-quality plant material to dead and living animals. If different individuals have experienced different nutritional conditions, a female that mates with a high chirp rate male may receive a fecundity benefit, incur a fecundity cost, or neither, depending upon her own nutritional history and the nutritional history of the male (Fig. 13). This is particularly a problem for low-nutrition females. Low-nutrition females could potentially solve this problem if they assess a nutrition-related male trait and then selectively mate with high chirp rate males that have experienced low-nutrition environments or low chirp rate males that have experienced high-nutrition environments (Section II.E). We do not know if there are male traits that are reliable predictors of a male's nutritional history, although such traits exist in a variety of animals (reviewed by Cotton et al., 2004). As a result, we also do not know whether low-nutrition females would change their chirp rate preferences based on the expression of a nutrition-dependent trait. In addition to the assessment of multiple traits by low-nutrition females, we might also expect high-nutrition females to ignore chirp rate, as there are few direct fitness consequences of mating with males that vary in chirp rate. However, neither diet quality nor diet quantity appears to affect female chirp rate preferences (Bulfer et al., unpublished).

IV. Conclusions

The evolution of female mating preferences is complicated, and our understanding of why females express signal preferences is surprisingly incomplete (Andersson and Simmons, 2006; Grether, 2010; Jones and Ratterman, 2009). Even in some of the best studied systems, such as guppies, a limited range of hypotheses have been explored, those that have been explored have only been partially tested, and the results are complex and ambiguous (e.g., Grether, 2010). I have argued that this is no less true for the direct benefits hypothesis, which if often thought to be the simplest of the major hypotheses for preference evolution. One reason for our incomplete understanding is the inherent complexity of biological systems. But there is another, sociological reason: an excessive focus on easy shortcuts that are of dubious value. Rather than testing the costs and benefits of female mating preferences, too many studies have tested whether preferred males are larger, older, more symmetrical, have higher immunocompetence, or are in better nutritional condition, with little evidence in the animal studied that females actually benefit from mating with males with these characteristics. A more direct and useful approach would be to test whether, when, and why females benefit (e.g., Qvarnström et al., 2006; Welch, 2003).

I have tried to outline some of the predictions of the direct benefits hypothesis, and what constitutes strong and weak evidence that females directly benefit from their mating preferences. Strong tests of all hypotheses for preference evolution are difficult, but we can make at least some progress with direct benefits by testing whether particular benefit mechanisms affect particular female fitness components in particular environments. It is important to recognize, however, that the inferences that can be made from such studies are limited to the specific benefit mechanisms, fitness components, and environmental conditions that are tested. An inability to detect direct benefits thus cannot be used to reject the direct benefits hypothesis, and the detection of direct benefits may or may not mean that females have higher fitness when they mate with preferred males. Ultimately, we need to measure the fitness consequences of preferences in a representative set of environmental conditions.

I have also argued that males might provide direct benefits to females, and produce signals that provide reliable information about benefit quality, because conditional female reproductive tactics incidentally penalize low-benefit males. The incidental sanctions hypothesis has the elegant economy of parsimony: rather than two separate evolutionary mechanisms—one that favors the evolution of direct benefits and one that favors reliable signaling of benefit quality—only one mechanism may be necessary. Despite this elegance, it may or may or may not have explanatory value. If nothing else, its formulation may help to clarify some of the gaps in our understanding of the male side of the direct benefits hypothesis. To understand the conditions under which females can directly benefit from their mating preferences, we need to also understand the conditions that determine whether males should provide direct benefits and whether male signals should provide reliable or unreliable information about benefit quality. Selection for male investment in females or offspring, while undoubtedly important in many animals, seems unlikely in species in which females engage in extensive multiple mating. And while the handicap hypothesis can contribute to reliable signaling, it must be accompanied by another mechanism that prevents males with attractive signals from cheating on the benefit.

Acknowledgments

I am grateful to Jane Brockmann for the invitation to write the chapter and to Alexandra Basolo and two anonymous reviewers for feedback on the ideas and comments on the chapter. The field cricket research was supported by an NSF Postdoctoral Fellowship in Environmental Biology and by NSF grants IBN 9604226, IOB 0521743, and IOS 0818116.

References

Adamo, S.A., Robert, D., Perez, J., Hoy, R.R., 1995. The response of an insect parasitoid, *Ormia ochracea* (Tachinidae), to the uncertainty of larval success during infestation. Behav. Ecol. Sociobiol. 36, 111–118.

Alexander, R.D., 1961. Aggressiveness, territoriality, and sexual behavior in field crickets (Orthoptera: Gryllidae). Behaviour 17, 130–223.

Alexander, R.D., Otte, D., 1967. The evolution of genitalia and mating behavior in crickets (Gryllidae) and other Orthoptera. Misc. Publ. Mus. Zool. Univ. Mich. 133, 1–62.

Andersson, M., 1994. Sexual Selection. Princeton University Press, Princeton, NJ.

Andersson, M., Simmons, L.W., 2006. Sexual selection and mate choice. Trends Ecol. Evol. 21, 296–302.

Arnqvist, G., Rowe, L., 2005. Sexual Conflict. Princeton University Press, Princeton, NJ.

Backus, V.L., Cade, W.H., 1986. Sperm competition in the field cricket *Gryllus integer* (Orthoptera: Gryllidae). Fla. Entomol. 69, 722–728.

Bailey, N.W., Zuk, M., 2008. Acoustic experience shapes female choice in field crickets. Proc. R. Soc. Lond. B 275, 2645–2650.

Bailey, N.W., Zuk, M., 2009. Field crickets change mating preferences suing remembered social information. Biol. Lett. 5, 449–451.

Balakrishnan, R., Pollack, G., 1997. The role of antennal sensory cues in female responses to courting males in the cricket *Teleogryllus oceanicus*. J. Exp. Biol. 200, 511–522.

Basolo, A.L., 1990. Female preference predates the evolution of the sword in swordtail fish. Science 250, 808–810.

Basolo, A.L., 1995. Phylogenetic evidence for the role of a preexisting bias in sexual selection. Proc. R. Soc. Lond. B 259, 307–311.

Beckers, O.M., Wagner, W.E., Jr., 2011. Mate sampling strategy in a field cricket: evidence for a fixed threshold strategy with last chance option. Anim. Behav. 81, 519–527.

Boggs, C.L., Gilbert, L.E., 1979. Male contribution to egg production in butterflies: evidence for transfer of nutrients at mating. Science 206, 83–84.

Borgia, G., 1981. Mate selection in the fly *Scatophaga stercoraria*: female choice in a male-controlled system. Anim. Behav. 29, 71–80.

Bro-Jørgensen, J., 2009. Dynamics of multiple signalling systems: animal communication in a world in flux. Trends Ecol. Evol. 25, 292–300.

Burley, N., 1986. Sexual selection for aesthetic traits in species with biparental care. Am. Nat. 127, 415–445.

Bussière, L.F., 2002. A model of the interaction between "good genes" and direct benefits in courtship-feeding animals: when do males of high genetic quality invest less? Philos. Trans. R. Soc. Lond. B 357, 309–317.

Bussière, L.F., Basit, H.A., Gwynne, D.T., 2005. Preferred males are not always good providers: female choice and male investment in tree crickets. Behav. Ecol. 16, 223–231.

Cade, W.H., 1975. Acoustically orienting parasitoids: fly phonotaxis to cricket song. Science 190, 1312–1313.

Cade, W.H., 1979. The evolution of alternative male reproductive strategies in field crickets. In: Blum, M.S., Blum, N.A. (Eds.), Sexual Selection and Reproductive Competition in Insects. Academic Press, New York, pp. 343–379.

Cade, W.H., 1980. Alternative male reproductive behaviors. Fla. Entomol. 63, 30–45.

Cade, W.H., Ciceran, M., Murray, A.M., 1996. Temporal patterns of parasitoid fly (*Ormia ochracea*) attraction to field cricket song (*Gryllus integer*). Can. J. Zool. 74, 393–395.

Christy, J.H., 1995. Mimicry, mate choice, and the sensory trap hypothesis. Am. Nat. 146, 171–181.

Cotton, S., Fowler, K., Pomiankowski, A., 2004. Do sexual ornaments demonstrate heightened condition-dependent expression as predicted by the handicap hypothesis? Proc. R. Soc. Lond. B 271, 771–783.

Cotton, S., Small, J., Pomiankowski, A., 2006. Sexual selection and condition-dependent mate preferences. Curr. Biol. 16, R755–R765.

David, P., Bjorksten, T., Fowler, K., Pomiankowski, A., 2000. Condition-dependent signalling of genetic variation in stalk-eyed flies. Nature 406, 186–188.

Dawkins, R., Carlisle, T.R., 1976. Parental investment, mate desertion and a fallacy. Nature 262, 131–133.

Dobzhansky, T., Holz, A.M., 1943. A reexamination of the problem of manifold effects of genes in *Drosophila melanogaster*. Genetics 28, 295–303.

Downhower, J.F., Brown, L., 1980. Mate preferences of female mottled sculpins, *Cottus bairdi*. Anim. Behav. 28, 728–734.

Drnevich, J.M., Papke, R.S., Rauser, C.L., Rutowski, R., 2001. Material benefits from multiple mating in female mealworm beetles (*Tenebrio molitor* L.). J. Insect Behav. 14, 215–230.

Dudley, R., 2000. The Biomechanics of Insect Flight: Form, Function, Evolution. Princeton University Press, Princeton, NJ.

Dussourd, D.E., Harvis, C.A., Meinwald, J., Eisner, T., 1989. Paternal allocation of sequestered plant pyrrolizidine alkaloid to eggs in the danaine butterfly *Danaus gillipus*. Experientia 45, 896–898.

Eisner, T., Meinwald, J., 1995. The chemistry of sexual selection. Proc. Natl. Acad. Sci. USA 92, 50–55.

Endler, J.A., Basolo, A.L., 1998. Sensory ecology, receiver biases and sexual selection. Trends Ecol. Evol. 13, 415–420.

Fedorka, K.M., Mousseau, T.A., 2004. Female mating bias results in conflicting sex-specific offspring fitness. Nature 429, 65–67.

Fisher, R.A., 1930. The Genetical Theory of Natural Selection. Clarendon Press, Oxford.

Freeman-Gallant, C.R., 1997. Parentage and paternal care: Consequences of intersexual selection in Savannah sparrows? Behav. Ecol. Sociobiol. 40, 395–400.

Getty, T., 1998. Handicap signalling: when fecundity and viability do not add up. Anim. Behav. 56, 127–130.

Gong, A., Gibson, R.M., 1996. Reversal of a female preference after visual exposure to a predator in the guppy, *Poecilia reticulata*. Anim. Behav. 52, 1007–1015.

González, A., Rossini, C., Eisner, M., Eisner, T., 1999. Sexually transmitted chemical defense in a moth (*Utetheisa ornatrix*). Proc. Natl. Acad. Sci. USA 96, 5570–5574.

Grafen, A., 1990. Biological signals as handicaps. J. Theor. Biol. 144, 517–546.

Gray, D.A., Cade, W.H., 1999. Sex, death and genetic variation: natural and sexual selection on cricket song. Proc. R. Soc. Lond. B 266, 707–709.

Greenfield, M.D., Rodriguez, R.L., 2004. Genotype-environment interaction and the reliability of mating signals. Anim. Behav. 68, 1461–1468.

Grether, G.F., 2010. The evolution of mate preferences, sensory biases, and indicator traits. Adv. Study Behav. 41, 35–76.

Gwynne, D.T., 1988. Courtship feeding and the fitness of female katydids (Orthoptera: Tettigoniidae). Evolution 42, 545–555.

Gwynne, D.T., 2001. Katydids and Bush-Crickets: Reproductive Behavior and Evolution of the Tettigoniidae. Cornell University Press, Ithaca, NY.

Haas, F., Gorb, S., Blickhan, R., 2000. The function of resilin in beetle wings. Proc. R. Soc. Lond. B 267, 1375–1381.

Hadfield, J.D., Burgess, M.D., Lord, A., Phillimore, A.B., Clegg, S.M., Owens, I.P.F., 2006. Direct versus indirect sexual selection: genetic basis of colour, size and recruitment in a wild bird. Proc. R. Soc. Lond. B 273, 1347–1353.

Halliday, T., 1978. Sexual selection and mate choice. In: Krebs, J.R., Davies, N.B. (Eds.), Behavioral Ecology: An Evolutionary Approach. Sinauer, Sunderland, MA, pp. 180–213.

Hebets, E.A., Papaj, D.R., 2005. Complex signal function: developing a framework for testable hypotheses. Behav. Ecol. Sociobiol. 57, 197–214.

Hedrick, A.V., Dill, L.M., 1992. Mate choice by female crickets is influenced by predation risk. Anim. Behav. 46, 193–196.

Heywood, J.S., 1989. Sexual selection by the handicap principle. Evolution 43, 1387–1397.

Higginson, A.D., Reader, T., 2009. Environmental heterogeneity, genotype-by-environment interactions and the reliability of sexual traits as indicators of mate quality. Proc. R. Soc. Lond. B 276, 1153–1159.

Hill, G.E., 1991. Plumage coloration is a sexually selected indicator of male quality. Nature 350, 337–339.

Hoback, W.W., Wagner Jr., W.E., 1997. The energetic cost of calling in the variable field cricket, Gryllus lineaticeps. Physiol. Entomol. 22, 286–290.

Hoelzer, G.A., 1989. The good parent process of sexual selection. Anim. Behav. 38, 1067–1078.

Howard, R.D., 1978. The influence of male-defended oviposition sits on early embryo mortality in bullfrogs. Ecology 59, 789–798.

Hunt, J., Bussière, L.F., Jennions, M.D., Brooks, R., 2004. What is genetic quality? Trends Ecol. Evol. 19, 329–333.

Hunter, F.M., Petrie, M., Otronen, M., Birkhead, T., Møller, A.P., 1993. Why do females copulate repeatedly with one male? Trends Ecol. Evol. 8, 21–26.

Iyengar, V.K., Eisner, T., 1999. Female choice increases offspring fitness in an arctiid moth (Utetheisa ornatrix). Proc. Natl. Acad. Sci. USA 96, 15013–15016.

Jennions, M.D., Petrie, M., 1997. Variation in mate choice and mating preferences: a review of causes and consequences. Biol. Rev. 72, 283–327.

Jia, F.Y., Greenfield, M.D., Collins, R.D., 2000. Genetic variance of sexually selected traits in waxmoths: maintenance by genotype x environment interaction. Evolution 54, 953–967.

Johnson, J.B., Basolo, A.L., 2003. Predator exposure alters female mate choice in the green swordtail. Behav. Ecol. 14, 619–625.

Johnstone, R.A., 1997. The evolution of animal signals. In: Krebs, J.R., Davies, N.B. (Eds.), Behavioural Ecology. Blackwell, Oxford, pp. 155–178.

Jones, A.G., Ratterman, N.L., 2009. Mate choice and sexual selection: what have we learned since Darwin? Proc. Natl. Acad. Sci. USA 106, 10001–10008.

Kirkpatrick, M., 1982. Sexual selection and the evolution of female choice. Evolution 36, 1–12.

Kirkpatrick, M., 1987a. The evolutionary forces acting on female mating preferences in polygynous animals. In: Bradbury, J.W., Andersson, M.B. (Eds.), Sexual Selection: Testing the Alternatives. Dahlem Conference Proceedings. John Wiley, Chichester, pp. 67–82.

Kirkpatrick, M., 1987b. Sexual selection by female choice in polygynous animals. Annu. Rev. Ecol. Syst. 18, 43–70.

Kirkpatrick, M., Barton, N.H., 1997. The strength of indirect selection on female mating preferences. Proc. Natl. Acad. Sci. USA 94, 1282–1286.

Kirkpatrick, M., Ryan, M.J., 1991. The evolution of mating preferences and the paradox of the lek. Nature 350, 33–38.

Knapp, R.A., Kovach, J.T., 1991. Courtship as an honest indicator of male parental quality in the bicolor damselfish, *Stegastes partitus*. Behav. Ecol. 2, 295–300.

Kokko, H., 1998. Should advertising of parental care be honest? Proc. R. Soc. Lond. B 265, 1871–1878.

Kokko, K., Heubel, K., 2008. Condition-dependence, genotype-by-environment interactions and the lek paradox. Genetica 134, 55–62.

Kokko, H., Brooks, R., Jennions, M.D., Morley, J., 2003. The evolution of mate choice and mating biases. Proc. R. Soc. Lond. B 270, 653–664.

Kotiaho, J.S., 2001. Costs of sexual traits: a mismatch between theoretical considerations and empirical evidence. Biol. Rev. 76, 365–376.

Kotiaho, J.S., Puurtinen, M., 2007. Mate choice for indirect genetic benefits: scrutiny of the current paradigm. Funct. Ecol. 21, 638–644.

Kvarnemo, C., 2006. Evolution of maintenance of male care: is increased paternity a neglected benefit of care? Behav. Ecol. 17, 144–148.

Lande, R., 1981. Models of speciation by sexual selection on polygenic traits. Proc. Natl. Acad. Sci. USA 78, 3721–3725.

Leonard, A.S., Hedrick, A.V., 2009. Male and female crickets use different decision rules in response to mating signals. Behav. Ecol. 20, 1175–1184.

Lindén, M., 1991. Divorce in great tits—chance or choice? An experimental approach. Am. Nat. 138, 1039–1048.

Markow, T.A., 1988. *Drosophila* males provide a material contribution to offspring sired by other males. Funct. Ecol. 2, 77–79.

Martin, C.M., Wagner Jr., W.E., 2010. Female field incur increased parasitism risk when near preferred song. PLoS ONE 5, e9592.

Matthews, I.M., Evans, J.P., Magurran, A.E., 1997. Male display rate reveals ejaculate characteristics in the Trinidadian guppy *Poecilia reticulata*. Proc. R. Soc. Lond. B 264, 695–700.

Maynard Smith, J., Harper, D., 2003. Animal Signals. Oxford University Press, Oxford.

Mills, S.C., Alatalo, R.V., Koskela, E., Mappes, J., Mappes, T., Oksanen, T.A., 2007. Signal reliability compromised by genotype-by-environment interaction and potential mechanisms for its preservation. Evolution 61, 1748–1757.

Mole, S., Zera, A.J., 1993. Differential allocation of resources underlies the dispersal-reproduction trade-off in the wing-dimorphic cricket, *Gryllus rubens*. Oecologia 93, 121–127.

Møller, A.P., Alatalo, R.V., 1999. Good-genes effects in sexual selection. Proc. R. Soc. Lond. B 266, 85–91.

Møller, A.P., de Lope, F., 1994. Differential costs of a secondary sexual character: An experimental test of the handicap principle. Evolution 48, 1676–1683.

Møller, A.P., Jennions, M.D., 2001. How important are direct fitness benefits to sexual selection? Naturwissenschaften 88, 401–415.

Møller, A.P., Thornhill, R., 1998. Male parental care, differential parental investment by females and sexual selection. Anim. Behav. 55, 1507–1515.

Murakami, S., Itoh, M.T., 2003. Removal of both antennae influences the courtship and aggressive behaviors in male crickets. J. Neurobiol. 57, 110–118.

Nur, N., Hasson, O., 1984. Phenotypic plasticity and the handicap principle. J. Theor. Biol. 110, 275–297.

Pampoulie, C., Lindström, K., St. Mary, C.M., 2004. Have your cake and eat it too: male sand gobies show more parental care in the presence of female partners. Behav. Ecol. 15, 199–204.

Pfennig, K.S., 2007. Facultative mate choice drives adaptive hybridization. Science 318, 965–967.

Pleszynska, W.K., 1978. Microgeographic prediction of polygyny in the lark bunting. Science 201, 935–937.

Pomiankowski, A., 1988. The evolution of female mate preferences for male genetic quality. Oxf. Surv. Evol. Biol. 5, 136–184.

Popov, A.V., Shuvalov, V.F., 1977. Phonotactic behavior of crickets. J. Comp. Physiol. 119, 111–126.

Price, T., Schluter, D., Heckman, N.E., 1993. Sexual selection when the female directly benefits. Biol. J. Linn. Soc. 48, 187–211.

Qvarnström, A., Pärt, T., Sheldon, B.C., 2000. Adaptive plasticity in mate preference linked to differences in reproductive effort. Nature 405, 344–347.

Qvarnström, A., Brommer, J.E., Gustafsson, L., 2006. Testing the genetics underlying the co-evolution of mate choice and ornament in the wild. Nature 441, 84–86.

Reynolds, J.D., Gross, M.R., 1990. Costs and benefits of female mate choice: is there a lek paradox? Am. Nat. 136, 230–243.

Robertson, J.G.M., 1990. Female choice increases fertilization success in the Australian frog Uperoleia laevigata. Anim. Behav. 39, 639–645.

Rodriguez, R.L., Greenfield, M.D., 2003. Genetic variance and phenotypic plasticity in a component of female mate choice in an ultrasonic moth. Evolution 57, 1304–1313.

Rodriguez, R.L., Sullivan, L.M., Snyder, R.L., Cocroft, R.B., 2008. Host shifts and the beginning of signal divergence. Evolution 62, 12–20.

Rodríguez-Muñoz, R., Bretman, A., Slate, J., Walling, C.A., Tregenza, T., 2010. Natural and sexual selection in a wild insect population. Science 328, 1269–1272.

Ryan, M.J., 1990. Signals, species, and sexual selection. Oxf. Surv. Evol. Biol. 7, 157–195.

Ryan, M.J., Keddy-Hector, A., 1992. Directional patterns of female mate choice and the role of sensory biases. Am. Nat. 139, S4–S35.

Ryan, K.M., Sakaluk, S.K., 2009. Dulling the senses: the role of the antennae in mate recognition, copulation and mate guarding in decorated crickets. Anim. Behav. 77, 1345–1350.

Sakaluk, S.K., 1984. Male crickets feed females to ensure complete sperm transfer. Science 223, 609–610.

Sakaluk, S.K., 1986. Sperm competition and the evolution of nuptial feeding behavior in the cricket, Gryllodes supplicans (Walker). Evolution 40, 584–593.

Sakaluk, S.K., Cade, W.H., 1980. Female mating frequency and progeny production in singly and doubly mated house and field crickets. Can. J. Zool. 58, 404–411.

Sakaluk, S.K., Avery, R.L., Weddle, C.B., 2006. Cryptic sexual conflict in gift-giving insects: chasing the chase-away. Am. Nat. 167, 94–104.

Searcy, W.A., 1979. Female choice of mates: a general model for birds and its application to red-winged blackbirds (Agelaius phoeniceus). Am. Nat. 114, 77–100.

Searcy, W.A., 1982. The evolutionary effect of mate selection. Annu. Rev. Ecol. Syst. 13, 57–85.

Searcy, W.A., Nowicki, S., 2005. The Evolution of Animal Communication: Reliability and Deception in Signaling Systems. Princeton University Press, Princeton, NJ.

Simmons, L.W., 1987. Sperm competition as a mechanism of female choice in the field cricket, *Gryllus bimaculatus*. Behav. Ecol. Sociobiol. 21, 197–202.

Simmons, L.W., 1988. The contribution of multiple mating and spermatophore consumption to the lifetime reproductive success of female field crickets (*Gryllus bimaculatus*). Ecol. Entomol. 13, 57–69.

Simmons, L.W., 2001. Sperm Competition and its Evolutionary Consequences in the Insects. Princeton University Press, Princeton, NJ.

Simmons, L.W., Parker, G.A., 1989. Nuptial feeding in insects: mating effort versus paternal investment. Ethology 81, 332–343.

Simmons, L.W., Wernham, J., García-González, F., Kamien, D., 2003. Variation in paternity in the field cricket *Teleogryllus oceanicus*: no detectable influence of sperm numbers or sperm length. Behav. Ecol. 14, 539–545.

Thornhill, R., 1976. Sexual selection and nuptial feeding behavior in *Bittacus apicalis* (Insecta: Mecoptera). Am. Nat. 110, 529–548.

Thornhill, R., 1983. Cryptic female choice and its implications in the scorpionfly *Harpobitacus nigriceps*. Am. Nat. 122, 765–788.

Thornhill, R., Alcock, J., 1983. The Evolution of Insect Mating Systems. Harvard University Press, Cambridge, MA.

Tinghitella, R.M., Zuk, M., 2009. Asymmetric mating preferences accommodated the rapid evolutionary loss of a sexual signal. Evolution 63, 2087–2098.

Tolle, A.E., Wagner Jr., W.E., 2011. Costly signals in a field cricket can indicate high or low quality direct benefits depending upon the environment. Evolution 65, 283–294.

Tregenza, T., Wedell, N., 1997. Definitive evidence for cuticular pheromones in a cricket. Anim. Behav. 54, 979–984.

Tregenza, T., Wedell, N., 1998. Benefits of multiple mates in the cricket *Gryllus bimaculatus*. Evolution 52, 1726–1730.

Vahed, K., 1998. The function of nuptial feeding in insects: A review of empirical studies. Biol. Rev. 73, 43–78.

Velez, M.J., Brockmann, H.J., 2006. Seasonal variation in selection on male calling song in the field cricket, *Gryllus rubens*. Anim. Behav. 72, 439–448.

Wagner Jr., W.E., 1996. Convergent song preferences between female field crickets and acoustically orienting parasitoid flies. Behav. Ecol. 7, 279–285.

Wagner Jr., W.E., 2005. Male field crickets that provide reproductive benefits to females incur higher costs. Ecol. Entomol. 30, 350–357.

Wagner Jr., W.E., Basolo, A.L., 2007a. The relative importance of different direct benefits in the mate choices of a field cricket. Evolution 61, 617–622.

Wagner Jr., W.E., Basolo, A.L., 2007b. Host preferences in a phonotactic parasitoid of field crickets: The relative importance of host song characters. Ecol. Entomol. 32, 478–484.

Wagner Jr., W.E., Basolo, A.L., 2008. Incidental sanctions and the evolution of direct benefits. Ethology 114, 521–539.

Wagner Jr., W.E., Harper, C.J., 2003. Female life span and fertility are increased by the ejaculates of preferred males. Evolution 57, 2054–2066.

Wagner Jr., W.E., Reiser, M.G., 2000. The relative importance of calling song and courtship song in female mate choice in the variable field cricket. Anim. Behav. 59, 1219–1226.

Wagner Jr., W.E., Kelley, R.J., Tucker, K.R., Harper, C.J., 2001a. Females receive a life span benefit from male ejaculates in a field cricket. Evolution 55, 994–1001.

Wagner Jr., W.E., Smeds, M.R., Wiegmann, D.D., 2001b. Experience affects female responses to male song in the variable field cricket, *Gryllus lineaticeps* (Orthoptera, Gryllidae). Ethology 107, 769–776.

Wagner Jr., W.E., Smith, A.R., Basolo, A.L., 2007. False promises: females spurn cheating males in a field cricket. Biol. Lett. 3, 379–381.

Walker, T.J., 1986. Monitoring the flights of field crickets (*Gryllus* spp.) and a tachinid fly (*Euphasiopteryx ochracea*) in north Florida. Fla. Entomol. 69, 678–685.

Walker, T.J., Wineriter, S.A., 1991. Hosts of a phonotactic parasitoid and levels of parasitism (Diptera: Tachinidae: *Ormia ochracea*). Fla. Entomol. 74, 554–559.

Wedell, N., 1991. Sperm competition select for nuptial feeding in a bushcricket. Evolution 45, 1975–1978.

Wedell, N., 1994. Dual function of the bushcricket spermatophore. Proc. R. Soc. Lond. B 258, 181–185.

Wedell, N., 1996. Mate quality affects reproductive effort in a paternally investing species. Am. Nat. 148, 1075–1088.

Weissman, D.B., Rentz, D.C.F., Alexander, R.D., Loher, W., 1980. Field crickets (*Gryllus* and *Acheta*) of California and Baja California, Mexico (Orthoptera: Gryllidae: Gryllinae). Trans. Am. Entomol. Soc. 106, 327–356.

Welch, A.M., 2003. Genetic benefits of a female mating preference in gray tree frogs are context-dependent. Evolution 57, 883–893.

Williams, G.C., 1957. Pleiotropy, natural selection, and the evolution of senescence. Evolution 11, 398–411.

Williams, G.C., 1966. Adaptation and Natural Selection. Princeton University Press, Princeton, NJ.

Wright, S., 1968. In: Evolution and the Genetics of Populations, Vol. I. Genetic and Biometric FoundationsUniversity of Chicago Press, Chicago.

Wright, J., Cuthill, I., 1989. Manipulation of sex differences in parental care. Behav. Ecol. Sociobiol. 25, 171–181.

Zahavi, A., 1975. Mate selection—a selection for a handicap. J. Theor. Biol. 53, 205–214.

Zera, A.J., Cisper, G., 2001. Genetic and diurnal variation in the juvenile hormone titer in a wing-polymorphic cricket: Implications for the evolution of life histories and dispersal. Physiol. Biochem. Zool. 74, 293–306.

Zera, A.J., Rokke, K., Mole, S., 1994. Lipid, carbohydrate and nitrogen contents of long-winged and short-winged *Gryllus firmus*: implications for the cost of flight capability. J. Insect Physiol. 40, 1037–1044.

Zera, A.J., Sall, J., Grudzinski, K., 1997. Flight-muscle polymorphism in the cricket *Gryllus firmus*: Muscle characteristics and their influence on the evolution of flightlessness. Physiol. Zool. 70, 519–529.

Zuk, M., Simmons, L.W., 1997. Reproductive strategies of the crickets (Orthoptera: Gryllidae). In: Choe, J.C., Crespi, B.J. (Eds.), The Evolution of Mating Systems in Insects and Arachnids. Cambridge University Press, Cambridge, pp. 89–109.

Zuk, M., Simmons, L.W., Cupp, L., 1993. Song characteristics of parasitized and unparasitized populations of the field cricket *Teleogryllus oceanicus*. Behav. Ecol. Sociobiol. 33, 339–343.

Zuk, M., Simmons, L.W., Rotenberry, J.T., 1995. Acoustically-orienting parasitoids in calling and silent males of the field cricket *Teleogryllus oceanicus*. Ecol. Entomol. 20, 380–383.

Zuk, M., Rotenberry, J.T., Tinghitella, R.M., 2006. Silent night: adaptive disappearance of a sexual signal in a parasitized population of field crickets. Biol. Lett. 2, 521–524.

Index

Note: The letters '*f*' and '*t*' following the locators refer to figures and tables respectively.

Contents of Previous Volumes